Crime and Punishment in Modern America

Edited By

Patrick B. McGuigan and Jon S. Pascale

THE INSTITUTE FOR GOVERNMENT AND POLITICS OF THE

FREE CONGRESS RESEARCH AND EDUCATION FOUNDATION

The Free Congress Research and Education Foundation is a 501 (c)(3) tax-exempt research organization, engaged in a variety of educational projects. Among the Foundation's many activities is the Institute for Government and Politics, which includes a Political Division, a Direct Democracy Division and the Judicial Reform Project. The Judicial Reform Project is designed to contribute to the debate on the proper role of the judiciary in a democratic society. The first phase of the Project included publication of *A Blueprint for Judicial Reform* in November 1981. A Conference on Judicial Reform was sponsored on June 14, 1982. The next phase of the project has included publication of *Criminal Justice Reform: A Blueprint* (1983), sponsorship of the Conference on Criminal Justice Reform on September 27, 1983 and, now, publication of *Crime and Punishment in Modern America*. The Project will next focus on tort reform, excessive litigiousness and other civil justice issues, with plans for publication of another major book in 1987-88. The Free Congress Foundation is located at 721 Second Street, N.E., Washington, D.C. 20002.

None of the statements in this book should be construed as the policy views of the Institute for Government and Politics or its Board of Advisors, nor should the policies advocated here be taken as necessarily the policy views of the Free Congress Foundation or its Board of Directors.

The Institute for Government and Politics
Stuart Rothenberg, Director, Political Division
Patrick B. McGuigan, Director, Judicial Reform Project

Board of Advisors
Jeffrey Bell, *Citizens for America*
Richard Rahn, *Chief Economist, U.S. Chamber of Commerce*
Newt Gingrich, *Member of Congress, Georgia*
William F. Harvey, *Carl M. Gray Professor of Law, Indiana University*
Richard Woodward, *President, Woodward and McDowell*

Library of Congress Cataloging-in-Publication Data

Crime and punishment in modern America.

Includes bibliographies.
1. Criminal justice, Administration of—United States. 2. Crime and criminals—United States. 3. Criminal law—United States. I. McGuigan, Patrick B. II. Pascale, Jon S.
HV9950.C74 1987 364'.973 86-82505
ISBN 0-942522-01-X (alk. paper)
ISBN 0-942522-00-1 (pbk. : alk. paper)

Distributed by arrangement with
University Press of America, Inc., 4720 Boston Way, Lanham, MD 20706 and 3 Henrietta St., London, WC2E8LU England

Second Printing: August 1987   Cover design by Barnett Danner.

for

William Bradford Reynolds

iii

CONTENTS

PREFACE

With this book, I complete nearly four years of intense involvement in the myriad issues of criminal justice reform. Like its predecessor, *Criminal Justice Reform*, this is an effort to find solutions to America's twin epidemics of crime and prison overcrowding.

I thank the many fine scholars who provided help and support in the production of this book. The contributors to *Crime and Punishment in Modern America* represent a cross-section of leaders from the judicial, scholarly and political communities. While the contributors to this book share many views on the best ways to deal with crime, incarceration and alternatives to incarceration, each author's chapter represents personal views and not necessarily those of the persons or organizations with which they are affiliated. In addition, none of the specific recommendations made here should be construed as representing the policy views of the Free Congress Foundation and its Board of Directors, or the Institute for Government and Politics and its Board of Advisors.

A number of colleagues provided assistance in the research and design of portions of this book. Deep gratitude is owed to Paul Summit of the Administrative Offices of the U.S. Courts, Dwight Rabuse and Terry Eastland of the Office of Public Affairs in the Department of Justice (DOJ), Katie Boyle of the Office of Justice Programs (DOJ), Terry Campo of the Department of Energy, Mark Barrett of the Assets Forfeiture Office (DOJ), Eleanor Hill of the Senate Governmental Affairs Committee's Subcommittee on Investigations, and Margaret Weber of Senator Bill Armstrong's staff. I also appreciated the helpful insights of Grover Norquist of Americans for Tax Reform.

For five years, I was privileged to accept the insightful counsel and advice of my friend, Randall R. Rader of the Senate Judiciary Committee's Subcommittee on the Constitution, who served as co-editor of both *Criminal Justice Reform* and its predecessor, *A Blueprint for Judicial Reform*. Although he did not participate in the editing of this book, his steady hand is reflected in many of the ideas developed herein.

Special gratitude is extended to five individuals. Kristin R. Blair and Jeffery D. Troutt of the Institute for Government and Politics cheerfully assisted in tracking down several obscure citations in the closing weeks of work on this book, while Curt Anderson, Vice President of Operations for the Free Congress Foundation, oversaw the final production. I owe a great deal to Patrick Fagan, Executive Vice President of the Foundation, for his understanding of the importance of this research. Paul M. Weyrich, the President of the Free Congress Foundation, invented the Judicial Reform Project in the winter of 1980–81 and has supported all my efforts in the years since. Now the liberals know exactly who to blame.

Naturally, I owe a special word to my good friend Jon S. Pascale, who ably served as Assistant Director of the Judical Reform Project for nearly two years, and who oversaw the editing of the book until he joined the U.S. Civil Rights Commission in March 1986.

Finally, my deepest gratitude goes to my wife Pam and to our four children. She has supported me and tolerated the late-night and weekend editorial sessions for six years now. She read this book and ably assisted with the final proof-reading. She understands that all these efforts are directed toward nurturing and sustaining justice in the land we both love.

pbm
Washington, D.C.
August 15, 1986

INTRODUCTION

MAN DOES NOT LIVE BY LAW ALONE
by J. Clifford Wallace

Law is the body of rules by which a society is disciplined or controlled. A physical law, such as the law of gravity, restricts our actions by making a fall the inevitable result of a dropped object. Anyone who has slipped from a ladder or dropped a breakable object of value has wished he could suspend that law, if only for a moment. However, while the law of gravity restricts our conduct, it also preserves the order that we enjoy by keeping objects in their place. In much the same way, the law that governs our actions in society restricts our behavior and thus preserves the order of society.

Just as the man falling from the ladder desires to suspend the law of gravity, many want to suspend the punishment or consequences of their disobedience of the criminal law. There have been many debates on the relative effectiveness or ineffectiveness of incarceration and other penalties as deterrents to crime. While I do not minimize the importance of deterrence to the would-be criminal as a proper function of punishment, deterrence aside, punishment as retribution is a necessary component of a system of law. The causal relationship between violation and punishment is the force that gives the law meaning and distinguishes it from mere social advice.

But we must always remember the limited role of law in our society. Because the purpose of the law is to preserve order by punishing the instigators of unacceptable conflict, it is based largely upon a concept of expediency rather than upon a total encompassing of ultimate right or wrong. The only aspects of right and wrong that the law reinforces are those which function to reduce conflict. Laws are, in a sense, reactions to society—as society becomes more complex, the opportunities for destructive conflicts increase, and the number of laws that are needed to prevent those conflicts grows.

For example, in a Robinson Crusoe-like society of one, there is no need for law because there is no possibility of conflict. But as soon as a "Man Friday" appears, the need for law to minimize conflicts arises. As our country grew and technology advanced, society reacted by developing laws to deal with the new complexities. We now have zoning laws to deal with increased population and industrialization, speed limits to minimize the dangers of high-speed travel and to reduce our consumption of diminishing resources, laws to restrict the use of nuclear power to protect society and the environment, and countless other laws that attempt to prevent or reduce the possibilities for conflict in a highly kinetic society.

Adding more laws, however, will not solve many of our societal problems. While the theory of reducing conflicts through the law is virtuous, it can be carried to unfortunate extremes. If, in an attempt to prevent even minor conflicts, the law becomes so restrictive that opportunities for meaningful growth and individual initiative were substantially curtailed, the execution of the law would destroy its ultimate purpose and our nation would be in jeopardy.

One of the great strengths of America's constitutional form of government is its limitations on the enforcement of the laws that restrict certain personal freedoms. For example, even though the right to free speech or the right to practice one's own religious beliefs may give rise to minor conflicts on occasion, the importance of those rights is so noble that they cannot be unduly limited—even to minimize conflict. This generation must recognize, as did the Founding Fathers, that a delicate balance must be maintained between the laws that would preserve freedom by protecting us from unacceptable conflict, and the laws that curtail freedom by abolishing individual agency and withholding fundamental rights.

Even if American society is successful in maintaining this balance, the law can unintentionally lead some to a warped sense of values. For example, the criminal law forces all community members to conform to minimum standards of conduct in order to secure a relatively pacific society. It is neither the intention nor the purpose of the criminal law to express the optimal standard of conduct, or to delineate a code for correct living. Unhappily, however, for many people the line of demarcation between criminal and non-criminal behavior becomes the definition of right and wrong. As long as conduct is not unlawful, or as long as unlawful conduct is not threatened with prosecution, many accept such action as proper, and sometimes even laudatory.

The story is told of a man who was charged with burglary and theft. After a long trial, the jury returned a verdict of not guilty and the judge advised the defendant that he was free to go. Although the man had been extremely quiet throughout the trial, after the judge's statement his eyes lighted up and he delightedly asked the judge: "Does that mean I get to keep the money?"

Although apocryphal, the story illustrates a feeling that is all too prevalent in our country. The "beat the system" philosophy is demonstrated by current authors who claim to have ways of avoiding the payment of taxes, of avoiding the probate procedures, and generally of exploiting the alleged "loopholes" of the law without getting caught. Far too often we forget that the law cannot guarantee individual or collective happiness or success. Even though lying is not always a violation of the criminal laws, a liar is still dishonest, and the fact that some derogatory statements may not be actionable slander does not make saying them any less obnoxious or unkind.

Thus, there are standards that promote general and individual well-being which are not, and should not be, part of our codified law. There is a lower law that forbids untolerated acts—but there is a higher ethic that asserts a positive force for the well-being of society. In other words, Man does not live by Law alone.

Aleksandr Solzhenitsyn, whom Malcolm Muggeridge has called "the greatest man living in the world today," confronted us with this uncomfortable truth in his historic commencement address at Harvard University in June of 1978. He identified the underlying difficulties of not only this country, but western nations in general, when he stated:

> People in the West have acquired considerable skill in using, interpreting, and manipulating law, even though the laws tend to be too complicated for an average person to understand without the help of an expert. Any conflict is resolved according to the letter of the law, and this is considered to be the supreme solution. If one is right from a legal point of view, nothing more is required; nobody may mention that one could still be not entirely right, and urge self-restraint, a willingness to renounce such legal rights, sacrifice, and selfless risk: it would sound simply absurd. One almost never sees voluntary self-restraint. Everybody operates at the extreme limit of the legal frames....
> I have spent all my life under a Communist regime and I will tell you that a society without any objective legal scale is a terrible one indeed. But a society with no other scale but the legal one is not quite worthy of man either. A society which is based on the letter of the law and never reaches any higher is scarcely taking advantage of the high level of human possibilities. The letter of the law is too cold and formal to have a beneficial influence on society. Whenever the tissue of life is woven of legalistic relations, there is an atmosphere of moral mediocrity, paralyzing man's noblest impulses.[1]

3

Solzhenitsyn spoke in extreme, sharply drawn terms in his stinging critique of a society where too many citizens strive merely to adhere to the "letter of the law." But the underlying verity of Solzhenitsyn's criticisms is difficult to refute: Too many Americans have forgotten that with rights come responsibilities.

Many members of the American community not only voluntarily obey the law but also accept the responsibility for individually and collectively contributing to the growth and development of society. They strive, each in their own unique way, to eradicate the moral mediocrity of which Solzhenitsyn spoke.

The contributions of these individuals take many forms but include: the encouragement of learning and culture; the protection of our physical and social environment; the provision of opportunities and support for the underprivileged; and the development of a spiritual awareness. I characterize this body of conduct as ethical—it focuses on meeting the higher needs of a changing society rather than on merely complying with the minimal code of conduct embodied in the law.

Ethical conduct is surely not divorced from the law because many of the reforms that take root in our collective conscience come to fruition as legislation which seeks to improve and to protect society. But the totality of ethics has a higher and more important societal value than law. Ethics involve the realm of ultimate "right and wrong" and as a consequence, the motivation for ethical conduct is not avoidance but attainment.

There are many examples of ethical forces in American society: the nation's citizens contribute millions of dollars annually to charities, churches, and civil service organizations; many individuals help directly and indirectly to set and to maintain high standards of morality and personal conduct; and a large number of business and professional groups adopt voluntary standards to guide and to improve their performances.

If both law and ethics are to perform their proper functions, there must be an appreciation that each has a separate goal. The problems of "moral mediocrity" are encountered when ethics rise to no higher watermark than does the law. A blurring of the law-ethic consideration can also occur when our country tries to fashion laws to become our ethics. It is not often recognized that there can be a debilitating effect on altruistic or ethical pursuits resulting from an over-reliance on the law.

Many Americans look to the law—especially to the courts—for all social change. We ask the courts and legislatures to resolve marital and racial disputes, to reduce poverty, to preserve our environment, to give us a right to live or a right to die, and in general to create a harmonious and comfortable setting for all members of society without infringing on the rights of anyone. When such reliance is placed on the law, people tend to reduce their own efforts to relieve any of the problems in society and to wait for a panacean law to create some sort of Utopia.

When the western frontier was young and a home was lost due to fire or storm, the whole community joined in an effort to assist the neighbor. Today, a similar occurrence often results only in a plea to the legislature for new laws and a community hope that already-enacted welfare laws will be of assistance.

In the 1960s and 1970s, a number of reform bills were enacted that attempted to deal with many of the country's problems. As laudable as they were in purpose, their result has been to inundate the courts with cases, and it is questionable whether their goals, even in part, have been reached. That the legislation has not eradicated pain, poverty, and prejudice is not the fault of the legislators who drafted the bills, or of the courts that attempt to enforce their provisions. The reality is that no matter how artfully worded the law is or how diligently it is enforced, formal rules in isolation cannot solve the fundamental ills of a society.

It is not unlike a parent trying to teach two unruly children to get along by knocking their heads together—pain rarely, if ever, teaches kindness. The real solutions to the problems of American society in general and the criminal justice system in particular cannot be found in the courts or in the legislatures alone. The hope for our society lies far less in the courts than it does in the hearts of those in our homes, offices, churches, and communities—where the problems have their sources and where their solutions must be found. While the law plays a fundamental and indispensable role in our society, we will never achieve greatness until we recognize its limitations. The true potential of America must be developed through ethical considerations that are in addition to and higher than our law.

In spite of our truly advanced culture, how close is America to inculcating a higher ethic, an ethic that would do more than anything else to spark lasting criminal justice reform? Americans today are better educated and better informed than any similar group in the history of the world. Thanks to our schools and excellent journalistic services, the citizens of America are relatively well informed about the key affairs of the country. As an optimist, I see signs that some things are better today than they were a decade ago. Yet, in the face of the advancements in education and transmission of information, in the face of a revitalized economy, there remains crushing cynicism and pessimism in some parts of America, particularly among our "best and brightest."

Never before have there been so many Americans who understand the irrationality of prejudice, who are aware of the dysfunctionalities of the criminal justice system, or who are capable of analyzing and dealing creatively with problems of the economy and the environment. But too many will not join in the efforts to solve these problems. Dismayed by the difficulty of the solutions, they assume a stance of cynicism and inaction.

For years, the numbers of citizens voting or taking part in civic affairs was declining. Many had convinced themselves that their role was too small to matter, or that our problems could never be remedied. Perhaps we have turned the corner on this problem—the 1984 election was the first in decades in which the voter participation percentage actually increased, if only slightly.

Some young people react to cynicism, pessimism or inaction with crime and violence. But cynicism, pessimism, inaction, crime, and violence will never do anything to spark solutions to ongoing problems. The path to development of the higher ethic requires both hope and resoluteness. In short, the challenge is *to begin*. The prospect of improving American society through the acceptance of individual responsibility and accountability merits our best efforts.

Happily, the contributors to this book have picked up the challenge to begin—to tackle the staggering problems of judicial misconstruction, of prison overcrowding, of just alternatives to incarceration, of proper allocation of crime-fighting dollars in the age of Gramm-Rudman-Hollings, of massive and debilitating drug abuse, and much more.

The essays of *Crime and Punishment in Modern America* deal largely with practical, specific questions of criminal justice policy. But underlying each of the works is the desire to develop policies that build on the best in our people—policies that support, if not require, ethical conduct.

Ethical conduct—conduct that builds and reinforces the truths which have contributed to the growth and development of our

6

nation since its inception—may again become the hallmark of American society. No longer can America afford the lethargy of social inaction. A few years ago, we were in danger of creating an American historical calendar that accounted for time in wars and riots rather than in scientific, social, moral, or religious achievements. Today, many Americans recognize that it is time to alter that perspective by recognizing and rewarding ethical conduct.

It is not clear what path America will take to solve its most pressing problems, including those of the criminal justice system. It is clear there is a need for new leadership to build on the awakening of recent years, leadership that demonstrates, and therefore promotes in others, a standard of conduct higher than that merely prescribed by law. Many of the realities that confronted the Framers are with us even now. As John Adams once observed: "We have no government armed with power capable of contending with human passions unbridled by morality and religion. Our constitution was made only for a moral and religious people."[2]

The new ethical leadership must emanate from people in all walks of life, who understand and believe in the dignity of individuals, and who recognize their own potential. Those of us who have benefitted from society, owe society. Through good fortune, we were born in a free country where a youth raised in near poverty around street gangs can, nevertheless, become a newspaper executive, a judge, a chief of police or a President. We only repay our debt when we help America achieve its greatness—by helping its people reach for the higher ethic. Our successes must be measured in terms of contribution rather than in terms of financial increase or media notoriety.

Some will say this call for continuing and improved ethical leadership in society as a whole and in the criminal justice system in particular overestimates what individuals can do in a large and complex society. I do not share their pessimism. Every human being is ultimately accountable and responsible. Every person can count if he or she will. The implications of this for each of us is clear—it is our job to strive for and promote that which is good. For policy makers, the question is how can the incentives and sanctions of the law best be structured to promote society's search for equal justice under law.

Some years ago, while I was attending a night football game, the stadium lights were turned off and each of us was asked to light a match. Had we all been pessimists, we would have stayed in darkness. Because most had the faith to try, the entire stadium was illuminated.

This book is an effort by many worthy individuals to reaffirm the higher values that are so essential to the vital pursuit of criminal justice reform.

REFERENCES

Man Does Not Live By Law Alone by J. Clifford Wallace

1. Aleksandr I. Solzhenitsyn, "A World Split Apart," The Commencement Address at Harvard University in June of 1978. The text here is taken from a booklet distributed shortly after the speech by the Young America's Foundation. For a stimulating debate on Solzhenitsyn's controversial speech, *see* Ronald Berman, ed., *Solzhenitsyn at Harvard: The Address, Twelve Early Responses, and Six Later Reflections* (Washington, D.C.: Ethics and Public Policy Center, 1980).

2. John Adams, quoted in Stanley Hauerwas, *A Community of Character* (South Bend, Indiana: Notre Dame University Press, 1981), p. 79. *See also,* Richard J. Neuhaus, *The Naked Public Square* (William B. Eerdmans Publishing Company, 1984).

1

CRIME AND PUNISHMENT IN MODERN AMERICA
by Edwin Meese III

In the classic novel *Crime and Punishment,* Dostoevsky focused on how crime can ultimately destroy not only its victim but the criminal himself. What was true in the time of this great writer remains true in the America of the 1980s. Crime exacts a horrible toll on all those who suffer its violence, intimidation, and deceit; while at the same time eroding the humanity of the person responsible for it. However, anyone who looks seriously at the nature of crime and punishment in contemporary society must go beyond the immediate evils crime works on its subjects and perpetrators. The price of crime in modern America cannot be measured simply in terms of the numbers of murders, robberies, and assaults committed each year, or the number of lives wasting behind prison walls. Today both crime and the fear of becoming the victim of crime are tearing the fabric of American society.

Several years ago an important study known as the "Figgie Report"[1] shed new light on this problem. According to this report, forty percent of all Americans harbor *concrete* fears that they will become victims of a violent crime, such as murder, rape, robbery or assault. Additionally, four out of every ten Americans have *formless* fears about the safety of their daily environments. This fear of crime extends across all demographic boundaries. It extends to every racial, ethnic, and income category. Moreover, certain groups, including women, residents of large cities, and minorities, have an especially acute fear of crime. The pervasiveness of the crime problem is disturbing enough. But an additional concern appears in evidence that public apprehension about crime appears to have increased over the last two decades.

A 1983 Gallup Poll found 45 percent of those questioned answering "yes" to the question "is there any area around here—that is, within a mile—where you would be afraid to walk alone at night?" In 1965 this same question got an affirmative answer from only 31 percent of those polled.[2]

Certainly, all Americans have good reason to be disturbed about the problem of crime, and many have ample reason to fear becoming a crime victim. Each year about 3.2 percent of our population—some 6 million Americans—become victims of violent crime. In 1984 the National Crime Survey reported more than 35 million victimizations for that year in the United States. In the same year some 22.8 million households, a figure representing about 26 percent of all American homes, were touched by crime in some way.[3]

These totals are disturbing. But perhaps more remarkable than the number of crimes is the evidence about the public's perception of crime. Public fear of crime has increased or held steady during a period when the number of crimes seems to have declined. For example, the number of victimizations for 1984, great as it was, was approximately 14 percent lower than the 1981 peak of 41.5 million. The number of households touched by crime was down from the peak of 32 percent measured in 1975.[4] What are the reasons for this disparity between public perception and the trends indicated in these statistics?

There are a number of plausible explanations: the greater immediacy with which television brings violent crime into our living rooms, greater publicity about the dangers of crime, and the fact that certain crimes, such as those involving substance abuse, are affecting a greater number of families, may bring greater awareness of the threat of crime to more people. On a deeper level, however, I believe that public concern about the danger of crime is rooted elsewhere. It grows out of a sense that some time back we took a wrong turn, that the basic institutions of our society fundamentally, and wrongly, changed their perspectives about how we should deal with the issues of crime and punishment.

The 1960s and '70s were decades of tremendous upheaval in many realms of American life. Long-accepted notions about personal morality, individual responsibility, and the role government should play in responding to social problems were among the casualties of these changes. The commission of a crime had traditionally been viewed as essentially a personal act for which the actor was both morally and legally responsible, and for which society could rightfully exact punishment. But precepts like these were discarded when our thinking about crime shifted from focusing on restraining and sanctioning criminals to finding "explanations" for criminal behavior. Social phenomena or societal conditions, economics, class conditions, education—all these factors and more became escapes for those eager to assign the blame for crime anywhere but to the criminal. The desire to shift blame became so pronounced, indeed, that in 1976 a Joint Economic Committee Report of the Congress could assert that a "1.4 percent rise in unemployment during 1970 is directly responsible...for 1,740 additional homicides."[5] Directly responsible? The implications of a philosophy that attributes "responsibility" for individual homocides to economic cycles is at the very least disturbing.

The law both reflected and abetted these changes. Fundamental changes in constitutional doctrine imposed punctilious procedural obligations upon both police and prosecutors. At the same time liberal parole and plea bargain practices and new sentencing practices combined to keep many offenders from doing jail time. Together, changing social mores, new legal attitudes and altered judicial practices worked fundamental changes in the American approach to crime and punishment. They also fed a growing public perception that government was sometimes more concerned with scrupulously protecting the criminally accused than with preventing and prosecuting crime.

Today, fortunately, there is a return to a better balance in our approach to the issues of crime and punishment. Many of the lessons gained in recent decades are certainly valid. We must be vigilant in our protection of fundamental rights. The protections enshrined in the Bill of Rights are among our society's most precious legacies. But what is sometimes missed in our praise for the protections these constitutional clauses afford against encroachments of government is the fact that these provisions are more than mere prohibitions against government misconduct. Many of the central provisions of the Bill of Rights, including the right to due process, the right to confront witnesses, to the assistance of counsel, and to trial by jury, are essential because they are intended to prevent the justice system from becoming arbitrary and capricious in its resolution of cases. In good measure, these provisions regularize and rationalize the criminal justice process, and help ensure that it is what it ought to be: a search for the truth.

The system of criminal prosecution, trial, and punishment will ultimately be judged unfair—and thus lose both legitimacy and public confidence—when the results it produces bear no relationship to actual guilt or innocence. This can occur when the innocent are unfairly prosecuted or punished. But it can also happen when the criminal justice system is perceived as wantonly and randomly freeing, or failing to convict or punish, those who have actually committed crimes.

This is the central challenge facing both state and federal law enforcement: how do we effectively identify, arrest, prosecute and punish criminals while preserving civil liberties? I believe there is a way. We can both combat crime and restore public confidence if we pursue a path marked by four key signposts. These markers are (1) a restoration of an authentic constitutional jurisprudence, one that respects the needs of effective law enforcement, (2) effective and realistic criminal law and statutes, (3) effective law enforcement policies, and (4) the public cooperation to make them work.

In some sense these elements may seem obvious. If they do, that in itself is a good sign, because not so long ago they were not. Courts often focused, to an extraordinary degree, on restraining "police misconduct." State and federal criminal statutes were often antiquated. Law enforcement often failed to appreciate the importance of cooperation, and the public's role in preventing crime was undervalued.

The lion's share of the battle against crime will continue to be fought by state and local law enforcement officials in state and local courthouses. But there is a vital federal role, a role touching each of these four elements. Federal courts make decisions that affect the conduct of state and local police and prosecutorial functions. Federal statutes control key areas of the criminal law. The federal government also stands in a unique position to provide national leadership in the battle against crime both in fostering cooperation between enforcement agencies and in facilitating public awareness and participation.

The first element, the task of aiding the evolution of constitutional jurisprudence conducive to effective law enforcement, is one that has been taken seriously by the Department of Justice in recent years. Both in cases in which the federal government is a party, and those cases in which we participate as a "friend of the Court," we seek to help the courts strike a proper balance. This is easier said than done.

For most of our history the bulk of criminal law, and especially the law of criminal procedure, was predominately a matter left to the states. Indeed, at least as originally intended, the strictures of the Bill of Rights applied only against the federal government, and not against the states. But over the last several decades, and particularly during the 1960s and '70s, Supreme Court decisions "federalized" the law of criminal procedure both by expanding the scope of procedural requirements and by imposing them against the states in the same manner they are applied to the federal government. Two of the best known of these decisions are *Mapp v. Ohio*,[6] which applied the so-called "exclusionary rule" for fourth amendment search and seizure rule violations to the states, and *Miranda v. Arizona*,[7] which revolutionized the law of police interrogation. Both decisions have significantly affected police practices and criminal prosecutions.

This "constitutionalization" of criminal procedure law has made the posture of the Department of Justice before the Supreme Court in criminal procedure cases more significant than ever before. Decisions coming out of these cases can affect the course of federal and state law enforcement equally. With this in mind, we have encouraged the Supreme Court, and other federal courts, to be cognizant of law enforcement needs when deciding cases involving criminal justice issues. And while progress has not been uninterrupted, I believe that in recent years we·have succeeded in helping move the law in the right direction.

Regarding the exclusionary rule, a major victory came with the Supreme Court's 1983 decisions in the *Sheppard* and *Leon* cases.[8] In these cases the Court established an important "good faith" exception to the exclusionary rule that permits evidence to be allowed in when it is obtained by a law enforcement officer who reasonably relied on a warrant, issued by a magistrate, which is later found to be defective. The Court wisely recognized that, in some situations, the exclusionary rule cannot be thought to discourage police misconduct—which even the Court now concedes is the only justification for evidence suppression. One such situation occurs when an officer, trying to conform his conduct to the requirements of the law, has obtained a warrant prior to making a search or arrest. This is an important advance. It recognizes the folly of penalizing police officers (and the public) when the police have acted reasonably.

Progress has also been made regarding the substantive interpretation of the Fourth Amendment. Car searches are now treated more rationally, and the Court has adopted a more reasonable "totality of the circumstances test" for determining probable cause.[9]

The Supreme Court in recent decisions, such as *New York v. Quarles*[10] and *Oregon v. Elstad*[11] has also emphasized that *Miranda's* rules are merely prophylactic measures rather than constitutional rights. In *Quarles*, for example, the Court announced a "public safety" exception to *Miranda* that realistically frees police from having to "read a suspect his rights" at the very moment a situation created by a suspect (such as an abandoned weapon) may be endangering innocent people in the area. Most recently, in *Moran v. Burbine*[12] the Supreme Court made it clear that it does not intend to extend further the non-constitutional right to have defense counsel present at police interrogations that was created by *Miranda*.

These and other cases have been important, both for their particular holdings, and for the fact that in deciding them the Court has shown a willingness to give more weight to the public's interests in crime prevention and law enforcement than in the past.

Changing the climate of the law through advocacy in important cases is essential. But it must be coupled with effective advocacy and action in our state and national legislative halls too. One example of the way that effective legislation can make a difference in law enforcement is the Comprehensive Crime Control Act of 1984.[13] This important legislation accomplished significant reforms in a number of areas, including bail and sentencing, asset forfeiture, and modification of the insanity defense to name but a few. The Act also created or modified federal criminal statutes in such areas as murder, hostage taking, drug tampering, and narcotics cultivation and distribution. The Comprehensive Crime Control Act contains the most significant series of changes in the federal criminal justice ever enacted at one time.[14]

One example of how these changes have made a difference is in the area of asset forfeiture. The forfeiture provisions of the Crime Control Act allow the federal government to seize assets which have been purchased with the proceeds of criminal activities. This law has become an important tool in the Department's efforts against drug traffickers and organized crime, as it allows us to deprive criminal rings of the assets to finance future criminal activities. Under this law more than $313 million in cash and property seized from criminals was in the custody of the U.S. Marshals at the end of November 1985. This amount is expected to grow to about $400 million during this year. Tangible assets seized include everything from banks to horse ranches and cars to condominiums.[15]

The assets seized under the forfeiture law are more than simply removed from the hands of criminals. They become resources for law enforcement, and can be shared with state and local law enforcement authorities to provide vital funding for the battle against crime. Not long ago I got to see one creative way the asset forfeiture program can work. New York Police Commissioner Benjamin Ward and I visited a group of sixth graders at P.S. 335 in the Bedford-Stuyvesant section of Brooklyn. There we observed a classroom demonstration of the city's new "School Program to Educate and Control Drug Abuse," or SPECDA. The program includes a film and specially designed "team teaching" curriculum taught by police officers and Board of Education drug counselors. What made this program even more special was that the money used to pay for it came from funds generated by the asset forfeiture program. Through this innovative measure we are really taking the profits out of drugs through forfeiture, and using them to profit our children through drug education.

Clearly the 1984 Act marked real progress. It gave us important new tools against crime. But it can only be viewed as a first step. There are other important legislative initiatives that deserve passage. One of these is the Administration's proposal for habeas corpus reform.

The "Great Writ," which began as a protection for federal prisoners against arbitrary detention by executive officers, has been radically changed by judicial innovations of the past 30 years. Today it is too often a device by which state prisoners seek endless review in the federal courts of convictions that have already been thoroughly reviewed and upheld in the state court system. In the past twenty years there has been an almost 700 percent increase in state prisoner filings of habeas corpus petitions in the federal courts.[16] In many cases these suits are brought solely as a means of harassing the authorities, or as a form of recreational activity by which prisoners pass the time. Although the federal courts regularly agree with the disposition of the state court, handling these cases is often difficult and time consuming. The difficulty posed by these cases is aggravated by the long lapses of time between state adjudication and the petition for review. A study funded by the Department of Justice in 1979 found that 40 percent of habeas corpus petitions were filed more than five years after the state conviction, and nearly one-third were filed more than a decade later. This same study documented the frivolous nature of most habeas petitions. The data showed that of 1,899 petitions filed only 3.2 percent were granted in whole or in part and that only 1.8 percent resulted in any type of release for the prisoner.[17]

In response to this situation the Administration's proposal would make major improvements. First, it would establish a one-year time limit for habeas corpus petitions that would normally run from the

15

time of exhaustion of remedies in state court. Under the current system there is no time limit whatsoever, and petitions have been filed as much as fifty years after conviction. Second, the proposal would establish a general rule barring the assertion in federal habeas corpus proceedings of a claim that was not properly raised before the state courts. Third, it would afford deference to "full and fair" adjudications of a petitioner's claims by the state courts. These reforms, if enacted, will redress the abuses of the current system in which criminal convictions are never truly final.[18]

These reforms would go far toward correcting the major deficiencies of the present system of federal habeas corpus in terms of federalism, proper regard for the stature of the state courts, and the needs of criminal justice.

Another area in which legislation is needed is that of tort claims. Currently most of the attention focused on this area concerns product liability and personal injury judgments, and the problems many individuals, businesses, and communities are facing in obtaining liability insurance. The administration has put forward a tort reform proposal addressing these problems.[19] While the impact of this legislation, if enacted, may be felt most in the civil area, it would also have some important repercussions for law enforcement. The prospect of unlimited liability can have a chilling effect on the performance of law enforcement duties at both the state and federal levels. Indeed, lawsuits against local police departments and municipalities can place an enormous strain on city budgets, and have sometimes impaired the ability of municipalities to obtain coverage. Proposals designed to address these and other tort issues did not make it into the Comprehensive Crime Control Act as it finally became law. But components of the tort reform package, including the proposals for capping awards for non-economic damages and limiting attorney fees, can go part of the way to addressing tort problems in the law enforcement area. These reforms deserve passage.

As important as constitutional and statutory law are, however, even good laws are useless tools unless they are placed in capable hands. That is why the design and execution of law enforcement policies are a critical element in the war against crime. One of the things we've discovered in recent years is that effective enforcement depends greatly on fostering cooperation both between various federal agencies, and between all levels of government. Crime is no respector of state or national boundaries. Because criminal activities cross many jurisdictions our response must involve cooperation on a broad scale.

Two areas in which an enforcement policy based on cooperation have yielded especially good results are themselves inextricably related: narcotics and organized crime.

No one needs reminding that drugs are one of the most serious problems our country faces. Combatting it on every level is a top priority of the Department of Justice. The extent of the problem is staggering. Approximately 21.6 million Americans have used cocaine. About four million are believed to use it currently. Among the young the crisis is particularly acute. Studies indicate that one out of every 20 high school seniors smoke marijuana on a daily basis. Approximately 2.7 million young Americans between the ages of 12 and 17 used it in the last month alone. According to the National High School Senior Survey at least 17 percent of the class of 1985 have tried cocaine.[20]

Faced with a crisis of this magnitude, we need both effective enforcement against the distribution and sale of illegal drugs and a concerted national effort to reduce America's enormous appetite for these harmful substances.

On the enforcement front, the battle against narcotics has been characterized by unprecedented cooperation and teamwork among federal, state, and local law enforcement agencies. Interdiction, investigation and eradication programs have emphasized inter-agency as well as intergovernmental cooperation. For example, we have brought the U.S. attorneys, the FBI, the DEA, the Coast Guard, Customs Service and the Criminal Investigation Division of the IRS together in the battle against drugs in regional task forces. They have compiled an outstanding enforcement record. Statistics as of January of 1986 show that the work of the regional Organized Crime and Drug Enforcement Task Forces has resulted in the indictment of over 7700 major traffickers during the three years these groups have been in existence. Tough enforcement policies are getting results. During 1985 federal drug arrests increased about 20 percent. Arrests of major traffickers increased 40 percent.

On the demand side, prevention and education campaigns are starting to reach more and more of our citizens, particularly young people. Efforts like those of the National Association Against Drug and Alcohol Abuse and the Sports Drug Awareness Program are just two examples of the more than 8000 organizations and activities devoted to this purpose. There is some evidence that drug use among the young is, in fact, finally starting to decline.[21]

Organized crime is deeply involved in the drug problem. New narcotics trafficking rings have grown up around the drug trade, supplementing those longstanding criminal syndicates who have for many years been active in the distribution of narcotics. Effective prosecution and punishment of organized crime is essential both as a component of the war against drugs, and to eradicate the influence these organizations have over other illicit activities. It is therefore encouraging that we've recently had some spectacular success against organized crime.

RICO prosecutions have resulted in the conviction of organized crime figures in a number of cities including Boston, Kansas City, Los Angeles, Chicago, Miami, New Orleans, New York and Philadelphia. These convictions have been made possible by the outstanding work of our organized crime strike forces, which combine the resources of a number of federal agencies and departments. A number of cases around the country are still being tried. We will continue to be aggressive in these cases, and help fulfill President Reagan's pledge to "bust up" the mob.

Finally, there is the matter of public involvement in the war against crime. One of the most encouraging developments of recent years has been the tremendous growth in citizen involvement in anti-crime activities. These efforts include participation of many kinds. Private businesses and civic organizations assist in the effort to find missing children. Parents, educators, and concerned citizens band together to educate our young people about the danger of drugs. Neighborhood watch groups help reduce crime in their communities. Victim assistance and support groups focus attention on the needs of the victims of crime, and provide genuine support to victims themselves. These efforts contribute to crime prevention in an especially meaningful and effective manner because they help reinforce and enhance the values of our society that say crime is simply unacceptable, and will not be tolerated.

After many years in which the crime rate soared, and society seemed tolerant, if not accepting, of much criminal activity, it is only natural that it will take some time before success against crime translates in to reduced public anxiety about crime. But I am convinced that it will occur. There is a sea change taking place in the attitudes of our lawmakers, our judges, and other public officials. They are finally catching up to the public's intolerance for crime.

With continued dedication, hard work, and cooperation, there will surely come a day when both crime, *and* the fear of crime, will be a far less pressing issue for America.

REFERENCES

Crime and Punishment in Modern America by Edwin Meese III

1. Figgie International Inc., *The Figgie Report Part IV: Reducing Crime in America* (1983).
2. *Gallup Report*, as presented in *Sourcebook of criminal justice statistics, 1984* (October 1985).
3. *Bureau of Justice Statistics Annual Report Fiscal 1985* (April 1986), p. 6.
4. *Id.*, p. 6.
5. *Quoted in* James Q. Wilson & Philip J. Cook, "Unemployment and Crime—What is the Connection?" *The Public Interest*, (Spring 1985) p. 3.
6. *Mapp v. Ohio*, 367 U.S. 643 (1961).
7. *Miranda v. Arizona*, 384 U.S. 436 (1966).
8. *United States v. Leon*, 104 S. Ct. 3405 (1984); *Massachusetts v. Sheppard*, 104 S. Ct. 3424 (1984).
9. *Illinois v. Gates*, 462 U.S. 213 (1983).
10. *New York v. Quarles*, 104 S. Ct. 2626 (1984).
11. *Oregon v. Elstad*, 105 S. Ct. 1285 (1985).
12. *Moran v. Burbine*, 54 U.S.L.W. 4265 (1986). [Editor's note: For additional analysis of key criminal law decisions in the 1985–86 term *see:* Peter J. Ferrara's overview in *Judicial Notice*, November–December 1986.]
13. Comprehensive Crime Control Act of 1984, Public Law No. 98-473, (1974). For the intellectual case for many of these reforms, *see:* Patrick B. McGuigan and Randall R. Rader, eds. *Criminal Justice Reform: A Blueprint* (Washington, D.C.: Free Congress Foundation, 1983).
14. *See generally: Handbook on the Comprehensive Crime Control Act of 1984 and Other Criminal Statutes Enacted by the 98th Congress*, (Washington, D.C.: U.S. Dept. of Justice, 1984).
15. *United States Marshals First Year Implementation of the Comprehensive Crime Control Act of 1984*, (Washington, D.C.: U.S. Dept. of Justice, U.S. Marshals Service, January 1986).
16. *Federal Review of State Prisoner Petitioners: Habeas Corpus* (Washington, D.C.: U.S. Dept. of Justice, Bureau of Justice Statistics, March 1984). *See also*, William French Smith, "A Proposal for Habeas Corpus Reform," in McGuigan and Rader, eds., *Criminal Justice Reform* (Washington, D.C.: Free Congress Foundation, 1983).
17. Paul H. Robinson, *An Empirical Study of Habeas Corpus Review of State Court Judgments* (Washington, D.C.: U.S. Dept. of Justice, Project JADAG-79-C-002, 1979).
18. *Habeas Corpus Reform: Hearing on S. 238 Before the Senate Comm. on the Judiciary*, 99th Cong., 1st sess. (Statement of Stephen S. Trott, Assistant Attorney General, Criminal Division).
19. The bills comprising the tort reform package are H.R. 4770, *Federal Tort claims Reform Act of 1986*; H.R. 4765, *Government Contractor Liability Reform Act of 1986*; 99th Cong., 2d sess. For another perspective on tort claims issues, *see* Charles E. Grassley, "Federal Tort Claims Act: Possible Reforms," in McGuigan and Rader, *supra* n. 16.
20. *ADAMHA UPDATE: Alcohol and Drug Abuse Among Adolescents* (Washington, D.C.: U.S. Dept. of Health and Human Services, Public Health Service, April 1986).
21. Address by Attorney General Edwin Meese III, National Press Club (February 15, 1985).

2

DRUGS AND CRIME:
A Legislative Perspective
by Paula Hawkins

As Chairman of both the United States Senate Subcommittee on Children, Family, Drugs and Alcoholism, and the Senate Drug Enforcement Caucus, this Senator has been made aware of just about every aspect of the problems caused by illicit narcotics use and trafficking. None is more devastating than that of drug related crime.

Well-financed, well-armed, well-staffed, and well-organized drug kingpins from all over the world focus their products, and their productivity, on the United States. The results of these activities include decreased national productivity, failed education, impaired national defense, corruption of our children, and increased violent crime.

The traffickers, the dealers, the pushers, the users—all share responsibility for the fact that America's streets are unsafe, American homes are vulnerable, and American citizens are regular victims of crime. By nature, the world of illicit narcotics is intricately tied to the criminal world, and this association affects each and every one of us. In fact, as indicated in evidence revealed in study after study, it is clear that a tremendous amount of the crime currently plaguing our society can be attributed directly to the ever-increasing problem of drug abuse in the United States.

DRUG CRIME DATA

As Chairman of the U.S. Senate Subcommittee on Children, Family, Drugs and Alcoholism, I have conducted numerous investigations and hearings into drug related crime. On May 10, 1984, for example, the Subcommittee addressed that specific question in the form of a congressional hearing. The witnesses testifying at this hearing were: Dr. John Ball of Temple University; Dr. David Nurco of the University of Maryland; Richard Lane of Man Alive Research, Inc.; Stanley Marcus, U.S. Attorney of the Southern District of Florida; Rudolph Giuliani, U.S. Attorney of the Southern

District of New York; and two young people who could testify directly of drug related criminal activity.[1]

Perhaps the most disturbing information of this important forum came from the testimonies of Drs. Ball and Nurco, when they revealed the results of their study of 379 heroin addicts in Baltimore, Maryland. The astounding results of this thorough study were that these heroin addicts had committed over 500,000 crimes in Baltimore during that 11-year period.[2]

In describing this study, referred to as one of the most extensive ever made of the addict population in a major American city, Drs. Ball and Nurco stated that those interviewed were equally divided between black and white, and were interviewed between 1973 and 1978. It was determined that the addicts actually committed an average of over 2,000 crimes each. While the most frequent crime was theft, at 40 percent of the total criminal activity, those studied were also guilty of illicit drug dealing, at 27 percent; violent crime, at 10 percent; and other crimes accounted for the remaining percentage.[3]

Drs. Ball and Nurco stated in their testimony that while not directly related to drug use, this criminal activity virtually became a 40-hour-a-week job for the addicts, who were hunting for money for a fix. It was estimated that these addicts committed crimes some 255 days a year.[4]

That was just one study—in one city—involving one kind of illicit narcotic. To multiply this situation nationwide begins to provide an accurate picture of the enormity of this problem.

GETTING SERIOUS ABOUT THE DRUG WAR

What can be done by legislators to try to break apart this symbiotic relationship between drugs and crime? There is fortunately, much that can be done.

Thus far in the ninety-ninth Congress, numerous pieces of legislation designed to deal with various aspects of the problem of drug related crime have been introduced. On April 4, 1985, I introduced the "Truth in Sentencing Act of 1985." This proposal would abolish the parole system as of the effective date of the Sentencing Reform Act of 1984, which would, in effect, do away with the five-year waiting period for the dissolution of the U.S. Parole Board, which is now called for in the Comprehensive Crime Control Act of 1984. If enacted, the "Truth in Sentencing Act of 1985" would force federal criminals to serve their full sentences almost immediately, and in so doing, begin to make our streets safe again. This proposal was introduced to guarantee truth and accuracy in the sentencing of convicted federal criminals, the necessity of which is indicated in most recent federal crime statistics. In this report, of all the crimes committed by the members of the study chronic offenders committed 61 percent of these crimes. This includes 76 percent of the rapes, 73 percent of the robberies, and 65 percent of the aggravated assaults. These statistics prove very clearly that the parole system, as it exists, allows perpetrators of crime back out on the streets to commit their offenses repeatedly against innocent citizens. And it is estimated that one-half of the criminal activity in the United States of America is drug related.[5]

Then, I introduced the "Drug and Violent Crime Sentencing Act of 1985." This legislation calls for greater penalties for large-scale drug activities, including life sentences and death penalties for drug traffickers involved in murder. Definitively, this proposal would do the following:

• for possession with intent to sell heroin or cocaine—ten kilograms or more—mandatory life imprisonment;

• for possession with intent to sell less than ten kilograms of heroin or cocaine, but more than 100 grams—mandatory sentence of 40 years, and a fine of $500,000, or both;

• and for possession of a quantity of marijuana of 100 kilograms or more—mandatory life imprisonment, and a fine of $500,000.

This legislation also calls for mandatory life imprisonment or punishment by death, if an individual convicted of drug trafficking activities kills or intends to kill any person in the commission of such an offense.[6]

The "Drug and Violent Crime Sentencing Act of 1985" specifies as well that the goods or property from illegal drug profits of convicted traffickers be subject to forfeiture.[7]

This legislation is designed to take the drastic steps necessary to ensure that drug traffickers know that we are serious about making them pay for their crimes. For too long, major drug traffickers have walked out of courtrooms with light bails and soft sentences. These people are nothing more than mass murderers, and should be legally treated as such. Supporters of these proposals strongly feel that individuals who commit crimes as heinous as trafficking in illicit narcotics must be punished as the murderers and saboteurs they are. This legislation, if enacted, will go far in putting drug traffickers and crime-prone addicts where they belong, which is away from where they can continue to do harm to innocent Americans.[8]

While violent crime is the most obvious aspect of the relationship between drugs and crime, there is also the white collar crime that results, such as money-laundering activities, and corruption of drug law enforcement officials. How this activity affects American citizens is not so obvious, but it is equally damaging. To counter the effects of this kind of criminal activity, I have introduced the following two bills.

The first, the "Money Laundering Prevention Act of 1985," would declare all currency in the denomination of $100 obsolete and not legal tender upon the expiration of three months after the date of enactment of the bill. Prior to the issuance of this order, the Secretary of the Treasury shall issue newly designed currency in this denomination. American citizens would be given a full three months in which to redeem their $100 bills for the newly designed currency. The massive amounts of cash needed in successful laundering operations would not be able to be exchanged in the process called for in this proposal, and money launderers would therefore be prevented from taking advantage of this provision in the legislation. Since latest estimates are that billions of dollars annually are laundered through American financial institutions, allowing drug traffickers to market massive amounts of drugs in our nation, we must use every means at our disposal to establish effective methods of prevention.[9]

Later in this Congress, I cosponsored, with Senator D'Amato, legislation entitled the "Money Laundering Crimes Act," which would, for the first time, make it a crime to assist in the laundering of money in the furtherance of a crime.

Because involvement of financial institutions and their personnel is an integral part of money-laundering operations, steps must be taken to end this cooperation on the part of banks and other financial institutions involved. This legislation would, specifically, subject whoever conducts or causes to be conducted a transaction or series of transactions involving one or more monetary instruments in, through, or by a financial institution which is engaged in, or the activities of which affect, interstate commerce, or attempts to do so:

- with intent to promote, manage, establish, carry on, or facilitate the promotion, management, establishment, or carrying on, of any unlawful activity; or
- with knowledge or reason to know that such monetary instru-

ments represent income derived, directly or indirectly, from any unlawful activity, or the proceeds of such income.[10]

For the first such offense, a fine of up to $250,000 or twice the value of the monetary instruments, whichever is greater, or imprisonment for up to ten years; and for each such subsequent offense, a fine of up to $1,000,000 or five times the value of the monetary instruments, whichever is greater, or imprisonment for up to 20 years, or both.[11]

To create their financial empires, drug traffickers need the cooperation of financial institutions and their personnel, and proposals such as the "Money Laundering Crimes Act" are the kind of action necessary to curb this corruption.

WORKING WITH THE 1984 CRIME BILL

Congressional colleagues obviously share my determination to curb drug related criminal activity, as in 1984 the most comprehensive crime control legislation in history was enacted into law.

Aspects of this legislation designed to affect drug related crime include sections:

• amending the Bail Reform Act of 1966 to permit courts to consider danger to the community in setting bail conditions and to deny bail altogether where the government proves by clear and convincing evidence that no conditions of release will reasonably assure the safety of the community and the appearance of the defendant at trial;

• amending the Bail Reform Act to tighten the criteria for post-conviction release pending sentencing and appeal;

• amending the Bail Reform Act to provide for revocation of release and increased penalties for crimes committed while on release;

• amending the Bail Reform Act to increase penalties for bail jumping;

• amending the Sentencing Reform law to establish a determinate sentencing system with no parole and limited good time credits;

• amending the Sentencing Reform law to promote more uniform sentencing by establishing a commission to set narrow sentencing ranges based on the offense and pertinent offender characteristics;

• amending the Sentencing Reform law to require courts to explain in writing any departure from sentencing guidelines;

- amending the Sentencing Reform law to authorize defendants to appeal sentences harsher, and the government to appeal sentences more lenient, than the sentencing commission guidelines;
- amending present forfeiture statutes by providing forfeiture of profits and proceeds of organized crime offenses;
- providing criminal forfeiture in all drug felony cases;
- transferring of forfeitured property to state and local enforcement agencies participating in the investigation leading to seizure and forfeitures;
- expanding procedures for "freezing" forfeitable property pending judicial proceedings;
- providing forfeiture of land used to grow, store and manufacture dangerous drugs;
- expanding use of efficient administrative forfeiture procedures in noncontested cases;
- expanding drug enforcement capabilities by strengthening federal penalties applicable to narcotics offenses;
- reducing the regulatory burden on law-abiding manufacturers and distributors of legitimate controlled substances;
- strengthening the ability of the Drug Enforcement Administration to prevent diversion of legitimate controlled substances;
- amending present Surplus Property laws to facilitate donation of surplus federal property to state and local governments for urgently needed prison space;
- amending current foreign currency transaction law by adding an attempt provision to existing law prohibiting transportation of currency out of the United States in violation of reporting requirements;
- strengthening penalties for currency violations and authorizing payment of rewards for information leading to the conviction of money launderers;
- clarifying the authority of U.S. Customs agents to conduct border searches related to currency offenses;
- establishing federal jurisdiction over solicitation to commit a crime of violence;
- expanding the felony-murder rule to include "escape, murder, kidnapping, treason, espionage, and sabotage;"
- establishing a minimum-mandatory 5-year sentence for use of a firearm in a federal crime of violence;
- expanding current laws to include kidnapping of federal officials;

- establishing a new federal offense for crimes against family members of federal officials;
- expanding authority to include attempted assaults and assaults upon United States intelligence and probation officers and to allow the Attorney General to designate other federal officials for coverage;
- creating federal penalties for escape from custody resulting from civil commitment;
- amending current law to cover warning the subject of a search;
- establishing federal sanctions for theft or bribery involving federal program funds;
- establishing federal sanctions for counterfeiting of state and corporate securities;
- amending current law to cover receipt of stolen bank property;
- adding a new section to current law to cover bank related bribery;
- adding to the current law to cover bank fraud including check kiting;
- lowering from 16 to 15 the age at which a juvenile may be prosecuted as an adult, by expanding the list of predicate offenses to include serious crimes of violence and drug trafficking, and by easing restraints on use of juvenile fingerprints;
- amending wiretap laws to permit emergency wiretaps in life-endangering situations and by expanding the range of predicate offenses to include wire fraud, illegal currency transactions and crimes against victims and witnesses;
- revising current law to permit prosecution of threat offenses in any district from, to, or through which the threat travels;
- authorizing civil injunctions against fraud pending criminal prosecution;
- authorizing government appeal of new trial orders;
- improving the Witness Security Program through codification of case laws and other changes;
- amending the Foreign Agent Registration Act to shift to the Attorney General powers now held by the Secretary of State;
- providing for federal jurisdiction over crimes by or against United States nationals in a place outside the jurisdiction of any nation;
- directing the Attorney General to report to the Congress concerning use by criminal defendants of internal Department of Justice guidelines as the basis for challenging criminal prosecutions;

- facilitating acquisition and admissibility of foreign evidence in connection with criminal proceedings;
- establishing a National Drug Enforcement Policy Board chaired by the Attorney General and made up of Cabinet Officers with drug enforcement responsibilities, to coordinate and oversee federal drug enforcement efforts by essentially codifying the drug enforcement program of that Cabinet Council under the new name of the National Drug Enforcement Policy Board;
- establishing a Crime Victim Fund comprised primarily of federal criminal fine collections from which up to $100 million per year may be allocated among the states, half for victim compensation (up to 35 percent of prior year state victim compensation payments) and half for victim assistance;
- authorizing up to $5 million per year to fund federal victim assistance activities;
- providing for forfeiture to the Fund of profits derived by convicted persons for the sale of their criminal stories;
- creating criminal penalties for those involved in trademark counterfeiting;
- strengthening civil sanctions by permitting seizure of allegedly counterfeit articles on an ex parte basis and allowing trademark owners to bring suit against trademark counterfeiters for treble damages or treble profits, whichever is greater;
- amending the felony firearm statute to authorize a minimum-mandatory fifteen-year prison sentence for defendants with three prior convictions who use a firearm in the course of a crime of violence;
- amending current anti-terrorism laws to strengthen federal aircraft piracy and kidnapping laws consistent with our obligations under international conventions on aircraft safety and hostage taking;
- amending current forfeiture statutes to create Justice and Treasury revolving funds into which forfeiture proceeds are channeled and from which forfeiture-related expenses may be paid.[12]

It is shocking to realize, but *every single provision just described addresses in some way the seemingly endless list of criminal activity by drug traffickers.* From international terrorism, to money-laundering, to aiding the innocent victim of an addict's assault, this encompassing legislation goes a long way in providing such necessary amendments to the law, such as higher penalties for drug traffickers, greater protection for witnesses, and additional power to drug law enforcement officers.

Further efforts are needed in the ninety-ninth Congress to strengthen certain aspects of the Comprehensive Crime Control Act, which did not go far enough.

THE PROBLEM HITS HOME

A constant spur to these efforts is the scope of the problem of drugs and crime in my home state of Florida. Sadly referred to as a "former" Paradise, Florida in many urban areas has developed rates of criminal activity that are among the highest in the nation. Cities in the sun-drenched state are frozen in fear.

These increased crime rates are almost all related to the increased narcotics trafficking activity in the state. Its geographical make-up, which on the one hand makes it beautiful and unique in our nation, also makes it a perfect haven for drug traffickers. There is a natural fallout from such activity, bringing results such as the designation of Miami as the "machine-gun murder capitol of the world."

Miami, in the last ten years, has become the point of entry for perhaps 75 percent of all the cocaine and marijuana smuggled into the United States. It has been primarily in South Florida that the criminal transactions of much of the American drug trade were taking place.[13]

The nature of the problem is staggering: more than 12,000 metric tons of marijuana enter the United States annually; between 40 and 48 metric tons of cocaine enter the United States annually. It has been estimated that there may be as many as 25 million regular users of marijuana in the United States, and more than 4 million regular users of cocaine. Between 13 and 18 million Americans have used cocaine at least once, and there are almost one half million heroin addicts in this country. The brutally serious nature of the drug problem in this country and its affect on crime is evidenced by the following statistic: a full one half of all jail and prison inmates regularly used drugs before committing their offenses. Other information reveals that 50 to 60 percent of all property crimes are drug related. Indeed, it has been estimated that one in four homicides in Miami is drug related.[14]

It is now abundantly clear to all of us that the real cost of drug smuggling and addiction in this country is staggering in human life and suffering. It is equally clear that South Florida has been and continues to be a main focus in the war against drugs.

The amounts of money involved in illicit drug transactions in a period of a year has been estimated to be in the billions of dollars, and the vast majority of this money must be laundered through a financial institution, or converted into non-cash assets. In both cases, some businesses are drawn into collaboration with, or outright domination by, the drug kingpins. It is unfortunately obvious that some of South Florida's financial institutions and personnel have aided and abetted these activities, and in so doing, not only violate the civic duties of responsible corporate behavior, but violate tax and currency laws as well.

There seem to be a great number of individuals who are willing to accept large amounts of cash for valuable assets, as this financial protection is another reason South Florida has become a haven for drug traffickers. The power of drug dollars to corrupt the civil integrity, indeed the very souls of a community's commercial life, cannot be overestimated. With the enactment of legislation calling for increased penalties for those involved in money-laundering activities, however, drug dollars will seem less attractive.

The primary problem in curbing money-laundering activities by financial institutions and their personnel is that the amount of money involved in the drug trade is so overwhelming that it has made the drug kingpins believe that no one, not in drug law enforcement, in banking, in transportation, is incorruptible. Perhaps it will help deter such activities on the part of financial institutions to have it made perfectly clear what kind of people are behind these drug dollars.

Drug traffickers and dealers are, very simply, vicious, brutal and violent to the extreme, even by the lowest standards of criminality. They are mass murderers, to whom even the crudest limits of decency are unknown. They are members of multiple-large-scale, criminal organizations who will open fire on a rival faction in a crowded mall, with total indifference to the lives of the men, women and children who may be caught in the cross fire. We are all in a position of having to deal with a collection of independent warring factions, an underworld who will stop at nothing and observe no law in their desire to reap profits. The international drug trade which has made South Florida its capital is not a single, established cartel; within each of these separate groups, though there exists a highly sophisticated structure, there is often anarchy within the ranks.

Not only does this situation place our families in a state of constantly increasing violence, but it also threatens the fundamental corruption of our society.

A constant concern of our justice system must be how long our basic institutions can maintain their integrity in the face of millions of drug dollars ready to be spent for the sole purpose of the corruption of these institutions. It is the obvious, and universal, intention of drug traffickers to corrupt public officials, and it is their genuine expectation that this corruption will be accomplished. We must all be cognizant of the fact that in the process of narcotics abuse, the bought-off official is no less guilty of the destruction of our children than is the drug trafficker.

INTERNATIONAL PROBLEMS IN THE DRUG WAR

Who are the drug traffickers? Where do they come from? Where do their products come from? These are questions I have dedicated my Senate career to resolving. For example, when I learned from a recent State Department report that the country of Bolivia had not, during Fiscal Year 1984, eradicated a single coca bush, and yet was slated to receive $48 million in U.S. aid, I decided to take action.[15]

On March 28, 1985, I introduced legislation designed to terminate all U.S. economic and military assistance for the Bolivian Government unless this nation eradicates 10 percent of its coca production. This is a drastic step, but one that is necessary after the information was revealed that this tiny nation is the supplier of 50 percent of the world's cocaine. Despite American financial assistance, American agricultural assistance, and American admonition, Bolivia did not, as was said in the State Department's Bureau of International Narcotics Control Strategy Report, "pull up a single coca bush." It is time to stop funding our own destruction; obviously, many Senators share this view—as of mid-1985 fifteen U.S. Senators had cosponsored this legislation.[16]

Then, it became clear that the Nicaraguan government was involved in narcotics trafficking activities, so the Senate Subcommittee on Children, Family, Drugs and Alcoholism conducted a hearing into this issue on April 19, 1985. It proved to be a very informative hearing, to understate things a bit.

Testifying at this hearing, along with officials of the U.S. Customs Service and the Department of Justice, were two individuals who had met with Nicaraguan government officials to implement drug trafficking activities. One of the witnesses was a former drug dealer who had been recruited by the Nicaraguans to teach their narco-traffickers the chemical process involved in cutting cocaine to gain a higher yield. The other, a former INTERPOL fugitive and major European hashish dealer, had been involved on numerous occasions with Nicaraguan government officials in various drug deals. Both men gave testimony about meeting with Robert Vesco to discuss Nicaraguan efforts to ship vast amounts of drugs to the U.S., and other Nicaraguan officials implicated by these witnesses included: Defense Minister Thomas Borge; his assistant Frederico Vaughn; and numerous police and military officials of the Sandinista government. As information, both the Department of Justice and the Department of the Treasury administered extensive lie-detector tests to these witnesses, and both men were found to be accurate and truthful in their statements.[17]

The government of Nicaragua is, it was revealed at this hearing, implementing a two-fold goal to raise vast amounts of money for the Sandinista treasury, and to corrupt American youth through drugs. Drug trafficking is a thriving concern in Nicaragua at the present time, with the focus of activity being the United States of America. To put a stop to this, the Reagan Administration should take the steps necessary to deny landing rights to Nicaragua, and to suspend trade as well.[18]

America cannot continue to allow itself to be victimized by nations like Bolivia and Nicaragua. Bolivia must be made to stop its drug production; Nicaragua, to stop its government-sponsored drug trafficking. Both these nations protect their drug kingpins, causing the drug trade in both nations to prosper. And this prosperity for drug traffickers and corrupt governments is being accomplished at American expense.

CONCLUSION

As the range of legislation discussed here indicates, the war against drug abuse must be fought simultaneously on a number of different fronts. The massive and intensifying federal response to the staggering, multi-faceted, problem of drug abuse involves the following coordinated efforts:
- stop drugs at the source;
- ensure existence of effective drug abuse education and prevention programs;
- increase interdiction efforts; and support local, state and federal drug law enforcement efforts.

As difficult and as expensive as this combination of efforts is, it is even more difficult to imagine the repercussions of not making this coordinated effort. We must remain a society unwilling to sacrifice our most precious resource, our children, to the horrors of drug abuse, and take whatever difficult steps we must to achieve the eradication of narcotics abuse. As we fight the war against drug abuse, unwilling to back down, we are preserving our future, and society.[19]

REFERENCE

Drugs and Crime: A Legislative Perspective by Paula Hawkins

1. "Impact of Drugs on Crime, 1984," Hearing before the U.S. Senate Subcommittee on Alcoholism and Drug Abuse of the Committee on Labor and Human Resources, May 10, 1984.
2. *Ibid.*
3. *Ibid.*
4. *Ibid.*
5. "Truth in Sentencing Act of 1985," S. 894, April 4, 1985.
6. "Drug and Violent Crime Sentencing Act of 1985."
7. *Ibid.*
8. *Ibid.*
9. "Money Laundering Prevention Act of 1985."
10. "Money Laundering Crimes Act of 1985" S. 572, March 5, 1985.
11. *Ibid.*
12. "Comprehensive Crime Control Act of 1984," P.L. 98-473, October 12, 1984. The intellectual case for many of these reforms can be found in the predecessor to this book. *See* Patrick B. McGuigan and Randall R. Rader, eds., *Criminal Justice Reform: A Blueprint* (Washington, D.C.: Institute for Government and Politics, Free Congress Foundation, 1983).
13. "Impact of Drugs on Crime, 1984," Hearing before the U.S. Senate Subcommittee on Alcoholism and Drug Abuse of the Committee on Labor and Human Resources, May 10, 1985, testimony by Stanley Marcus, U.S. Attorney for the Southern District of Florida.
14. *Ibid.*
15. "Legislation to Terminate U.S. Aid to Bolivia," S. 790, March 28, 1985. *See also* Amy Belleau, "Two Senators Wage War on Drugs," *Judicial Notice*, May/June 1985, pp. 12–13.
16. *Ibid.*
17. "Role of Nicaragua in Narcotics Trafficking," Hearing before the U.S. Senate Subcommittee on Children, Family, Drugs and Alcoholism of the Committee on Labor and Human Resources, April 19, 1985.
18. *Ibid.*
19. [Editor's note: As this book was published in the fall of 1986, Senator Hawkins' six years of work in this area seemed near fruition. The Congress was on the verge of enacting sweeping anti-drug provisions.]

3

JUVENILE JUSTICE:
Is It A Kid's Game?
by Benedict J. Koller

Suppose an eleven-year-old was arrested for the brutal murder of a nine-year-old who had been left, after an afternoon of play, with 15 stab wounds and a crushed skull. How would this case be handled within the ordinary workings of the current juvenile court system? Typically, the youngster would be declared a "status offender," a special category of offenders created by the juvenile court system. Status offenders are minors who commit acts, such as truancy, which would not be crimes if committed by adults. As such, the eleven-year-old child is not considered a delinquent, and is likewise exempt from having a criminal record.

The situation above is based upon a case now pending in Wisconsin in which an eleven-year-old girl and two boys, ages 12 and 14, are accused of slaying their 9 year-old playmate. According to an August 19, 1985 news column, "If the boys are convicted, they could be sentenced to a youth facility only until age 19. They then must be freed under Wisconsin law. Because the girl is younger than 12, she cannot be charged....A petition...declares the girl 'a child in need of protection and services' and seeks to have her placed in a foster home or youth treatment center."[1]

This story reflects not only the inability of the juvenile court system to deal satisfactorily with serious juvenile offenders, but also demonstrates the scope of the crimes juveniles are committing. This story may be shocking, but it is not as unusual as some might think.

By way of further illustration, the following stories appeared on the same page of a local newspaper. Two Washington, D.C. youths, both age 12, lured a seven-year-old child into a park where they allegedly struck him in the head with a baseball bat and then pushed him into the Potomac River. They reportedly threw rocks at the child forcing him into deeper water where he drowned. Their motive: they wanted his bicycle.

Another seven-year-old child, a Maryland resident, was brutally beaten and left lying face down in the water while playing in a creek near his home. His 10-year-old playmate, with him when the alleged attack took place, could think of no motive for the vicious attack. The suspects were believed to be two area youths. (It was later determined that the 10-year-old playmate committed the attack. There have been claims that he attacked the youth because of an Ethiopian tradition where manhood is proven by use of the fists.)

Finally, a 17 year old District of Columbia youth was reported in good condition after being shot. The apparent reason for the shooting: the youth was discovered talking to the perpetrator's girlfriend. The teenage gunman is still being sought.[2]

THINKING ABOUT YOUTH CRIME

Is it any wonder that the juvenile justice system in our country has become the focus of so much concern and criticism? Headlines scream out at us daily of crimes committed by juveniles. Bernard Goetz achieved celebrity-status for his reaction to the mugging he received on a New York subway at the hands of juveniles. Juvenile crime—violent and non-violent, against persons and property—extends to every corner of America. Whether one lives in rural or metropolitan America, the effects of juvenile crime are bound to be felt.

Statistically, juveniles commit a disproportionate amount of crime. Six percent of the total population is comprised of juveniles in the 15 to 17 age group, however, this group accounts for approximately 10 to 15 percent of arrests for forcible rape, and between 20 to 25 percent of arrests for robbery. Likewise, eight percent of arrests for criminal homicide are accountable to these older juveniles, as are 11 percent for aggravated assault.[3] Statistics for 1983 further demonstrate that, although those between the ages of 5 and 17 only make up about 20 percent of the total population,[4] they account for over 50 perent of arrests for burglaries and motor vehicle thefts.[5]

In seeming contradiction to these startling data, other recent statistics indicate that the actual number of arrests for those under 18 has *decreased* for nearly all types of crime. Does this apparent shift signal that the fight against juvenile crime is actually succeeding? Or is there another, more realistic explanation for this decrease?

John K. Van de Kamp, the Attorney General of California, recently held a crime conference to address the issue of falling crime rates. Various researchers and noted scholars formed panels to discuss the causes of this trend. Among factors cited were differences in accounting methods, reduced police forces, and demographic changes.

As regards accounting methods, when looking at crime records, we are bound by the figures compiled by each state individually. Unfortunately, the methods used to gather these records vary from state to state, and may be subject to independent alteration. Furthermore, within each state itself, counties may change their methods, rendering a precise accounting of juvenile arrests impossible. Dr. Barry Krisberg, the President of the National Council on Crime and Delinquency, gave two examples of this in his testimony at the crime conference:

> I was . . . alarmed to discover that the highest per capita rate of juvenile crime is traditionally in Wisconsin. I feel sorry for the people of Milwaukee, but it turns out that Wisconsin's crime reporting of minor and trivial juvenile offenses is a lot more honest than in other places. I also noticed that there were dramatic declines in youth crime in Washington State during a key period. . . . I was disturbed to find out that, for a couple of years the City of Seattle was not included in the juvenile arrest data for Washington State.[6]

Second, the size of the police force plays a determining role in crime rate figures. In the late 1970s many jurisdictions had to lay off police officers because they lacked sufficient funds to pay them. Given this fact, police were obviously hampered in efforts to combat crime, and it is clear that, with a smaller police force, arrests are sure to decrease.

The above factors, although recognized as contributing to the overall decline in juvenile arrests, were not thought to be of major import to those attending the California conference. Rather, they believed demogaphics to be the most significant factor. In fact, Alfred Blumstein, the Director of the Urban Systems Institute School of Urban and Public Affairs, predicted many years ago that we could expect drops in the juvenile crime rates.

Dr. Blumstein based his predictions on his studies of demographic conditions. Previous studies had shown that the peak age of criminality for property crimes is 16. The baby boom having peaked, it was expected that there would be a declining juvenile population. Thus, juvenile crime rates should decline. And this is exactly what has happened.

However, additional factors exist which were not considered by those attending the conference but which offer insights into an accurate interpretation of the statistics. For instance, as states pass new legislation with regard to juvenile offenders, police practices change. A particular example: having passed legislation requiring that status offenders be processed through diversion programs and not through the courts, Washington state police are now hesitant to arrest runaways knowing they will be back on the streets in a few hours. To complicate matters further, these runaways are frequently prostitutes. A computer check in Seattle revealed 587 juvenile prostitution charges since 1979 (after changes in the code became effective). A random survey of ten of these cases found that eight were multiple offenders, some of which had as many as 15 previous convictions for various crimes: *yet they were still on the streets.*[7] Hence it is clear that diversion legislation is hindering police in the practice of their duty. This in turn leads to misleading arrest records and fosters misconceptions about the scope of juvenile crime.

Another consideration is that the above data tabulates arrests only. Taken at face value, it reveals nothing about how many crimes a juvenile has committed before his first arrest. In point of fact, however, one study has shown that juveniles committed from eight to 11 serious crimes for each time they were arrested.[8]

In addition, the probability that a person will be arrested for a crime increases with age and criminal experience. Although it seems that criminal experience would help the offender avoid detection, this does not appear to be the case because the more crimes one commits, the more detailed police profiles become. Thus, arrest and conviction rates increase with each criminal act.[9] Also, because fingerprints, photographs, and other adult records are readily available to police agencies, whereas juvenile records are not, law enforcement personnel are better able to get the evidence needed to solve crimes committed by adults. Hence it is likely that juveniles, being less likely than their adult counterparts to get arrested, are committing substantially more crimes than arrest records indicate.

It is clear from the above that juvenile arrest statistics can be misleading. Nonetheless, public perception of juvenile crime as a serious problem is prevalent, and the "treatment and rehabilitation" model in today's juvenile courts is under increasing attack. Tougher sentencing laws and increased incarceration are being urged by many citizens. Californians, for example, voted into law an initiative, the Victim's Bill of Rights, in response to their crime problem. A major component of this measure, passed in 1982, referred to juvenile criminals.

The seriousness of the juvenile court problem can be further appreciated by looking at the crime history of chronic adult offenders. The adult being arrested for crime, more often than not, began as a juvenile delinquent. A study prepared under a grant from the Office of Juvenile Justice and Delinquency Prevention by Peter W. Greenwood and Franklin E. Zimring makes this clear:

> Only two percent of those with no juvenile convictions experienced more than three convictions as an adult. Most chronic adult offenders will also have been frequent offenders when they were juveniles. Most chronic juvenile offenders will go on to commit crimes as adults. The probability is extremely remote that any individual who was never arrested as a juvenile will become a chronic offender as an adult.[10]

Taking into account, then, the scope of the juvenile crime problem and the ineffectiveness of the juvenile court system, as demonstrated above, it is clear that something more needs to be done. What, then, are and ought to be the state legislatures' responses to juvenile crime? To understand these, a quick look at the history of the juvenile law and how it operates would be helpful.

The juvenile court is unique, joining traditional legal powers with purposes and functions inherently social in nature, and designed to promote individualization of justice through evaluation and treatment. In other words, it is civil rather than criminal in nature. Law enforcement agencies, county probation departments and state rehabilitation facilities are all integral parts of the juvenile court process.

America's juvenile court system is the result of developments begun in the 1300s in England. The *parens patriae* theory was a legal doctrine created to give the King authority to protect certain people incapable of caring for themselves. Lunatics, idiots, and children were among those designated for protection. From this beginning, the "parental" relationship between the state and the child developed into a separate legal system.

THE ILLINOIS MODEL, AND ITS VARIATIONS

The first comprehensive code developed on our shores was the pioneer "Juvenile Court Act of 1899" in Illinois. Separate hearings, lesser punishments, segregated facilities, and probation were already realities in certain parts of the country. Illinois put them all together into one code for the purpose of treating and rehabilitating juveniles.

Recognizing the need for a uniform set of laws aimed at dealing with juvenile delinquency, every state eventually followed the Illinois example. It is interesting to note that the explicit purpose of each of these codes is quite similar. They are also alike in that the stated goals are to protect juveniles rather than to punish them, and to rehabilitate and treat juveniles so that they become respected and productive members of the community.

On the other hand, although the purposes and goals of the various state courts are very similar, the methods of accomplishing these goals are quite different. Nearly all of the states created a separate court to deal with juvenile delinquency. Nine states, however, gave the existing Family Court jurisdiction over juvenile cases.[11] They reasoned that delinquency, being a family problem, should be treated in the family courts. Two states not wanting to confuse delinquency with family problems such as divorce, and not wanting it to be a part of the criminal court, placed jurisdiction in the Probate Court.[12]

Other differences (discussed below) include: minimum and maximum ages for jurisdiction; time at which jurisdiction attaches; length of jurisdiction; whether the juvenile is entitled to bail or trial by jury; and whether the public should be excluded from the hearings.

All juvenile courts must begin by addressing the initial question of the age at which jurisdiction attaches. However, this question of minimum age, or age of culpability, has never received much attention in the state juvenile codes. Under common law, a child under seven was deemed incapable of committing a criminal act because he lacked the ability to form the requisite criminal intent. Eight states have set the minimum age at which jurisdiction attaches at 10 years.[13] One state has set the minimum age at 12,[14] and another has set it at six.[15] The remaining states have either not mentioned a minimum age or use the common law presumption of seven years.

The maximum age for jurisdiction is a crucial decision because it determines whether a youth comes under the jurisdiction of the juvenile or the criminal court. And it can make a significant difference in the ultimate disposition of the case. Five states set the maximum age of jurisdiction at 16 years.[16] For these states, once a person reaches the age of 17 and commits a crime he is tried in criminal court. Eight states have original jurisdiction up to 17 years,[17] and one state allows jurisdiction to continue until the youth is 19 years old.[18] The remaining states set 18 years as the maximum age.

Since 1974, revisions on the maximum age at which jurisdiction attaches have changed upwards. Alabama raised its maximum age from 16 to 17 years, and then a few years later from 17 to 18. Florida, Maine, and New Hampshire raised their maximum ages from 17 to 18 in 1976. South Carolina raised its jurisdictional maximum from 16 to 17 in 1977. Such revisions have served to increase the power of the juvenile court.

The time at which jurisdiction attaches is important for the same reason because for youths close to the maximum age limit it determines whether they will be tried as juveniles or as adults. According to such considerations, if a juvenile commits a crime while he is under the maximum age at which jurisdiction attaches but is not detained until after that age, and if jurisdiction attaches at the date of detention (which is the law in six states),[19] he will be tried as an adult. If jurisdiction attaches at the date of the crime (the law in the remaining states), then the youth will be tried as a juvenile.

The final jurisdictional difference deals with the duration of the jurisdiction of the juvenile court. This issue is becoming increasingly important when we consider the number of serious juvenile offenders and, again, because of its decisive role in determining whether the offender will be tried in juvenile or adult court. Almost all states make statutory provision to continue jurisdiction at least two or three years beyond the maximum age at which jurisdiction attaches in their state, establishing a pattern such that jurisdictions with higher maximum ages have higher ages for continuing court jurisdiction. In concrete terms, this means that a juvenile alleged to have committed a serious crime at age 16 in a state where continuing jurisdiction is to age 18, will more than likely be transferred to adult court because the sentence for that type of crime is more than two years.

California has addressed the problem of jurisdictional duration with a blanket extension of the jurisdiction of juvenile courts to age 25, to allow as many youths as possible access to the rehabilitative services of the juvenile system. On the other hand, if it becomes evident in that time that rehabilitation is not occurring, the offender may be transferred to the California State Adult Corrections Department.

Now, the transition from juvenile to adult court has advantages and disadvantages. If the youth is tried in the adult court, the sentence may be harsher than he would receive in juvenile court. And, as we have all seen, rehabilitation is not an important component of the adult system; thus, facilities and programs available to the youth in the juvenile court are absent in the adult jail and prison system. On the other hand, the adult court provides advantages missing at the juvenile level. These include the due process rights that have become a fixture in criminal proceedings, such as the right to trial by jury, the availability of bail, and the right to a speedy and impartial trial.

Some states extend to the juveniles more due process rights than have been mandated by United States Supreme Court decisions. Sixteen states allow for bail at the discretion of the court.[20] Thirteen states give juveniles the right to trial by jury.[21] Finally, the states are split evenly whether the public should be allowed to view hearings. In most states that do allow the public access to the hearings, courts still have the power, when necessary, to exclude them.

Turning now to a more specific problem area within juvenile crime, in recent years states have been attempting to solve the dilemma of what to do with violent and chronic offenders. These offenders pose serious problems to public safety. It is these sophisticated, persistent, or violent juvenile offenders that pose the most difficult problem to the administration of juvenile justice. As noted by Barry C. Feld, a law professor at the University of Minnesota, Minneapolis: "This small but important class of youths challenges both the rehabilitative assumptions of the juvenile court and the propriety of informal, nonpunitive and relatively short-term social control."[22]

State legislatures have recognized this shortcoming within the juvenile system, and so have made it easier to transfer juveniles to adult courts. These transfer mechanisms allow states to retain jurisdiction for longer periods while simultaneously keeping the door open to the possibility of transference of serious juvenile offenders to adult court.

In 1975, for example, California substantially modified the waiver, or transfer, provisions. These provisions introduced more specificity into the waiver process, and in effect made it easier to waive juveniles to adult court. Then, in 1976, more provisions listing target offenses were added, which created a presumption in favor of waiver. Hence, the burden of producing evidence to show that he is amenable to treatment has been shifted to the juvenile. California also allows juveniles who have not been rehabilitated to be transferred to an adult correctional facility in the region where they committed their serious crime.

Colorado has attempted to deal with serious offenders in another way, by creating legislative classifications for violent juvenile offenders which are designed to handle the "repeat juvenile offender" and the "violent juvenile offender." In effect, these new legislative classifications provide a mandatory sentencing policy for youths who fall into one of the new delinquency classifications. According to such classification, the period of placement within an institution may be indefinite, but must be for more than one year.

Delaware likewise added a provision for mandatory sentencing in the 1976-77 legislative session. Title 10, Section 937(c) of the Delaware Code sets out prescribed periods of confinement for specified crimes. Coupled with existing jurisdictional provisions, this broadens Delaware's range of punishment and narrows the rehabilitative aspects of its juvenile court.   ·

One of the most drastic responses to serious juvenile offenders is New York's limitation on jurisdiction. Jurisdiction in New York cannot attach after the youth reaches 16 years of age. Youths 16 years and older are automatically considered adults. It is only if the person can demonstrate that he is amenable to treatment or rehabilitation that he will be allowed to be transferred down to the juvenile courts.

Other jurisdictions are following the lead of these states and are setting up new categories to deal with problem delinquents. Pennsylvania, for example, is considering legislation which defines the "dangerous juvenile offender."[23] The effect of this bill would be to make it easier to transfer youths to adult court, to allow certain law enforcement agencies easier access to juvenile records, and to open hearings to the public.

As we have just seen, the states are attempting to handle the serious juvenile crime problem by creating new classes of offenders, by making it easier to transfer the offender to adult court, and by legislating mandatory sentencing. These responses represent a significant movement away from the traditional notion of the juvenile court and, more importantly, from the stated purpose of each state code.

The trend towards specificity in sentencing and ready transferral to adult court reveals another, perhaps less obvious weakness within the juvenile court system, namely the decision-making process. These changes have been made necessary by the fact that judges are not able to administer discretionary statutes consistently and evenhandedly. As Donna Hamparian, principal investigator of a youth and adult court study and a fellow in social policy at the Academy for Contemporary Problems, in Columbus, Ohio, states:

> The juvenile justice system centers on a predictive process by which judges make estimates of a youthful delinquent's future. Our research was only one of many studies which led to the same conclusion: the power to predict is too weak to be a basis for decision-making.[24]

At present any disposition or decision to transfer to adult court depends on a judge's ability to assess the youth's amenability to treatment. Having first found an adequate treatment program, the judge must then decide whether the juvenile before him would be suited to that program. To date there has been no valid or reliable clinical basis according to which juvenile court judges can make the necessary individualized determinations of amenability or dangerousness. Such broad and ill-defined guidelines, leaving so much to the discretion of the judge, result in inconsistent and discriminatory applications.

A final weakness of the juvenile court system lies in the ineffectiveness of rehabilitation, which has been elevated over other justifications for punishment in the juvenile court. Unfortunately, juveniles are not being rehabilitated. As John Monahan, a professor of law, psychology, and legal medicine at the University of Virginia School of Law, stated in testimony before the U.S. subcommittee on Juvenile Justice: "In terms of prevention of future crime, in terms of demonstrated results, . . . as I have read the literature there has yet to be an intervention to *treat* demonstrated criminal tendencies that has resulted in a significant decrease in later violent crime."[25]

To sum up, then, current practices are not only ineffective but, according to Barry Feld, serve to undermine the preventative effects of sanctions:

> . . . by characterizing dispositions as treatment rather than penalty, by preventing the communication of the threat of punishment to other potential offenders because of closed proceedings and restricted publicity, by individualizing dispositions and reducing any certainty that specific sanctions will be applied, and by obscuring any relationship between an act and its consequences.[26]

THE "JUSTICE MODEL" AS A REFORM

By way of resolution many authors who have experience with juveniles and juvenile crime argue for a "justice" model of juvenile justice founded upon the twin pillars of *system accountability* and *individual responsibility*. According to this argument the system itself must be accountable to the public, which it is supposed to protect, and the juvenile must be held individually responsible for his actions. Only in this way will the juvenile system be rendered consistent and predictable.

Having a predictable juvenile system is an essential factor in combatting serious juvenile crime, because it will serve to clarify for young people what it is the court is about, namely, enforcement of the law. All too often a youth is thrown into the system ignorant of precisely why he is there or what will happen to him. Predictability will "assure that the consequences of anti-social behavior demonstrate to the offender and all who know about him that certain kinds of behavior are not to be done."[27] Once we can say to the juvenile, "If you persist in your delinquency these are the consequences within the system" then we can be assured of some deterrent effect.

Proportionality is the notion that violent crime will be treated more seriously than minor crime and that similar crimes will be dealt with in a like manner. This should be fundamental to the juvenile system, because certain actions, by their very nature, are more serious than others. It is the act itself, and its effect on the victim, which defines how serious a crime is.

The present system, however, puts greater emphasis on the actor than the act. When juveniles are treated inconsistently and when they see the occasional outrageous system abuse, even discrimination, brought about by "individualized" justice, they lose respect for the system. This lack of respect almost inevitably leads to disobedience.

Furthermore, discretionary justice has allowed juveniles to "play" the system. Juveniles know that if they can make the judge think they are amenable to treatment, then, no matter how serious the crime, they will be placed in a rehabilitation program. Predictability and proportionality would mean that the juvenile justice system is no longer a game.

In order to assure predictability and proportionality within the state systems, legislatures should make the courts accountable to the public as well as to the juvenile. To accomplish this end, hearings should be opened to the public, allowing them access to courtroom proceedings. Additional procedural checks and balances may also be installed. For instance, if a judge or prosecutor deviates from the normal procedural guidelines of the juvenile system, he must explain in writing the reasons for his action. Then, if abuses occur, evidence is available which can be used to hold an individual official responsible and accountable to the public.

In order for such measures to be implemented, the principles and purposes of juvenile courts must be re-evaluated and revised. Rehabilitation should remain as a concern, *but not the purpose*, of the system. Instead, the responsibility of the individual must become the starting point for the state codes. A system based on this "justice" model serves to emphasize fairness, uniformity, and proportionality.

The present juvenile court system has had 86 years to work out its bugs. In the meantime, and most unfortunately, people young and old suffer unnecessarily while state legislatures and the court continue to struggle with the delinquency problem. Equality of treatment, firm expectations of good citizenship, and individual responsibility are the messages state juvenile codes ought to be sending to young people. If adults expect them to behave as responsibile citizens it is only fair to children that they know the rules and that these rules be evenly enforced. Their teenage years are the critical time for learning to integrate into the human family as adults, and it is crucial that society effectively form them in moral, or right, behavior instead of relying on the dubious chances of success with psychological roulette.

REFERENCES

Juvenile Justice: Is It A Kid's Game? by Benedict J. Koller

1. Chicago *Tribune*, August 19, 1985.
2. Washington *Times*, July 22, 1985.
3. California Department of Justice, *Proceedings of the Attorney General's Crime Conference 1985*, March 28, 1985, p. 34.
4. U.S. Department of Commerce, Bureau of the Census, *State Population Estimates, by Age and Components of Change: 1980–1984*, June 1985.
5. "Age-Specific Arrest Rates, 1965–1983," *Uniform Crime Reporting Program*, September 1984, (Washington, D.C.: U.S. Department of Justice). For an informative discussion of juvenile justice issues, *see also* Patrick B. McGuigan and Teresa L. Donovan, eds., *A Conference on Criminal Justice Reform: The Proceedings* (Washington, D.C.: Institute for Government and Politics, Free Congress Foundation, 1984).
6. *Supra*, n. 3, p. 30.
7. Peyton Whitely, "Troubled Kids in a Troubled System," Seattle *Daily Times*, June 18, 1985, p. 44.
8. *Attorney General's Task Force on Violent Crime, Final Report*, August 17, 1981, (Washington, D.C.: U.S. Department of Justice), p. 81.
9. *Ibid.*

10. Peter W. Greenwood and Franklin E. Zimring, *One More Chance: The Pursuit of the Promising Intervention Strategies for Chronic Juvenile Offenders*, The Rand Corporation, May 1985, p. 13. [Editor's note: For an overview of the campaign surrounding the Victims Bill of Rights initiative, *see* John Fund, "Canal Rejected as Voters Approve Tax Cuts and Anti-Crime Measures," *Initiative and Referendum Report*, June 1982 special.]

11. CT, DE, HI, MS, NJ, NY, RI, SC, VA.

12. MI, MN.

13. CO, KS, MN, MS, PA, SD, TX, VT.

14. WI.

15. NC.

16. CT, NY, NC, VT, OK (Males only).

17. GA, IL, LA, MA, MI, MO, SC, TX.

18. WY.

19. AZ, CT, DE, MO, OR, WI.

20. AR, CO, DE, GA, KS, LA, MD, MA, MI, NE, SD, TN, VT, VA, WA, WV.

21. AK, CO, KS, MA, MI, MN, MT, NM, OK, TX, WV, WI, WY.

22. Barry C. Feld, "Delinquent Careers and Criminal Policy: Just Deserts and the Waiver Decision," *Criminology*, May 1983, p. 196.

23. House Bill No. 577, Pennsylvania House of Representatives, Session of 1985.

24. Donna Hamparian, Hearing Before the Subcommittee on Juvenile Justice of the Committee on the Constitution, United States Senate, 97th Congress, October 22, 1981, p. 104.

25. John Monahan, *Supra*, n. 24, p. 13 (Emphasis added).

26. Barry C. Feld, *Supra*, n. 22, p. 208.

27. Donna Hamparian, *Supra*, n. 24, p. 107.

4

THINKING ABOUT JUVENILE CRIME

by Alfred S. Regnery

A theory prominent at the turn of the century claimed that juvenile delinquency is a condition subject to treatment. The trouble with theories is that unless flatly refuted, they can linger for years as vaguely functional rules. Such is the case with that turn-of-the-century theory about delinquency. Its validity is by no means clear, but then neither is its invalidity. The time comes, however, when even those notions long considered viable must withstand the test of practicality before they should continue to be applied.

When the first juvenile court act was passed in Illinois in 1899, it put theory into law.[1] The juvenile court was established to treat a condition rather than punish a wrongdoer; to adjudicate delinquency instead of delinquents. Since that time, the juvenile justice system has expanded in structure, though not in substance. The juvenile courts have increased in number, and have thus kept pace with increases in the juvenile population, but the philosophy of the system is lagging behind. The juvenile justice system has held fast to a theory about delinquency that has yet to be proven, while society impatiently waits for something to be done about juvenile crime.

Each year, there are 28,000 aggravated assault arrests among males aged 15 to 17 (police estimate that there is one arrest for every ten crimes) and 368,000 arrests for burglary, larceny and vehicle theft.[2] Our children under 18 years of age account for approximately one third of all arrests for serious crime, yet the 10 to 17 age group constitutes less than 14 percent of the total population.[3] Because youth are responsible for such a large proportion of serious crime, the juvenile justice system could play an important role in addressing the overall crime problem. Unfortunately, the juvenile court is ill-equipped to meet such a responsibility. Crime calls for justice—to the offender and to society—and justice is noticeably absent from the conceptual framework of the juvenile court.

The goal of the first juvenile court was to save children from the environmental and psychological factors that were believed to cause delinquency. Because adolescence was viewed as a period of dependency, juvenile judges assumed a parental role throughout court proceedings. Rulings were designed to ensure that "the care, trust, custody and discipline of a child" should "approximate as nearly as may be that which should be given by its parents."[4] The court justified this family intervention by adopting *parens patriae*, a doctrine dating back to feudal times, which granted the state fatherly authority in legal disputes.

The newly established juvenile court represented a considerable departure from the characteristics traditionally associated with a court of law. Juvenile court had jurisdiction over poor, neglected and delinquent youth, all of whom were believed to be in need of treatment and a reasonable facsimile of parental control. The court's mandate made no mention of punishment. The same sort of treatment could be prescribed for children who broke the law as it was for those who were poor or neglected. This custodial rather than punitive orientation included the presumption that the best interests of the state naturally coincided with the best interests of the child. Consequently, juvenile court was not conducted within the procedural guidelines normally associated with the judicial process. Juvenile judges conducted civil proceedings rather than criminal; hearings rather than trials. There were no defense counsels, no juries of peers, and no formal rules of evidence. Juveniles faced delinquency petitions instead of criminal charges. Deliberation was not a matter of determining guilt or innocence, but of finding the condition of delinquency. Because the new court claimed original jurisdiction in all cases involving children under the age of 16, there were essentially no juvenile criminals.

The juvenile justice system experienced rapid growth. By 1920, all but three states had established juvenile courts, all of which were based on the original design. The system continued to operate in this fashion until the 1960s, when the U.S. Supreme Court affected a number of changes in the juvenile court process. The Court applied some of the procedural safeguards to the juvenile court which had been previously guaranteed to defendents in criminal court by *Mapp v. Ohio*.[5] Finding that juveniles also had certain rights to due process when facing the possibility of institutionalization, *In re Gault* provided for the rights of counsel, confrontation and cross examination.[6] The Court further ruled in *Gault* that juveniles were entitled to notification of their charges and of their privileges concerning self-incrimination. Additional procedural guidelines were set in by *in re Winship* (1970),[7] which introduced the notion of guilt "beyond a reasonable doubt," and *McKeiver v. Pennsylvania* (1971),[8] which denied juveniles the right to trial by jury.

In *Gault*, the Supreme Court described the juvenile justice system as "peculiar" due to its "debatable" constitutional and theoretical bases. The Court succeedeed in revising the system somewhat by limiting the discretion juvenile judges had previously exercised under the doctrine of *parens patriae*. Nevertheless, the juvenile court continued to direct its efforts towards the treatment of whatever 'condition' appeared before the court, whether poverty, neglect or delinquency. The Supreme Court had moved the juvenile justice system one step closer to the judicial process procedurally, but philosophically it remained virtually unchanged.

The juvenile justice system has remained collectively devoted to its foundation theory. The ways in which the courts have attempted to treat delinquency vary, but all share a common basis. *Something other than the methods employed by the adult criminal court should be applied to juveniles.* The justification behind differential treatment for young offenders grew out of a debate that has continued since the system began. The debate centers on two conflicting viewpoints concerning what can best provide justice for our young people: social welfare or law enforcement. The social welfare mentality frees juveniles of any moral and legal responsibility for their actions. Aberrant behavior is believed to be the fault of society, the family, or some other influence beyond a juvenile's control. Conversely, the arguments for a law enforcement approach to juvenile crime are based on the assumption that juveniles are capable of choosing to obey the law and therefore, they should be held accountable when they break it. The law enforcement approach involves a concept of justice not found in the social welfare approach, but central to the adult criminal court. Justice is what is due to both the offender and society. It is the guarantee of punishment as a consequence of crime.

The fact that the juvenile court operates in conjunction with the law enforcement system is merely a technicality. Although the debate between these two viewpoints continues, the system primarily adheres to the social welfare approach. Juvenile court dispositions have been largely based on the assumption that punitive measures do more harm than good. If the court labels a child "delinquent," for example, the child will allegedly try to live up to his designation. This notion of a self-fulfilling prophecy is furthered in the belief that a juvenile stands to become an even better delinquent if he is

51

institutionalized. At one time, various studies seemed to support these contentions. One body of research in particular indicated that youth who had contact with the juvenile justice system recidivated at least once. There was no apparent difference in the recidivism of youth who were thus 'punished' and youth who were left alone—both resorted to further crime.

Today, the proponents of the juvenile justice system's social welfare orientation still enjoy a considerable amount of popular support. Because of the supposedly damaging effects of punitive measures, rehabilitation is the system's primary goal. Unfortunately, it has proved to be elusive. The benign form of rehabilitation most commonly attempted requires the juvenile court to identify the various factors believed to be responsible for a particular case of delinquency, and intervene in an effective way at an effective moment. The system further seeks to reach beyond the rehabilitation of existing delinquency by intervening at an earlier stage in a child's development. Because the causes of delinquency are considered identifiable, they need only be remedied *before* causing a juvenile to go astray. Thus, the proper targeting of some chosen facet of a child's life is supposed to prevent delinquency from ever occurring.

The efforts of the juvenile justice system in the areas of treatment, prevention and rehabilitation have been tireless, even though the viability of such efforts has repeatedly come under question. Delinquency prevention is, according to the National Council on Crime and Delinquency, an "excessively ambitious if not pretentious" idea and a "fruitless or even naive" belief.[9] Assessments of rehabilitation efforts have been similarly discouraging. In 1975, Robert Martinson reviewed approximately 200 evaluations of the impact of rehabilitation programs, and concluded that with "few and isolated exceptions, the rehabilitative efforts that have been reported so far have had no appreciable effect on recidivism."[10] Martinson stated further that regardless of the method employed—vocational or academic education, individual or group counseling, therapy with social workers or psychiatrists—the results were disappointing. In fact, some psychotherapy programs actually produced an increase in the rate of recidivism. The length of the programs did not seem to matter; neither did the use of probation versus parole, nor community versus institutional settings. Martinson's conclusions were validated by the National Academy of Sciences in two reports issued in 1979 and 1981.[11] However, the Academy stated that Martinson's findings did not necessarily mean that rehabilitation itself was ineffective, but that a successful formula for a rehabilitation program had not yet been discovered.

A workable rehabilitation method may emerge at some point and it remains incumbent upon the juvenile justice system to find the correct formula. The time has come, however, when further efforts based on these unproved theories are unwarranted. Today there is considerably less conviction that the causes of deviant behavior can be fully understood. As yet, they have defied identification. Thus, authorities are beginning to lose confidence in the viability of treatment and the wisdom of rehabilitation as the system's primary goal. James Q. Wilson, Professor of Government at Harvard University, finds fault in the whole concept of rehabilitation, in that it "requires not merely optimistic but heroic assumptions about the nature of man to lead one to suppose that a person, finally sentenced after (in most cases) many brushes with the law, and having devoted a good part of his youth and young adulthood to misbehavior of every sort, should, by either the solemnity of prison or the skillfulness of a counselor, come to see the error of his ways and to experience a transformation of his character."[12] However, coupled with this declining faith in previous efforts is a growing sense of confidence in the potential of the juvenile justice system. Those who have faithfully held to the social welfare design of the juvenile court are facing increasing opposition from experts who favor more of a law enforcement approach to juvenile crime.

In recent years, the arguments for enforcing the law in juvenile court have gained credibility, partially because evidence is mounting against the old beliefs that punishment and contact with the system have negative effects on recidivism. Studies in the past typically examined recidivism on the basis of an either/or proposition. If a youth had been rearrested even once, he was statistically classified a failure. Only those youth who had no further contact with the law were counted as successes. In 1979, Charles Murray and Louis Cox redefined "success" in a way that appeared to measure the impact of various programs with a greater degree of accuracy.[13] Instead of basing success or failure on whether a program participant recidivated, they counted how often he recidivated. Murray and Cox studied several programs for chronic offenders in Chicago in order to determine the frequency of rearrest among program participants. When they examined the recidivism of incarcerated juveniles in the traditional way, they found that the Illinois Department of Corrections had failed—82 percent of the cohort was rearrested sometime after being released. But when they examined the frequency of rearrest for the same cohort, they found a significant reduction in criminal activity. Although the juveniles studied had been arrested an average of 6.3 times each during the year before incarceration, they were arrested an average of 2.9 times each during the 17 months following their release. This finding clearly fit Murray and Cox's new definition of "success." The incarceration of this cohort resulted in a decrease in subsequent criminal activity of nearly 70 percent. Moreover, Murray and Cox discovered a definite relationship between the degree of confinement and the amount of the cohort's subsequent criminal activity. The data generally indicated that the likelihood of "success" after release was greater when the institutional setting was more restricted and structured. The average number of crimes committed was higher among juveniles who had been released from less secure settings.

Additional research in this area is needed, partially because Murray and Cox only followed their cohort for 17 months and did not record the type of crime for which their subjects were rearrested. Nonetheless, their conclusions are consistent with those of several other studies conducted during the same period, and obviously have important implications for the juvenile justice system in terms of its rehabilitative efforts.

Contrary to suppositions concerning the damaging effects of contact with the system, successful rehabilitation efforts are often related to deterrence and punishment. The use of such measures would not be a matter of sacrificing the rehabilitation goal, but of merging it with another important goal: administering justice. For years, the concept of personal accountability has needlessly separated these goals. Justice is not served by telling an offender that he broke the law due to some factor beyond his control. But, as recent studies have shown, neither is rehabilitation accomplished. Because the purpose of rehabilitation is to turn juvenile offenders into useful or, at least, non-troublesome members of society, personal accountability is of the utmost importance. In order to successfully integrate with society, children need to learn the values society expects of adults. Yet, the juvenile court fails to instill these values in offenders when it fails to consider personal accountability. Indeed, one of the juvenile court's primary obligations is to act in the best interest of juvenile offenders by disposing of cases in a manner which will best mend errant ways. However, another obligation is to act in the best interest of society by upholding the law. These obligations both seek to control juvenile crime as a common end, but they also share a common means: justice.

The need for justice in juvenile court is critical. Juvenile criminals are not all minor offenders, the type of youth who may respond to the gentle persuasion of today's juvenile justice system. Of the approximately 1.3 million delinquency cases juvenile courts dispose of each year, 42.4 percent are violent crimes and serious property offenses.[14] Most serious juvenile crime can be attributed to a small core of youthful offenders, many of whom commit literally hundreds of felonies per year and usually continue this pattern as adults. The juvenile court has contact with these offenders early in their criminal careers, and could presumably be a valuable tool in the overall reduction of crime. Unfortunately, this small group of chronic offenders has posed a problem to the juvenile justice system. As a result, state after state has made statutory provisions so these offenders can be placed in a system that should be, but is not necessarily, better equipped to handle them—the criminal justice system.

The specific reasons behind the use of waiver and transfer of youth to adult criminal court may vary slightly, but all are due to the shortcomings of juvenile court. In some instances, a juvenile judge will employ waiver and transfer in the hope—sometimes false—that adult criminal court will deal more severely with a serious juvenile offender. In addition to the presumed punitive advantages of criminal court, waiver and transfer sometimes occurs because there is not enough space in existing juvenile institutions. Consequently, some juveniles are tried in criminal court so they can be sentenced to adult prisons. At the end of 1982, over 6000 inmates aged 18 or younger were housed in adult prisons in this country, and the number increases each year.[15] However, the transfer of a youthful offender to criminal court does not insure that his incarceration will be more certain, or that his sentence will be more just than the disposition he would have received from a juvenile judge. In a court which predominantly tries adults, a youthful offender is more likely to win both the leniency of the judge and a light or suspended sentence. The use of waiver and transfer may appear to be a move toward the application of punishment appropriate to serious juvenile crime—in some cases, juveniles convicted in adult court are indeed appropriately sentenced—but in order to improve juvenile dispositions overall, attention needs to be devoted to the sentences themselves, regardless of the court in which they are imposed.

Waiver and transfer is also used to bypass juvenile record confidentiality. When youthful offenders reach legal age, the records they have accumulated in juvenile court are often sealed. Since these records are not generally available in the criminal courts, particularly in the early stages of the process, the vast majority of juvenile criminals are, in effect, given clean slates. Thus, offenders with juvenile records who are tried in adult court are not likely to be sentenced in a manner which adequately reflects their repeated violation of the law. A 1980 Rand Corporation study indicated that this is a common situation.[16] The study revealed that only three percent of the prosecutors in criminal court have access to complete juvenile records when needed. Juvenile records can be made available for future use, however, if an offender is transferred to adult criminal court before reaching legal age. Prior offense records are essential to the key decisions in both the juvenile and criminal processes, such as arrest, bail determination, charging, plea negotiation, and sentencing. When complete records are not available, the entire criminal justice system is compromised as a viable crime control mechanism, in that the incarceration of repeat offenders is dangerously delayed. While most serious crime is committed by men under the age of 23,[17] career criminals peak at 29 years of age when they are finally incarcerated in programs tailored for such offenders.[18] The Bureau of Justice Statistics (BJS) reported in 1983 that most criminals are not incarcerated at all until well after the years in which they are most crime prone.[19] BJS attributed this lag to the time it takes for an offender to develop a record which justifies a prison sentence.

Protective policies such as record confidentiality may prove to be the undoing of the juvenile court. Such policies exemplify the court's general reluctance to punish criminal offenders, thereby diminishing the public's confidence in the system as well as its deterrence value. Serious offenders find little to fear or respect in a court which repeatedly tolerates illegal behavior and is more likely to employ waiver and transfer than impose punishment. There is, in fact, little reason for serious offenders to fear the juvenile justice system. The system is preoccupied, and has been for several years, with one-time and minor offenders.

The passage of the Juvenile Justice and Delinquency Prevention (JJDP) Act of 1974 contributed to the focus of the system today. The Act constituted Congress' response, in part, to a 1967 report of the President's Commission on Law Enforcement and Administration of Justice.[20] The report claimed that "delinquency is not so much an act of individual deviancy as a pattern of behavior produced by a multitude of pervasive societal influences well beyond the reach of the actions of any judge, probation officer, correctional counsellor, or psychiatrist." In order to accomplish what was purportedly impossible through the individual efforts of juvenile authorities, this classic Great Society document recommended typical Great Society solutions. The report concluded that the weapons in the fight against delinquency should be social and economic, because the Commission viewed the existence of crime as prima-facie evidence that society had failed. Thus, new social and economic arrangements would best combat delinquency—not attempts to affect change in individual offenders. The report urged improvement in schools, housing, employment opportunities, and occupational training programs, as well as the strengthening of the family by the social welfare community.

When Congress passed the JJDP Act, it not only upheld the Commission's conclusions, but supported them with the significant force of federally mandated reform. The Office of Juvenile Justice and Delinquency Prevention (OJJDP) was established to encourage compliance by awarding funds to states which adopt the Act. Participating states must concentrate on the deinstitutionalization of status offenders,[21] the separation of juveniles from adults in jail, the removal of juveniles from jail, and the development of community based alternatives to institutionalization. The Act also encourages the development of youth bureaus and youth advocacy programs designed to increase the rights of juveniles; programs which seek to correct the ills of society to which the Johnson Administration report attributed crime and delinquency.

Judging the Act singularly, on the basis of intent and implementation, it has been a success. The deinstitutionalization mandate, for example, has inspired the participation of 53 states and territories, resulting in an 88 percent reduction in the number of institutionalized status offenders. But in the larger context of juvenile crime and delinquency, the federal effort has been less than successful. In an effort to divert juvenile offenders from the system and protect them from punitive dispositions, serious juvenile crime has not received adequate attention.

To the extent that federal spending is indicative of official priorities, the focus of the juvenile justice system today is largely misplaced. Over half of OJJDP's budget is still awarded to states for compliance with reforms that are already in place and would remain in force without federal funding. Inasmuch as Act money is insufficient to cover the full cost of implementation, compliance requires a state to make a financial commitment which would not be made without an ideological commitment as well. In other words, the cooperating states adopted the Act because they believed it was the right thing to do, there being no reason to believe they would withdraw from this commitment in the absence of the Federal Government's monetary inducement. Therefore, the diversion of juvenile offenders from the justice system is no longer a problem which should consume a major portion of federal resources. The major effort of the juvenile justice system should be revised in accordance with current needs and continually revised as those needs change. Juveniles have long been accountable for a proportion of the total arrests for violent crimes and serious property offenses which is two to four times their proportion of the U.S. population.[22] Yet, it took Congress until 1980 to acknowledge (in one of a series of amendments to the JJDP Act) that there was such a thing as serious juvenile crime. In 1982, OJJDP finally acted on this belated acknowledgement and began funding programs geared toward serious juvenile offenders.

Of course, the fact that a problem has won the attention of the federal government does not guarantee that a solution is imminent. The underlying reasons for juvenile crime and delinquency are too complex and too numerous; they are beyond the comprehension, much less the expiation of the federal government. Many experts agree that delinquency is at least partially influenced by the social institutions which children encounter early in life. A series of government programs and a portion of the overburdened federal budget will not produce a panacea for disintegrating families and other symptoms of social distress. The federal government *can* build more prisons, train more policemen, help improve public awareness, fund research efforts, and assist state and local governments in the improvement of their law enforcement systems. In other words, the federal government can provide assistance when it is needed and limit interference when it is not. Many of the needed changes in the juvenile justice system must come from the system itself. For example, making juvenile records available to all levels of the judicial process, and opening juvenile court proceedings are two reforms that are long overdue. Further improvements can be made by involving the private sector in the system to improve the efficiency of public resources. The federal government can play a part, but members of the juvenile justice community and state legislatures must assume major roles in instituting these reforms.

One of the most critical reforms needed in the system today is increased awareness of the real victims of juvenile crime; not to be mistaken for the offender as many believers in the treatment philosophy have done in the past. In the JJDP Act, Congress defined "treatment" as "including, but not limited to, medical, educational, special education, social, psychological, and vocational services, corrective and preventive guidance and training, and other rehabilitative services designed to protect the public." As repeated attempts have shown, the expectation that society can be protected through the use of such measures is unreasonable. First and foremost, the juvenile justice system should be accountable to the victims of juvenile crime. Indeed, the system is obliged to uphold the inalienable rights of children. If a juvenile offender has been deprived of medical care, education, etc., the court should provide whatever services are necessary—*after* justice has been served. The court's primary responsibility, insofar as the offender is concerned, is to uphold that child's right to a moral education, the right to learn the kind of behavior which is acceptable to society. This can best be accomplished through the aggressive use of the juvenile justice system for prosecution and punishment, in order to succeed where we have previously failed: in the rehabilitation of young criminals.

OJJDP is currently doing what it can to encourage reform of the juvenile justice system by participating in various projects which emphasize the accountability of juvenile offenders according to age, seriousness of offense and prior record. Through such efforts, the Office hopes to help reconcile Congress' ideal with reality, to "treat" delinquency in a manner "designed to protect the public."

REFERENCES

Thinking About Juvenile Crime by Alfred S. Regnery

1. Illinois Session Laws, April 21, 1899, p. 131. For recent discussion on the history of the juvenile courts, *see* John L. Hutzler, "Canon to the Left, Canon to the Right: Can the Juvenile Court Survive?," 1 *Today's Delinquent* 25–38 (1982). *See also* Joseph B. Sanborn, "The Rise and Fall of Juvenile Court: The Separation and Reunion of Constitution and Juvenile Defendant," in Gene Stephens, ed., *The Future of Criminal Justice* (Cincinnati, Ohio: Anderson Publishing Company, 1982), pp. 122–157.

2. *Crime in the United States, 1984*, FBI Uniform Crime Reports (Washington, D.C.: U.S. Department of Justice, 1985).

3. *Report to the Nation on Crime and Justice*, Bureau of Justice Statistics (Washington, D.C.: U.S. Department of Justice, 1983), p. 32. *See also* Bureau of Census estimates as of July 1, 1983.

4. S. J. Fox, *Law of Juvenile Courts in a Nutshell* 3rd ed., (St. Paul, Minnesota: West Publishing Company, 1984).

5. *Mapp v. Ohio* 367 U.S. 643, 81 S. Ct. 1684; for a discussion of *Mapp, see* R. G. Hall and C. Dempsey, "Alternatives to the Exclusionary Rule," 3 *Criminal Justice Journal* 303–321 (No. 2, Spring 1980).

6. *In re Gault*, 387 U.S. 1 (1967); for a discussion of *Gault, see* A. L. Bailey, "Waiver of Miranda Rights by Juveniles—Is Parental Presence a Necessary Safeguard?" 21 *Journal of Family Law* 725–743 (No. 4, 1982–83). *See also* A. Donahue, "Juvenile Justice," 2 *Children's Legal Rights Journal* 6–12 (No. 5, March/April 1981).

7. *In re Winship*, 397 U.S. 358 (1970). For a discussion of *Winship, see* R. J. Allen and L. A. DeGrazia, "Constitutional Requirement of Proof Beyond a Reasonable Doubt in Criminal Cases," 20 *American Criminal Law Review* 1–30 (No. 1, Summer 1982). *See also* J. P. Kenney, *et al.*, *Police Work With Juveniles and the Administration of Justice* (Springfield, Illinois: Charles C. Thomas, 1982).

8. *McKeiver v. Pennsylvania* 403 U.S. 528 (1971).

9. *National Evaluation of Delinquency Prevention Programs*, National Council on Crime and Delinquency (Washington, D.C.: U.S. Department of Justice, 1979).

10. Douglas Lipton, Robert Martinson and Judith Wilks, *The Effectiveness of Correctional Treatment: A Survey of Treatment Evaluation Studies* (New York: Praeger Publishers, 1975).

11. Lee Sechrest, Susan O. White and Elizabeth D. Brown, eds., *The Rehabilitation of Criminal Offenders: Problems and Prospects* (Washington, D.C.: National Academy of Sciences, 1979). *See also*, Susan E. Martin, Lee Sechrest and Robin Redner, eds., *The Rehabilitation of Criminal Offenders: New Directions for Research* (Washington, D.C.: National Academy Press, 1981).

12. James Q. Wilson, *Thinking About Crime*, revised edition, (New York: Basic Books, Inc., 1983), p. 163.

13. Charles A. Murray and Louis A. Cox, Jr., *Juvenile Corrections and the Chronic Delinquent* (Washington, D.C.: American Institute for Research, 1979). *See also* Charles A. Murray and Louis A. Cox, Jr., *Beyond Probation: Juvenile Corrections and the Chronic Delinquent* (Beverly Hills, California: Sage Publications, 1979).

14. Howard N. Snyder and John L. Hutzler, *The Serious Juvenile Offender: The Scope of the Problem and the Response of Juvenile Courts* (Pittsburgh, Pennsylvania: National Center for Juvenile Justice, 1981), p. 3.

15. American Correctional Association, Report to the Office of Justice Programs, U.S. Department of Justice, 1984.

16. Peter Greenwood, Joan Petersilia and Franklin E. Zimring, *Age, Crime and Sanctions: The Transition from Juvenile to Adult Court* (Santa Monica, California: Rand Corporation, 1980).

17. *Crime in the United States, 1982*, FBI Uniform Crime Reports (Washington, D.C.: U.S. Department of Justice, 1983), p. 176.

18. *Prevalence of Imprisonment*, Bureau of Justice Statistics (Washington, D.C.: U.S. Department of Justice, 1985).

19. Patrick Langan and Larry Greenfeld, "Career Patterns in Crime," *BJS Bulletin*, June 1983.

20. *Indexed Legislative History of the Juvenile Justice and Delinquency Prevention Act of 1974*, LEAA, Office of General Counsel, U.S. Department of Justice.

21. *Report of the National Institute of Juvenile Justice and Delinquency Prevention: Fiscal Year 1981–82*, Office of Juvenile Justice and Delinquency Prevention, U.S. Department of Justice, p. 1.

22. Preliminary estimates of Bureau of the Census as of July 1, 1983.

5

"EQUAL JUSTICE UNDER LAW":
Time to Apply the Hobbs Act
to Union Violence
by Charles E. Grassley[1]

Federal law required Bob Wohlsen to prove that the picketers at his eastern Pennsylvania construction site were blocking the entrance before he could get a court order to limit their number. So, Bob took his lawyer and son-in-law with him, along with a video camera that morning in June of 1983. "After all," Bob thought, "what could better prove to the federal judge the harassment" his employees faced than pictures? Bob was not new to the construction business and realized that there was some possibility of trouble. His lawyer, Rick Harmon, called the state police and told them what they had planned. He also asked them to be present in case there was any trouble. There was.

Within minutes of arriving at the job site, there surfaced the name-calling and verbal threats that too often accompany labor/management differences. And then it happened. As he was taking pictures of the picketers blocking the entrance with an instamatic camera, someone or something hit Bob on the side of the head. It knocked his hard-hat and glasses off. As he fell to the ground, Bob remembers thinking, "Oh God, please do not kick me too hard."

A few seconds later, the videotape ends. The camera containing film of the attack on Bob was knocked to the ground and destroyed. The cameraman, Bob's son-in-law, was also beaten. But the film survived as evidence of a brutal physical attack on Bob Wohlsen and his party. The instamatic camera was gone from his coat pocket. The state police had never arrived.

As a result of the incident, doctors diagnosed a subneural hematoma and Bob underwent two brain surgery operations. When Bob told his story at a Senate Judiciary Committee hearing on October 25, 1983, portions of his scalp had not yet healed.

Nothing ever happened to the people who attacked Bob Wohlsen. Nor did anything ever happen to the people who beat up Sygmund Kaye in Philadelphia a few weeks later. And in Hawaii, when Cher and Walter Mungovan found that the local authorities would not help them against union harassment, they turned to the United States Attorney for help, but were told that the federal government could not do anything because of the *Enmons* loophole in the Hobbs Act. Cher and Walter had never heard of the Hobbs Act.

Some people think what happened to Bob Wohlsen, Sygmund Kaye and the Mungovan family is just a risk they accepted when they decided to do business with non-union workers. But this type of violence and property damage is something that can no longer go unpunished in this country, where we believe in "equal justice under law."

Bob Wohlsen, Sygmund Kaye, Cher and Walter Mungovan are just a few of the people who fall through the *Enmons* loophole in the Hobbs Act. The Hobbs Act is an almost unbelievable law that actually bars federal prosecution of union violence. Many concerned public officials, including this writer, seek to close that loophole forever through S. 462, a bill introduced in the Senate on February 3, 1983.

THE ENMONS LOOPHOLE

In 1973, the Supreme Court ruled that extortionate violence or threats of violence are not punishable under federal law if the purpose of the violence was a "legitimate union objective."[2] This five-to-four decision misconstrued the Hobbs Act,[3] the federal law prohibiting robbery and extortion in interstate commerce.

S. 462[4] would end this special privilege of union officials to terrorize employers and non-union workers into complying with their demands. Congressional action would reverse the Supreme Court's astonishing decision in *United States v. Enmons.*[5] We have already enjoyed some success. For the first time, committees in both houses of Congress held hearings on a federal law to ban union violence.[6] Also, for the first time, a committee of the Congress has given its approval to reversing the *Enmons* decision.[7] But passage of such a law will require Congress to muster the courage to say "no" to leaders of big labor.

FEDERAL LAW PRIOR TO THE HOBBS ACT

As much as the bill to amend the Hobbs Act responds to a Supreme Court decision exempting unions and union officials from the federal extortion law, the Hobbs Act itself was a response to a prior Supreme Court decision[8] which exempted unions from the federal Anti-Racketeering Act of 1934.

Section 2 of the Anti-Racketeering Act of 1934 defined racketeering as a crime whereby:

> any person who...obtains or attempts to obtain, by the use of force, violence, or coercion, the payment of money or other valuable consideration ...*not including, however, the payment of wages by a bona-fide employer to a bona-fide employee....*[9]

The Supreme Court ruled that this exception covered members of New York City Teamsters Local #807 which had exacted payments from out-of-town truckers for the unwanted and superfluous service of driving the trucks, or allowing them to be driven, within the city of New York.[10]

The *Local 807* case saw union members, with the apparent approval of the union's officers, stopping out-of-town truckers at shotgun-point in the Holland Tunnell and other points of entry into New York City. There the gun-toting Teamsters would offer the out-of-town truckers a choice: they could either pay the local union a sum for the privilege of driving their truck on the streets of New York, or they could hire a member of the local union to drive the truck for them. The shotgun made the out-of-town trucker's other choice clear.

Incredibly, the Supreme Court of the United States held that the union could not be prosecuted for extorting the payment of money to the union at the threat of physical harm, because the federal racketeering law contained the language "not including...the payment of wages by a bona fide employer to a bonafide employee...." In the view of the Supreme Court, the fact that the out-of-town truckers had been forced at gunpoint to hire the local's drivers was irrelevant. The mere fact that the payment to the union had taken the form of wages was enough to remove it from the racketeering law.

The language of the racketeering statute was not intended to exempt such coercion from the law. Rather, it was intended to protect the right of union members to engage in a strike or similar concerted activity to obtain their goals. A strike is inherently coercive in an economic sense, but we, as a society, have made a decision of public policy to allow strikes against employers. This coercion loses, however, its legal and protected status when the strikers resort to violence and intimidation. Then, the coercion flows not from the worker's refusal to work until their demands are met, but rather from the fear of property damage or physical harm. This is what the court failed to distinguish in the *Local 807* case. As a result, the Court construed Congress' decision to shield economic coercion as a decision to exempt violent coercion from prosecution whenever the payment took the form of wages.

The Court's decision, in effect, exempted all violent activity and coercion from the federal law if it had as its basis a labor-management quarrel. This clearly was beyond what Congress had intended to do in the 1934 Act and "Congressional disapproval of this decision was swift."[11] Several bills were introduced with the purpose of overturning the Supreme Court's decision in the *Local 807* case.[12] The bill which eventually passed and became known as the Hobbs Act,[13] eliminated the "wage clause" that had been the basis of the Supreme Court's decision in that case.

Nevertheless, in 1973, the Supreme Court again disregarded Congress' desires and exempted union violence from federal law as long as the purpose of the violence was to benefit the union, rather than a non-union third party.[14]

THE ENMONS DECISION AND THE HOBBS ACT

The Supreme Court's decision in *United States v. Enmons* construed the legislative history of the Hobbs Act to be nothing more than reversal of the specific holding of the *Local 807* case. While the court could no longer excuse the union's extortion because it took the form of wages, it would not look to the desirability of the extortionist's gain. Consequently, only if a union's end sought by violence was itself illegal would the violent conduct be illegal. If the union had a legal right to seek the employment of its members, nothing the union did to accomplish its goal could be punished. The Court did not attempt to explain why one rule should apply to labor union members and another to all other sectors of society.

The *Enmons* case arose in the early 1970s when striking workers at the Gulf States Utilities Company in Louisiana fired high powered rifles into company-owned transformers and drained the engine coolant from the transformers causing them to burn up at a great financial cost. All this was done to force the utility to accede to the union's demand for higher wages. The U.S. Attorney brought federal charges against the union for violating the Hobbs Act's extortion provisions since they had used violent destruction of company property to coerce the employer to accept the union's demands at the bargaining table.[15]

But the United States District Court in Louisiana dismissed the indictment without allowing a trial.[16] The federal court ruled that no valid criminal charge existed, because "the indictment alleged *the use of force to obtain legitimate union objectives*."[17] In the eyes of the court, as long as the ultimate objective of the union's use of violence, force, and intimidation was legally permitted—in this case a collective bargaining contract—then no act of violence could be prosecuted under the Hobbs Act—and the Supreme Court agreed!

The Court read the congressional action that followed the *Local 807* case as narrowly as possible. It reasoned that the Congress only intended to prohibit the use of union force or violence designed to force the employer to pay for workers he did not want to hire. But if the employer was willing to hire the workers without being forced to, the union could use any amount of force or violence to get higher pay or benefits under the Supreme Court's reasoning.

The Court did not even consider the fact that federal law *required* the utility to negotiate with the union and, therefore, it could not refuse to negotiate over the wage it would pay the workers.[18]

As a result, federal law required Gulf States Utilities to negotiate in good faith with the electrical workers union for the wages that the company would pay the union's members, and it could not refuse to negotiate with them without violating federal law—while the union was free to have its members destroy company property until the utility agreed to pay what the union demanded, without fear of being charged with breaking the federal criminal laws. This result is even more incredible when one considers that as a result of the court's construction of the law, a man who was not a union member could walk up to the company's personnel chief at gunpoint and demand a job paying $20 an hour and would be committing extortion. But if the man with the gun also had a union card, he would be bargaining with the company.

This anamoly was based on the Court's construction of the intent of Congress when the Hobbs Act was passed in reaction to the *Local 807* decision.

Unfortunately, these violent bargaining tactics can be ruthlessly effective. Businesses make a cost/benefit analysis whenever a union demands higher wages or benefits. Businesses decide whether the dollar price of the union's demands outweighs the cost of enduring a strike by the company's workers. But, when the union is able to add to the business' cost the replacement of extremely expensive equipment which it has destroyed, it changes the equation in its favor. The National Association of Manufacturers recently explained how this tactic works in a statement to the Senate Judiciary Committee:

> Premediated strike violence against the employer becomes a factor in contract resolution since it raises the employer's cost of disagreeing with a union's demands, adds other costs through lost production by the strike itself, and can result in serious property damage and in injuries to the employer, his non-striking workers, and others. An employer who is faced with mounting strike violence must begin to calculate the cost of the expected future disturbances. Such violence can raise the employer's cost of disagreeing with the union's demands above his cost of agreeing. The employer thus finds himself making concessions that he would not ordinarily make. It is clear that strike violence can and does enhance the union's bargaining strength and often leads to more employer bargaining concessions than would otherwise be the case.[19]

This practical implication, however, was ignored by the Supreme Court in *Enmons*. Instead, it focused solely on its own misconstruction of Congress' intent. While the legislative history that the Court examined in the *Enmons* case was at times ambiguous, when it was clear, it left no doubt that unions were intended to be subject to the same laws as anyone else. As Justice William Douglas' dissent points out, the Court examined the legislative history of a predecessor bill considered by the seventy-eighth Congress, while the bill that passed and became known as the Hobbs Act was enacted by a much different seventy-ninth Congress.[20]

The House debate between Congressmen Marcantonio and Hobbs, in the seventy-eighth Congress, was cited in the Court's opinion as showing the intent of Congress. In response to a question from Marcantonio: "In connection with a strike, if an incident occurs which involves—", Congressman Hobbs interrupted, "This bill does not cover strikes *or any question relating to strikes . . . because a strike is perfectly lawful* and has been so described by the Supreme Court and by the statutes we have passed. This bill takes off from the springboard that *the act must be unlawful to come within the purview of this bill."*[21] While Congressman Hobbs' first highlighted statement might be construed to mean that nothing related to a strike is punishable by the law (which defies logic), the second clause seems to clearly suggest that an unlawful act taking place during a strike could be punished. This unfortunate exchange was the sole basis for the majority's interpretation of congressional intent.

But in the seventy-ninth Congress which actually passed the Hobbs Act, three amendments sponsored by Congressmen Celler and LaFollette, which would have preserved a union exemption from the extortion law, were rejected by the House.[22] Even the seventh-eighth Congress, which was more favorably disposed to the union's wishes, defeated a Celler Amendment which would have preserved the union's exemption.[23] The majority opinion of the Supreme Court completely ignored this fact.

Union supporters in the seventy-ninth Congress attempted three times to preserve organized labor's special privilege with amendments that would have retained the "wage clause" in some form. But each time the amendments were defeated in the House of Representatives. They even turned back a move by Congressman LaFollette to send the bill back to Committee. This effort was defeated by a margin of nearly 3 to 1![24] Each time a vote was taken, a majority of Congress made clear that the federal criminal laws were to apply equally to everyone. Even so, the Supreme Court in the *Enmons* case ignored the defeat of these amendments as an expression of congressional intent. Instead, the Court focused on Congressman Hobbs' remarks in the floor debate that "this bill does not cover strikes or any question relating to strikes." The Court apparently ignored his elaboration of that statement that the bill did not cover strikes "because a strike is perfectly lawful. . .the act must be unlawful to come within the purview of this bill."[25]

Justice William O. Douglas, hardly an antiunion zealot, focused on this misreading of the legislative history in a stinging dissent:

> The Court today achieves by interpretation what those who were opposed to the Hobbs Act were unable to get Congress to do. . .the opposition lost in the 79th Congress [a union exemption] what they win today.[26]

It was a differently composed Congress in 1945 which passed the Hobbs Act than it was that debated it in 1943. In the seventy-seventh Congress, Democrats outnumbered Republicans in the House 267 to 162. But in the seventy-eighth Congress that passed the Hobbs Act, a coalition of Southerners and conservatives among the 222 Democrats joined with most of the 209 House Republicans to pass the bill and defeat the union exemption amendments. But President Harry Truman vetoed the bill and a third Congress acted to pass the Hobbs Act and attached it to another measure that avoided the Presidential veto.[27]

In short, while an examination of the legislative history of the seventy-eighth Congress might leave some question as to whether unions were intended to be exempt because of the possible contradiction of Congressman Hobbs' remarks, the rejection of union exemption amendments by the seventy-ninth Congress, and President Truman's attempt to block passage of the Hobbs Act, make clear that no one was intended to be exempt.

EXTORTION UNDER THE HOBBS ACT

Extortion is defined by the Hobbs Act as the taking of property from another, with the person's consent, but with that consent having been obtained by the "wrongful" use of force or violence, or threats of same. In essence, the Court's *Enmons* ruling was that if the ends sought by the violence were "legitimate union objectives" it was not "wrongful," and therefore the violent means could not constitute extortion.

Specifically, the Hobbs Act states, in pertinent part:

(A) *Whoever in any way* or degree, obstructs, delays or *affects commerce* or the movement of any article or commodity in commerce, *by robbery or extortion* or attempts or conspires so to do, or commits *or threatens physical violence to any person or property in furtherance of a plan* or purpose to do anything in violation of this section shall be fined not more than $10,000 or imprisoned not more than twenty years, or both.

(b) As used in this section . . .

(2) The term "extortion" means the obtaining of property from another, with his consent, induced by *wrongful* use of actual or threatened force, violence, or fear, or under color of official right.[28]

The plain language of the statute states that "whoever" uses violence or threats against "any person" commits the crime prohibited by the Hobbs Act. The Court, in essence, read the law as saying "whoever is not a union member" could be charged with the crime of extortion, but that a union member could commit the same acts and not be charged with violation of the Act. Neither does the law as written by Congress state that anyone who threatens "any person not an employer of bona fide unionized workers" or "any person not engaged in negotiation with a union" can be prosecuted for extortion. Congress, whatever its shortcomings, is capable of creating express exceptions to the federal laws when it wants to. It is not necessary, or desirable, for the Supreme Court to do it for us.

There is, therefore, some parallel between contemporary efforts to amend the Hobbs Act in order to overturn the *Enmons* decision and the Hobbs Act's passage in the seventy-ninth Congress to overturn the Supreme Court's *Local 807* decision. Congress, in this instance, seeks to apply the law equally, but the federal courts keep presenting obstacles to these efforts. The influence that union leaders have with many members of Congress imposes an additional obstacle.

There have been prior attempts to reverse the *Enmons* decision. A presidential commission was formed in 1966, known as the Brown Commission, to study the federal criminal laws and develop proposed reforms of the law.[29] The Brown Commission report and proposed recodification of the criminal law was submitted to the Congress in 1971;[30] legislation along the lines recommended by the Commission was introduced as S. 1 only a few days before the *Enmons* decision. But after the *Enmons* exemption for labor violence was handed down, congressional proposals to change the criminal code included a reform of the extortion law that would do away with the labor violence exemption.[31] That is, until a change in the Democratic leadership of the Senate Judiciary Committee in 1979.

Senator Kennedy proposed the first criminal code revision that would have codified the *Enmons* ruling in the Criminal Code Reform Act of 1979, S. 1722. Efforts of the House Judiciary Committee also sought to codify *Enmons*. But unable to pass a total reform of the federal criminal code, Democratic Congresses have made no effort to reverse the *Enmons* decision.

In the ninety-seventh Congress, Republicans controlled the Senate for the first time in twenty-five years. Senator Strom Thurmond (R-SC) became Chairman of the Judiciary Committee and introduced the first Hobbs Act amendment designed solely to overturn *Enmons*.[32] The bill was referred to the Criminal Law Subcommittee of the Senate Judiciary Committee. Two subcommittee hearings on the Thurmond bill were held, but it was not reported out of the subcommittee.[33] Instead, it became necessary for Chairman Thurmond to introduce a new bill and have it held at full committee.[34] Even at full committee, however, opponents of the Thurmond bill prevented the Judiciary Committee from getting the quorum necessary to vote on the bill before the ninety-seventh Congress adjourned, thus killing the bill.[35]

THE GRASSLEY BILL AND ITS RATIONALE

On February 3, 1983, this writer introduced S. 462 in the ninety-eighth Congress. Chairman Thurmond and 25 other Senators joined as cosponsors of the bill,[36] which differs from the Thurmond proposal in that it specifically excludes from coverage minor picket line violence and property damage under $2500.[37] In so doing, it takes into account concerns expressed by the Justice Department as well as the *Enmons* court's concern that minor incidents of violence might result in a federal extortion charge.[38]

Two companion bills have been introduced in the House by Congressman J. Kenneth Robinson (R-VA)[39] and Philip M. Crane (R-IL).[40] Together, nearly 70 members of the House are sponsors of these two bills.[41,42] For the first time since the *Enmons* decision, a committee of the Congress gave its approval to changing the Hobbs Act when the Senate Subcommittee on Separation of Powers gave its endorsement to S. 462 by a vote of 3 to 2 to recommend the bill to the full Judiciary Committee.[43]

So that another Supreme Court may not rewrite the law or change the intent because of an ambiguity in the legislative history, in S. 462 the traditional definition of extortion is restated and then the measure specifically expresses the intent of Congress that nothing in the bill excludes from federal jurisdiction violence occurring in the course of a "legitimate business or labor dispute" or "in pursuit of legitimate business or labor objectives."[44] The bill provides that it is an affirmative defense to prosecution that the violence was minor and occurred as part of otherwise peaceful picketing.[45] The result of this provision is that it shifts the burden to the government to prove an intent to extort if the violence was minor and along the picket line, but prevents the picket line from becoming a subterfuge for extortionate activity.

AFL-CIO publications have denounced this bill as the product of the "National Right to Work Committee" and "its right-wing allies."[46] They claim that the bill subjects union members to federal prosecution for extortion "when they exercise their right to walk a picket line."[47] This claim is plainly untrue. First, a specific provision in the bill provides for an affirmative defense that the conduct "was incidental to picketing."[48] Mere picketing is not punished—but the use of violence or threats of violence as part of a plan to coerce the employer while picketing is fully covered.

Another allegation of the AFL-CIO unions that was contained in the Carpenters union magazine is also not true. In their July 1983 issue, the union claimed:

> Under S. 462, an employer or strikebreaker and a striking worker can commit the same offense but be treated far differently. The employer or strikebreaker would be prosecuted for violating a state law, but the striker would face federal prosecution for "extortion". The penalties facing the striking worker will be far more severe than those facing the employer or strikebreaker.[49]

This is simply untrue. Even though there has never been an exception to the Hobbs Act created for employers (which means they can be prosecuted by both the state and federal governments), the Grassley bill specifically includes violence occurring in pursuit of a "legitimate *business or labor* objective."[50] All strike-related violence aimed at coercing a person to "pay" to stop this violence is treated equally under my bill. Current federal law and some state laws treat strike related violence differently based on who commits it; and they punish *only the employer and not the union*.

The two union arguments are provably false by simply reading the bill itself. Union publications go even further, denying the *Enmons* decision creates an exemption for union violence:

> Union members are currently subject to the same laws as all other citizens...The Grassley bill would change this by subjecting workers to far harsher federal penalties.[51]

For ten years, between 1961 and 1971, when I worked at the Waterloo Register Company in Cedar Falls, Iowa, I carried a union card and was a voluntary member of a labor union. When the union went out on strike, I went out on strike. The men and women I worked with and went out on strike with did not believe that they had a right to use violence to get their way. I do not believe that the overwhelming majority of American's working men and women union members do either.

Frankly, I resent the American workforce being deceived about my intentions with this bill and the manner in which union leadership apparently disregards their ability to understand the truth when fairly and objectively presented. We can argue over whether S. 462 should become the law, but we should at least start with an honest discussion of what the law is now and what the bill would do if it became law. Union members deserve better than what they have been told about this issue in union publications.

Another argument the union has raised is that strike-related violence is extremely rare. As proof of this, the AFL-CIO points to "the fact that the Federal Bureau of Investigation maintains no statistics on strike-related violence is strong evidence of the peaceful nature of most strikes."[52]

But the FBI has no reason to keep these statistics when the Federal government cannot prosecute union violence as a result of *Enmons*. The fact is, however, the Bureau of Alcohol, Tobacco, and Firearms (BATF) of the Treasury Department does keep this data. In 1981 and 1982, the BATF listed 64 bombings with a cost to the economy of $320,600[53], as well as 9 arson incidents[54] as "labor related," and this may be just the tip of the iceberg.

Union violence is not a theoretical problem.

THE GREY BUS

As wrong as the *Enmons* exemption appears in the abstract, it is even more unjust when one confronts the human cost of labor violence. In hearings before the full Senate Judiciary Committee in 1983 and 1984, eleven victims of union violence from eight different states made evident this cost.[55]

Robert Wohlsen, Sr. is the third generation president of a family-owned construction company that operates in eastern Pennsylvania and in Delaware. His company used to operate "as an entirely union organization."[56] His employees decided in 1962 to become non-union. Since then, Wohlsen Construction has been an open-shop company. In Bob's own words "it is no concern of ours as to whether a man, a carpenter or a laborer is a union individual; we do not ask . . . it makes no difference to us whether you belong to the union or not."[57]

On June 8, 1983, Bob went to his company's Brandewine River Museum Construction site because he had been told that union picketers were blocking access to it. If true, Bob would have to prove that his employees were being physically prevented from working by the pickets before he could get a court order limiting the number of picketers. Bob described what he saw:

> When we arrived at the job site, we were denied access, and there was a volatile demonstration of anger at our being there. . .They beat on the car, and they allowed us to pass through. . .I found out at that point that we were in

the job site and we were surrounded on both sides of the road, the access to the job, by picketers...I looked up and I saw that Mr. Rick Harmon [Wohlsen's company attorney] was being assaulted by Mr. Earl Henninger, who is the head of the Philadelphia Building Trades Council union members...Someone had hold of his foot, and at that time they were pouring hot coffee on him...they were attacking the cameraman. And out of nowhere...someone came up and gave me a roundhouse blow to the side of my head. And the hardhat went flying...the hardhat came in and made an indention on my skull.[58]

The picketers did not stop, however, A few moments later they attacked Bob and his party a second time:

After the camera was destroyed, the only thing I remember after that, someone blindsided me. It did not come from the front. It is like a football player being blindsided. And I went to the ground. There were several people on top of me. And the only thing that went through my mind was, please God, do not kick me too hard.[59]

The picketers, including the head of the union, had beaten Bob, his lawyer Rick Harmon, and Bob's son-in-law. They had stolen the camera that Bob had been using to gather evidence, and they had totally destroyed the video camera. Pennsylvania State Police had never arrived. Because the police were not present and did not witness the attack, only a single assault charge was filed against the picketers and a misdemeanor theft charge for stealing the instamatic camera.[60] The charges were later dropped as part of a deal to end picketing.

As Rick Harmon, Wohlsen's lawyer pointed out, the failure of local police in the area to protect job security and prevent violence "is a continual problem throughout the construction industry...it does not do a lot of good after a gentleman such as Mr. Wohlsen has been attacked to file a simple assault charge."[61]

Bob went to the doctor that afternoon and was thought to have suffered no serious injuries at the time. But over the Fourth of July weekend, he began experiencing severe headaches and a blood clot in his brain was discovered. He has since undergone two brain surgery operations and is recovering from his physical injury.[62]

But the injuries Bob Wohlsen suffered go beyond physical damage to his person. His business has been harmed because some of the owners of large construction projects are afraid of union troubles if they hire Bob's company.[63] In his testimony, Bob cited the example of some hospital construction underway in his area. Normally,

Wohlsen construction would be prime competition for this work. Now the possibility of unchecked union violence dogs his company:

> We go before their boards and we have not been able, in some instances, to be chosen or asked to bid because of the incrimination and the harassment that the boards get from such people. It scares them half to death.[64]

One of the other costs of what happened to Bob Wohlsen, as Bob told the Committee on October 25, 1983, was that he was unable to travel long distances. As a result, Bob was unable to visit his son, whom he had not seen for over a year, while his ship was docked in Japan. His son, Thomas, is an officer aboard a guided missile cruiser in the United States Seventh Fleet in the South China Sea. The significance of the loss was brought home that October morning as the number of American Marine deaths in the Beirut bunker topped 200, and other American military units were landing on the island of Grenada.

THEY SHUT HIM DOWN[65]

One of the witnesses the Committee has heard from is Cher Mungovan, a Hawaii woman whose husband is now in hiding in the federal witness protection program because he went to federal authorities with proof of illegal union activities when they tried to unionize his company by terrorist tactics.

After 13 years as a union carpenter, Walter Mungovan went into business for himself in 1979. Within two years, he was doing over a million dollars of business. His work was high quality and his rates were competitive. After a union organizing effort began, C & W's employees voted unanimously not to join a union.[66] Under federal law,[67] that should have ended the pickets; but instead the labor strife turned violent.[68] Cher and Walter's construction company began losing business from builders who had been threatened not to hire Mungovan.

Then business agents for the Carpenters Union and the state president of the Hawaii AFL-CIO, offered Walter Mungovan a deal. His problems would be over if he signed a contract with the union and hired only union workers. The violence would end and he would be able to get jobs again.[69]

Walter Mungovan was not the kind of person to back down to threats. He is a 6'7" decorated veteran of the U.S. First Air Cavalry in Vietnam and recognized extortion. As a result, he tape recorded his meeting with the union officials. Walter then took the evidence to federal authorities. That's when Cher and Walter learned that the Hobbs Act had been interpreted to say that the union could legally extort him.

The only thing the federal government could do is use Walter's tape recordings as evidence of perjury based on the union officials' false statements to the National Labor Relations Board (NLRB). During the trial of some of the union officials, two men found Walter Mungovan at his hidden location and falsely identified themselves as FBI agents who were to accompany him to a meeting.[70] They were imposters who had found out how to get to him. Federal authorities immediately withdrew Walter into the super-secret world of the witness protection program out of fear for his life.

As a result of Walter's standing up to the union, Walter Kapau, the president of the Hawaii State AFL-CIO and three others have been convicted on multiple felony counts of perjury.[71] Another official of Hawaii's unions has been indicted for murdering rival union leaders on instructions from both union and organized crime figures.[72] The investigation begun because of the courage of Cher and Walter Mungovan has unearthed a web of "mob" control of Hawaii's unions, which in turn gain control on legitimate businesses. But, Cher and Walter have paid a high price to the union leaders. Hawaii's U.S. Attorney, Dan Bent described what the union leaders had accomplished:

> They were the driving forces behind the destruction of a man, a family, a business and an ideal. They transformed Walter Mungovan, a combat veteran, a carpenter and a successful contractor, into a man whose business and family life were virtually destroyed, and into a man who feared for the safety of himself and his business. They bullied him, they threatened him, they shut him down...[73]

While Walter Mungovan, the victim, has lost his freedom to the witness protection program and lost his family life and business, the convicted union leader, Walter Kapau, remains free pending appeal of his conviction. Kapau has taken a leave-of-absence from his unsalaried post as AFL-CIO president of the Hawaii Chapter and left a man described as his "bodyguard" in charge of the state union federation.[74] But, Kapau retains his $83,000 a year position as the Secretary-Treasurer of the state's Carpenters Union.[75]

The union made its point with Hawaii's non-union builders. They shut down Walter Mungovan.

These are not the only cases which the Judiciary Committee has come to know, and those, I fear, are just the tip of the iceberg.

Mr. Mike Ashby, a lumber worker in northern Idaho, and Sheriff Ron Smith of Boundary County, Idaho, told the Judiciary Committee of firebombings, gun shots, rocks and bottles being hurled at non-striking workers at the Louisiana Pacific Company.[76] Both brought into the hearing "captured weapons" that had been used by the union to "deter" non-strikers from working. These included Molotov cocktails, homemade devices casually known as "frisbees" and "spiders" as well as items resembling punji sticks from Vietnam. Steel ball bearings were fired from "wrist rocket" slingshots at car and truck windows, *and at people!*

What is most frightening is that Mr. Ashby testified to being present at the union's meeting when an officer of the international union actually encouraged the strikers to engage in violent harassment of the non-striking workers and to destroy company property.

Sheriff Smith proved himself to be an exceptional and courageous man. His Sheriff's department did try to stem the tide of violence, but, as he told the Committee, his six deputies were simply not enough to control the violence that occurs when an entire segment of the community chooses to disregard the law.

Mr. John Pickell of the Brinderson Corporation of Irvine, California, told the Committee of death threats and firebombings of company facilities, *while they were on the premises of a United States Air Force Base* in Montana. Local and state officials were either unable or unwilling to prevent the violence there.[77]

Mr. Horace Guyton of New Jersey continued to work at his janitorial job because he could not afford to participate in the strike and the union officials refused to tell him why they were on strike. His wife was followed and subjected to verbal harassment while he was at work and while she was with their child. On one occasion, Mr. Guyton was threatened at knifepoint and called the police. When the police arrived, they met first with the union picketers and then threatened to arrest Guyton—the victim—for harassing the picketers if he ever called the police again.[78]

I have met Horace Guyton. He is a courageous young man, but he is not particularly large or threatening in appearance or manner. I seriously doubt that he had threatened a group of picketers. The calculated brutality of the union in this case went even further. A "hit list" of Horace and other non-striking workers was maintained and posted at the union hall. The "hit list" contained not only the name of the non-striking workers, but also their home addresses. *When Guyton was forced to move out of concern for his family's safety, the list was updated with his new address!*

Mr. David Young of Florida was doing construction work when a mob of union supporters trapped him and several other workers in a room and threatened to kill them.[79] Heavy equipment was dropped from upper levels of the construction site. One of the pieces of equipment came through the roof of David's pickup truck while he was driving away. Had the equipment landed just a few inches nearer to the driver's side of the truck, David probably would have died.

Yet another construction incident involved Gerry Bartow.[80] He was doing construction work in Port Huron, Michigan with non-union labor. More than 400 union picketers stormed the construction site and destroyed his company equipment. He and several of his employees were trapped on the rooftop of a building for several hours by an angry mob. When Bartow was rescued by the Sheriff's police and a handful of the mob's leaders were arrested, an aide to Michigan's Governor asked that the union leaders be released from jail. On another occasion, the Governor's office applied pressure on the Sheriff to remove Bartow and his workers from the job site.

When 28-year-old graduate student Sygmund Kaye stopped at a building he had invested in to check on the remodeling work that had been done, he found 15 men wearing yellow tee shirts doing a little remodeling of their own. The men were beating and ripping apart the work that had been done by the non-union crew Sygmund had hired. When Sygmund demanded to know what they were doing, several of them beat Sygmund Kaye to the point that he is now partially paralyzed. As they were leaving the scene, Sygmund saw the men board a grey bus—the same grey bus that brought thugs to Bob Wohlsen's job-site—and he took down the license number. The grey bus was registered to the Philadelphia Area Buildings and Trades Council, and the union admitted responsibility. But the police would do nothing. The district attorney told him that "it is an election year" when he refused to do anything. So bold are the thugs in the Philadelphia area that the men who beat Sygmund Kaye into paralysis wore tee-shirts proclaiming their creed: "Union Carpenters, We Hit Harder."[80]

These stories are only a few of the incidents. Others are afraid to testify to the Senate Judiciary Committee. However, newspaper accounts of labor troubles elsewhere indicate a nationwide pattern of violence.

Recently, I received a letter from an Iowa constituent:

> ...the first time I was asked to join a union was at gun point, on highway 63 south of Ottumwa, on a hill, at night.
>
> The goon holding the gun in my ribs smelled of alcohol. (that "scared" me). He told me it would be mighty hard on my head if I didn't join the union, out *here* on these hills at night, alone. Because of his alcohol breath, and gun, I was 100% agreeable.
>
> ...I was advised by my employer to join. I believe he was trying to keep the peace. He had already lost a truck or two by the union organizer...[81]

When I received the letter, I contacted the person who wrote it. I thought surely he was talking about the 1930s. I thought that sort of thing cannot be happening in my state. That sort of thing could not be happening in the 1980s, and fortunately he was talking about the "old days." But after meeting the victims of union violence who have testified at Senate hearings and studying other incidents, I have concluded that in many parts of this country, the "bad old days" of the 1930s are back!

There are two other arguments in support of the *Enmons* decision that have been raised that are at least worthy of debate. They are that union violence is not a matter for federal law and that state and local officials are adequate to handle the problem.[82] These are really two prongs of the same argument.

THE FEDERALISM ARGUMENT

As a strong supporter of a state's right to control its own affairs, this writer is always suspect of any attempt to increase the power and authority of the federal government. The federal government should not normally be in the business of policing strikes and preserving the peace in the local community.[83]

But, half a century ago America chose to provide, at the federal level, a right to organize labor unions and to bargain collectively.[84] One of the fundamental findings of the Congress in the Wagner Act was that labor strife was disruptive of the interstate commerce.[85] A decision to provide a minimum standard for the conduct of labor-management relations was made. For this reason, some aspects of labor law are preempted by the federal government while others are left to joint jurisdiction by both the federal and state laws.[86]

One of those minimum standards that federal law should maintain is that an employer or non-striking worker should not be placed in fear of being beaten or having his life threatened or his property firebombed if he does not accept the union's demand. Indeed, the very fact that most labor-management matters are in the jurisdiction of federal authorities provides an adequate justification for many local and state authorities to avoid the controversy of strike-related violence. This is really the heart of the need for federal jurisdiction.

While the AFL-CIO asserts "state's rights" and claims that there is no need for federal jurisdiction to curb union violence, it sings a different tune when the tables are turned. AFL-CIO President Lane Kirkland urged the federal government to intervene *against* local law enforcement in the Las Vegas strike by hotel and casino employees. In a letter to Attorney General William French Smith, Kirkland stated that "*local police have proven unable or unwilling to maintain order* and protect worker's rights."[87] Kirkland's letter also claimed that striking workers had been beaten and "otherwise abused" by private security guards and police.

Sometimes, using Kirkland's words, "local police have proven unable or unwilling to maintain order" and protect *both* non-striking workers and strikers, as well as employers. When local authorities fail to act because of undue political pressure, or inadequate resources, then strikers as well as non-striking workers and employers have a right to ask for help from the federal government. The states have the right to be the first to act and the duty to do so. But when these states do not act, the federal government has the obligation to punish violent conduct, especially within the sphere of labor law *which it has created.*

I believe in federalism and in state's rights, but I also believe that the law should be applied equally to those who walk a picket line and those who cross it.

The federal government cannot prosecute unions for extortion if the goal of the violence was a "legitimate union objective."[88] Nearly all state Attorneys General have no independent criminal prosecutorial powers with which they can initiate prosecutions.[89] All state laws are really enforced by locally-elected, county district attorneys. Even if the local prosecutor has the staff and budget to prosecute an action of this kind, the political realities render such prosecution unlikely. In short, the rationale for federal jurisdiction is the same as in the area of organized crime, or for that matter, interstate extortion by anyone.

As Judiciary Committee Chairman Strom Thurmond explained in a speech on the Senate floor:

> In reality, state and local authorities are not equipped or strongly motivated to deal with the consequences of clashes between powerful competing interest groups in their communities.

> This is particularly true with regard to labor disputes...the political implication may be overwhelming to a local official who appears to take sides in a labor dispute by vigorous enforcement of criminal laws. I am sure the most comfortable position is one of non-involvement.[90]

This writer recently learned of a situation that involved violent strife against an Alabama company working on a project in Kentucky. According to the president of that company, the local sheriff stated that "we had his sympathy but since he depended on local people to elect him to office and we were from Alabama he was not going to take any action."[91]

Furthermore, in Montana, the Haines Pipeline Company of Oklahoma had been involved in the construction of a public utility pipeline with out-of-state non-union labor.[92] In that highly unionized state, local officials did not protect the out-of-state company's right to do business. When several hundred angry workers stormed the construction site of the pipeline, state authorities did nothing.[93] At one point, the only charges filed in the violent labor strife were against two of the out-of-state company's employees who had been forced to fire gun shots over the heads of a charging mob to deter their attack.[94]

Some colleagues in the Senate have suggested that the ability of individuals in some states to act as private Attorneys General is a sufficient "back-up" when local authorities fail to act to restrain union violence and to punish those who perpetrate it.[95] But this mechanism is, in reality, no "back-up" at all.

The most obvious problem with expecting a businessman who has been beaten or extorted by a union (or a nonstriking worker in a similar situation) to bring and prosecute criminal charges against those who attacked or threatened them is *the sheer cost of providing private legal counsel to do the government's job* of prosecuting criminals. When a local prosecutor fails to prosecute a criminal, it is not the responsibility of the victim to hire a lawyer to prosecute. But that is, in essence, what colleagues who suggest this as an alternative to restoring federal jurisdiction suggest.

A more subtle problem also arises that exposes this alternative to be no alternative at all. In every jurisdiction that allows a private citizen to act as a public prosecutor, they are limited to *participating* in the prosecution only.[96] They cannot indict the criminal themselves. The actual charges must always be brought by the government. It is here that the "private attorney general" alternative becomes no alternative at all. For in the cases that the Judiciary Committee has investigated, as well as the hundreds which we have not dealt with, no charges are ever brought by politically intimidated public officials. Absent the police conducting the investigation and the local prosecutor bringing charges or securing an indictment, the private Attorney General-victim can do nothing at all.

This "alternative" is merely a sham. Unless the locally elected prosecutor possesses the courage and budget to prosecute, nothing will happen to union officials engaged in extortion. Statewide law enforcement authorities lack the authority to initiate criminal prosecutions in nearly all states, witness the table accompanying this chapter.[97]

Even where local officials are *willing* to preserve the peace against the interest of powerful groups, they may lack the financial resources and manpower to do so. The October 1983 Senate Judiciary Committee hearing saw Sheriff Ron Smith of Boundary County, Idaho, tell of the near-impossible task of preserving the peace during the violent strike at the Louisiana Pacific Company.[98] Sheriff Smith told the Committee that he had a department of only six deputies responsible for covering a territory of several thousand square miles. This is respresentative of most of the country. According to the Bureau of Justice Statistics, most parts of the country have fewer than three police officers per one thousand residents.[99]

When a union decides to use a wide spread pattern of violence against an employer, local officials are virtually powerless to conduct the necessary investigation and prosecutions, even when they possess the courage to do so.

Indeed, the Judiciary Committee's hearings have demonstrated that strike-related violence most often occurs in states and localities where unions are powerful and are able to intimidate local political officials, not where the unions are weak and struggling to survive.

Prosecutorial Powers of State-Wide Authorities[97]

State	Atty. General has power to initiate criminal prosecutions
Alabama	has "selected" trial-level authority
Alaska	NO
Arizona	Can "take-over" trial at direction of Governor, but cannot initiate prosecution
Arkansas	NO
California	NO
Colorado	NO
Conn.	NO
Delaware	YES
Florida	NO
Georgia	Only in actions which carry the death penalty
Hawaii	Atty. Gen. "may assume. . .on a selected basis" a criminal trial, but cannot initiate prosecution
Idaho	NO
Illinois	Atty. Gen. may prosecute "when in the interest of the general public"
Indiana	NO
Iowa	NO
Kansas	NO
Kentucky	NO
Louisiana	Atty. Gen. "may intervene *for* the District Attorney" but cannot act without approval of local prosecutor
Maine	Atty. Gen. "may assist" the local prosecutor, but cannot initiate prosecution
Maryland	NO
Mass.	NO
Michigan	Atty. Gen. may prosecute "only at request" of local prosecutor, or in exercise of statutory authority at the request of state or local officials
Minnesota	NO
Miss.	Atty. Gen. may "assist in prosecution," but cannot initiate
Missouri	NO
Montana	NO
Nebraska	YES

State	Atty. General has power to initiate criminal prosecutions
Nevada	"may take exclusive charge of criminal prosecution"
New Hampshire	Atty. Gen. may prosecute cases involving the death penalty or prison sentences of 20 years or more
New Jersey	Under "special circumstances" proscribed by statute
New Mexico	"has authority...but in practice" does not initiate cases
New York	Only in securities fraud and monopolies
North Carolina	NO
North Dakota	NO
Ohio	Atty. Gen. may act only when requested by the Governor or the legislature
Oklahoma	NO
Oregon	NO
Penn.	NO
Rhode Island	Atty. Gen. can act in "some bizarre cases"
South Carolina	NO
South Dakota	Atty. Gen. has "concurrent" jurisdiction but under this authority he may only prosecute "for" the local prosecutor when requested or deemed necessary
Tenn.	NO
Texas	Atty. Gen. has authority to act but seldom does, as a practice, only acts when requested by a grand jury or district attorney
Utah	Atty. Gen. "exercises more limited jurisdiction"
Vermont	Atty. Gen. has concurrent jurisdiction, but has not exercised it
Virginia	NO
Washington	Atty. Gen. exercises prosecutorial authority "only in infrequent circumstances"
West Virginia	Atty. Gen. has authority, "but in practice it does not" prosecute criminal cases
Wisconsin	NO
Wyoming	NO

Witness the "grey bus" terrorizing the construction industry in the Philadelphia area, the Hawaii AFL-CIO president allegedly tied to both organized crime and local political officials as well as union violence problems in New Jersey, Dade County (Florida), Michigan, Montana and Northern Idaho. This suggests the violence happens not because unions are desperate, rather violence occurs *because they are powerful enough to get away with it!*

UNION EXEMPTIONS IN STATE LAW

In testimony before the Criminal Law subcommittee in 1981,[100] in a formal statement submitted to the Senate Judiciary Committee in 1983,[101] and in their publications,[102] the AFL-CIO has stated that union violence is already subject to state law. In the past other supporters of restoring federal Hobbs Act jurisdiction, have assumed that it was the inadequacy of local budgets and political pressures that have prevented the prosecution of union violence. Even the Supreme Court assumed this to be the case in the *Enmons* decision.[103] But many local officials are legally restrained from prosecuting union violence by their own state laws as well.

Not only has organized labor succeeding in exempting itself from the same federal law the rest of us must obey, but they have achieved similar special treatment under the laws of at least a dozen states.

At least eight states contain extortion statutes with either a "wage clause" or "wrongfulness" element in their laws, and thereby grant special privileges to union extortion. These states include New York,[104] Washington,[105] Hawaii,[106] Maryland,[107] Oregon,[108] Connecticut,[109] Nebraska,[110] Utah[111] and my own state of Iowa.[112] Together, these states contain one out of six[113] of the nation's work-force and generate one-fifth[114] of the nation's interstate commerce.

Tennessee has used the *Enmons* analysis of "legitimate union objectives" in a recent extortion case, implying its approval of the *Enmons* loophole as an appropriate test under its state law.[115]

At least four other states including Massachusetts,[116] Montana,[117] Alaska[118] and Indiana[119] restrict the use of the police or other state law enforcement when unions are involved in violence.

Consequently, an employer or non-striking worker in one of these eighteen states may call for help from the authorities and find that no one, not the Local, State or Federal government, can come to his aid. Where there is no law, lawlessness reigns supreme.

The New York state extortion law was the basis of the original

Hobbs Act definition of extortion and was considered by the Supreme Court in *Enmons* when it reached its decision to exempt union violence.[120] New York now defines extortion as a form of the crime of larceny and, making *sure* unions are exempt, contains *both* a "wage clause" and a "wrongfulness" element. The express language of the statute exempts union extortion:

> A person steals property and commits larceny when...he *wrongfully* takes, obtains or withholds such property...in any of the following ways...By extortion: A person obtains property by extortion when he compels or induces another person to deliver such property to himself or a third person by means of instilling in him a fear that, if the property is not so delivered, the actor or another will:
> (i)   Cause physical injury to some person in the future; or,
> (ii) Cause damage to property, or,...
> (iv) Cause a strike, boycott or other collective labor group action injurious to some person's business; *except that such a threat shall not be deemed extortion when the property is demanded or received for the benefit of the group* in whose interest the actor purports to act;...[121]

New York thereby excludes from its criminal extortion law violence and threats of violence "when the property is demanded or received for the benefit" of a labor group *and requires that it be sought for a "wrongful" purpose*. This closely parallels the Supreme Court's *Enmons* rationale of exempting violence undertaken as a means of achieving "legitimate union objectives." In addition, New York courts have acted to restrain the issuing of court injunctions against union violence, under the theory that they had the effect of restraining the federal collective bargaining rights of employees.[122]

Our largest state, California, follows this New York rule and refuses to issue injunctions against strike-related violence.[123]

Neither has organized labor been satisfied by just one bite of the apple. In at least one federal court action, they have attempted to extend the *Enmons* union violence exemption to other federal criminal laws as well.

In *United States v. Thordarson, et al.*, (1982)[124] members and officers of the Teamsters Union sought court protection for arson, the use of explosives, misappropriation of union funds and racketeering, in addition to the *Enmons* protection for their acts of extortion.

After being chosen as the bargaining agent for employees of Redman Moving and Storage Company of California, Teamsters

85

Local 186 ordered a strike against the company in July of 1978. Because the union did not by itself have the manpower it felt necessary to conduct the strike, "it obtained the assistance" of Teamsters Local 389.

"Between July and December of 1978, Redman's truck fleet was the object of vandalism, including tire slashings and truck burnings." Trucks owned by the California company were burned while in Arizona and Connecticut. Explosives were used, and the Treasury of the local union was used to pay for travel, telephone calls, and "unspecified expenses" for trips to Arizona and to Connecticut for the purpose of "locating and destroying two Redman trucks." The United States Attorney for central California charged the unions and their officers with violating federal laws against arson, travel in interstate commerce with explosives, misuse of union funds and racketeering. Because of the *Enmons* decision, he could not charge them with extortion even though it was clear that violence and the threat of further violence was being used as pressure on the company to comply with the union's demands.

Then the union moved to dismiss the ten-count indictment because the purpose of the violence had been to force the employer to agree to the union's demands; and it based its argument on the Supreme Court's "legitimate union objectives" rationale in the *Enmons* case. The frightening thing is, the United States District Court agreed with the union and dismissed the indictments without a trial![125]

The district court ruled that *Enmons* "precludes federal criminal prosecution for violent activity which occurs during the course of a strike." Explaining why it chose to dismiss the charge of misuse of union funds for union funding of trips to Arizona and Connecticut to destroy Redman's trucks, the court stated:

> ...the use of this broad interpretation in the context of labor organizational activities and strikes is troubling. Taken to its logical conclusion, the government would consider as an embezzlement...union expenditures made to *reimburse members or other individuals who* ultimately *violate* certain *state laws through acts that* might *reasonably occur during the labor dispute, such as* disturbance of the peace, *assault, or vandalism*...*unions often hire professional picketers. If these picketers participate in "unlawful activities"* that occur during legitimate labor activities, *the union officials who authorized the expenditure* for the hiring of the picketers *could conceivably be prosecuted*...*If a union officer reimbursed organizers for* gasoline, hotel and other expenses, and these organizers participated in *the identical activities as* did the union workers in

86

> *Enmons (blowing up a transformer substation, firing high-powered rifles* at three company transformers, and *draining the oil from a company transformer) there would exist the anomalous situation wherein the federal government* would be precluded from indicting the union officials (for extortion)...but *would be able to convict the union officials* on the basis that the funds expended...constitute an embezzlement.[126]

In the district court's view, the fact that the several criminal laws were violated by a course of violent conduct, and that the Supreme Court had seen fit to exempt the unions from one of those laws, their prosecution of the union for any of the other laws created an "anamalous situation."

I disagree with the district court's premise. While I do not believe that the Supreme Court was right when it read a congressional choice to exempt unions from the extortion law, I certainly do not believe that such an exemption should be applied to exempt unions from all of the criminal laws.

Fortunately, the Court of Appeals agreed with my view and reversed the district court. *But the fact that any federal judge was willing to expand the union exemption to all other federal criminal laws makes even more urgent the need for Congress to move to do away with the union's special privilege in the extortion laws.* The Court of Appeals saw this danger as well:

> To uphold (the lower court)...we would be required to create an exemption for labor violence that would necessarily be applicable to all federal criminal statutes...if an *Enmons* doctrine were to immunize a union official from federal prosecution under the...(statutes involved), it would, in all logic, immunize from federal prosecution a union official—or, indeed, an employer—desperate enough to resort to kidnapping to achieve collective bargaining objectives.[127]

THE ENMONS LOOPHOLE PROTECTS ORGANIZED CRIME

According to the Annual Report of the Inspector General at the Department of Labor, "over 400 labor organizations are associated, influenced, or controlled by organized crime."[128] Extortion, kickbacks, and illegal payments by employers to union officials are a major problem in areas where federal law requires companies to deal with mobsters who control these unions. According to the Labor Department report:

Employers who want their cargoes unloaded or to keep their business open too frequently are forced to bow to extortionate demands. Although the problem is perhaps more prevalent in the construction industry, no business is immune...[129]

This report discusses at length the successful investigation of New York's Fulton Fish Market, which generates approximately 25 percent of all seafood business on the Atlantic Coast. There, three officials of Local 359 of the United Seafood workers union and its associated welfare and pension funds were indicted on as many as 167 felony counts by a federal grand jury in New York.[130]

Citing law enforcement sources, the report states that Carmine Romano, executive administrator of the market's welfare and pension fund, and formerly the secretary-treasurer and business agent of Local 359, is an "alleged high-level organized crime figure."[131]

A scenario under which organized crime working through a union can gain substantial influence over a legitimate business is easy to construct. Union leaders with organized crime ties could threaten an employer with "labor troubles" if he does not do what the union official/mobster demands. Such demands could include requiring the company to grant a concession to a mob-controlled company for vending machines or cafeteria services, or a strike will be called at the end of the contract period, or immediately, alleging a contract violation. What does the honest businessman do?

Does he turn to the federal authorities only to be told that the Hobbs Act bars prosecution of the union official for extortion aimed at "legitimate union objectives"? If the union official is smart enough to "cover" his personal objective with a legitimate one, what federal prosecutor with limited resources is going to wade into that quagmire?

If this employer tries to resist the union official's demands, his property may be destroyed. He may be beaten, his life may be threatened. *If he stops negotiating and hires non-union workers, he may, in addition to the violence, face a federal charge of engaging in unfair labor practices and be fined by the Federal government and commanded to hire the union workers back* at full pay!

If the honest employer turns to state authorities, he is likely to find them unwilling to play David to the union's Goliath. And if he is in New York or one of the other states that have such *Enmons*-type laws, he will find that even the courageous law enforcement officer can do nothing but prosecute him for fighting back.

The combination of the federal requirement that the employer deal and negotiate in good faith with a union, and the Enmons *exemption forces the honest businessman to "cut a deal" with organized crime in one of those 400 unions. And, of course, honest and hard-working union members have their interests thwarted by union leadership that works for the Godfather, not for them.* The Enmons loophole makes a labor union too attractive a cover from which organized crime may operate with impunity.

The Federal Bureau of Investigation has cited several cases in which the investigation or prosecution of organized crime figures have been blocked or impeded by the Enmons loophole of the Hobbs Act. In testimony before the Senate Judiciary Committee this year, the FBI stated:

> While there are several statutory tools available to us, *only the Hobbs Act proscribes a local act of extortionate violence.* As a result of the Enmons decision, our investigations of extortionate violence are limited...[132]

One of the key officials of the FBI's criminal investigative unit then cited several examples of where "mob" figures got away with their crimes because of *Enmons:*

> In 1981, a North Carolina construction company...was laying 10 miles of natural gas pipeline using non-union labor. The job site was being picketed by a local union...Subsequent pressure testing of the pipeline revealed that 15 small holes had been drilled into sections of the pipeline. The construction company suffered about $15,000 to $20,000 in damage to its equipment from sabotage and was forced to pay approximately $50,000 in overtime and salary to repair the pipeline...*The United States Attorney's office declined prosecution because of the Enmons decision. Local authorities were unsuccessful in identifying the saboteurs.*

● ● ●

> During June 1983, a construction company began construction of an office building complex in Ohio. The construction firm adhered to a best bid-low bid policy, which resulted in the hiring of union and non-union contractors...the construction company hired a non-union firm to install plumbing at the construction site. After telephone threats by anonymous callers who suggested that *the house of the vice president of the plumbing company would be blown up if the company started the job,* the plumbing company cancelled its contract...Again, based upon the bidding system, the construction company firm hired a second non-union plumbing company...On the day before the plumbing company was to begin work, *the owner of the first received four telephone calls.* One of the callers *threatened the owner's life* if he began construction. These four telephone *calls were traced to the residence*

of the secretary-treasurer of the local union. The United States Attorney's office determined that federal prosecution in this matter could not be initiated because of the Enmons decision.

• • •

A local union of the Hotel Employees and Restaurant Employees International Union is located in Philadelphia, Pennsylvania and Southern New Jersey. This local union has been identified as being corrupted by organized crime. It was alleged that on two occassions the vice president of the local union has hired persons to vandalize businesses...FBI investigation of these incidents were forestalled by an existing policy statement from the United States Attorney's office citing the Enmons decision.[133]

"Other examples exist as well," the FBI told the Committee, "our field offices...reported several cases in which *Enmons* precluded FBI investigation or federal prosecution."[134]

The FBI made clear that it, like myself, has no desire:

to interfere with the right of labor and management to pursue legitimate goals. We do desire to bring to justice those who resort to violence and other criminal acts to pursue their legitimate goals....Corrupted businesses negotiating with labor unions should not have the right to extort rank and file members and use the union for their personal benefit.[135]

Neither, in the FBI's view, is this an uncommon practice. The FBI told the Committee that four unions, including "the International Longshoremen's Association, the Hotel Employees and Restaurant Employees International Union, the Laborers International Union of North America, and the International Brotherhood of Teamsters", are "substantially influenced and/or controlled by organized crime."[136] And that in these four unions, "*organized crime figures routinely extort employers or companies whose employees are represented by these unions. And the result has been a significant influence of certain industries as employers succumb to this extortion in order that they may survive.*"[137]

The ability to legally extort employers helps organized crime maintain control of the unions it dominates. The FBI informed the Judiciary Committee:

As a result of their ability to get better pay and benefits from an employer by the use of these extortionate methods, organized crime figures in leadership positions in labor organizations have been able to maintain those positions. However, the influence and control of labor unions by organized crime is such that even the membership would be fearful of threats or acts of violence should they oppose the union leadership. . .*We believe that the Enmons loophole in the Hobbs Act has helped organized crime figures retain their control of legitimate labor organizations and they are better able to secure benefits for the union membership in that regard.*[138]

While the FBI was able to present these examples of organized crime elements working under the shield of the *Enmons* decision to the Senate Committee, it made clear that the type of organized crime involvement that might permit the use of Racketeering (RICO) and similar laws does not always readily present itself:

Frequently we have intelligence information from informants that identify particular organized crime groups that are behind these types of activities. And under the current state of the law, *we are precluded from conducting any investigation* because of the *Enmons* decision. There can be no prosecution if these individuals state as their purpose a, quote legitimate labor objective. So we are forstalled from even initiating an investigation. . .[139]

There are other reasons why the federal racketeering (RICO) statute and the Travel Act are inadequate to "get at" organized crime in the extortion situation. As pointed out by the FBI in the Senate testimony, the Travel Act[140] requires a showing of actual travel across state lines as part of the crime.[141] However, extortion can and usually does, take place in one area and in one state. Neither is the RICO[142] statute enough. First, as the FBI noted in its testimony, it requires proof of more than one event.[143] Second, it defers to state laws to define the elements of the crime, which, as I have pointed out, sometimes exempt union violence as well.[144] Third, and I would suggest most importantly, RICO requires the approval of high-level political officials at the Department of Justice in Washington before an investigation can proceed.[145] Senator Biden pointed out in the Senate Judiciary Hearing that political officials at the Justice Department, are sometimes encouraged to "look the other way" when a powerful union is involved—and that this happens in Republican and Democratic Administrations alike.[146]

OTHER REMEDIES FOR VIOLENCE

It is true that union violence can still be prosecuted as other crimes. If the extortion was not for "legitimate union objectives," it may still be prosecuted as extortion by the federal government.[147] This, however, has been confined to cases where the union officials sought a personal pay-off or the hiring of persons for services that the employer did not want.[148] If an employer does agree to hire them, he is presumed to have wanted their services under federal law, so there is no extortion.[149] Obviously, a federal prosecutor will be reluctant to enter this quagmire. The prosecutor is also hindered by the fact that the current law requires the victim to test the sincerity of his assailant's threat of violence before anything can be done.

Also at the federal level, union violence can give cause for an unfair labor practices charge against the union under the Wagner Act.[150] But the enforcement tool for this is a "cease and desist" order which has no criminal penalties, and it can only be brought by the National Labor Relations Board (NLRB).[151] If the union ignores the order, the NLRB can seek a contempt citation in court.[152] An injunction can be sought,[153] once again, only by the NLRB. "In aggravated cases," the union may be required to demonstrate its majority status.[154] Unbelievably, union violence only amounts to an unfair labor practice when it has the effect of coercing employee rights. If union members just "beat up" the boss or threaten his family without coercing fellow employees in the process, the violence is beyond the scope of the labor laws.[155] The NLRB has consistently refused to grant monetary penalties against the union for lost wages or property damage.[156] It is a small wonder that union officials believe that they can disregard the law with impunity.

Because local law enforcement officials often lack the courage or resources to act to stem strike related violence, and the state authorities cannot, one segment of our society has been able to put itself beyond the reach of the law. As power corrupts, the power possessed by some union officials as a result of their special status has led to serious abuse, and the ruination of innocent lives and businesses. The time has come to reign in that power to commit acts of violence without fear of legal penalty.

But even if local officials were able and willing to act to restrain violence by militant labor officials, there is still no justification for the federal criminal laws treating one class of citizens differently from all others. A fundamental tenet of our society is "Equal Justice Under Law," but today we provide no justice at all to a person injured because of crossing a picket line or hiring non-union workers. The theme of this book is *Crime and Punishment in Modern America*. Perhaps today a more appropriate title would have been *Crime and the Lack of Punishment*. The time has come to restore federal jurisdiction over extortion—without regard to who commits it.

REFERENCES

"Equal Justice Under Law": *Time to Apply the Hobbs Act to Union Violence* by Charles E. Grassley

1. I wish to express my gratitude to Terry T. Campo, former counsel on my subcommittee staff for his assistance and research in preparation of this article.

2. *United States v. Enmons, et. al.* 410 U.S. 396, at 398 (1973). (Hereinafter *Enmons.*)

3. 18 U.S.C. 1951 (1970).

4. S. 462, 98th Cong., 1st Sess.; *Cong. Rec.*, February 3, 1983, daily ed., at S. 1072-73.

5. *Supra.* n. 2, *Enmons.*

6. The Senate Judiciary Committee Subcommittee on Separation of Powers held hearings on S. 462, "Union Violence and the Hobbs Act" on March 23, 1983. The full Senate Judiciary Committee held a series of hearings on October 25, 1983, April 30, 1984 and on May 1, 1984. The House Republican Study Committee held a hearing on February 8, 1984.

7. The Senate Judiciary Committee's Subcommittee on Separation of Powers voted to recommend passage of S. 462 on July 19, 1983 by a vote of 3 to 2. Senators John East (R-NC), Alan Simpson (R-WY) and Jeremiah Denton (R-AL) were present and voted in favor of passage. Senators Howard Metzenbaum (D-OH) and Max Baucus (D-MT) voting against passage by proxy.

8. *United States v. Local 807, International Brotherhood of Teamsters,* 315 U.S. 521 (1942).

9. 48 Stat. 979 (Emphasis added).

10. *Supra,* n. 8, *Local 807.*

11. *Enmons,* 410 U.S. at 402 *(Douglas, J. dissenting).*

12. S. 2347, 77th Cong., 2d Sess.; H.R. 6872, 77th Cong. 2d Sess.; H.R. 7067, 77th Cong., 2d Sess.; H.R. 653, 78th Cong., 1st Sess.; H.R. 32, 79th Cong., 1st Sess.

13. 92 *Cong. Rec.* 7308.

14. *Enmons.*

15. *United States v. Travis Paul Enmons, et. al.* 335 F. Supp. 641 (E.D. L.A. 1971); *aff'd* by 410 U.S. 398 (1973).

16. 335 F. Supp. at 646.

17. *Enmons,* 410 U.S. at 398 (Emphasis added).

18. Under Section 8(a) of the National Labor Relations Act, 20 U.S.C. 151, *et seq.,* it is an unfair labor practice for an employer "to refuse to bargain collectively with the representatives of his employees."

19. Statement of the National Association of Manufacturers, in S. 462, *"Union Violence and the Hobbs Act"*: *Hearing before the committee on the Judiciary,* 98th Cong., 1st and 2nd Sess. (1983-1984); (hereinafter cited as the Judiciary Committee Hearings). *See also* A. Thiebolt, Jr. and T. Garrard, *Union Violence: The Record and the Response by Courts, Legislatures and the NLRB* (University of Pennsylvania: The Wharton School, Industrial Research Unit, 1983).

20. *See Enmons, (Douglas, J., dissenting)* at 413.

21. *Enmons,* at 405. *See also* 89 *Cong. Rec.* 3213 (1943) (Emphasis added).

22. 91 *Cong. Rec.* 11917 (Celler Amendment); 91 *Cong. Rec.* 11922 (LaFollette Amendment). *See also, Enmons* at 414-417 *(Douglas, J. dissenting).* The record vote on Congressman LaFollette's amendment was 56 in favor and 174 opposed.

23. 89 *Cong. Rec.* 3225. The record vote on Congressman Celler's (D-NY) Amendment was 126 in favor of the amendment and 167 against it.

24. The vote on Congressman LaFollette's (R-IN) motion was 62 in favor and 164 against. *See:* 91 *Cong. Rec.* 11922 (1945).

25. *Enmons,* at 405; *See also* 89 *Cong. Rec.* 3213 (1943).

26. *Enmons,* at 413, *(Douglas, J., dissenting).*

27. For a more detailed discussion of the legislative history of the Hobbs Act, *see generally*, Thiebolt and Gerard, *supra*, n. 19, pp. 254–300.

28. 18 U.S.C. 1951, *et seq.* (1970) (Emphasis added).

29. Thiebolt and Gerard, *supra* n. 19, p. 285.

30. *Ibid.*

31. S. 1400, 93rd Cong., 1st Sess., (1973), Section 1722 (a); S. 1, 94th Cong., 1st Sess. (1975); S. 1437, 95th Cong., 1st Sess. (1977).

32. S. 613, 97th Cong., 1st Sess. (1981).

33. *Supra* n. 19, p. 299.

34. S. 2189, 97th Cong., 1st Sess. (1981).

35. *Supra*, n. 19, p. 300.

36. Senators sponsoring S. 462 were:

Nickles (R-OK)	Humphrey (R-NH)	Armstrong (R-CO)
Thurmond (R-SC)	Hatch (R-UT)	Kassebaum (R-KS)
East (R-NC)	Helms (R-NC)	Wilson (R-CA)
Symms (R-ID)	Abdnor (R-SD)	Tower (R-TX)
Jepsen (R-IA)	Denton (R-AL)	Mattingly (R-GA)
Simpson (R-WY)	Trible (R-VA)	Domenici (R-NM)
McClure (R-ID)	Goldwater(R-AZ)	Hecht (R-NV)
Laxalt (R-NV)	Dole (R-KS)	Wallap (R-WY)
Warner (R-VA)		

37. S. 462, Section (d) (4), 98th Cong., 1st Sess. (1981).

38. Testimony of the Honorable Jonathan C. Rose, Assistant Attorney General, Office of Legal Policy, Department of Justice, on S. 613, *A Bill to Amend the Hobbs Act: Hearings before the Subcommittee on Criminal Law of the Committee on the Judiciary*, 97th Cong., 1st and 2nd Sess. (1981–1982), p. 5.

39. H.R. 287 (98th Cong., 1st Sess.).

40. H.R. 49 (98th Cong., 1st Sess.).

41. The sponsor of H.R. 287 was J. Kenneth Robinson (R-VA) along with 68 cosponsors, including:
Stangeland (R-MN), Bliley (R-VA), Marriott (R-UT), Hansen (R-ID), Wolf (R-VA), Ireland (D-FL), Martin (R-NC), Roberts (R-KS), Archer (R-TX), Oxley (R-OH), Broyhill (R-NC), Hammerschmidt (R-AK), Spence (R-SC), Rudd (R-AZ), Badham (R-CA), Stump (R-AZ), Hansen (R-UT), Bilirakis (R-FL), Livingston (R-LA), Montgomery (D-MS), O'Brien (R-IL), Chappel (D-FL), Vander Jagt (R-MI), Loeffler (R-TX), Myers (R-IN), Dannemeyer (R-CA), Whitehurst (R-VA), Shumway (R-CA), Holt (R-MD), Winn (R-KS), Erlenborn (R-IL), Vucanovich (R-NY), Gingrich (R-GA), Parris (R-VA), Frenzel (R-MN), Lloyd (D-IN), Sunia (D-AS), Sundquist (R-TN), Won Pat (D-Guam), Forsythe (R-NJ), Hartnett (R-SC), Kramer (R-CO), Dickinson (R-AL), Bateman (R-VA), Corcoran (R-IL), Coats (R-IN), P. Crane (R-IL), D. Crane (R-IL), Nielson (R-UT), Weber (R-MN), Porter (R-IL), Craig (R-ID), Sawyer (R-MI), McCollum (R-FL), McCain (R-AZ), Stenholm (D-TX), Bartlett (R-TX), Cheney (R-WY), Campbell (R-SC), Lewis (R-FL), Moorhead (R-CA), Siljander (R-MI), Walker (R-PA), Packard (R-CA), Whittaker (R-KS), Lagomarsino (R-CA), Roth (R-WI), McCandless (R-Ca).

42. The cosponsor of H.R. 49 was Charles Bennett (D-FL).

43. *Supra*, n. 7.

44. S. 462, Section (c) (2), 98th Cong., 1st Sess. (1983), p. 2, lines 11–13.

45. S. 462, Section (d) (1) and (2), 98th Cong., 1st Sess. (1983).

46. *See* "A union member exercising his or her right to picket could face federal prosecution for 'extortion' under proposed law," *Carpenter*, July 1983, pp. 19, 38; *See also* "U.S. Senate considers Bill to Threaten Just Workers in Picket Line Disturbances," *The Ironworker*, September 1983, pp. 9–10; "News from the General Secretary-Treasurer, Cecil O. Clay:

Your Letters and Post Cards Are Needed!," *Sheet Metal Workers' Journal*, July 1983, p. 4; Anti-Labor Forces At It Again," *Signalman's Journal*, July/August, 1983, p. 7; "They're At It Again," *Labor Union*, August 1983, p. 6; "AFL-CIO and APWU Hit S. 462 and Urge Union Members to Oppose," *American Postal Workers News Service*, p. 1.

47. *Ibid.*

48. S. 462, Section (d) (1), 98th Cong., 1st Sess. (1983).

49. *Supra*, n. 46.

50. S. 462, Section (c) (2), 98th Cong., 1st Sess. (1983).

51. *Supra*, n. 46.

52. *Ibid.*

53. *Ibid.*, Sum of "Labor Related" incidents in: "Table 9—Bombing Incidents by Motive, Including Property Damage for 1981–1982" and "Table 10—Incendiary Bombing Incidents by Motive, Including Property Damage for 1981–1982," *Explosives Incidents 1982, 7th Report by the Bureau of Alcohol, Tobacco and Firearms*, Department of the Treasury p. 11 (hereinafter cited as "*Explosives Incidents 1982*").

54. "Table 27—Motivations for Arson Incidents Investigated by ATF for 1981–1982," "*Explosives Incidents 1982*," p. 31.

55. S. 462, "*Union Violence and the Hobbs Act:*" *Hearings before the Committee on the Judiciary,* 98th Cong., 1st Sess. (1983); (hereinafter cited as the Judiciary Committee Hearings).

56. Judiciary Committee hearings, Testimony of Robert Wohlsen, Sr., p. 15 (unofficial transcript).

57. *Ibid*, pp. 15–16.

58. *Ibid*, pp. 17–19.

59. *Ibid*, p. 21.

60. *Ibid*, p. 24.

61. *Ibid*, p. 25.

62. *Ibid.*

63. *Ibid.*

64. *Ibid*, p. 27.

65. I wish to note that this subtitle is drawn from a column written by nationally syndicated columnist, Jack Anderson, about the Mungovans. Jack Anderson, "They Shut Him Down," *The Washington Post*, September 23, 1983, p. 15e.

66. *Ibid.*

67. Under Section 8 (6) 7 (B), of the National Labor Relations Act, 29 U.S.C. 151, *et seq.*, it is an unfair labor practice for "a labor organization or its agents...to picket or cause to be picketed...any employer where an object thereof is forcing or requiring an employer to recognize or bargain with a labor organization...where within the preceeding twelve months a valid election...has been conducted...."

68. *See:* Jack Anderson, "They Shut Him Down," The Washington *Post*, September 25, 1983, p. 15e.

69. *Ibid.*

70. Walter Wright, "Hunt on for Fake Lawmen," Honolulu *Advertiser*, June 2, 1983, page A-3; and Walter Wright, "Contractor put under protection," Honolulu *Advertiser*, June 1, 1983, p. 1.

71. Charles Memminger, "Kapau Convicted on 6 Perjury Counts," Honolulu *Star-Bulletin*, November 18, 1983, p. 1; and Charles Memminger, "2 Union Leaders Found Guilty of Perjury Charges," Honolulu *Star-Bulletin*, May 24, 1983.

72. James Dooley, "Huihui Murder charges: Indicted in going-style killings," Honolulu *Advertiser*, March 30, 1984; and Ken Kobayashi, "Convict says he killed Lii on Huihui orders," Honolulu *Advertiser*, March 27, 1984, p. 1.

73. Sentencing Memorandum filed by United States Attorney for the District of Hawaii in *United States v. Torres, et. al.*; *See also* Jack Anderson, *supra*, n. 65.

74. Charles Turner, "Kapau: Stepping down, but its only temporary," Honolulu *Advertiser*, January 27, 1984; and Robbie Dingeman, "Kapau Says He's Only on a 'Vacation'," Honolulu *Star-Bulletin*, January 27, 1984, p. 8a.

75. Charles Turner, "Kapau to yield state union office: Business agent named successor," Honolulu *Advertiser*, January 26, 1984, p. 3a.

76. *See generally* Judiciary Committee Hearing, *supra*, n. 19.

77. *Ibid.*

78. *Ibid.*

79. *Ibid.*

80. *Ibid.*

81. I retain the letter in my files and avoid revealing the identity of the writer at his request (Emphasis added).

82. Prepared Statement of the AFL-CIO, Submitted for the Record of Judiciary Committee Hearings, October 25, 1983, p. 5.

83. *See, Enmons* at 411. *See also, supra*, n. 41.

84. Section 7 of the National Labor Relations Act, 29 U.S.C. 151, *et seq.*, was enacted in 1935.

85. Section 1 of the National Labor Relations Act, 29 U.S.C. 151, *et seq.*, declares: "the denial...of the rights...of employees...lead[s] to strikes and other forms of industrial strife or unrest, which have the intent or the necessary effect of burdening or destructing commerce...It is hereby declared to be the policy of the United States to eliminate the causes of certain substantial obstructions to the free flow of commerce and to mitigate and eliminate these obstructions...."

86. *See, Sears, Roebuck and Co., v. San Diego County District Council of Carpenters*, 436 U.S. 180 (1978); *See generally* A. Cox, D. Bok and R. Gorman, *Labor law*, 9th Ed., (Foundation Press Inc., 1981), pp. 916–920.

87. "U.S. Intervention Urged: Police, Guards attack strikers in Las Vegas," *The AFL-CIO News*, April 7, 1984, p. 1 (Emphasis added).

88. *Enmons.*

89. *State and Local Prosecution and Civil Attorney Systems.* Law Enforcement Assistance Administration, National Criminal Justice Information and Statistics Service. U.S. Department of Justice.

90. Cong. Rec., daily ed., February 3, 1983 at S. 1073 (remarks of Senator Grassley).

91. I retain the letter in my files. As this was written, I had not acquired permission to identify the writer.

92. "Murray MPC Provoked Project Violence" *Great Falls (Montana) Tribune*, August 8, 1983, p. 11-A.

93. "Protesters Gather Again at Pipeline," Montana *Standard*, July 25, 1983.

94. Thomas Schmidt, "Shots, blasts bring arrests," Montana *Standard*, August 6, 1983.

95. Senate Judiciary Hearings, *supra*, n. 19, comments of Senators Joseph Biden and Arlen Specter.

96. Andrew Sidman, "The Outmoded Concept of Private Prosecution," 25 Am. U. Law Rev., 754–794 (1976).

97. Based on information contained in Department of Justice publication, *supra*, n. 89.

98. Prepared Statement of Mr. Ron Smith, Sheriff of Boundary County, Idaho, in Judiciary Committee Hearings, October 25, 1983.

99. *Report to the Nation on Crime and Justice: The Data*, Bureau of Justice Statistics (U.S. Department of Justice, 1983), p. 48.

100. Testimony of Laurence Gold, Special Counsel, AFL-CIO, in S. 613, *A Bill to Amend the Hobbs Act: Hearing before the Subcommittee on Criminal Law of the Committee on the Judiciary*, 97th Cong., 1st and 2nd Sess. (1981–1982), p. 17.

101. *Supra*, n. 82.

102. *Supra*, n. 46.

103. 410 U.S. 411. *See also: Enmons*, 410 US 411, 412, (Blackmun, J., concurring).

104. N.Y. Penal Law, Sect. 155.05.

105. Wash. Crim. Code, Sect. 9A.04.110.

106. Hawaii Penal Code, Sect. 707-764(1)(j).

107. Maryland Crimes and Punishment, Art. 27, Sect. 562B.

108. Oregon Rev. Stat. Sect. 164.075 (1)(f).

109. Conn. Penal Code, Sect. 53a-119 (5)(F).

110. Nebr. Crimes and Punishments, Sect. 28-513 (1)(e).

111. Utah Crim. Code Sect. 76-6-406 (2)(h).

112. Iowa Code, C.732, Sect. 732.1, para. 3.

113. Sum of listed states Total Civilian Labor Force, 1st Quarter 1983, not seasonally adjusted. Source: Bureau of Labor Statistics, U.S. Department of Labor.

114. Sum of listed states Personal Income, 1st Quarter 1983, seasonally adjusted. Source: U.S. Department of Commerce, Survey of Current Business.

115. *Moore v. Tennessee*, 519 S.W. 2d 604 (Tenn. App. 1975), *cert. den.*, 519 S.W. 2d 604 (1975).

116. Mass Ann. Laws, Ch. 22, Sect. 9A.

117. Montana Code Ann., Sect. 31-110.

118. Alaska Stat., Sect. 26.05.340.

119. Indiana Code, Sect. 10-1-1-10.

120. *United States v. French*, 628 F. 2d. 1069, at 1073 (8th Cir. 1980), *cert. den.*, 449 U.S. 956 (1980).

121. N.Y. Penal Law, Sect. 155.05. (Emphasis added).

122. *See: Opera on Tour, Inc. v. Weber*, 285 N.Y. 348 (1941), *May's Furs and Ready to Wear, Inc. v. Bauer*, 282 N.Y. 331 (1940); *Goldfinger v. Feintuch*, 359 N.Y.S. 2d 143 (1937). *See also: People v. Vizzini*, 359 N.Y.S. 2d 143 (1974) (public sector).

123. *Musicians Union Local No. 6, et al. v. Superior Court of Alameda County*, 69C. 2d 695, 447 P. 2d 313 (1968).

124. *U.S. v. Thordarson, et. al.*, 646 F. 2d 161 (1982). A New York Firefighter's Union advanced similar arguments in *People v. Vizzini*, 359 N.Y.S. 2d 143 (1974).

125. 487 F. Supp. 991 (1980).

126. 487 F. Supp. at 997 (1980). (Emphasis added).

127. 646 F. 2nd at 1330 (1982).

128. *Semiannual Report of the Inspector General*, U.S. Department of Labor, Office of the Inspector General, April 1, 1981–September 30, 1981, p. 64.

129. *Ibid*, pp. 64–65.

130. *Ibid*, p. 65.

131. *Ibid*.

132. Judiciary Committee Hearings, *supra*, n. 19, Testimony of Floyd I. Clarke, Deputy Director, Criminal Investigative Division, Federal Bureau of Investigation, pp. 22–23.

133. *Ibid*, pp. 23–25 (Emphasis added).

134. *Ibid*, p. 25.

135. *Ibid*, pp. 26,27.

136. *Ibid*, p. 31.

137. *Ibid*, p. 32 (Emphasis added).

138. *Ibid*, p. 36–37 (Emphasis added).

139. *Ibid*, p. 41 (Emphasis added).

140. 718 U.S.C. 1952.

141. *Supra*, n. 132, p. 51.

142. 18 U.S.C. 1962 (d).

143. *Supra*, n. 132, p. 51.

144. *Ibid*, p. 57.
145. *Ibid*.
146. *Ibid*, p. 53.
147. *United States v. Green*, 350 U.S. 415 (1956).
148. *Enmons*, 410 U.S. 400 (1973).
149. *NLRB v. Gamble Enterprises, Inc.* 345 U.S. 117 (1983).
150. Section 8 (b)(4) was added to the National Labor Relations Act, 29 U.S.C. 151, *et seq.*, by the Taft-Hartley Act in 1947.
151. Under Section 10 of the National Labor Relations Act, 29 U.S.C. 151, *et seq.*, only the National Labor Relations Board can bring an action to enforce the Act. *See also* A. Cox, D. Bok and R. Gorman, *Labor Law*, (Foundation Press, Inc.), pp. 808–809.
152. *Ibid*.
153. *Ibid*.
154. *Ibid*.
155. Section 8(b)(4) of the National Labor Relations Act, 29 U.S.C., *et seq.*
156. Supra, n. 151.

6

THE EPIDEMIC OF THE EIGHTIES:
Missing and Exploited Children
by William E. Spaulding

Child sexual exploitation is an increasingly relevant social problem which has existed in some form or another for thousands of
years. The problem of child exploitation is extensive, nationwide,
and potentially harmful for child victims and their families. The
general public hears only of occasional isolated incidents involving
children through media reports of the more sensational cases.

This tends to skew public understanding of the issue and precipitate inappropriate reactive responses from public agencies responsible for addressing the issue. The fact that must be dealt with in a
logical, non-emotional, proactive manner beneficial to the immediate needs of the child victim and his family, as well as, the future development of the child is that children are being continuously
subjected to sexual exploitation through a variety of scenarios—*the
majority of which are not of the magnitude of the sensationalized media
accounts.* It seems imperative that the issue be dealt with systemati-
cally by examining the dynamics of child sexual exploitation rather
than responding to the sensationalism.

Understanding the dynamics of child sexual exploitation makes
possible a variety of desirable results; investigators may use the ob-
sessive compulsive behavior of the pedophile to obtain evidence
and build substantive cases, prosecutors can more effectively present their cases, realistic prevention efforts can be undertaken, children can be interviewed under conditions where they are more
likely to provide needed answers, informed and responsible replies
can be made to queries from the public and the media to counter allegations of unacceptable agency performance, and sound legislation can be passed to aid in coping with the problem. Successfully
obtaining such objectives can fall miserably short of accomplishing
the goal of adequately treating such a vital and complex issue as
child sexual exploitation. The little that is known regarding the
alarming probabilities of child victimization and the devastating
long-term consequences to many of those child victims as well as the

apparent identification of what is being termed "the cycle of victimization" and its geometric expansion places an additional burden on those persons who would institute programs, conduct training, provide technical assistance, propose legislation, or select to work in positions to assist child victims. Such persons must acknowledge and internalize a philosophy that recognizes the youth as a victim and permits response to instances of missing and exploited children that is in the best interest of the victimized youth. Failure to do so makes efforts in this area a further exploitation of the child victim.

Therefore this article will briefly address the exploited and missing child problem in hope of providing an overview that will include some of the definitional difficulties of the issue, an estimate of the extent of the problem, an examination of the child as a willing participant or a victim, a typology of the offender, and recommendations for action.

PROBLEMS OF DEFINITION

Perhaps the best starting point for this article is to discuss some of the problems that exist when professionals gather to talk about the issue, to propose legislation, to provide technical assistance, to seek grants, to design treatment programs, etc. Each of these professionals bring specific knowledge and personal commitment to focus on aspects of the problem. The difficulty arises when one realizes that very often these professionals come from different disciplines, different geographical areas, different personal backgrounds, and different exposure to the issue. The result is a type of definitional bedlam where a particular term will possess a consensus as to its general meaning but there remains a vagueness about its specific meaning. For example, one currently used definition of child sexual exploitation refers to commercial sexual misuse of a child. The difficulty with this definition is that it would not include the child who has become the exploited victim through a bond of affection with a pedophile. Another definition, particularly favored, defines child sexual exploitation as sexual misuse that occurs to those persons statutorily recognized as juveniles where, because of their position as youth, they: a) possess an inability to knowingly assess or resist such contact, b) are in such a situation that they become dependent on the adult, c) lack the capacity to consent by statute. The problem with this definition, if it is a problem, is that it does not separate the incest victim from the exploited victim. It is true that *both* types of victims are certainly victims of sexual misuse—but the dynamics of the victimization require different methods of investigation as well as different treatment approaches for the victim and offender. This examination of terminology could continue for pages but the two examples cited do call attention to a need to reach agreement on the terms used. Perhaps more important is to understand that current terminology may have different shades of meaning depending on who is using it, and to approach the differences in a tolerant open-minded manner.

In a similar manner the vast majority of the research that has been accomplished in this area has been local, or regional, and may possess the same problems when trying to apply it in other geographical areas. Again it is necessary to understand that differences may exist and at the same time not discredit or invalidate the work.

Additionally, the extremely emotional nature of the missing and exploited child issue has fed an increasing national interest in the child protection movement. The tragic story of Adam Walsh, a six year old who was abducted and killed in 1981, and the heroic effort of Adam's parents John and Reve Walsh, in challenging the conscience of this country to obtain better response for the protection of other children was dramatized on national network television in 1983. This dramatization let many see, perhaps for the first time, the power of this issue. Recently political candidates have used what they are doing for missing and exploited children in successful bids for public office. Organizations and individuals have blatantly commercialized on the effort to locate missing children. Others have designed and marketed prevention programs. Many of those who have profited from the power of the issue, or politics of children, have made significant contributions and deserve the benefits they receive. But there are others who are interested in what the politics of children can do for them instead of what they can do for the children, and these people serve to confuse the issue, to be alarmists, to create a lot of hype not for the purpose of constructive improvement but rather for personal gain. As such the power of the missing and exploited child issue may, ironically, become one of the major obstacles to progress in the protection of children.

THE EXTENT OF THE PROBLEM

A combination of the difficulties already discussed has resulted in vastly different statistical data when attempting to gauge the extent of the missing and exploited child problem, particularly in the area of missing children. Those called to task for inadequate response tend to minimize the extent of the problem while those trying to profit from the issue tend to sensationalize. Both tend to confuse a concerned but largely uninformed public. As Ernie Allen, director of Public Safety for Louisville, Kentucky and Chairman of the Board of the National Center for Missing and Exploited Children, is fond of saying "What's counted counts."

With such difficulties in mind efforts must still be made to gauge the extent of the problem. The National Center for Missing and Exploited Children, which was established to address these specific issues and to assist families, citizens groups, law enforcement agencies, and governmental institutions in a new national effort to ensure the safety and protection of our children, has provided these alarming estimates that indicate the magnitude of the problem:

• at least 1,500,000 children are missing from their homes each year;

• apparently 1,000,000 of these children are voluntarily missing or labeled as "runaways" or "throwaways." This is an endangered group, the frequent victims of street crime or exploitation. Unfortunately, many end up as homicide victims;

• estimates of the number of children who are the victims of non-custodial parental kidnapping vary from 25,000 to 500,000. This, too, is an endangered group of children who are often exposed to emotional and physical abuse;

• between 20,000 and 50,000 children disappear each year and their cases remain unsolved at the end of the year. Included in this group are the victims of stranger abduction and foul play; parental abduction; children who remain voluntarily missing for months; and the victims of accidental deaths;

• between 70 and 90 children of this statistic above are actually thought to be stranger abductions;

• pornography and prostitution of children are highly organized multi-million dollar industries;

• recent studies have shown that 85% of the children who have been criminally or sexually exploited were missing from their homes at the time of the act of exploitation; and,

• each year, at least 3,000 persons are buried unidentified, in "John" or "Jane Doe" graves. Hundreds of these unfortunates are children.[1]

It is very difficult to provide an accurate figure on the number of sexually exploited children either locally or nationally. However knowledgeable persons have made some estimates. Robin Lloyd, author of *For Love or Money: Boy Prostitution in America*, estimates that there are 300,000 active boy prostitutes under the age of sixteen in the United States.[2] The Los Angeles Police Department has identified 30,000 boy prostitutes in that city with 5,000 of that number under the age of fourteen and several hundred as young as eight.[3] There is no estimate of the number of girls involved in prostitution but experts agree that there are probably equal numbers. If one totalled both of these estimates there would be an estimated one half million children involved in prostitution nationwide. Some experts referred to by Lloyd estimate that there are easily twice that number actually involved, a number in excess of 1.2 million children under the age of sixteen that are being exploited as child prostitutes. According to the United States General Accounting Office, estimates of the number of teenage prostitutes, male and female, range from tens of thousands to 2.4 million.[4] Such estimates show child prostitution to be a staggering problem in and of itself, but in addition to these youths engaged in prostitution as it is traditionally defined, there is an inestimatable number of youth who are being exploited through a non-traditional type of prostitution where the payoff is attention, affection, shelter, food, clothing, alcohol or drugs, or access to a video game.

It is incomplete to discuss child prostitution without considering child pornography. From personal investigative experience the two appear closely related. Although it is true that every child molester is not a child pornographer, every child pornographer is a sexual exploiter of children and the pornography product is the pictorial evidence of that exploitation. Also it appears that most pedophiles employ some type of child pornography in the course of their sexual exploitation of the child victim. The pornography that is available is used for several purposes: sexual self gratification, to arouse the curiosity of potential victims, to lower victims inhibitions, to illustrate a desired type of sexual activity, as a unit of barter for new material, to relive the actual experience, and sometimes, as a method to intimidate the victim either to insure silence or to encourage an ongoing victimization. Congress has indicated that child prostitution and pornography have become organized industries with a national scope of operation.[5] Such enterprise has been estimated to gross between a half billion and a billion dollars a year. Experts suggest that seven percent of the total United States pornography market consists of child pornography.[6] Sgt. Lloyd Martin, of the Los Angeles Police Department, testified that child pornography was a multimillion dollar business and estimated that between 40,000 and 120,000 children were involved annually.[7] It appears that the vast majority of the professional quality child pornography is produced overseas and distributed from outside the United States. However it has been suggested that much of this product is shipped from the United States to Europe, reprocessed then sent back to the United States.[8] Local experience shows the existence of "cottage industry" type of child pornography where production takes place in the home or motel room. The pornographer is not a commercial producer and uses self developing film or video which makes discovery less probable and the protection of the child victims much more difficult.

Although the initial focus on the issue of child sexual exploitation centered on child prostitution and pornography, as these problems were addressed collateral problems such as in-family sexual abuse, parental abductions, stranger abductions, and the particular vulnerability to exploitation of the abducted child, the runaway, and those children recently described as "latchkey" and "throwaway" children appeared as inseparable elements to the central issue in that they can be the precursors to the victimization/exploitation of the child. Therefore it is appropriate to include in an estimate on the extent of the problem some additional estimates regarding our "at risk" youth. Acknowledged experts in the area of child sexual victimization have provided some frightening data regarding the susceptibility of youth to sexual assault. In a 1953 study Alfred Kinsey states that at least one in every four females is a victim of sexual assault before age thirteen.[9] According to the Children's Hospital National Medical Center at least ten percent of the children sexually assaulted are less than five years of age.[10] More youth between eight and twelve years are reporting sexual assault than teenagers according to a study by the National Committee for Prevention of Child Abuse.[11] The Child Sexual Abuse Prevention Project of the Hennepin County Attorney's Office reports that thirty to forty percent of all children are sexually assaulted in some degree before the age of eighteen.[12] As unpleasant as it is to do so, based upon such information, all children must be considered as vulnerable to sexual exploitation.

THE DYNAMICS OF EXPLOITATION

Understanding the dynamics of the exploitation that is involved in the victimization of these sometimes seemingly compliant child victims is crucially important to adequately addressing the problem. There is a great deal of misunderstanding surrounding the child victim of sexual exploitation. In the past there has been, at least in some cases, a tendency to look towards the child as somehow contributing to the adult's abusive sexual behavior. This concept of the child contributing to his victimization is one of many factors that add to the child's psychological burden. Such a concept may also contribute to a lack of investigative effort by the agencies responsible, as well as have a negative effect on the support the child needs from those closest to him.

Several reasons exist that may help to understand why the child is considered as an active participant or at least a compliant victim. Previous research statistics were often obtained from the adult offender who had been convicted of sexual misuse of a child and was incarcerated. The fact of facing a parole board or appearing in a different light to fellow inmates could be reason enough to minimize his participation and maximize that of the child (often the child is described as a seducer and fully participating). Sometimes the lack of resistance on the part of the child is perceived as willing participation. Children are inclined not to resist the adult because childhood is a natural state of innocence characterized by a lack of experience, the inability to perceive consequences, lack of judgment and moral sense, and an inclination to indiscriminately absorb all events impinging on the senses (kids love stimulation). The adult may offer rewards such as the opportunity for a free range of behavior, gifts, or affection in return for the desired behavior. The desire to please the adult, which many of us instill in our children, may cause the child not to resist. Fear of punishment for non-compliance with the wishes of the adult may often be an important reason for not resisting. The type of punishment involved here may be more subtle than an overt threat. Perhaps an analogy can be drawn to the scenario of a youngster disliking to clean his room—yet he straightens it every day because he was told to do so by an adult authority figure. Although he was not directly told he would be punished for not complying, he does it anyway as he senses the possible consequences. A child's unknowingly seductive behavior (the media of today teaches us that seduction is an important part of American culture—if we want to be happy we have to have sex appeal) in an effort to receive adult attention or affection may be perceived as "willingness" on the child's part.

The fact that the sexually exploited child usually does not come forward and volunteer information often has a negative effect on investigative personnel perceiving the child as a victim. Many reasons exist for the child victim's reluctance to discuss his victimization. One of the most difficult of these reasons for law enforcement to understand is that the child may want to guard or protect the offender from harm. Upon reflection about the dynamics involved in the enticement used in some instances it should be understood that the child may well perceive the offender as the only person who has treated the child with affection and understanding, i.e., as a friend, sentiments the child has not found elsewhere. The child victim may also be concerned about embarrassment from his family or peer group. A very similar reason for not disclosing information is the fear that disclosure would disrupt his family life (a very real fear particularly when the offender is a member of the family or a family friend). The fear of being disbelieved is another reason that some child victims do not come forward with information. Other children feel that they would be blamed or held responsible for the incident. And there are some unfortunate victims whose self worth is so low that they see themselves as being at fault.

Even if investigators do not understand or do not believe the dynamics of the child's sexual victimization as just explained, they must acknowledge that legislative bodies acting with their collective wisdom and on behalf of their constituents recognized an imbalance of power where a child is incapable of making a knowledgeable consent regarding sex with an adult. Legislators have consistently enacted statutes that do not permit the child to make that choice.

Who makes up this at risk population of youth? Because runaways comprise such a large percentage of the exploited and missing problem it is appropriate to look first at them. While aware of the difficulty of obtaining sound statistical data upon which to draw inferences because of despicable reporting practices, there do exist some staggering estimates on the size of the runaway population. The National Center for Missing and Exploited Children estimates that a million children are missing from home every year. Happily, approximately 90 percent of this number return home. However, the remaining 10 percent that decide life on the street is better than their home situation become potential victims of sexual exploitation. It is important to understand that the act of running away from home does not necessarily indicate anti-social behavior on the part of the child. Dr. Douglas Huenergardt, supervisor of the Runaway Youth Crisis Shelter in St. Petersburg, Florida says, "Runaways are very different now from what they were when so much was being written about them ten years ago. During that time we had kids seeking alternative lifestyles. That's not what's happening today. The child who's running is one who simply can't stand it at home any longer."[13] Many of these children are confronted with the dilemma of an unbearable home life (sexual or physical abuse, unwanted, etc.) on one hand and an unsympathetic community (inadequate, difficult to obtain, or non-existent support systems) on the other. This is an extremely difficult choice to make particularly for a child under sixteen whose options are limited to returning home to the intolerable home environment or to attempt to get by on the street. "The incidence of criminal activity rises sharply with the length of time a kid is away from home," says Robbie Calloway, executive director of the National Youth Work Alliance. Calloway also says that although only 40 percent of runaways report legal difficulties before leaving home almost all children who have been gone more than two weeks get involved in crime, either as perpetrator or victim.[14]

Likewise the children who are victims of parental abduction are also an at risk group. Parental abduction normally does not activate the full resources of the law enforcement community. Usually the child snatch will occur before custody orders are finalized, in which case each parent has an equal right of access to the child. The majority of the children that are parentally abducted are between three and twelve years old and have little or no resources with which to protect themselves from the snatch. Child snatching is a traumatic experience for the child and may leave long lasting scars. The snatched child may experience isolation, anger, resentment, loss of stability, and the lack of opportunity to have normal peer relationships. It is important to keep in mind that there are many reasons for parental abductions and many of those reasons have nothing to do with the best interests of the child.[15]

This epidemic number of children missing from their homes through a voluntary act of running away, being pushed out by their parents, abducted by a stranger, or snatched by a non-custodial parent constitutes an endangered, high risk group that is easy prey for those in our society who would exploit children. It is difficult to estimate how many of this group end up involved in prostitution, pornography, or other forms of exploitation. Local experience showed that approximately 80 percent of the case load of the Louisville and Jefferson County Exploited and Missing Child Unit had been sexually exploited while a runaway. The New York City Police Department similarly reported that ninety percent of the runaways apprehended by that agency may have been involved in prostitution.[16]

Law enforcement has viewed these children as "problem kids" and treat them as a nuisance. Not surprisingly, social service and law enforcement agencies have generally performed their respective duties often unaware of adult pimp juvenile prostitute networks that thrive on victimization of youth through sexual abuse and exploitation. There is also a common community attitude that prostitution is a "victimless" crime which results in a low law enforcement priority compared to other offenses. Additionally an attitude permeates law enforcement that views children as small stature adults. Such attitudes continue to be a major obstacle in addressing the exploited and missing child problem despite the fact that a growing cyclic pattern of victimization has been found in which juveniles become first the victims of child abuse (both physically and sexually), then run away from home, enter into prostitution for survival needs, or are recruited into such exploitation by peers, father-surrogates, and business managers (pimps) and from there enter into even more endangering situations. Such a pattern has been termed "progressive victimization" by John Rabun, Deputy Director of the National Center for Missing and Exploited Children.

Although runaways and child prostitutes are identified as a major portion of the problem of child sexual exploitation and missing children, additional threats are posed to all children by child molesters. According to *Newsweek*, one out of ten children are sexually abused each year, often by a trusted authority figure, i.e., teacher, doctor, camp counselor, minister, relatives, or other known and trusted authority figures.[17] Such victimization cuts across all social, economic, and racial divisions. Irving Prager has stated that "child molestation is probably the most common serious crime against the person in the United States."[18]

TYPOLOGY OF THE OFFENDERS

Who are the exploiters of these children? Society has misconceived the source of threat to children as being the ominous stranger

108

in black raincoat with a sack of candy lurking in the playgrounds and school yards of our nation and warn its children of such a threat. Many parents believe that their children will be safe if they simply do not talk to strangers. According to research, child molesters are almost always someone that the child knows.[19] Probably one-third of the time the molester is a relative, and at least another third of the time the molester is an acquaintance of the child's parents who recruits the child right out of the parent's house.

The pedophile, a particular type of child molester, is an adult whose conscious sexual interests and overt sexual behavior are directed either partially or exclusively toward children. Typically pedophiles with whom the author has had contact tend to be white, male, often unmarried, collectors of pornography and erotica, who find it far easier to relate to children than to adults. Frequently such persons seek employment, offer volunteer services, or simply just linger in places where they will have access to children. Many pedophiles appear to have an "ideal" victim, that is a preference for a specific age range, developmental stage, or physical features, and his attraction for that ideal type may be specifically rigid. Such rigidity may account for multiple victim phenomenon which is all too familiar in cases of child sexual exploitation. Although such a profile as that just suggested may be helpful from an investigative standpoint, *it should be understood that available research suggests pedophilia cuts across the entire social spectrum having little correlation with such demographics as race, religion, education, vocation, intelligence, socioeconomic level, etc.* There does appear to be a common denominator in the psychological basis of pedophilia. The sexual involvement with the child is an attempt to fulfill the pedophile's needs for acceptance, validation, mastery, and control. Groth refers to this as essentially a "pseudo-sexual act" where the act itself represents a sexual expression of non-sexual needs and unresolved life issues.[20] Groth divides pedophiles into two basic categories, fixated and regressed. The fixated pedophile's primary sexual orientation is toward children. This attraction to children often emerges during adolescence and continues as an obsessive-compulsive behavior pattern throughout later life. Frequently this individual is the product of an abusive chaotic home life and may himself have been sexually victimized. The fixated pedophile has little contact with age-mates, neither sexually nor socially. Male children are most frequently the fixated pedophile's primary targets. The regressed pedophile's primary sexual orientation is toward age-mates and his pedophilic interests emerge as a response to a stress situation. The victim's of this individual are usually female. The regressed pedophile treats this victim as if the victim were an age-mate, *i.e.*, as an adult. Groth terms both types of behavior as maladaptive response to life situations.[21] Because the regressed offender's involvement with children is a departure from otherwise normal activity due to life stress activity there has been some success in treating these offenders. Treatment of fixated pedophiles on the other hand has been generally unsuccessful. A growing body of evidence and an increasing number of medical, sociological, and legal experts are concluding that child molesters with a lifelong history of sexual involvement with children are not curable.[22] Others who would minimize the problem say that pedophilia is nothing more than a sexual preference, similar to homosexuality. However, the problem is that the sexual activity is *never* consensual because if the child is incapable of foreseeing the consequences of the act the child is unable to consent to it.

Pedophiles are also mainly responsible for child pornography produced, distributed, or sold in the United States for without the demand there would be no market. The pedophile's obsession with child pornography stems from many different factors. Many take photos of their victims to show other pedophiles, much in the same manner that one takes in displaying a picture of a spouse or lover. Pedophiles take pride in displaying their victims. Child porn is also used as a lure to introduce other children to the desired activity as well as to lower inhibitions of potential victims. This type of material is also sexually stimulating to some pedophiles. Child molesters often have thousands of photographs in treasured collections. Such collections have a particular value as the pedophile relives the sexual encounter with his victim and recalls each and every relationship.

Misconceptions regarding the dynamics of child sexual exploitation, coupled with an unwillingness to admit the potential vulnerability of all children, are the most difficult hurdles to overcome in taking steps to deal with the missing and exploited child problem. Parents who quite properly warn their children about not taking candy from strangers or getting into a car with a stranger fail to explain why this is inappropriate or what the dangers could be—and fail completely to warn children about the very real threat of a relative, friend of the family, neighbor, minister, teacher, doctor, or police officer. In much the same manner many organizations designed to serve children, yet failing to understand the pedophile's need for access to children, often fail to screen prospective employees and volunteers. The court system, failing to understand the harm to the victim and the compulsion or drive of the pedophile, humanely sentences convicted offenders with out-patient treatment programs. Law enforcement, confronted with what is deduced as apparent consentual behavior of the participants, assigns low priority to missing children (considering them "just runaways") and often selects not to aggressively investigate offenses. Cross-jurisdictional and cross-agency information sharing is nearly nonexistent. The territorial imperative of guarding one's own turf takes precedence over the pooling of resources to attack the problem.

It is the opinion of the author that this issue is a community problem that only the community as a whole can deal with effectively. No one agency—be it local, state, or federal—can effectively solve the problem. Understanding, education, and cooperation are the keys to unlocking the grip that the problem of missing and exploited children has on our future. Parents must understand the threat and prepare their children in a non-frightening manner to realize that parts of their bodies are private and no one has the right to intrude on that privacy. Victims must know that agencies will support and believe. Families of victims must understand the need to be supportive. Social service must plan treatment for victim support. Law enforcement must aggressively investigate the abuse.

POLICY RECOMMENDATIONS

The preceding pages have provided a very brief overview of the exploited and missing child problem. What follows are some recommendations to combat the problem. The majority of these recommendations are a result of The Kentucky Task Force on Exploited and Missing Children.

Recommendation 1: A state missing children's act should be passed requiring law enforcement agencies to accept, investigate, and relay to a state clearinghouse all reports of missing children and requiring the state department of education to establish a program to identify and locate missing school children.

Recommendation 2: A state child sexual abuse and exploitation act should be established that creates a Child Victims Trust Fund to finance local prevention programs which will educate children and adults about the dangers of sexual abuse and the lures of sexual exploitation.

Recommendation 3: Legislation should be passed requiring youth serving agencies to request criminal record checks on all persons who apply for employment, or volunteer, for positions in which they would have supervisory or disciplinary authority over children.

Recommendation 4: Legislation should be passed to establish certain sexual offenses against children as offenses where probation cannot be granted and the imposition or execution of sentence cannot be suspended.

Recommendation 5: Legislation should be passed permitting the pretrial videotaped testimony of children age twelve and under to be used as evidence in sexual abuse cases.

Recommendation 6: Legislation should make provision to allow child victims of sexual abuse to claim compensation for psychological as well as physical bodily injuries.

Recommendation 7: Custodial interference should be a felony in all cases so that extradition of the person interfering with the lawful custody is possible.

Recommendation 8: Legislation should make it a felony offense where a person knowingly induces, assists, or causes a minor to engage in sexual activity.

Recommendation 9: Juvenile Justice Commissions should be charged with investigating and recommending possible changes in procedures associated with termination of parental rights.

Recommendation 10: Child fingerprinting programs should be organized to insure that every child is properly fingerprinted and that the child's parents are provided with the fingerprints to be kept in a safe place along with a recent photograph of the child and other identifying information in order to raise the level of public awareness about the problem of exploited and missing children and to help law enforcement authorities locate the child if the child ever turns up missing.

Recommendation 11: Call back programs should be instituted in every school whereby parents are immediately notified (and also the police if suspicious circumstances are involved) when a child fails to report to school as scheduled. Also, school boards should institute sign-out and identification procedures governing permission of students to leave school during the school day with an adult.

Recommendation 12: Sexual child abuse or body safety programs should be provided in all schools by trained volunteers in order that children are properly informed about sexual abuse, the lures of sexual exploitation, and how to protect themselves from sexual abuse and exploitation. Teachers should be trained to recognize the subtle signs of child sexual abuse and exploitation and should be fully supported by the school administration and local police when reporting possible abuse or exploitation under a procedure that does not permit disclosure of the teacher or the person reporting the suspected abuse.

Recommendation 13: Educational television should develop and produce a series of television programs appropriate for viewing by children of different age groups relying on the expertise of those with experience in runaway prevention and child sexual abuse and exploitation.

Recommendation 14: Local task forces should be established in counties or multi-county areas, combining resources and focusing on the missing and exploited child problem from an interdisciplinary, cooperative approach, in order to expose the problem, raise public awareness, and initiate efforts to improve local services for exploited and missing children and better protect all children.

Recommendation 15: Exploited and Missing Child teams of police and social workers should be established in cities, counties, or multicounty areas that can afford them in order to focus combined law enforcement and juvenile court efforts on the prevention of child tragedies.

Recommendation 16: Volunteers should organize locally into groups similar to SLAM (Society's League Against Molestors) and ECHO (Exploited Children's Help Organization) in order to provide such services as court watch, child fingerprinting, victim counseling, and body safety education.[23]

REFERENCES

The Epidemic of The Eighties: Missing and Exploited Children by William E. Spaulding

1. Interview with John Rabun, The National Center for Missing and Exploited Children, 1835 K Street, N.W., Suite 700, Washington, D.C. 20006.
2. *Final Report of the Kentucky Task Force on Exploited and Missing Children: Child Sexual Abuse and Exploitation and the Particular Vulnerability of Runaway and Abducted Children — Kentucky's Response to a Growing National Tragedy*, by Mitch McConnell, Chairman (Louisville, Kentucky: Jefferson County Print Shop, 1983), p. 9 (hereafter cited as McConnell).
3. *Ibid.*

4. *Ibid.*

5. U.S. Congress, House Committee on Education and Labor, *Sexual Exploitation of Children*, hearings before the Subcommittee on Select Education, Ninety-Fifth Congress, First Session, Washington, U.S. Government Printing Office, 1977. Hearings held May 21–31 and June 10, 1977.

6. Shirley O'Brien, *Child Pornography* (Dubuque, Iowa: Kendall/Hunt, 1983), p. 19. [Editor's note: *See also*, David Alexander Scott, *Pornography: Its Effect On the Family, Community and Culture* (Washington, D.C.: The Child and Family Protection Institute, Free Congress Foundation, 1985).]

7. *Ibid*, p. 19.

8. *Ibid*, p. 44.

9. Caren Adams and Jennifer Fay, *No More Secrets* (San Luis Obispo, California: Impact Publishers, 1981), p. 4.

10. *Ibid.*

11. *Ibid.*

12. *Ibid.*

13. Katherine Barrett and Jack Fincher, *Ladies' Home Journal*, August 1982, pp. 81–83, 128–130.

14. James Mann, *U.S. News and World Report*, Jan. 17, 1983. p. 64.

15. Dorinda N. Noble and C. Eddie Palmer, "The Painful Phenomenon of Child Snatching," *Social Casework: The Journal of Contemporary Social Work* (June 1984), pp. 330–36.

16. McConnell, *supra*, n. 2, p. 9.

17. Eloise Salholz, et. al., "Beware of Child Molesters," *Newsweek* (August 9, 1982), pp. 45–47.

18. Irving Prager, "Sexual Psychology and Child Molesters: The Experiment Fails," *Journal of Juvenile Law*, Vol. 6, No. 1, (1982), pp. 47–79.

19. Adams, p. 8.

20. Jon Conte and David Shore, *Social Work and Child Sexual Abuse* (New York: Hawthorne Press, 1975), p. 134.

21. *Ibid.*, p. 135.

22. *Ibid.*, p. 140.

23. McConnell, *supra* n. 2, pp. 33–35.

7

FAMILY VIOLENCE:
Mistaken Beliefs About the Crime
by Lois Haight Herrington

For more than two years, a mother and her children lived in fear of the man they loved, the man they thought loved them. On numerous occasions the family called the police for relief from his abusiveness, only to be told he could not be arrested unless the officers had actually seen the violence. The threats and beatings escalated. The man was taken to a mental hospital, then was released unbeknownst to his family. Enraged and intoxicated, he returned home to bash the windshields of three cars. Now having destroyed property, he was charged and a court date was set. He retaliated by holding his son hostage for four days, denying him food and sleep. When he came to court, he attacked his wife, and the judge ordered him to be evaluated at a mental health clinic. Still, he was not arrested.

Then one day his wife went to meet her husband to discuss the mortgage payments she was making on the house she had been forced to flee and where he continued to live. She never returned. That afternoon she was found dead, shot by her husband as she sat in her car parked at the police station. Her family surmised that she had driven there for help.

"He was considered dangerous by two hospitals, at least one judge and a sheriff," said the dead woman's sister. "Why was he continually allowed to roam free and blatantly show the world what he was capable of doing? Did someone think he was bluffing?"[1]

For decades, abuse in the family has been the crime no one sees or hears or acts upon until it is too late—until a wife, husband or child is found shot or beaten to death. Nearly 18 percent of the murders in 1984 were committed within the family.[2] There is little disagreement about the role of the criminal justice system when one family member kills another. But most cases are not that clear cut. How does one differentiate between a one-time loss of temper and one of many episodes of brutal one-sided abuse? How does one know whether a child is recanting a sexual story because it is not true or because he is too frightened to continue talking about it? Is recently increased attention and reporting of child and spouse abuse a result of an actual increase in these crimes or an increase in the victims' willingness to come forward?

These are serious issues facing Americans. Television, movies, billboards, public service announcements, publicized research and several notorious cases have prompted the public call for action against abuse perpetrated by relatives or trusted adults. But whose responsibility is it to take this action? If they come to light, these acts have traditionally been the province of medical and mental health professionals if any action at all was taken. Recently there has been a concern that social workers have become overzealous in their allegations of suspected child abuse and that their intervention disrupts and can destroy families.[3] Some have worried that refuges offering safety to battered spouses encourage them to leave their families rather than try to repair the damage.[4] Given the rising divorce rate, there is a legitimate concern that it has become easier for families to dissolve rather than work out their differences and stay together.

A new approach offers an alternative between doing nothing and relying solely on solutions provided by the social service professions. There is growing support for the justice system to intervene more decisively in family abuse cases, to treat them as serious crimes. The President's Task Force on Victims of Crime brought a national focus to this problem after seeing that many people were being violently victimized not only by strangers—but by loved ones.[5] Recognizing that the violence often had very different motives and solutions, it recommended the creation of the Attorney General's Task Force on Family Violence in September 1983 to study these issues and recommend ways to stop the violence and heal the family unit if possible. The Task Force held hearings in six cities and spoke to more than 1,000 victims, abusers, law enforcement officers, prosecutors, judges, doctors, nurses, clergymen, counselors and victim service providers. In September 1984, the Task Force published a report with 63 recommendations, based upon the fundamental conclusion that the nature of the act not just the relationship of the victim to the abuser should guide the criminal justice system's response.[6] Family violence is a crime.

While this broad conclusion has been widely accepted and praised,[7] implementing particular policies to achieve its objectives have provoked more debate.[8] The Task Force challenged tenaciously held beliefs about family violence that have caused the crime to be denied, ignored or explained away until it escalates into serious injury or death. On close examination, however, one sees the facts do not support these beliefs.

Family violence is not a serious problem. Task Force testimony and FBI statistics indicate that family violence is a problem of alarming magnitude. In 1984, 2,928 people were killed by a member of their family.[9] Of female homicide victims alone, nearly one in three died at the hands of a husband or partner.[10] Husbands were responsible for 20.6 percent of the women killed in 1984; while boyfriends were the offenders in 9.5 percent of female homicides for that year.[11] Law Enforcement surveys report family violence cases are among their most frequent calls.[12] Battery is a major cause of injury to American women.[13] One major study of family violence indicated that as many as two million Americans are beaten by a spouse every year.[14]

The misconception that family violence is not a widespread problem has been perpetuated in part because, with the exception of murder, crimes committed among family members cannot be neatly tallied. The Uniform Crime Report of the FBI does not discern the relationship of victim to offender for crimes less than homicide. When the Bureau of Justice Statistics conducts its survey of homes for information about crime, interviewers usually speak with the entire family at the same time and include only children 12 years or older. Therefore the survey has difficulty obtaining data on inter-family abuse. The Task Force recommended reforms in statistical collection, and the FBI and BJS currently are redesigning their efforts to obtain more detailed information on family crimes.

There are special problems in gathering data on child physical and sexual abuse. Because of the nature of child abuse, often child deaths are originally recorded as resulting from an accident. If the fact pattern evolves and indicates abuse, the original reported cause of death may remain unchanged. Therefore there is no reliable data on child homocides as a result of maltreatment.

Reporting of child abuse has experienced a large and yet unexplained increase during recent years. Since 1976, reported child abuse has increased 142 percent.[15] Reported estimates of child sexual abuse have grown more than 900 percent during that period.[16] Still other research indicates most abuse never comes to the attention of the authorities. A large random survey of adult women which elicited information regarding previous sexual abuse found that only two percent of the victims had reported to the authorities

117

when the offender was a relative, and only six percent had reported when the offender was not related.[17]

Is child maltreatment increasing or are more people reporting it? There is no way to answer that question definitively at this time. So many abuse cases were hidden before the recent surge in reporting that there is not a reliable benchmark from which to assess the meaning of the increase. Some critics are concerned that excessive mandatory reporting laws have caused the increase. It should be noted that these laws were passed in the late 60s and early 70s, more than a decade prior to the recent dramatic increase in reporting.[18]

Some have expressed concern that the child abuse problem has been exaggerated and that most of the reported cases turn out to be unfounded.[19] But recent studies show the term "unfounded" should not necessarily be equated to mean "untrue." Nationwide, from 35 to 55 percent of child abuse fatalities and tens of thousands of injuries involve children previously known to the authorities as victims of abuse.[20] An analysis of children who died due to maltreatment in New York City uncovered 18 out of 47 deaths in which abuse had been previously investigated and then determined to be unfounded.[21]

This large increase in reporting, the percentage of cases which are determined to be unfounded, and the number of the so-called unfounded cases which eventually result in a death indicate serious problems with the investigation of child physical and sexual abuse. Some reforms have been proposed to remedy the problem. They include defining child abuse more clearly and refining screening procedures so that the most serious reports receive the most attention.[22]

Even with changes in data collection procedures, a great amount of abuse is likely to remain unreported by the victims of family violence. They wrestle with conflicting feelings of love and anger, fear and loyalty, shame and self-blame—emotions generally not experienced by victims of stranger crimes.[23] Family violence is the ultimate betrayal. Rather than disclose it to friends or the authorities, the victims often choose to suffer in silence.

Only the poor and uneducated are battered. Those cases which are reported to the authorities often involve individuals from lower socio-economic backgrounds because they have fewer private resources for safety. Temporary residences are generally filled by women with little or no money to pay for other refuge or to seek professional marital counseling. The statistics obtained from shelters therefore do not necessarily reflect the actual incidence of spouse abuse among various classes.[24]

The Attorney General's Task Force learned of serious abuse endured and committed by doctors, teachers, lawyers, and other professionals as well as non-professionals. One study found that men with a college education were as likely to be abusers as those with a seventh or eighth grade education.[25] "When I tell people I am a former battered wife, it is a real eye-opener," testified one victim. "They say things like 'you are too smart, too professional, too middle-class.'"[26] When unspeakable violence strikes the upstanding professional, often the victims hesitate to seek help because they feel they have more to lose by leaving. If they decide to report the crime, they can often be discouraged from following through with prosecution. One woman lawyer who had been beaten severely by her husband, a C.P.A., told the Task Force that friends and even law enforcement urged her not to press charges. "They did not want me to file a complaint against my husband," she said. "They'd say, 'Well you don't want to ruin his career, now, do you?'"[27]

Just as spouse abuse is often seen to only strike the lower classes, child physical and sexual abuse is often perceived to affect single parent households more than traditional families. Common sense suggests that the added pressures of single parenthood might heighten the potential for violent situations. However, there are no statistics to support or refute that statement at this time.

When victim advocates try to make the point that all abusers are not step-fathers, step-mothers or single parents, critics have responded that this challenge is, in effect, an attack on middle-class and traditional values. But it should be noted that when victim advocates speak of the classlessness of abuse, they are not saying that it occurs *equally* among all classes.[28] Furthermore, accepting that violence occurs in all types of household lifestyles is not a judgement on these particular lifestyles. It simply keeps others from dismissing from the realm of possibility that someone who is educated, professionally successful and married is not capable of abusing family members.

A battered spouse must have provoked the assaults. If she didn't like the violence, she could leave. This misconception appears to stem from a belief that wives nag their husbands who are then justified by retaliating with violence. This thinking is wrongheaded for two reasons. First, no provocation short of a violent assault should condone a violent response in self-defense. Second, victims told the

Attorney General's Task Force that the "provocation" for violence is usually a minor incident such as burnt dinner, dirty kitchen, an evening with girl friends or a perceived slight. Furthermore, a recent study found no support for the "mutual combat" theory that holds both parties to be equally culpable. In the overwhelming majority of the cases, it is women who are being routinely victimized by men.[29]

Even in the face of random brutal attacks, it is extremely difficult for abused victims to pack their belongings and go, even if they could afford to leave. Battered women do not wish to break up the family; just stop the violence. They may have been taught that a good woman can change a man. If he beats her she must not be good enough or he must be sick, and she is therefore obligated to stay, improve her behavior and make him better. To leave would be to admit defeat, to fail as a marriage partner. Moreover, a violent outburst by a mate is usually followed by a "honeymoon" period of remorse and begging for forgiveness. This cyclical pattern of tension build-up and violent explosion, followed by apologies and promises that it will never happen again leaves the victim with false hope. So she stays and neither she nor her husband receive much-needed help.[30]

"He promises that he will do anything, sheds lots of tears and says, 'I'm so sorry, and I love these children. I love you. I would never do it again,'" testified one woman. "You want to believe that it's just a mistake, but it's not."[31]

Ashamed, fearful that any resistance or attempt to leave will incite greater violence, isolated from family and friends, often without any means of support other than from her husband, the battered spouse often sinks into submission, a stage of "learned helplessness" in which she avoids any act that may provoke the abuser's rage.[32] She is too terrified to leave and has nowhere to go.

Family violence is not a problem requiring action by the criminal justice system. Any intervention should be by the health and social service professions. The criminal justice system historically has hesitated to intervene in violent family disputes for several reasons. Its professionals have not wanted to interfere in what they perceived as being private family matters, or have felt such action was not their responsibility.[33] They have not been trained sufficiently to handle these volatile and complex calls. They view them as being among the most dangerous to their own safety.[34] The health and social services fields have not wanted to thrust an already injured family into an adversarial justice system at the risk of causing even greater damage.

There has been a belief that criminal justice action would not serve the best interests of the family.[35] And finally, communities have not expressed to their lawmakers and law enforcers that citizens believe family violence is serious criminal behavior and should be treated as such.[36]

As a result of these attitudes, the criminal justice system has responded inconsistently to acts of family violence. Police dispatchers have frequently screened out family violence calls[37] or given them a low priority.[38] Felonious assaults may be recorded as misdemeanors or not recorded at all. When one study examined non-stranger misdemeanors assaults in three cities, it found that more than two-thirds of the victims had been injured and a full quarter required medical attention. Furthermore, weapons such as guns, knives and clubs had been used in more than a quarter of the assaults.[39] Prosecutors have been generally less strict in applying the criminal law to spousal assault cases compared to other assaults. This prudence may seem wise given the sensitive dynamics of the family. However, most law enforcement officers have usually already screened cases to take action on only the most serious assaults. Despite this preselection, prosecutors have been seen to reject the majority of cases brought to their attention.[40] The judiciary has also been criticized for lenient sanctions against offenders who abuse spouses and children.[41]

This underenforcement of the law tells victims and assailants that abuse in the home is not really a serious crime, if a crime at all. It is this perception that has helped to perpetuate family violence. Moreover, it compounds the blame felt by the victim. Victims of any kind of crime often feel somehow responsible for the incident,[42] but victims of family violence are plagued by a more profound guilt. Battered spouses realize they chose to live with their victimizers. Abused children may believe they are being punished for a wrong they committed. The laws and their enforcement are one of the clearest expressions of society's disapproval of a behavior. A strong response by the justice system is essential to send the message that violence in the family will not be tolerated.

"Many of the people across the country have looked at this as a civil problem, as a family problem, as a social problem," testified a New York prosecutor. "We believe it is a criminal problem and the way to handle it is with criminal justice intervention."[43]

The Task Force did not suggest that law enforcement lock up every abuser; many alternatives exist between doing nothing and imposing a prison sentence. Protection orders can be imposed and enforced. One arrest may be sufficient to halt the violence. Prosecution and/or incarceration can be deferred pending completion of a therapy program. Treatment is essential. As is discussed in more detail later, it works most successfully when it is carefully monitored and enforced by at least the threat of a criminal sanction, which may be the only real incentive for the abuser to change the behavior.[44]

"It was such an extreme experience having actually been arrested and dealt with harshly...that I sought help," said one former abuser.[45]

The Attorney General's Task Force found that as more research is conducted and more new policies are implemented, criminal justice professionals are realizing that it is possible to protect the victim, sanction the abuser and preserve the family unit. These results are best achieved with sure, swift action by the justice system to signal the gravity of offenses against family members.

Arrest exacerbates violence. Adhering to the social science literature of the sixties that stressed the role of officers as conflict resolvers, law enforcement training has taught them not to respond surely and swiftly to family violence.[46] A 1984 survey of major law enforcement agencies found approximately 40 percent of the agencies instructed officers to mediate violent family situations and about one half gave the officer complete discretion.[47] Officers have been told to mediate situations out of the legitimate concern that harsher intervention will only incite more violent reprisals from the abuser. But this directive in effect instructs officers to play the role of psychologist, marriage counselor or referee, not assertive law enforcer. As a result, they have been able to issue only a tenuous peace often lasting until the officer leaves the premises.

Police and sheriff's deputies have expressed frustration at performing what they perceive to be social work roles; they are instructed to mediate the dispute and sometimes legally prevented from making an arrest to handle what is typically one of the most frequent calls to American police departments.[48] It is also the call which is generally the most feared by law enforcement. Data formerly showed "disturbances" to be the number one cause of police homicide. More specific breakdown of this category, however, has shown that family fights are among the least likely of police calls to result in death of an officer.[49] One reason that officers have not arrested abusers is that in 17 states they are prohibited from making arrests for misdemeanors unless they have a warrant or witness the assault. (As stated earlier, most spousal assaults are classified as misdemeanors.[50]) To enable more assertive action by law enforcement, as of 1983, 33 states passed laws permitting warrantless arrests for misdemeanors. Some of these laws apply only to domestic violence situations, while other states allow warrantless arrests in any situation where there is probable cause and the arrest is needed to avoid a violent situation, injury or destruction of evidence.[51]

New studies are reinforcing the need to change the laws. An experiment conducted in Minneapolis, Minnesota found that of three law enforcement responses—arrest, mediation, and separation—arrest is the most effective deterrent to future outbursts. When ordered to leave the home, 24 percent of the abusers repeated the violence within six months. When officers mediated the dispute, 19 percent of the spouses continued to batter. When arrested, which in Minneapolis includes overnight incarceration, only ten percent of the abusers had repeated the violence again within six months.[52]

Other research has shown that if the abuse is permitted to continue unchecked, often it may escalate into severe violence. In one city, police had been called at least once before in 85 percent of spousal abuse and homicide calls.[53] In half of the cases which resulted in homicide, the police had responded previously five times or more.[54]

"He would have stopped the violence long before if the police had arrested him in the beginning," testified one victim. "In the beginning he was afraid of the police, afraid of going to jail and losing his job. But when he saw that the police were not going to touch him, he came right back and the violence got worse as he got bolder."[55]

Law enforcement officers have the first opportunity to send the message to the abuser that his behavior is criminal and will not be tolerated. Therefore, the Task Force recommended that arrest be established as the preferred response, and that state laws be changed which hamper officers from making an arrest.

The decision to arrest involves several variables, including a previous history of violence. Accordingly, the Task Force also recommended that police file a report for every family violence call answered, whether or not an arrest was made. Furthermore, law enforcement should keep complete records of protection orders, violations of which would be grounds for arrest. Oregon experienced a 10 percent drop in domestic homicides after the state passed a law requiring arrest for the violation of a protection order.[56] When

Washington state passed a mandatory arrest law, reported spouse abuse increased by more than one half and the number of arrests increased by four times. Significantly, both the number of cases set for trial and successful prosecutions increased 300 percent.[57]

Arrest should be established as the preferred response, but it may not be appropriate in every case. At the very least officers should interview the parties separately, read the victim and abuser their respective rights, and refer them to services. If the husband and wife must separate, the Task Force supports—and common sense dictates—that the abuser, not the innocent victim, should leave the home.

Sometimes, however, making the abuser leave is neither feasible nor enforceable. Talking has failed. Self defense may be futile or exacerbating. The safety of the children likewise may be at risk. When frustration or confusion or intoxication erupt into violence, the victims may need temporary emergency refuge.

The Attorney General's Task Force found this haven can take many forms: facilities run by churches or other private organizations as well as shelters receiving some public assistance. Family life centers offer immediate counseling to precede violence and promote family stability and self-esteem. Respite day care centers for elderly relatives and crisis nurseries provide services to parents and children seeking temporary relief from stress. In addition, Safe Home Networks have been established by individual families to offer temporary housing and emotional guidance to victims of family violence. Some of these options for refuge are not widely known in communities. The Attorney General's Task Force recommended that localities develop several programs to better serve victims whose needs, other than immediate safety, can vary greatly.[58]

Battered women won't press charges against their husbands. In the strictest sense, this is not a mistaken belief. It is in fact a sad state of affairs. However, the Attorney General's Task Force concluded that this is generally the result of an insensitive justice system rather than a victim unwilling to cooperate.

Victims of spouse abuse have felt little support from the justice system in seeking prosecution.[59] They have been frustrated by the prosecutor's failure to take the violence seriously and/or attempt to discourage the victim from pressing charges.[60] Prosecutors have often required victims to come to their offices and sign formal complaints in order to prove their willingness to cooperate.[61] A victim of robbery or burglary is not required to personally press charges against the assailant. It is unfair to treat a victim of family violence any differently, especially when these victims are already subject to intense pressure to drop the charges. As a result, often fewer than 10 percent of cases referred to a prosecutor's office are adjudicated.[62] Once in court, they are handled inconsistently. Assistance in filling out paper work and understanding the procedure has been seen to vary.[63] Continuances can extend for months.[64] As a result, many victims give up and request to drop the charges. Studies in the past from several jurisdictions have shown that 50 to 80 percent of abused spouses will cause the charges to be dropped by failing to appear or requesting dismissal.[65] It should be noted that a respected study found the likelihood of full prosecution did not depend on the victim, the defendant or the severity of the violence. "The probability of victim cooperation is in fact better predicted by the conduct of the prosecutor than by the conduct of either the victim or defendant."[66]

The Task Force suggested that teams specially trained to handle family violence cases can ensure that the victim will be able to cooperate thereby helping to hold the offender accountable for his behavior.

In addition, the Task Force made two other key recommendations to expedite successful prosecution. First, victims of family violence should not be required to testify at a preliminary hearing, unless their testimony may lead to a finding that there is no probable cause for prosecution. At this stage of the proceedings, the defense's questioning is not restrained by a desire not to alienate the jury, and victims told the Attorney General's Task Force that it is often their most unpleasant interrogation. Yet there is no constitutional right of confrontation at this stage of the proceedings.[67] The sufficiency of hearsay evidence at a preliminary hearing is firmly established in the federal courts as well as in 25 states.[68]

In addition to accepting the sufficiency of hearsay at preliminary hearings, limiting case continuances and keeping victims informed about the case proceedings, there is a more direct and controversial step which a few prosecutors have taken to ensure the victim's cooperation. In 1981, about a dozen programs in the country limited victim discretion in prosecuting their assailants; that practice is becoming more common and its implementation varies. In some areas, the prosecutors do not force the victim to testify but rather they attempt to make the case with other evidence. Other prosecutors will try to persuade the victim that prosecution will help

125

protect the family. Still other jurisdictions strictly enforce "no-drop" policies, and will hold victims in contempt of court for failure to testify.[69]

The Attorney General's Task Force endorsed "no-drop" policies provided they do not penalize victims.[70]

"I have seen relief on a woman's face when I've said, 'I am sorry, I am not waiving prosecution.' . . .It works, it really does work," testified one assistant district attorney.[71]

Children lie about sexual assault. The recent publicity given to investigations into child sexual abuse that have ended in acquittal or dismissal have perpetuated this belief. The Minnesota Attorney General closed the investigation of 21 adults accused of molesting children in Jordan, Minnesota.[72] After a 17-month preliminary hearing in Los Angeles, the district attorney dropped charges against five of seven adults accused of torturing, sexually abusing and performing satanic rituals with children during the past 10 years at McMartin Pre-school.[73] A top aide to a state attorney general was recently acquitted from charges that he molested his daughter's friend at a slumber party.[74]

One should not automatically assume, however, that therefore children lie about being sexually assaulted. Common sense suggests that children lie to get out of trouble but not into trouble. Moreover, when cases are dismissed, the legal reasons given do not always malign the truthfulness of the children, rather they manifest the inability of the justice system to respond to child abuse. When the Minnesota Attorney General closed the Jordan investigation, he stated that it was not possible to continue the case, although there was "no doubt that a number of children in Scott County were victims of sexual abuse."[75] No one denied the abuse occurred. The problem was the ineffective manner of eliciting the circumstances in which it occurred.

Even those mistakenly accused of molestation recognize more often than not, children are telling the truth. When acquitted, the state official said, "There's no question that we ignored for far too long abuse within families. A dramatic well-publicized acquittal like mine suggests that all of these things are ill-founded. And that's wrong. It's just simply wrong. The vast majority of people who get accused of this are guilty as hell."[76]

According to one expert very few children (no more than two or three per thousand) have ever been found to invent claims of molestation.[77] It has become a maxim among child sexual abuse investigators and counselors that children cannot fabricate the kinds of explicit sexual manipulations they divulge during questioning.[78] Further, of the children who were found to have misrepresented their complaints, most had sought to *understate* the frequency or duration of sexual experiences, even when reports were made in anger and in apparent retaliation against violence or humiliation. One psychiatrist has drawn a vivid metaphor for the automatic assumption that when a case is dropped, the child must have lied. This fallacious thinking is tantamount to saying, "we should discard any culture for strep throat if it merely diagnoses the illness without proving who is to blame for infecting the patient. By further analogy to the theories of the courtroom, if the doctor can't prove where the infection came from, then we'll blame the doctor for implanting the germs."[79]

Most dismissed cases have failed because there was not enough reliable evidence obtained to present a case beyond a reasonable doubt in a court of law. Obviously, there are difficulties inherent in getting the truth about crimes for which there are no witnesses. The only evidence is often the word of the child against an adult. The physical evidence of child abuse, especially sexual, is often very difficult to gather. By the time the victim reports the abuse, the evidence may have healed or been washed away. Sexual abuse may or may not cause visible injury. Only recently have more progressive diagnostic methods such as the colposcope been more widely used to detect minute physical evidence on a child's body.

Probably the strongest argument denying the credibility of child witnesses is the frequency with which they recant their stories. A landmark paper identifying the characteristics of sexually abused children made this point: "Whatever a child says about sexual abuse, she is likely to reverse it."[80]

When children are abused often they are told they must keep it a secret. "Don't tell anyone." "Don't tell your mother." "She won't believe you." "She'll hate you." "She will send you away." "If you tell I won't love you anymore." "I'll spank you." "I'll kill your puppy." "I'll kill you," were common ploys cited to the Attorney General's Task Force. These are serious threats to young children, and they help to explain the painstaking process required to enable children to discuss the molestation. The pioneer in identifying the Child Sexual Abuse Accommodation syndrome explains a typical disclosure process.

In a typical pattern of investigation of suspicions of group exploitation, an interviewer may receive convincing denial from all of the children interviewed. In a subsequent round of interviews one child may implicate the children who have continued to deny. The child who breaks the secret, often somewhat older than the others, may claim that he resisted involvement or even fought back against the assaults, but that he knows things happened to other kids. With progressive interviews and with increasing reassurance and rapport, the specialist interviewer may pry open this ten[t]ative 'window of disclosure': 'He did it to me too...but only once.' 'He did it to me a lot of times.' 'He made me do it to him once...a lot of times.' 'She did it too.' 'They all did it.' 'They made me do it to the other kids.' 'They took pictures.' 'They wore funny clothes.' 'They killed birds.' 'They killed babies.' 'They made me kill the baby.' Such admissions are rarely volunteered. They are confessed in response to questions that focus on a presumption that such things might be possible. On encountering outrage or disbelief, the admissions will evaporate in reverse order.[81]

A great deal of skill therefore is required to elicit accurate testimony from children. The following transcript of one case is illustrative of this point.

Defense Attorney:	And then you said you put your mouth on his penis?
Five-year-old:	No.
Attorney:	You didn't say that?
Child:	No.
Attorney:	Did you ever put your mouth on his penis?
Child:	No.
Attorney:	Well, why did you tell your mother that your dad put his penis on your mouth?
Child:	My brother told me to.

At this point, it appeared the child had recanted his earlier report of being sexually abused. However, an experienced prosecutor recognized the problem and clarified the confusion.

Prosecutor:	Jenny, you said that you didn't put your mouth on daddy's penis. Is that right?
Child:	Yes.
Prosecutor:	Did daddy put his penis in your mouth?
Child:	Yes.
Prosecutor:	Did you tell your mom?
Child:	Yes.
Prosecutor:	What made you decide to tell?
Child:	My brother and I talked about it, and he said I better tell or dad would just keep doing it.[82]

128

The purpose here is not to suggest that the constitutional safeguards to protect against unjust accusations should be weakened. Conviction of a crime requires proof beyond a reasonable doubt that the accused is indeed guilty. That standard should be no less for children than it is for adults. The argument here is that one should not look at the number of acquittals and unfounded cases and immediately assume that the children were lying about the abuse.

Most of the reforms that would ease the child's passage through the justice process require no change in law; simply an exercise in discretion. "Too much attention is presently directed to legislative reforms permitting innovative practices that benefit only a handful of the growing number of children enmeshed in the criminal justice system. A large portion of the effort now devoted to statutory reform might be more productively focused toward alternative techniques that are less dramatic (such as testimony by videotape or closed-circuit television) yet equally—or even more—effective."[83] These techniques generally include aids to communication, such as using anatomically correct dolls and vocabulary appropriate to the child's level of development. In addition the physical environment can be modified. For example, a smaller chair can be provided for child witnesses. The judge can wear business clothes rather than black robes. Finally, assuring that the child is adequately prepared for court by the prosecutors or victim aides can eliminate the need for elaborate procedures so they do not have to face their attacker.[84]

The purpose is to assure that case dismissal occurs because the accused is innocent and not because the victim is handled so poorly that the parents pull the child from the proceedings in the interest of sparing him any further trauma. Or if the parents themselves are responsible for the abuse, the reforms intend to protect a child from collapsing under pressure due to the lack of parental support coupled with an insensitive justice system.

Youngsters are caught in a paradox within the justice system. If they commit crimes, they are handled with care by a separate juvenile justice system that considers their cases behind closed doors. Their names are not released. Sentences are more lenient. Rehabilitative therapy is virtually assured. But when children are the victims of crime, they are afforded little or no protection by the criminal justice system. The following two measures recommended by the Attorney General's Task Force would aid child victims.

• *Accepting hearsay at preliminary hearings.* Just as for victims of spouse abuse discussed earlier, the requirement to testify at the preliminary hearing can be the most difficult part of the criminal justice process for children. Allowing an investigator, therapists or physician to testify on behalf of the child victim would spare the child victim from this interrogation. As stated earlier, there is no constitutional right of confrontation at the preliminary hearing.[85]

• *Limiting Continuances.* In child sexual abuse cases, youngsters are subjected to repeated questioning by investigators, doctors, nurses, therapists, family members, lawyers, social workers and judges. Needlessly postponing the case exacerbates this problem. In New York City, for example, children are interviewed an average of 27 times during the process.[86] Preliminary findings of a study of child sexual abuse victims, conducted by the University of North Carolina, suggest that court delay can be a causal factor in the pattern of retracting statements that is typical among sexually abused children.[87] The President's Task Force on Victims of Crime as well as the Attorney General's Task Force on Family Violence recommended that prosecutors and judges limit continuances.[88]

Treatment—rather than incarceration—is the best means to change an abuser's behavior. Particularly in cases of molestation committed by someone outside the family, the sentence generally imposed has been commensurate with the harm done to victims. A study by the American Bar Association has found 68 percent of sexual assault offenders against children were sentenced to probation. Of those cases, 89 percent involved mandated treatment as a condition of probation and 56 percent were also sentenced to some jail time, with the most frequent duration being one year or less. Alternatively, only 29 percent of offenders against adults were sentenced to probation.[89]

This disparity in the sentencing of those who sexually assault children versus those who sexually assault adults seems to stem from a belief that pedophiles are mentally ill and therefore not criminally responsible for their acts. If the offender is a stranger or unrelated but trusted adult, experts agree there is no known proven successful method for changing his behavior. "You can't say pedophilia is an illness anymore than you can say bank robbery is an illness," one expert has said. "Treatment has been used as an escape from responsibility."[90]

Both Task Forces recommended that judges handle child molestation cases as serious criminal offenses rather than as the product of mental illness. The search should continue for successful means to change the deviant behavior, but therapy must be administered under conditions sequestering the molester from potential prey. "There is no such thing as a reformed child molester," said Patty Linebaugh, president of Society's League Against Molestation. Her granddaughter was molested, mutilated and murdered by a pedophile who had been released less than six weeks from a mental hospital where doctors had recommended he no longer be treated in a maximum secure facility. The doctors declared that he "had developed enough inner strength" to return to the community. Moreover, they said releasing him would be the only means to determine the results of his treatment program.[91]

When the sexually abused victim is related to the offender, the motive for the abuse and methods for stopping it may vary. There is greater hope that treatment will change the behavior. The directors of programs treating incest offenders told the Attorney General's Task Force, "We see results. We see how families are put back together. We are satisfied that incest will not occur again."[92] One respected counseling group reports one percent of fathers completing their incest treatment program recidivate.[93] One graduate said, "We've reunited our family...It's not a real quick process. It took us a period of 14–16 months to get the family reunited."[94]

This and other anecdotal evidence supports the effectiveness of certain therapy programs for incest offenders and spouse abusers. However, much more research is needed in this area. A pioneer in the development of a model court-mandated treatment program for batterers has pointed out that spouse abuse manifests a long-term, complicated behavior pattern that is not easily changed. Even counseling for 18 months may not be sufficient to stop the violence.[95] Arguing that counseling works only if batterers truly want to change their behavior, some therapists accept only batterers who of their own volition seek treatment.[96] A majority of counselors believe combining the court-ordered and non-court ordered batterers into a single group benefits both types of abusers. "Court-ordered men introduce a degree of reality to the non-ordered men by showing them they, too, could be subject to the criminal justice system if their battering continues. At the same time, the non-ordered men demonstrate the fact that there are other reasons for [taking steps to change their behavior]."[97] Current research by the National Institute of Justice is examining the effectiveness of various treatment programs for batterers, to help guide criminal justice professionals in their response.

In serious cases, incarceration is the only punishment that fits the crime.[98] It is rarely ordered for the first offense, but it should be viewed as appropriate if the violence causes serious injury or if the offender has repeatedly violated protection orders and/or has continued to be abusive despite counseling.[99] The Attorney General's Task Force recommended creative sentencing, such as overnight or weekend incarceration, so that abusers may still provide financially for the family. Split sentences are sometimes used, whereby the offender serves a portion of the jail or prison term, with the remainder suspended upon his compliance with certain probation requirements, such as treatment or restitution to the victim.

Statements from victims attest to the need to recognize the option for using criminal sanctions against abusers. This threat may be the only incentive for the offender to change his behavior. "My husband was never a person who had respect for the law. [Then] he knew he would not get away with it and he was punished. He's a totally different man now, he is a totally different person."[100]

Most of the preceding discussion has focused on the proper criminal justice *response* to family violence. Obviously, it is preferable to be able to prevent and not have to respond to abuse within the family. Treating alcohol abuse is frequently cited as an effective means to stop the violence before it starts. Some data do suggest that a large number of violent abusers have alcohol abuse problems. One survey found alcohol involvement in as many as 38 percent of child abuse cases and 60 percent of all spouse abuse cases.[101] However, the prevalence of alcohol abuse should not be seen as the only precipitating factor in family violence cases. One psychologist with extensive experience counseling batterers has said, "while some men who batter also abuse drugs or alcohol, there are many other batterers who are social drinkers or abstainers."[102] There are also many men who drink and never assault their spouses. With this perspective, the existence of alcohol abuse among batterers can be viewed as an overlap of two major social problems. Acting against one will not necessarily cause the other to cease as well. The treatment of substance abuse should be used in conjunction with other efforts to prevent family violence.

These efforts include education for new parents, instruction on anger-control for children and adults, child safety education for youngsters, greater emphasis in schools, churches and other institutions on the value of strong families, and better training for professionals on preserving the family unit and recognizing the signs of

family violence. The media plays an important role both in accurately reporting the extent of the problem, as well as in reducing the depiction of violence which may foster aggressive behavior.

Much more could be said regarding various approaches to preventing family violence. The purpose of this article, however, has been to build the case to support the new approach of criminal justice intervention to stop abuse. Proper action by justice professionals, in fact, can be seen as a prevention technique. Experts agree that violence is learned behavior.[103] Those who assault strangers or loved ones have often witnessed or been victims of family violence as children.[104] Acting now to stop violence in families will help prevent it from recurring in future generations.

The ideas posited above are a new approach to combatting a problem that has existed for centuries but has recently begun to receive increased attention. There is a danger that it will be exaggerated and prompt overly aggressive intrusion by the state and community into private family life. Public concern about problems seems to swing like a pendulum, from ignorance to hysteria. Therefore, it is imperative both that common sense and caution guide the debate about the best means to end violence within the family. There can be no short cut to justice. The criminal justice system must investigate all cases of family violence with the care that it examines every crime. The same criteria for charging and the same burden of proof must hold true for all acts of violence, whether they occur on the street or in the home, by a stranger or by loved one. With the guidance provided by the Attorney General's Task Force, communities will reach solutions that will strike a balance of the interests for all.

REFERENCES

Family Violence: Mistaken Beliefs About the Crime by Lois Haight Herrington

1. Testimony of Janice before the Attorney General's Task Force on Family Violence, New York City hearing, December 1, 1983. The members who served on this one-year commission were: Chairman, Chief William Hart, The Honorable John Ashcroft, Dr. Ann Burgess, The Honorable Newman Flanagan, Ursula Meese, Catherine Milton, Dr. Clyde Narramore, Chief Ruben Ortega, Frances Seward.

2. Federal Bureau of Investigation, *Uniform Crime Reports for 1984* (Washington, D.C., U.S. Department of Justice, 1985).

3. Allan C. Carlson, "The Child Savers Ride Again," *Persuasion At Work*, Vol. 8, No. 8 (August 1985), pp. 1–9.

4. Sandra McDade, "Government Aid Can Destroy Families," *USA Today*, September 25, 1984.

5. *Final Report*, The President's Task Force on Victims of Crime, (Washington, D.C.: USGPO, 1982). Members of this Task Force were: Chairman Lois Haight Herrington, Garfield Bobo, Frank Carrington, Doris L. Dolan, Kenneth O. Eikenberry, Robert J. Miller, Reverend Pat Robertson, Stanton E. Samenow.

6. *Final Report*, The Attorney General's Task Force on Family Violence, (Washington, D.C.: U.S. Department of Justice, 1984), p. 4.

7. The New York *Times*, September 29, 1984; *The Christian Science Monitor*, September 21, 1984; *USA Today*, September 25, 1984; in addition to numerous editorials in local papers throughout the nation.

8. *Newsday*, June 14, 1985; several stories in the Washington *Times* and the Washington *Post* during July 1984.

9. *Supra* n. 2.

10. *Ibid.*

11. *Ibid.*

12. Eric J. Scott, *Calls for Service: Citizen Demand and Initial Police Response*, (Washington, D.C.: U.S. Department of Justice, 1981); Raymond Parnas, "Police Discretion and Diversion of Incidents of Intrafamily Violence," 36 *Law and Contemporary Problems*, 546 (1971).

13. Testimony of Dr. Evan Stark, New York hearing of the Attorney General's Task Force, December 3, 1983. Evan Stark and Anne Flitcraft, "Women Battering, Child Abuse and Social Heredity, What Is the Relationship," *Sociological Monographs*, London 1984.

14. Murray Strauss, Richard Gelles, and Suzanne Steinmetz, *Behind Closed Doors: Violence in the American Family* (Garden City, NY: Anchor Press, 1980) pp. 32–36.

15. The American Humane Association, Child Protection Division, *Highlights of Official Child Neglect and Abuse Reporting, 1983.* (Denver, Colorado: The American Humane Association, 1985) p. 2.

16. *Ibid.* p. 12.

17. Diana Russell, "The Incidence and Prevalence of Intrafamilial and Extrafamilial Sexual Abuse of Female Children," *Child Abuse and Neglect*. Vol. 7, 1983.

18. Cited in letter from Anne Cohn, Executive Director of the National Committee for the Prevention of Child Abuse, *The Progressive*, November 1985.

19. David Kirp, "Hug Your Kid, Go To Jail," *The American Spectator*, June 1985.

20. Douglas J. Besharov, "An Overdose of Concern: Child Abuse and Overreporting Problem," *Regulation Magazine*, November/December 1985, p. 27.

21. "Report on the Preliminary Study of Child Fatalities in New York City," by the Mayor's Task Force on Child Abuse and Neglect, November 21, 1983, p. 51.

22. *Supra* n. 20, p. 28.

23. *Supra* n. 15; Lenore Walker, *The Battered Woman*, (New York: Harper & Row, 1979), p. 31.

24. National Institute of Justice, *Confronting Domestic Violence*, (Washington, D.C.: U.S. Department of Justice, 1986), p. 3.

25. *Supra* n. 14, p. 129.

26. *Supra* n. 6, p. 11

27. Testimony of Margaret Embry before the Attorney General's Task Force, San Antonio hearing, February 1, 1983.

28. *Supra* n. 16.

29. Richard Berk, Sarah Fenstermaker Berk, Donileen R. Loseke, and David Rauma, "Mutual Combat and Other Family Violence Myths," *The Dark Side of Families: Current Family Violence Research*, David Finkelhor, Richard J. Gelles, Gerald T. Hotalling, and Murray A. Straus, eds. (Beverly Hills: Sages, 1983), pp. 197–212.

30. Lenore Walker, *The Battered Woman* (New York: Harper & Row, 1979), pp. 42–70.

31. *Supra* n. 6, p. 28.

32. *Supra* n. 30.

33. D. Bell, "The Police Response to Domestic Violence: A Replication Study," *Policy Studies*, Vol. 7, No. 3, (Fall 1984), pp. 136–144.

34. David N. Konstantin, "Homicides of American Law Enforcement Officers, 1978–80," 1 *Justice Quarterly* 29–45 (March 1984).

35. *Supra* n. 24, p. 2.

36. *Supra* n. 6, pp. 6–7.

37. *Supra* n. 12.

38. Roger Langley and Richard C. Levy, "Wife Abuse and Police Response," 4 *FBI Law Enforcement Bulletin*, No. 7 (May 1978).

39. Barbara E. Smith, National Institute of Justice, *Non-Stranger Violence: The Criminal Court's Response*, (Washington, D.C.: U.S. Department of Justice 1983), p. 89.

40. U.S. Commission on Civil Rights, *Under the Rule of Thumb: Battered Women and the Administration of Justice* (Washington, D.C.: USGPO, 1982); Lisa G. Lerman, *Prosecution of Spouse Abuse: Innovations in Criminal Justice Response* (Washington, D.C.: Center for Women Policy Studies, 1981), p. 4.

41. Raymond Parnas, "Judicial Response to Intra-Family Violence," 54 *Minnesota Law Review* 642 (1970); Beverly Jacobson, "Battered Women—The Fight to End Wife Beating," 9 *Civil Rights Digest* 13 (Summer 1977).

42. M. Bard and D. Sangrey, *The Crime Victims Book*, (New York: Basic Books, 1979).

43. *Supra* n. 6, p. 11, Testimony of Jeanine Pirro, District Attorney of Weschester County, New York.

44. *Ibid.*

45. *Ibid.*, p. 22.

46. N. Loving and M. Quirk, "Spouse Abuse: The Need for New Law Enforcement Response," 5 *FBI Law Enforcement Bulletin*, No. 12 (December 1982), pp. 10–16

47. Survey cited in editorial written by its researchers, Lawrence Sherman and Anthony Bouza, "The Need to Police Domestic Violence," *Wall Street Journal*, May 22, 1984.

48. *Supra* n. 12.

49. *Supra* n. 34.

50. *Supra* n. 39.

51. L. Lerman, F. Livingston, and V. Jackson, "State Legislation on Domestic Violence," *Response*, Vol. 6, No. 5 (September/October 1983).

52. Lawrence Sherman and Richard Berk, National Institute of Justice, "The Minneapolis Domestic Violence Experiment," (Washington, D.C.: The Police Foundation, 1984).

53. Police Foundation, *Domestic Violence and The Police: Studies in Detroit and Kansas City* (The National Institute of Justice, 1977).

54. *Ibid.*, p. 9.

55. *Supra* n. 6, p. 21.

56. *Ibid.*, p. 104 (Annette Jolin, researcher).

57. Joanne Tulonen, "Impact of the Domestic Violence Prevention Act," a special report by the Seattle City Attorney's Office, Seattle, Washington, August 1985.

58. *Supra* n. 6, pp. 47–50.

59. M. H. Field and H. F. Field, "Marital Violence and the Criminal Process: Neither Justice Nor Peace," 47 *Social Service Review*, 221–240 (1973); D. A. Ford, "Wife Battering and Criminal Justice: A Study of Victim Decision-Making," 32 *Family Relations*, 463–475 (1983); Walker, *supra* n. 30.

60. Ford, *supra* n. 59; T. L. Fromson, "The Case for Legal Remedies for Abused Women," 6 *N.Y.U. Review of Law and Social Change* 135–174 (1977).

61. L. Lerman, *Prosecution of Spouse Abuse: Innovations in Criminal Justice Response* (Washington, D.C.: Center for Women Policy Studies, 1981), p. 4.; Ford, *supra* n. 59.

62. D. A. Ford, "Battered Wives and the 'Dropped Charge Syndrome: Why Not Prosecute?' " Paper presented at the annual meeting of the North Central Sociological Association, April 27, 1985.

63. Ford, *supra* n. 59.

64. *Supra* n. 61.

65. Field and Field, *supra* n. 59; Ford, *supra* n. 59; R. I. Parnas, "Judicial Response to Intra-family Violence," 54 *Minnesota Law Review* 585–644 (1970); J. Bannon, "Law Enforcement Problems with Intra-family Violence," Speech presented at the annual meeting of the American Bar Association, Montreal, Canada, August 12, 1975.

66. *Supra* n. 60, p. 4.

67. *Gerstein v. Pugh*, 420 U.S. 103 (1975).

68. This comes from a yet unpublished survey of statutes as of July 1985 conducted by the Criminal Justice Subcommittee of the American Bar Association, the Victims Committee of the National Association of Attorneys General, and the Office for Victims of Crime, U.S. Department of Justice.

69. "No Drop Policies Sometimes Backfire Against Victims," *Response*, The Center for Women Policy Studies, May/June 1984.

70. *Supra* n. 6, pp. 29–30.

71. *Ibid.*, p. 30.

72. "Minnesota Halts Child-Sex Investigations, Washington *Post*, February 2, 1985.

73. "A Child-Abuse Case Implodes," *Newsweek*, January 27, 1986.

74. "Child's Charges Brand Innocent Man," Washington *Post*, March 19, 1985.

75. Attorney General Hubert Humphrey III, "Report on Scott County Investigations," February 12, 1985, p. 17.

76. *Supra* n. 74.

77. Personal communication, Hank Giaretto, Founder of Parents United.

78. L. Muldoon, Ed., "Incest: Confronting the Silent Crime," A Minnesota Program for Victims of Sexual Asault, (Saint Paul, MN. 1979).

79. Roland Summitt, "No One Invented the McMartin Secret," Los Angeles *Times*, February 5, 1986.

80. Roland Summitt, "The Child Sexual Abuse Accommodation Syndrome," 7 *Child Abuse and Neglect*, 177–193 (1983).

81. Testimony of Roland Summitt before the Attorney General's Commission on Pornography, Miami, Florida, November 20, 1985, p. 9.

82. Lucy Berliner and Mary Kay Barbieri, "The Testimony of the Child Victim of Sexual Assault," 40 *Journal of Social Issues* 132 (1984).

83. Debra Whitcomb, Elizabeth R. Shapiro, and Lindsey D. Stellwagen, Esq., National Institute of Justice, *When the Victim Is A Child*, (Washington, D.C.: U.S. Department of Justice, 1985), p. 111.

84. *Ibid.*, pp. 112–115.

85. *Supra* n. 67.

86. E. Tracey, "Investigating/Interviewing Techniques for the Child Victim," New York: Workshop conducted by The Detective Bureau, New York City Police Department, October 29, 1985.

87. *Supra* n. 83, p. 105.

88. *Supra* n. 5, pp. 67–68 and 75; *supra* n. 6, pp. 31–33 and 41.

89. Soon to be published study for The National Institute of Justice, "Comparison of Sentences for Sex Offenses Against Children and Adults," by Jane R. Chapman, The American Bar Association, 1986.

90. *Supra* n. 5, p. 81.

91. *Protecting Our Children: The Fight Against Molestation* (Washington, D.C.: U.S. Department of Justice, 1985), pp. 12–23.

92. Testimony of Pat Bates and Jim DeChant, Metropolitan Organization to Counter Sexual Assault, Kansas City hearing of the Attorney General's Task Force, January 12, 1984.

93. Testimony of Dr. Henry Giaretto, founder of Parents United, Sacramento hearing of the Attorney General's Task Force, February 15, 1984.

94. *Supra* n. 6, p. 58.

95. *Supra* n. 24, p. 107.

96. *Ibid* pp. 105–106.

97. *Ibid*, p. 107.

98. *Supra* n. 6, p. 36.

99. *Supra* n. 22, p. 85.

100. *Supra* n. 6, p. 23.

101. Fifth Special Report to the U.S. Congress on Alcohol and Health, U.S. Department of Health and Human Services, Public Health Service, National Institute of Alcohol Abuse and Alcoholism.

102. Anne L. Ganley, *Court-Mandated Counseling for Men Who Batter: A Three-Day Workshop for Mental Health Professionals—Participant's Manual* (Washington, D.C.: Center for Women Policy Studies, 1981), p. 2.

103. Albert Bandura, *Aggression: A Social Learning Analysis* (Englewood Cliffs, N.J.: Prentice Hall, Inc., 1973). *See also, supra* n. 6. The statement that family violence is learned behavior was heard repeatedly by the Attorney General's Task Force.

104. *Ibid.; supra* n. 14, pp. 101–122.

8

PUBLIC BAIL–A NATIONAL DISASTER?
by Gerald P. Monks

Bail is designed to guarantee the appearance of a criminal defendant in court at a time the court directs. The bail bond is a surety bond and is not designed to cover fines, attorney fees, court costs, or other extraordinary expenses. It is designed to protect the taxpayer from loss in the event a criminal defendant does not appear in court when the court is ready to try the case. More importantly and essentially, bail is designed to guarantee a defendant will be brought back to court so the case can be tried. The criminal justice system fails if, when a case has come before the court, the prosecutor is ready to try the case, the witnesses have left their jobs in order to testify, the judge is on the bench, the jury has been seated, the prosecutor is ready to make his motions, as is the defense—and no defendant is available to be tried! When this happens—as it does too many times in our country—the real cost is borne by the victim taxpayer. The above scenario occurs most frequently when public bail is used in a jurisdiction instead of the free enterprise private bail agents.

Our forefathers formed the unique American system, among other reasons, to receive the benefits of due process and law. They designed a system which assumed accused persons are innocent until proven guilty. The system was and is designed to make sure when accused are arrested that the arrest itself is not tantamount to a guilty verdict. Lack of bail in "due process" makes arrest almost a finding of guilt. Provisions for due process and reasonable bail for each of the citizens of the United States have been guaranteed to our citizens by the Fifth and Eighth amendments.

PUBLIC BAIL EXPLAINED

In the present era, bail has developed into several different forms, but essentially bail bonds given in the United States are either public bail or private bail. Public bail, generally known as the personal recognizance (p.r.) or release on recognizance bonds, allows the judge to say to the defendant, "I know you have been charged with a crime, however, I will trust you to come back when it is necessary to go to trial, and if you do not, I expect you to pay a certain forfeiture amount, for example, $10,000.00." Pre-trial research is very limited, yet this form of public bail comprises nearly half of the people in jail today. Personal recognizance bonds in some states and areas are given by judges, sheriffs, and others who are responsible and accountable, yet in some jurisdictions those granting p.r. bonds are not at all responsible to the public. For certain offenses, personal recognizance bonds are given by bail commissioners.

A second type of public bail bond given is the limited deposit bail bond. In this case, the judge says to the defendant, "You must put up ten percent of the bond to show good faith that you will come to court. If you do come to court, you will get ninety percent back of what you put up and ten percent will be charged as a service fee." Therefore, on a $10,000 bond the criminal defendant will put up $1,000. If he comes to court on time, the case will be disposed of, and he will get back $900. If he fails to show up for court, he will lose the ten percent, and allegedly he can be sued for the other ninety percent. This type of bond can either be a judicial option or a defendant option, depending on the jurisdiction. In some states, the judges have the right to determine whether or not this type of bond will be available to the incarcerated party. In other states and jurisdictions, the defendant must *always* be offered the option of the ten percent. In "defendant option" states, the judge has really lost his ability to make bond determinations and only can set the *amount* of the bail bond.

PRIVATE BAIL EXPLAINED

Private bail bonds also follow two general models. First are bonds for which the defendant puts up cash to guarantee his appearance. When he shows up for court, the cash is returned to him. The second type of private bond is one which uses commercial bail bonds handled by commercial bail bond agents. In this instance the bail bond agents use surety companies to guarantee to the state that they will pay the bond forfeiture. Alternatively, property owned by the bail agent is pledged to guarantee the defendant will show up for court as agreed. If the defendant does not show up for court, the bail agent will go get him and bring him to court. For this service the defendant is charged a premium. In the commercial bail bond case, if a defendant fails to appear, the commercial bail agent knows he may have to pay—thus he has the incentive to go out and either rearrest, or talk the defendant back to court.

DISCUSSION OF THE COMPETING MODELS

Theoretically, the good points of a p.r. bond (also sometimes known as o.r. for "own recognizance") are that it will allow the judge to offer the indigent an opportunity to get out of jail without expense. It requires only the payment of the bond forfeiture by the indigent person if he does not show up. The payment of the forfeiture is a quixotic thought at its best. According to the American Criminal Justice Research Institute, there is no evidence that shows this bond has ever "paid off" anywhere in the United States of America. ("Paid off" is a term used for collection of bond forfeitures). This personal recognizance bond also could be used for prominent people in the community who are well known and who may have little reason to leave the community. Local elected judges, however, found that high failure to appear rates cause a great deal of criticism, particularly during election year. Therefore, some local governments developed, or worked for the development of, the pre-trial release agency's "direct release and monitor" system.

Personal recognizance bonds are designed to get the criminal defendant to take some quasi-responsibility for his failure or success. In practice, however, pre-trial release agencies in many areas, we have found, are headed by lawyers who, for all practical purposes, believe that everyone will just naturally show up for court trial. In spite of determined efforts and their attempts to sophisticate these systems, "failure to appear" rates have never dropped much below twenty percent for misdemeanor bonds and fifteen percent for felony bonds.[1] To offer an illustration of how such p.r. systems can grow, just like other government bureaucracies, the Washington D.C. pre-trial bail agency started out in 1967 with a budget of $75,000 and a staff of four. In 1981, they had a $1,100,000 budget with a staff of over sixty-one.[2] The cost for personal recognizance bonds utilizing pre-trial release agencies has been estimated at $356 per release.[3] This has produced a substantial cost to the victims, the taxpayers, and a substantial relief to criminals! In addition, the pre-trial release agencies do not address the indigency problem, nor have they ever proven that they reduce the jail population.

Some of us involved in the criminal justice system argue that pre-trial release agencies have actually become criminal welfare agencies,

141

with lots of benefits and entitlements for criminals but little benefit to taxpayers. The pre-trial personal recognizance bond provides no one to monitor or watch the criminal defendant while out on bail, and relies solely upon the overworked police forces as those who will somehow bring the defendant back to justice and incarcerate them. It is estimated that ninety percent of the people incarcerated are found guilty.[4] While only four percent of those go to long term sentencing, the rest theoretically are subject to substantial fines or probation, which reduces the cost to the victims and taxpayers.[5] The personal recognizance program, while once intended for the indigent, may actually discriminate against the indigent in many instances because of the various "point systems." These point systems may allow the wealthy criminal to qualify to get out of jail because the bureaucrat, in his desire to enhance his position through more releases, will spend more time interviewing and getting a rich man out, not taking time to determine if the indigent accused is likely to remain in the community for trial. The pre-trial release programs have been a bonanza for many criminals and criminal attorneys. As an example, in Austin, Texas, a criminal attorney can get a defendant out of jail at night by just showing his bar card and promising to bring him back the next morning for a hearing before the judge. At that time he will get a pre-trial personal recognizance bond for his client. The lawyer charges the criminal defendant for getting him out of jail just as much as it would cost to make a surety bond. Instead, he persuades the judge to give a personal recognizance bond, and *no one has any liability whatsoever on the accused*, certainly a position that any private surety would welcome for private bails! These programs have turned into little more than programs releasing rapists, murderers, robbers, drug addicts and other criminals in the world without the public's knowledge. It is not abnormal to see a judge, on the recommendation of pre-trial release agency, set a $200,000 personal recognizance bond on a defendant with a drug charge even though that defendant has only been in the community for a short period of time. Many times the release is recommended by an attorney who asks for a personal recognizance bond from the judge. Because there is no one properly to monitor the program, and everyone benefits except the victim taxpayer, who's to say anything? It is interesting to note that a convicted supreme court judge in Texas was given a personal recognizance appeal bond. He proceeded to forfeit the bond and go to Grenada, and it took several years before he was captured at the cost of nearly $1,000,000 to the taxpayers. No one has ever found out if he paid the $5,000 which he agreed to pay when he made the bond.[6]

After years of experience in this field, this writer is not aware of a single instance in which a personal recognizance bond has ever paid off. Therefore, whenever one of these bonds is recommended to the public, it is truly a fraud perpetrated on the public. The bond should be reclassified and no longer considered a bond. Forty percent of the bail made in the United States are made by public bonds. When one considers the tremendous number of personal recognizance bonds given every day in the United States, one can easily understand why taxpayers should be concerned. This is truly a hidden tax imposed on the people by the criminal justice system—some believe it may be in excess of $30 billion a year.[7]

The ten percent deposit plan, designed by a Yale Professor and passed by the United States Congress in 1966,[8] is really a personal recognizance bond in disguise. With this bond, the defendant may post only ten percent of the bond amount. If he shows up for court, he will get his money back. In the federal judiciary and in some states, it is allowed solely at the discretion of the judge. This, at least, leaves the option in the hands of the judge. In states such as Illinois and Kentucky, the judges have had even these options taken away from them. The only option the judge has now in these states is how high to set the bond. The American Bar Association believes that only the judge should have the final discretionary responsibility of the defendant's options of bail. The ten percent plan allegedly helped the indigent and encouraged him to come to court because he would get nearly all of his money back. If he did this, the money then could be used, allegedly, to pay the fine or it could be assigned to his attorney to pay attorney fees. Research in Florida, with an $80,000 governor's investigation and a $100,000 California Legislature Research program, showed that this ten percent deposit program primarily benefited criminals who could quickly pay their way out and never have to return for trial.[9]

The ten percent deposit plan was enforced in California for five years and was thrown out (effective January 1, 1986) as unworkable. The courts in some cases have not even found a way to collect the ten percent when the defendant does not show up, much less the other ninety percent that the criminal promises to pay. During the August 1984 meeting of the American Bar Association in Chicago, Illinois, personal conversations with criminal attorneys included the ten percent plan. During a seminar on how to collect money from defendants, the attorneys from the "ten percent states" scoffed at the idea that the ten percent deposit would help pay their fee, except on very large bonds. These attorneys were not hesitant to tell other attorneys from other states, "Don't expect the ten percent to help you to collect your fee."[10] If the people show up for court, in practice the cash deposit normally goes for increased fines. It does not help the indigent because the judges have raised the bond in most areas as high as ten times what they were before a ten percent deposit was put into effect. For example, the prostitution bond in California, before the ten percent plan was put in, was $500; after it was put in, it was raised to $5,000. This, in effect, meant a $500 cash bond. The same thing has occurred in DWI, shoplifting, etc. After the ten percent plan goes into effect, the bond is raised ten or fifteen times. Ironically, this has actually caused jail overcrowding because there is no alternative allowed. In states using the ten percent deposit plan, jail population crowding has been most profound.[11] The most distressing problem with the ten percent program is that it is deceptive. There has never been any evidence to show that the 90% not deposited was ever collected from the defendant by the court when the ten percent plan was used. In actuality, it is an automatic reduction of ninety percent to benefit the criminal defendant. This is very deceiving to the taxpayer and certainly circumstances have shown that it only benefits the criminal and sometimes the criminal's advocate. Peace officers everywhere, including the National Sheriff's Association,[12] oppose this type of bond in part because it is most effectively used by the very well financed criminals who want to buy their way out of the criminal justice system.

The private types of bail bonds include, first of all, the full cash bond. This is a much more honest bond than the ten percent deposit bond. It is certainly more truthful to the public. The cash bond program requires the criminal defendant to post cash to guarantee his appearance. The cash bond does an excellent job of paying off. However, its weakness is that it does not help at all in picking the criminal up or tracking him down if he should "skip" to avoid trial. Pursuit, again, is left to the overworked police officer. It is important to remember that the normal pick-up cost on a criminal is about $800 to the taxpayer.[13] This bond also does not provide for the issuance of notices to the accused when he is due in court, therefore resulting in a high bond forfeiture rate. However, if the bond is set high enough, it does pay the government for peace officer's pick-up expenses, as well as judicial expenses, district attorney expenses and witness expenses. Another weakness is that this bond can be easily forfeited. It will not pay over the stated amount, will not pick the party up, and will not pay for extra court costs. The weakness of this bond is that sometimes the judge will set the bond too low, and therefore expenses cannot be covered; or set it too high with the result that the indigent or poor person cannot get out of jail awaiting trial.

The last type of private bond is the commercial surety bond, which is marketed by the free enterprise crime control bail agent. This originally went into effect around 1907 when the Supreme Court held that such indemnity agreements were not against public policy. A bail surety bond is designed to guarantee performance. In the case of the private bail industry, it is used to guarantee that the surety or its agent will get the criminal defendant to court and to trial on time and, if not, eventually will find him so the criminal defendant can be brought to justice as soon as possible. It is similar to a performance bond. The surety bond has become even more important in the United States as the population has become more transient and people have moved from one place to another to take advantage of new jobs and new opportunities. When people move into a community and have only resided there for a short period of time, they are considered "transient" people. Communities need a guarantee that those transient people who become criminal defendants will not overload the jails in their area. Along with this guarantee, the communities need to be assured that once a criminal defendant is released, he will show up for court.

The commercial bail agent can provide these guarantees by securing the involvement of the defendant's family, if possible, wherever the family is located. In most cases, the family's involvement is an excellent guarantee for the defendant's appearance at trial. The bail agent issues an indemnity agreement and secures collateral from the family. An example would be the following scenario: A $10,000 bond is set by a judge. To secure this bail, the defendant's mother, father, brother, sister, cousin or other friend/relative contacts a commercial surety bail agent. The bail agent would secure proper collateral or indemnity agreements from these parties to guarantee that if the criminal defendant does not go to court he will have these people available to assist in finding him. If the criminal defendant does not go to court, these relatives will pay the surety back for the loss suffered. The surety normally charges ten percent of the value of the bond. Of *that* ten percent, ten percent of the bond goes to losses, and ninety percent goes to the expenses of tieing up the collateral, going out and recovering the criminal defendant and, hopefully, making a profit.

Sometimes sureties, in order to help unload jails, will secure or "make" certain risky bonds and will take property of any kind as collateral. The property is returned to the defendant or indemnitors when the criminal defendant goes to court and the case is disposed of.

ADVANTAGES OF THE FREE ENTERPRISE BAIL AGENT

The commercial free enterprise bail agent has a tremendous advantage over any other type of bail bond because the free enterprise bail agent can go across state lines to secure or arrest defendants who have escaped, saving the counties and states a great deal of money on extradition. In addition, with the free enterprise incentive program, the surety *only* profits if the defendant goes to court. If the defendant fails to show up for trial, the surety is penalized in one manner or another, either by the court costs or by additional cost to pick the defendant up—or in full payment of a judgment. In theory, the surety should be able to recover from the co-signer, however, in practice the bail agent requires extensive periods of time to recover the liquidation of collateral. Liquidation of collateral is not easy and sometimes the collateral will even evaporate. The reality is that the surety must monitor the person on a weekly basis to make sure he is at the same address he gave. The bail agent must send the criminal defendant his court date, and send the defendant's criminal attorney the court date. The surety must work very closely with other members of the criminal justice system to guarantee the defendant's appearance. In short, the bail agent's position in the criminal justice system is much like that of the offensive lineman on a football team: He does the job, but gets very little acclaim.

The commercial free enterprise bail agent today is normally licensed by state laws. Bail agents have to take license examinations, in some cases go to school, and are very carefully regulated by bail bond boards. A commercial bail agent cannot have a felony against him or a misdemeanor involving moral turpitude.

The free enterprise bail agent has another advantage which benefits taxpayers. He got the defendant out of jail; consequently, he is in a much more objective trust position with the criminal defendant than anyone else in the criminal justice system. Therefore, he can many times "arrest" a man without a problem due to the fact that the criminal defendant may have to use the bail agent again, as long as the criminal defendant is cooperative and can pay the fee that is required. Free enterprise bail agents all have in their agreements items stating that in the event an accused is arrested for any other type of crime other than traffic violations, he can be surrendered to the courts and lose the premium he paid. This means that the criminal defendant, while on bail under the scrutiny of the free enterprise bail agent, does not want to commit any additional crime because he knows he can be turned in and lose the premium he has put up to the surety.

The trend of recent years throughout the United States has been carefully to select free enterprise bail agents to serve the criminal justice system and to reduce or eliminate the ten percent deposit plan. The ten percent deposit plan has been thrown out of California after five years of use as a drain on the taxpayer which was not getting accused persons to show up for court. The two states relying totally on public bail face substantial problems in effective law enforcement. In Illinois, we hear continual complaints from police officers, sheriffs, and all parties involved saying that the ten percent plan is not working. In Kentucky, the jails are completely overloaded and the direct cost to the taxpayer for their system is as high as $3,400,000.[14]

The commercial surety or the commercial free enterprise bail agent puts the burden strictly on himself as well as the defendant's family and friends to guarantee that he will go to court. Membership requirements for the Professional Bail Agents of the U.S. include a pledge they will *never* give up a chase and will make sure the fugitive is returned to the community.[15] In the Alexander Grant study, commercial bail agents were shown to have a .7% fugitive rate as opposed to a 7.0% fugitive rate for public bail.[16] This means that when a person did jump bond, and truly meant to jump bond, the commercial free enterprise bail agents normally got the jumper back within a period of two or three years, while the personal recognizance bond only got him back eight percent of the time. Many personal recognizance and ten percent research projects show a forfeiture rate as high as sixty-six percent with no one paying off.[17] Figures from surety companies in their profit/loss statements indicate that no more than a two percent failure to appear rate can be allowed or they will go broke.[18] Consequently, the eight percent rate by the public bonds would indicate that certainty of punishment is not in effect whenever these type of bonds exist. A free enterprise bail company could never exist under these circumstances. Victims are entitled to know where the criminal defendant is at all times, to be protected from the criminal defendant, and to be guaranteed the criminal defendant will go to court. The best method devised so far to guarantee this, and other aspects of equity in the pre-trial criminal justice system, is the free enterprise crime control bail agent.

Commercial free enterprise bail agents have proposed a guaranteed misdemeanor jail reduction program and a felony *pro bono* program to help indigents, similar to the assigned risk plan used by automobile insurance companies in the United States today. The problems of fighting crime in America and still protecting our freedoms are difficult to balance, but the pre-trial burden must be shouldered by the criminal, his friends and his family. The greatest danger to the free enterprise crime control bail agents and to the victim taxpayers is public bail (exemplified by personal recognizance bonds and the ten percent deposit bonds) which promotes favoritism and cronyism in the criminal justice system and has foisted a fraud on the public with hidden cost to taxpayers. As previously stated in this work, the cost of each public bail bond has been calculated at $356 per defendant, a cost which is borne by the non-criminal taxpayer/victim.[19] In contrast, the cost of private bail is paid by the accused.

PROBLEMS IN THE FEDERAL SYSTEM: ONE EXTREME OR THE OTHER

The public bail is just another federal CETA type program that has not worked out. The federal system has completely gotten out of control in the area of pre-trial detention. Bail agents supported the 1984 federal crime bill which allows a federal judge to hold a defendant who is dangerous to the community without bond. Under the old federal bail laws, there was no basis for denying bail. The bonds were set by the judges to reflect what the judge felt was necessary to cause the defendant to appear in court. This amount also showed inherent consideration for the defendant's dangerousness to the community. This system did, at least, always allow the defendant a bail bond amount. In several drug cases, unfortunately it allowed dangerous criminal types the right to escape the community's judgment by paying the high bail amount. With the support of professional bail agents around the country, the 1984 legislation revised the old bail standards to include likely dangerousness to the community as a basis for *denying* bail. The congressional hearings on the legislation, many of which were attended by this writer, made it very clear that Congress intended bail would be denied in those cases where a released defendant, in a judge's reasonable opinion, would pose actual physical danger to victims, witnesses or other citizens. However, judges and federal magistrates are, to put it mildly, interpreting these provisions in a frightening and inconsistent way. Today, many are concerned that a majority of the people arrested by the federal government are being held without bond. This absolutely violates the Fifth and Eighth Amendments.

In Kansas City, a federal magistrate held a person without bond due to a credit card violation scheme. The pre-trial officer said that the fellow *might* flee which *might* cause him to be some sort of economic danger to the community. There is not one bail bond made where a person *might* not flee. To contend that this economic crime is "dangerous" to the community promotes dictatorship by disallowing the right to reasonable bail.

At totally the other extreme, a magistrate in Houston, Texas, let several suspected drug peddlers out on public bail with *no* guarantees to the public. This was one of the largest drug busts ever made in Harris County.[20] Another federal magistrate allowed an ex-convict out on public bail even though the man's wife pleaded with the magistrate not to let him out as he would kill her. The magistrate still let him out on public bail. The wife was found two days later, dead, in the trunk of a car.[21]

The federal bail system now seems to sanction either one of the two extremes: public bail at great cost to the taxpayer and the victim, or keep the criminal defendant in jail without bail. Federal magistrates would be wise and the country well served if the federal courts would allow no more than four percent of the people arrested detained pre-trial, and let the rest out on private bail based on the amount needed to get the defendant to court, with the *defendant* paying the expense. Under *Blunt v. United States*,[22] a man is entitled to due process of law, but the presumption of innocence starts when the trial begins, and not before.

CONCLUSION

Public bail does not reduce jail population.[23]
Public bail does not reduce public attorney costs.

Public bail does not address indigency.

Public bail does not increase fines.

Public bail may impede the early release of prisoners.

Public bail may reduce the use of private attorneys.[24]

In addition, twice as many crimes may be committed by those criminal defendants out on public bail than those out on private bail.[25]

The bottom line on the effective difference between public bail and private bail can best be explained in the following vignette: In October of 1985, John Burns, President of the Professional Bondsmen of Texas, spoke before a public bail audience, the National Association of Pre-trial Services Agencies in Lexington, Kentucky, and said: "Really, there are very few differences between public bail and private bail. In spite of the fact that I am the only free enterprise bail agent in this room. Let me give you an example. Would all of you please hold up your hand when you agree that you do similar things that I do? How many here interview and get people out of jail? Please hold up your hand." Everyone in the room, including John, raised up their hand. Next question, he asked, "How many here pay for their house notes, their groceries, etc., because of the work that we do?" Everyone in the room held up their hand, including John. He continued, "How many of you go out if the man does not show up for court, find the man, and bring him to court or are personally responsible to pay the bond if it forfeits?" Lo and behold, John was the only one in the room who held up his hand. He looked at the crowd and said, "You see, the only difference is that we are responsible." Then he sat down.

REFERENCES

Public Bail – A National Disaster? by Gerald P. Monks

1. J. Michael Monks, *St. Louis Bail Research Project*, American Criminal Justice Research Institute, October 22, 1982, p. 6. *See also*, J. Michael Monks, *A Study of Bexar County Personal Recognizance (PR) Bonds in 1981: System Abuses and Forfeiture Rate*, American Bail Research Institute, 1981.

2. *Bail, You Be the Judge*, Accredited Surety & Casualty Co., Inc., January 3, 1981, p. 14.

3. J. Michael Monks, *Harris County Pre-trial Services Agency Research Project*, American Bail Research Institute, February 1983, p. 13.

4. Independent Bail Agent's Association of California, *The Bailetter*, December 1985–January 1986, p. 14.

5. Carol B. Kalish, ed., *Bureau of Justice Statistics Bulletin*, U.S. Department of Justice, Bureau of Justice Statistics, May 1981.

6. Glenn Smith, "Marshals Nab Don Yarbrough," Houston *Chronicle*, March 17, 1983.

7. J. M. Monks, *Harris County Pre-trial Services Agency Research Project*, American Bail Research Institute, February 1983, p. 13. Figure of $356 per bond multiplied by an estimated three million bonds made per year plus estimated cost of crime. *See also: Report to the Nation on Crime and Justice*, Bureau of Justice Statistics, October 1983, (Washington, D.C.: U.S. Department of Justice), p. 99.

8. The 1966 Bail Reform Act, 18 U.S.C. 3146 *et seq.*

9. James Austin and Barry Krisberg, dirs., *Bail Reform Act of 1979 (AB2): An Evaluation Report to the California Legislature*, Office of Criminal Justice Planning, September 1983. *See also*, Phil Bronstein, "Bail Jumpers: New State Law Lets Them Make Low-cost Escape," San Francisco *Examiner*, January 30, 1983.

10. *Criminal Lawyer Seminar*, American Bar Association Convention, August 1984, Chicago, Illinois, Hyatt Regency Hotel.

11. Paul E. Dow, "Bail Bonding Reform in Kentucky—Folklore For the Indigent Defendant," *Kentucky Bar Association Journal*, October 1976.

12. *Resolution*, National Sheriff's Association, June 20, 1979, Rochester, Minnesota, Mayo Civic Auditorium.

13. Aric Press, Janet Huck and Elaine Shannon, "The Long FIST of the Law," *Newsweek*, March 26, 1984, p. 58.

14. Mr. Hicks, Treasurer of Kentucky Pre-trial Release Division, Personal Telephone Interview. April 15, 1986. Figure from 1986 budget for Kentucky Pre-trial Release Division.

15. Professional Bail Agents of the United States, Membership Application, National Association office, Houston, Texas.

16. Alexander Grant & Company, *A Report on the Dallas County Pre-trial Release Program*, Professional Bail Agents of the United States, Jail Reduction Committee, October 21, 1983, pp. G-19, G-20.

17. Celes King III and Marvin Byron, *An Analysis of the Impact of AB2 (Berman Bail Reform) Effective January 1, 1981*, July 1982 Los Angeles County.

18. *Best's Key Rating Guide*, A.M. Best Company, Inc., 1985, p. 3.

19. J. Michael Monks, *Harris County Pre-trial Services Agency Research Project*, American Bail Research Institute, February 1983, p. 13.

20. Tom Moran, "Harris County's Largest Drug Bust," Houston *Chronicle*, December 12, 1985.

21. Tom Moran, "Judges Criticized By Missing Mom's Father," Houston *Chronicle*, January 1986.

22. *Blunt v. United States*, 322 A. 2d (1974).

23. "Jail Does Not Have to Reduce Inmate Population, Judge Rules," St. Petersburg *Times*, April 1, 1986.

24. J. M. Monks, *Definitive and Comparative Analysis of the Effects of Public Bail on Jail Reduction, Fines, Public Attorney Costs and Indigents in Harris County, Texas*, Houston, Texas, (American Criminal Justice Research Institute), March 4, 1986.

25. Martin D. Sorin, *Out on Bail*, National Institute of Justice, January 1986, (Washington, D.C.: U.S. Department of Justice).

9

FORFEITURE OF ATTORNEYS FEES:
Caveat Juris Doctor
by Patrick B. McGuigan

One of the major accomplishments of the Reagan Justice Department is the rediscovery and implementation of the ancient legal practice of forfeiture. The term "forfeiture" is best defined as the divestiture without compensation of property used or acquired in a manner contrary to the laws of the sovereign. It is a particularly useful weapon against economically motivated crime such as narcotics trafficking. Effective assets forfeiture provisions, like most other tough on crime legislation, are consistent with American traditions of compassionate, limited but effective government.

Nevertheless, of late, there have been attempts to thwart the effectiveness of this vital crime fighting tool. These attempts have come from those who, second only to the criminals themselves, stand to gain the most from a weakened forfeiture policy—the criminal defense bar.

Before plunging directly into this controversy, it would be useful to set forth the types and functions of federal law in this area.

Under the laws of the United States, there are two types of forfeiture statutes: criminal and civil. Although the purpose of both types of forfeiture is to deprive criminals of the profits and tools of their trade, the two approaches attack the problem from different perspectives.

Criminal forfeitures, like traditional criminal prosecutions, are actions against individual defendants *in personam*. The criminal forfeiture of property is imposed against the person as a penalty for the crime committed by that person. Therefore criminal forfeitures, under the two United States statutes that provide for it,[1] require indictment of a person and a listing in the indictment of the property interests to be forfeited, as well as proof of the crime beyond a reasonable doubt and a special jury verdict forfeiting a defendant's interest in that property. This is the type of forfeiture today most often challenged for its impact on the ability of attorneys to be paid from the proceeds of crime.

Civil forfeitures, on the other hand, are actions against property, not people, *i.e.* they are *in rem*. The theory of prosecution under the many civil forfeiture statutes in the United States law[2] is that the property has violated the statute. Consequently, the civil forfeiture proceeding is not dependent upon the success or failure of any criminal prosecution. Civil forfeiture may proceed in cases where the violator is a fugitive or is otherwise unavailable for criminal prosecution. Additionally, there is an easier burden of proof. The United States need only demonstrate probable cause of the property's statutory violation, not proof beyond reasonable doubt. The claimant to the property then has the burden to show by a preponderance of the evidence that the property in question should not be forfeited. In some cases, the United States may even accomplish civil forfeiture of the property administratively without having to pursue the matter in court.

Another concept vitally important to both the operation and understanding of federal forfeiture law is the "relation back" doctrine, which holds that forfeitable assets become the property of the United States at the time of the illegal activity that makes them subject to forfeiture. Simply put, the government's ownership of illegal proceeds (such as those exchanged for illegal drugs) "relates back" to the moment the crime is committed. Thus, after property is used or obtained in certain illegal ways, it no longer belongs to the violator. Just as you do not have a right to sell or give away the property of your next door neighbor without his permission, those who run afoul of the forfeiture laws can no longer deal with such property as they see fit.

DISCUSSION OF THE FORFEITURE CONCEPT AS APPLIED TO ATTORNEYS FEES

Consider this scenario: a criminal steals your car. He has no other assets except your car. Should a special exception be allowed to let him pay his lawyer with your car or with the proceeds from the sale of your car? Of course not. Illegal drug profits are no different than the car used in this scenario. Under the crime fighting legislation discussed at length below, illegal drug profits become the property of the U.S. government (read that: you, the taxpayer) at the moment of the crime. In sum, drug profits are blood money and not the property of the drug dealer.

Forfeiture provisions disallow criminals from enjoying the fruits of their illegal activities. Applying to this issue some straight-forward economic analysis, it is surely true that every society has as constituents individuals for whom moral questions come down to a matter of dollars and cents.

If the financial rewards of crime are great, these individuals feel that risks of imprisonment are worth taking. Conversely, if such persons risk not only prison but also the possibility that their ill-gotten gains (and even legitimately acquired assets used illegally) will belong to Uncle Sam, the incentives are greatly diminished.

As long as due process guarantees remain in place, forfeiture of assets for criminal activity can be consistent with personal freedom, economic liberty, and our traditions—and can do much to reduce organized crime for profit. On the other hand, if cracks begin to appear, if loopholes open, then the nation risks the loss of whatever gains in crime prevention and punishment have been made since the landmark crime bill of 1984 was enacted.

Such a loophole has indeed appeared in the handful of federal court decisions discussed at length in this essay. This potential loophole involves the forfeiture of assets earmarked to be paid to criminal defense attorneys. Economic and historic analysis can reveal the danger of a possible misapplication of the Sixth Amendment's right to counsel.

Consider another scenario: You are an indicted drug dealer. You have, in fact, done nothing but peddle drugs for many years, and have amassed staggering wealth from the trade. Your expensive lawyer tells you that, indeed, everything you earned in recent years (because it is all derived from drug trafficking) is forfeitable to the government. You look at your lawyer and say to yourself, "I'd rather give even a substantial portion of my wealth to my attorney than give it all to Uncle Sam." If you can do this, you know your $250-an-hour lawyer will work tirelessly, take numerous appeals, use every trick in the book to see that you keep at least some portion of your drug proceeds.

In the big picture, the end result of this scenario is obvious. Many defense lawyers will get very rich—and some drug dealers will get off. Why? Not necessarily because justice dictates it, but because against the limited resources and manpower of prosecutors, the seemingly limitless wealth of the drug lords will surely overwhelm even the most earnest prosecutorial efforts.

Some will say, "What's wrong with that?" Even the venerable William F. Buckley, Jr. seems to have given up on the drug war.

Others will say, "If you want to pay your attorney with your money, that's your business." But this is precisely the point. *If you are a drug dealer, the money you "earned" is not yours to keep.* As explained above, the law allows the government's ownership to "relate back" to the time you obtained the money from an illegal activity. You are no more entitled to pay a lawyer out of forfeitable drug proceeds than you would be out of stolen money or out of kidnapping ransom.

The whole "attorneys fees" issue in assets forfeiture (the focus of this essay) is a red herring designed, by invoking the Constitution, to cow into submission those who intend seriously to attack organized crime for profit, particularly in the area of narcotics.

No one is contending that drug dealers, or anyone else, should be deprived of the right to counsel. What *must* be stopped, however, is the sieve-like exception advocated by some criminal defense lawyers—and upheld so far in five federal court decisions—that would be created by allowing forfeitable assets to be exchanged for anything, including the services of top-flight defense attorneys.

In the words of one federal district judge hard-nosed enough to disallow such an exception, "In the same manner that a defendant cannot obtain a Rolls Royce with the fruits of a crime, he cannot be permitted to obtain the services of the Rolls Royce of attorneys from these same tainted funds."[3]

U.S. law has always recognized the vital "relation back" doctrine in the civil forfeiture context.[4] Not until the passage of the landmark Comprehensive Crime Contol Act of 1984—perhaps the least heralded major accomplishment of the Reagan Administration—did this principle have explicit application to federal criminal forfeitures. On October 12, 1984 it became codified in both the "RICO"[5] and "CCE"[6] statutes that the interest of the United States in criminally obtained property vests at the time of the illegality and is not extinguished simply because the defendant subsequently transferred the property to another person.

Despite this clear message from Congress, the criminal defense bar has led a great hue and cry to carve out an exception for fees paid to attorneys from illegal proceeds, regardless of whether the counsel knows of the source of the funds. Presently, both criminal and civil forfeiture laws allow people who deal with criminals (including third parties such as bail agents) to have their interest in forfeitable property protected. As long as the third party can show that he has obtained an interest in the forfeitable property through an "arms length" transaction (engaged in a commercially reasonable bargain) *and* that he was reasonably without cause to believe that the property was subject to forfeiture, the third party will receive or be allowed to keep the benefit of his bargain. Those who urge that an exception be made for attorneys would remove burdens shared by every other provider of good and services.[7]

SOME CASES EXEMPTING ATTORNEYS FEES

Because the reasons put forward for creating an exception to the principle that only innocent parties (in the sense noted above of not knowing about the illegal source of the funds) should receive the benefit of the bargain are highly technical in nature, it is imperative that the handful of cases that dealt with the matter be examined. As of May 1, 1986, a few courts had dealt with the forfeiture of assets which have been transferred to attorneys as fees for services.[8] There has been a split in these authorities on whether such forfeitures are permissable, with most of the courts ruling they are impermissable.

The first court to rule on the new forfeiture provisions was the U.S. District Court for Colorado. The case, *U.S. v. Rogers*,[9] was decided on February 22, 1985. District Judge John Kane first found that the new federal RICO forfeiture laws were not unconstitutional in the face of *ex post facto* and vagueness attacks. However, he went on, through a rather tortured reading of the section dealing with third party transfers, to hold that section 1963 (c) of the law was meant only to avoid fraudulent or "sham" transactions. Section (c) reads as follows:

> All right, title, and interest in property described in subsection (a) vests in the United States upon the commission of the act giving rise to forfeiture under this section [this is the "relation back" doctrine spoken of above]. Any such property that is subsequently transferred to a person other than the defendant may be the subject of a special verdict of forfeiture and thereafter shall be ordered forfeited to the United States, *unless the transferee establishes . . . that he is a bonafide purchaser for value of such property who at the time of purchase was reasonably without cause to believe that the property was subject to forfeiture under this section.*[10]

A careful reading of the above language would lead one to believe that there are two criteria to be met if property transferred to any third party is not to be forfeitable. First, for a purchaser to be "bona fide" the transaction must be a real one (*i.e.* reasonable value must be given in an arm's length business arrangement). Second, and just

157

as important, the transferee must not have knowledge or even reason to know the tainted sources of funds. Thus, even if the transaction is not a sham, the transfer of property to a third party will be forfeitable if the transferee knows of the illegality that produced the property.

The reason for this two-fold criteria is easy to understand: Congress did not want to allow lawbreakers to remove property from the reach of forfeiture, and it wanted to discourage persons from knowingly dealing with and profitting from criminals. This is analogous to the situation in which a kidnapper attempts to purchase a car with ransom proceeds. No one would contend that if the car dealer knows that the purchase price was paid with ransom money he should be allowed to keep the money simply because the transaction was "arms length" and not a sham. Nevertheless, Judge Kane chose to ignore the statute's plain language (and even common sense) in arriving at his decision.

After dispensing with the statutory language, Judge Kane examined the legislative history of the Crime Control Act. Students of the law know the legislative history is what the framers, through reports or comments in the record, said about the law they were attempting to pass (or in some cases had already passed). Suffice it to say that Judge Kane's interpretation of the legislative history was equally as unpersuasive as his reading out of the statute the requirement that third parties who claim an exemption from forfeiture be without knowledge of the source of the funds.

Perhaps cognizant of the weakness of his statutory analysis, Judge Kane proceeded to search for any constitutional infirmities lurking in the forfeiture provisions. The court found that *if* Congress intended to forfeit property transferred to an attorney as a fee for actual legal services rendered, then the forfeiture provision would be unconstitutional. To Judge Kane's thinking such a policy would so disrupt the "attorney-client privilege" as to deprive a defendant of complete representation by counsel of his or her choice—because the government could pry into the matters "essential" to preparation of a defense. Furthermore, because a fee is not assured, Judge Kane argued that not many members of the criminal defense bar, except already overworked "public defenders," would take a case under such circumstances.

The short answer to these constitutional concerns is, "If the money is not the defendant's in the first place, it is unfortunate (for the defendant as well as his well-heeled attorney) that it interferes with the selection of counsel—unfortunate, but certainly neither unjust *nor* unconstitutional." Because the constitutional challenges to the new forfeiture provisions are the ones most frequently aired in the media, perhaps the Sixth Amendment analysis of the issue deserves a bit more exposition through later case law.

United States v. Badalamenti[11] was the next reported case dealing with and rejecting the attempt to forfeit funds transferred by a defendant to his attorney. In *Badalamenti*, Judge Pierre Leval of the federal court for the Southern District of New York also addressed constitutional questions, but did so only in *dicta.*[12] After adopting the *Rogers* analysis of legislative intent on the forfeitability of assets transferred to an attorney as fees,[13] Judge Leval opined that *if* Congress intended the scope of forfeiture laws to encompass a defendant's transfer of illegal funds to his attorney, it would be nearly impossible to get *any* representation for that defendant. This is a serious charge which, if true, would be fatal to attempts to forfeit ill-gotten gains transferred to attorneys as fees. Thus, Judge Leval's assertion deserves closer examination.

The Sixth Amendment to the Constitution reads, in pertinent part:

> In all criminal prosecutions, the accused shall enjoy the right . . . to have the assistance of counsel for his defense.

The Supreme Court has long held that an individual has an absolute right to counsel.[14] It is also the operative law of the land that the Sixth Amendment protects the right to obtain counsel of the defendant's choice. However, that right is a qualified one; as explained by a federal circuit court:

> While it is clear that an accused who is *financially able* to retain counsel of his choosing must not be deprived of a reasonable opportunity to do so, it is also clear that the right to retain counsel of one's choice *is not absolute.*[15]

Because the right to counsel of choice is a qualified one (dependent upon the ability and willingness of the accused to pay), does the threat of attorneys fee forfeiture make it impossible to obtain *any* counsel, as Judge Leval charges? Of course not, no more than does indigency spark such a result.

The Criminal Justice Act (CJA)[16] provides that for those who are financially unable to mount their own defense, adequate representation of defendants via representative "plans" will be assured at the public expense. Defendants covered under this law are those, among others

for whom the Sixth Amendment to the Constitution requires the appointment of counsel or for whom, in a case in which he faces loss of liberty, any Federal law requires the appointment of counsel.

The sorts of crime for which forfeiture is a penalty invoke this law. No defendant, even if all of his assets are under indictment for forfeiture, will be deprived of counsel. Furthermore, the law mandates:

Representation under each plan shall include counsel and investigative expert, and other services necessary for an adequate defense. Each plan shall include a provision for private attorneys.

Recognizing that such representation plans are financed through the general Treasury, several prosecuting attorneys have acceeded to motions to have reasonable attorney fees exempted from forfeiture. But comprehensive exemption of sky's-the-limit fees has never been, nor should it ever be, the policy of federal law enforcement. Judge Leval's musing that federal forfeiture law will render the accused defenseless, therefore, has validity *only* if $250+ an hour attorneys are the sole counsellors considered competent to raise a viable defense.

The next case after *Rogers* dealing directly with the forfeitability of property transferred to an attorney as fees was *U.S. v. Matthew Ianiello, a/k/a "Matty the Horse", et al.*[17] Judge Constance Baker Motley of the U.S. District Court for the Southern District of New York rendered the *Ianiello* decision in this case on September 3, 1985. Judge Motley took much the same approach as the *Rogers* court. Here (almost incredibly in the face of the plain language of the statute and legislative history) Judge Motley found a congressional exemption from forfeiture of illegally acquired or used assets which, it just so happens, are paid to an attorney. Perhaps realizing that her statutory interpretation would not pass the "straight face" test, Judge Motley proceeded, in the spirit of Judge Kane, to a discussion of Sixth Amendment considerations.

Judge Motley used an ingenious variation of Judge Leval's "forfeiture will deprive defendants of any counsel" argument. Employing 18 U.S.C. § 3006 A—the very statute guaranteeing an accused effective representation—Judge Motley held that if forfeiture of attorneys fees is permitted (except in the course of sham transactions where, according to Motley, apparently representation by counsel is not an issue), the defendant will have neither counsel of choice nor court-appointed counsel available. The reasoning runs thus: "Because a defendant who has money, albeit subject to forfeiture, cannot lawfully swear under oath that he is indigent, the Criminal Justice Act representation would not be available. And because we already know that no private attorney will take the case unless he can be handsomely paid, the defendant is defenseless."

This is an ingenious argument, somewhat contradicted in her next move—to release from restraint those proceeds the grand jury indicted as forfeitable. Her rationale for this action was that proceeds to pay high-priced, high profile attorneys are a "necessity of life" akin to food and medicine. (Such a finding shows with astonishing clarity the lengths to which some judicial minds must go to do away with legislation they would not have enacted themselves. It also shows that Judge Motley cannot be serious about fearing that the defendant before her would possibly be without representation.)

Any judicial body in America would approve the appointment of CJA counsel to a defendant whose entire assets were under indictment for forfeiture. This is all the more true if the assets were subject to restraining order—as they were in this case before Judge Motley dissolved it. The argument that forfeiture can be used both as "a sword and a shield" by the government is thus without merit.

Two cases arose in the spring of 1986 which had the practical effect of assuring that high powered defense lawyers will continue to be well compensated at the expense of the law abiding public. These cases embody much of the interpretive nonsense of the preceding case law; nevertheless, they also contain fresh "insights" that merit a closer look.

Judge James C. Cacheris, in the case of *U.S. v. Christopher F. Reckmeyer, III*,[18] followed the legislative and constitutional reasoning of *Rogers*, *Badalamenti* and *Ianiello*, but took one giant step beyond. In the previous cases, none of the assets in which both the government and defense attorneys claimed an interest were yet forfeited. Some judges expressed that this "presumption of innocence" was a factor persuading them that, despite the clear intention of Congress, the government should not tamper with a defendant's assets prior to conviction,[19] and that, therefore, those same assets should be available for payment to a defense attorney. In *Reckmeyer,* Judge Cacheris actually ordered that out of assets *already forfeited* the government must pay some $170,000 to the defendant's attorneys. Certainly, Reckmeyer's lawyers doubtless did a fine job defending him—but that is small consolation when one considers that they were paid out of assets which the government proved, beyond a reasonable doubt, belonged to the people of the United States.

It is hard to single out for blame Judge Cacheris. His expansive reading of the law is really the logical conclusion of the reasoning in *Rogers* and its progeny. In fact, the court's view on attorneys fees actually complements an earlier decision in the Reckmeyer matter, in which Judge Cacheris ruled that *all* general creditor third parties were entitled to have their claims litigated to determine whether they deserved a share in forfeitable and already forfeited assets.[20] Such a holding obviously provides no disincentives for either criminals or those who deal with them freely to trade in assets in which the government has a superior interest. This renders the government little more than a collection agency for the creditors of *convicted* criminals.

U.S. v. Bassett[21] is the one other case, through May 1, 1986, which exempted from forfeiture assets transferred to an attorney as fees. Judge James Rogers Miller Jr. of the U.S. District Court for Maryland did not have the benefit of Judge Cacheris' decision in *Reckmeyer,* that decision having been rendered only two weeks earlier. Nevertheless, there was by this point a groundswell of case law with which creative judges might work. Unhappily, the district court of Maryland was up to the task of emasculating the criminal forfeiture laws via the increasingly familiar analytical gambit: You see, Congress intended to exempt attorneys fees from forfeiture (despite the fact that a common sense reading of the statute dictates otherwise) but even if Congress did not, then by golly, the *Constitution* will not stand for it (despite the fact that the only demonstrable harm is to the defense attorney's wallet). Without re-echoing the errors of the cases discussed above, analysts might note here that it was not sufficient merely to jump on the bandwagon—a judge interested in stretching the Constitution as thin as has been accomplished here must add his own embellishments. After all, this is judge-made law, the creation of precedent. Each milestone must have its own distinctive signature.

Judge Miller's distinction was not only that he absolved the defendant from any responsibility to pay his attorney out of legitimate assets (which arguably at least one of the defendants, Bassett, had)—but also that he enjoined the government from seeking *civil* forfeiture of the tainted assets. (As noted in the earlier discussion, this is often the only recourse left to prosecutors and is a legally viable, albeit more lengthy, alternative to criminal forfeiture.)

Judge Miller did not even bother to discuss the differing burdens of proof and such other considerations as the inapplicability of the Sixth Amendment right to counsel in a civil setting and the fact that the legislative history and case law surrounding the appropriate sections of the criminal code[23] do not intertwine. He simply enjoined the government from pursuing *any* forfeiture remedy against assets which the defendants' attorneys claim as their fees. This is merely the consequence of a bench bending (to the breaking point) well-established forfeiture law, in order to adjust the law to fit the judge's personal predilections.

One is tempted to say that if this remains the "state of the art" in judge-made forfeiture law, prosecutors will be well-advised to seek some other remedy, such as the hefty fines levied by the RICO and CCE statutes. But repetition of an error only serves to make it more diffuse, not any less false. In late spring 1986, appeals of some of these decisions were under consideration in the Department of Justice. Perhaps scrutiny at the more lofty heights of the Circuit Court of Appeals, far removed from the hurly-burly of trial, will produce saner results.[24]

In fact, as case law builds and more and more judicial embellishments—along with their logical consequences—come to light, the skaky underpinnings of these pro-defense bar (in intention)/pro-criminal (in result) cases will become all the more evident.

ASSET FORFEITURE: LAWYER BASHING OR COMMON SENSE?

Granted that there are no statutory or constitutional reasons to exempt attorneys fees from forfeiture, there does remain the question of whether such a procedure is desirable. In other words, it is reasonable to ask if the policy to seek forfeitable assets in the hands of defense counsel is good public policy—and whether it is nothing more than a thinly veiled "attorney bashing."

The fact is, advocates of a strong yet just forfeiture policy, such as this writer, want only *that attorneys be accorded the same responsibilities as all other providers of goods and services.* Attorneys should not be

163

permitted to "launder" dirty money simply because they worked for it—any more than a carpenter or grocer who knowingly takes forfeitable proceeds should be able to keep them simply because they were earned.

There are compelling reasons why forfeitable proceeds should not be permitted to slip away, *particularly* to certain attorneys who engage in lucrative criminal defense work stemming from the drug trade and other forms of racketeering. A case which addressed the attorney's fees issue in the wake of *Rogers*, and the only federal case through publication of this book to approve the forfeiture of such fees in a criminal context, is *United States v. Payden*.[25] The deciding Judge David Edelstein addressed the challenges and issues raised in *Rogers*, particularly with regard to attorney-client privilege, saying:

> In the context of addressing the scope of the attorney-client privilege, the Second Circuit voiced its concern over the possible use of attorneys to launder money. In *Shargel* the court stated:
>
>> It seems evident to us that a broad privilege against the disclosure of the identity of clients and of fee information might easily become an immunity for corrupt or criminal acts. . . . Such a shield would create unnecessary but considerable temptations to use lawyers as conduits of information or of commodities necessary to criminal schemes or as launderers of money. The bar and the system of justice will suffer little if all involved are aware that assured safety from disclosure does not exist.
>
> The court cannot stand by and open the door to such abuse. In this light and after a review of the opinion, *Rogers* cannot be accepted as the law in this district.[26]

Nor did the court make such statements in the abstract. Judge Edelstein realized full well the implications of his opinion when he wrote:

> One who receives funds with the knowledge that the funds are subject to forfeiture cannot be said to have entered into an arms length transaction regardless of the price paid for the good or service. The court has little sympathy for transferees in this group even though the results of forfeiture may be harsh. . .Third parties who obtain tainted assets with knowledge of the forfeiture proceedings assume the risk that the government may obtain superior title and reclaim those assets.[27]

Was this judge engaging in attorney bashing? No—statements such as the above have general applicability outside of the attorney fee context. Nevertheless, rather than bending over backwards, as did other courts, to find a constitutional violation where none existed, Judge Edelstein in *Payden* used common sense to observe that any abuses will be on the part of criminals. In the most publicized statement of this, Judge Edelstein concluded:

> Fees paid to attorneys cannot become a safe harbor from forfeiture of the profits of illegal enterprises. In the same manner that a defendant cannot obtain a Rolls-Royce with the fruits of a crime, he cannot be permitted to obtain the services of the Rolls-Royce of attorneys from these same tainted funds...To permit this would undermine the purpose of the forfeiture statutes, which is to strip offenders and organizations of their economic power.[28]

Therefore, it is most certainly an open question as to whether assets transferred to an attorney by a criminal defendant as fees for legal services are beyond the reach of forfeiture statutes. Judge Edelstein's decision took into account the legitimate needs of defendants as well as the compelling needs of society. Through a careful and common sense legal analysis, such as the above, the needs of both can be satisfied to the true detriment of neither.

Even if the prosecutor is not fortunate enough to encounter an enlightened judiciary in a criminal case, there is another weapon in the federal arsenal which, if used in conjunction with a criminal prosecution, can achieve the same result of depriving a defendant of benefits flowing from ill-gotten gains. (However, it must be noted that *Reckmeyer*, as discussed above, is a threat even to this approach.)

As noted in the discussion at the outset of this essay, U.S. law contains civil as well as criminal forfeiture provisions. Under a civil theory, the *property* is deemed to have broken the law and is, therefore, subject to confiscation on that basis. Although not so broad in scope as the criminal forfeiture statutes, civil forfeiture is particularly effective against narcotics criminals because virtually all valuable property used (or intended for use) to facilitate illegal drug dealing is subject to forfeiture.[29]

Further, because a Sixth Amendment right to counsel is not guaranteed in a civil context, the constitutional "problems" with the forfeiture of property assigned to an attorney as fees simply do not exist in any reasonable analysis.[30]

Therefore, a wise prosecutor has the capability of using either one or both of these approaches to see to it that the public's assets (for, remember, that is what the "relation back" doctrine provides) are not permitted to dissipate or be transferred to third parties who have knowledge of their illegal origins.

DISCRETION AT THE DEPARTMENT OF JUSTICE

Just how the United States Department of Justice (DOJ), the enforcer of these provisions, chooses to implement these potent weapons is thus the next logical inquiry. DOJ has, in fact, set down in writing what it will seek to forfeit and under what circumstances. The "Policy with Regard to Forfeiture of Assets Which Have Been Transferred to Attorneys as Fees for Legal Services" (hereinafter in the text: *Policy*), the official government guidelines covering the matter, has been in general circulation for some time now.[31]

Clearly, DOJ has an interest in issuing these guidelines to the world at large. The *Policy* not only puts criminal defendants and their attorneys on notice as to what will be sought from them, it also gives the federal bench an opportunity to see that the government's litigators are not overzealous in their pursuit of ill-gotten gains. In this writer's view, DOJ has taken a middle course between, on the one hand, treating attorneys as if they were any other third party transferee and, on the other hand, exempting forfeitable attorneys fees altogether.

In its published *Policy*, DOJ reviewed the existing case law through fall of 1985 and rightly concluded that "there are no constitutional or statutory prohibitions to application of the third party forfeiture provisions to attorneys fees."[32] Notwithstanding this, DOJ acknowledged the potential adverse effect such forfeitures could have on the attorney-client relationship. The *Policy* thus set forth that "it is the policy of the Department that application of the forfeiture provisions to attorneys fees be carefully reviewed and that they be uniformly and fairly applied." The *Policy* thereafter, at length, discussed the various standards of knowledge to employ in analyzing whether a given transfer to a given attorney will be sought in forfeiture. All such attempts at forfeiture (or even subpeonas of attorney's fee records) are subject to the personal and prior approval of the Assistant Attorney General for the Criminal Division.[33]

The DOJ position may be prudent given what has proven to be the proclivity of certain courts to find a constitutional violation "under every bed." Furthermore, as the addage goes, hard cases do make bad law: it would indeed be tragic to have an instance of prosecutorial abuse set a negative standard in this area, so prior approval at DOJ is no doubt warranted.

But these are policy considerations, not matters of fundamental law. The DOJ, while understandably cautious, cannot be considered as codifying the outside limit of the rearch of forfeiture in the matter of attorneys fees. Thus, states contemplating adding or modifying their own forfeiture statutes would be well advised to create *no exceptions* for assets transferred to attorneys as fees. To do so would reward those who profit the most from criminal activity.

Those interested in equal justice under law can hardly find desirable a state of law in which the small-time hood (say, a shop-lifter) must be content with what some courts obviously consider inferior representation while organized criminals get special protection to pay "cream of the crop" attorneys who will help them beat the rap.

Given the harm to society that these two classes of criminals present, any sympathetic treatment of drug lords over small time crooks seems quite skewed at the least. This is not to suggest there should be a "preferential option" for those individuals of lesser means who find themselves accused of crime. If *any* criminal defendant has otherwise "clean" assets, he is (and should be) free to obtain the counsel of his choice within his price range. If such assets are not clean, however, they belong to the people of the United States—and no defendants (*Mafioso* or corner drug peddlers) have the right to spend such assets as they see fit.

Students of the economics of Adam Smith, such as this writer, can well appreciate the motivation of those who would have attorneys fees exempted from asset forfeiture provisions. Those who would gain the most from such an exemption are members of the criminal defense bar. As things stand now, win or lose, criminal lawyers collect their fees. In fact, unlike their civil counterparts, ethical rules prevent criminal lawyers from taking cases on a contingent basis. Thus, a crucial question involves whether the potential client has the wherewithall to pay the defense fee.

One certainly cannot blame the defense bar for seeking its own interests. Nevertheless, in certain circumstances even legitimate self-interest (and that may not always be the driving force in this area) must yield to larger concerns. The safety of American streets and the health of our citizens are such concerns.

One of the most effective means of removing the financial incentive to commit crime is to prevent criminals from enjoying *any* benefit from their illegal activities. Forfeiture of the proceeds of organized crime for profit accomplishes this end. Only an exception such as one for a provider of legal services can undermine the effectiveness of such a weapon.[34]

In conclusion, asset forfeiture provisions are consistent with American traditions of compassionate and limited yet effective government. As noted above, there is a constitutional right to counsel—but there is no constitutional right to $250 an hour lawyers when the money used to pay them is ill-gotten. *The right to counsel in a criminal setting is absolute—the right to counsel of choice is not.* Therefore, lawmakers at the federal and state level should be urged not to create such an exception in representative bodies, while federal, state and local prosecutors should aggressively oppose judicial creation of the same.[35]

REFERENCES

Forfeiture of Attorneys Fees: Caveat Juris Doctor by Patrick B. McGuigan

1. 18 U.S.C. 1963 and 21 U.S.C. 853.
2. Including most notably, the drug forfeiture statute—21 U.S.C. 881. The discussion of the rationale for asset forfeiture which follows sparked a useful critique from a good friend who is also an excellent attorney and legal scholar. This friend wrote to me: "I have a little difficulty in [empathizing] with your argument concerning the limited resources and manpower of prosecutors vis a vis drug dealers. I know very little about drug dealers, but I do know something about the resources of the federal government in litigation matters. They often seem limitless. Indeed, one of the problems with litigating against the government is that government attorneys are under no client-imposed discipline concerning cost. I am firmly convinced that the court system would deal with cases much more expeditiously if the government, like ordinary citizens, were subject to the discipline of cost." While this argument deals with the edges rather than the heart of the forfeiture issue, my friend has a point. My own observation is that an astonishing amount of government resources are wasted on civil matters, although Assistant Attorney General Richard Willard in the present Justice Department has made a good deal of progress in this area. However, particularly on street crime and violent crime (including drug trafficking), the "good guys" are consistently outnumbered, especially in the court room where the odds remain against the forces opposing societal breakdown. I do agree with my friend that the discipline of cost could improve the efficiency and efficacy of government litigators, but I would not be willing to sacrifice assets forfeiture as a means of achieving that discipline.
3. *See below*, n. 25.
4. *U.S. v. Stowell*, 10 S. Ct. 244, 1890, and cases cited therein.
5. Racketeer Influenced and Corrupt Organizations, 18 U.S.C. 1961 *et seq.*
6. Continuing Criminal Enterprise, 21 U.S.C. 853.
7. For a short analysis of the issues raised in this chapter, *see* Patrick B. McGuigan, "New Tool in the War on Drugs," Washington *Times*, November 26, 1985. Note the response of Scott Wallace, Legislative Director of the National Association of Criminal Defense Lawyers, "Criminal Defense Bar Deserves More," *Friday Forum*, Washington *Times*, December 20, 1985.
8. Of course, cases had emerged dealing with other aspects of assets forfeiture. For example,

in a proceeding related to the *Reckmeyer* case discussed below, U.S. District Judge James Cacheris held that a father could retain portions of an estate built by two leading drug distributors in Northern Virginia, despite plea agreements specifying the property would be forfeited to the government. *See*, "Judge Rules on Drug Figures' Assets," Washington *Post*, February 20, 1986.

9. *U.S. v. Rogers*, 602 F. Supp. 1332 (filed February 22, 1985).

10. Emphasis not in the original. *Supra* n. 5.

11. *U.S. v. Badalamenti*, 614 F. Supp. 194. [S.S. 84 CR. 236, dated July 10, 1985.]

12. *Dicta:* "opinions of a judge which do not embody the resolution or determination of the court." *Black's Law Dictionary* (5th ed., 1979).

13. Judge Leval nevertheless acknowledged "that a literal reading of the two forfeiture statutes would seem to encompass the legal fee." *Badalamenti, supra* n. 11 at 196.

14. *Powell v. Alabama*, 287 U.S. 45, at 66 (1932).

15. Emphasis not in the original. *Cerquhart v. Lockhart*, 726 F. 2d 1316, at 1319. (8th Cir. 1984).

16. 18 U.S.C. § 3006 A.

17. *U.S. v. Matthew Ianiello, a/k/a "Matty the Horse," et al.*, No. S 85 CR 118, filed September 3, 1985.

18. *U.S. v. Christopher F. Reckmeyer, III*, Crim. No. 85-00010-A (E.D. Va., March 27, 1986).

19. As a slight digression, the presumption of innocence for an accused individual does not preclude his arrest, indictment and confinement *prior* to trial [*see* Randall R. Rader, "Bailing Out a Failed Law," in Patrick B. McGuigan and Randall R. Rader, eds., *Criminal Justice Reform: A Blueprint* (Washington, D.C.: Free Congress Foundation, 1983)]. Perhaps those judges who are offended by the relation-back doctrine feel that a person's property should be accorded more deference than his liberty or reputation.

20. *U.S. v. Reckmeyer*, 628 F. Supp. 616 (E.D., Va. 1986). Previously, it has been held that only secured creditors, *i.e.* those with a recorded interest in the specific piece of property sought for forfeiture, could seek exemption from forfeiture. Even then, such creditors had to be ignorant of the illegal source or use of the property in which they held an interest.

21. *U.S. v. Ronald Burnell Bassett and Clarence Meredith*, Crim. No. M-85-0541, April 11, 1986.

22. Both Miller and Cacheris sit in district courts within the Fourth Circuit Court of Appeals. As such, Cacheris would doubtless have welcomed the co-jurisdictional support.

23. 21 U.S.C. §§ 853 and 881.

24. If *Reckmeyer* and/or *Bassett* are appealed, it will be before the Fourth Circuit which has already indicated a disinclination to exempt attorneys fees from forfeiture. *See*, *U.S. v. Raimondo*, 721 F 2d 476 (1983).

25. *U.S. v. Payden*, 605 F. Supp. 839 (S.D.N.Y. 1985) revd. on other grounds, 767 F. 2d 26 (2d Cir. 1985).

26. *Payden* at 849, n. 14. The citation for *Shargel* is 742 F. 2d at 64. A portion of the material Judge Edelstein cited is omitted. *See* "Lawyers Called Organized Crime 'Life Support,' " *N.Y.L.J.*, March 11, 1985, p. 1, col. 5, in which is described the debriefing of an attorney/informant who claimed mob lawyers receive property "all the time" on behalf of mafia clients.

27. *Ibid.* Judge Edelstein cited "Criminal Forfeiture: Attacking the Economic Dimension of Organized Narcotics Trafficking," 32 *American University Law Review* 227, 242 (1982).

28. *Ibid.* A portion of Judge Edelstein's citation is omitted: *see* "Lawyers Called Organized Crime 'Life Support,' " *N.Y.L.J.*, March 11, 1985, p. 1, column 5. (President's Commission on Organized Crime reports that " 'a small group of lawyers' have become a 'critical element in the life support system of organized crime.' ")

29. *See* 21 U.S.C. § 881.

30. *See*, *U.S. v. One Parcel of Land*, 614 F. Supp. 183 (D.C. Ill., 1985).

31. The full text of the guidelines appeared in the Bureau of National Affairs publication, "The Criminal Law Reporter," October 2, 1985, p. 3001 (38 CrL 3001).

32. 38 CrL 3003, 9-111.230. The latter number is an internal numeration keyed to the U.S. Attorneys Manual of which the new attorneys fees policy now forms a part.

33. 38 CrL 3003, 9-111.700.

34. It must also be noted that asset forfeiture is the single most effective weapon for impacting upon the minority of criminal defense lawyers who actually serve as financial advisors and money launderers for the mob. For an intriguing look inside the dark world of mob lawyers, see John McCaslin, " 'Mob lawyer' tells panel of lucrative practice," Washington Times, January 30, 1986. See also, George Lardner, Jr., "Mob Stable of Lawyers Described: Witness Says Attorneys Perform Dirty Work," Washington Post, January 30, 1986. Earlier references to this phenomenon include the authorities cited in Payden, supra n. 26 (Payden n. 14).

35. It looks as if this issue will spark meaningful debate in the 100th Congress, slated to enter office in January 1987. "Senator Howard Metzenbaum [D-OH], with support from The American Bar Association, has proposed codification of the exemption for legitimate attorneys fees... Strom Thurmond [R-SC] has countered with a bill to clarify that forfeiture applies to all illegal proceeds, including attorney fees except when the attorney has no reason to know the source of the funds." See Randall R. Rader, "1984 Act: Changing the Course of Federal Criminal Law," forthcoming in Federal Bar Journal in late 1986. Forfeiture of attorneys fees has already drawn scholarly attention as well. The best essay I have seen thus far on this issue came to my attention just as work on this book was completed. See Kathleen F. Brickey, "Forfeiture of Attorneys' Fees...," 72 Virginia Law Review 493–542 (1986).

10

CONGRESSIONAL AND EXECUTIVE CHALLENGE OF *MIRANDA V. ARIZONA:*
A Strategy for Correcting Error or Excesses in the Supreme Court
by Bruce E. Fein

To check misuse or aggrandizement by the executive, Congress, or the Supreme Court, the authors of the Constitution divided power among the three branches of the federal government.[1] Historically, Congress has ordinarily employed two tactics to check judicial excesses or to rectify erroneous constitutional interpretations of the Supreme Court: the initiation of amendments to the Constitution,[2] and the enactment of statutes to precipitate reconsideration of constitutional pronouncements of the High Court.[3] The use of the latter tactic is essential to an enlightened evolution of constitutional jurisprudence, and to curbing abuse of judicial power.

Constitutional checks and balances are necessitated by ambitions and imperfections of individuals which incline each branch of government to usurpations and ill-conceived actions. The Supreme Court is no less prone to ambition and error than is the executive or Congress. As Justice Robert Jackson observed, the High Court was not made final because of its infallibility, but is deemed infallible because it is final.[4] The accuracy of the observation is confirmed by the approximately 250[5] cases overruled by the Supreme Court. Justice Oliver Wendell Holmes elaborated on a paramount reason for judicial misinterpretations:

> Judges are apt to be naif, simpleminded men, and they need something of Mephistopheles. We too need education in the obvious—to learn to transcend our own convictions and to leave room for much that we hold dear to be done away with short of revolution by the orderly change of law.[6]

In 1968, Congress sought by statute[7] to correct what it believed was an erroneous Supreme Court interpretation of the Fifth Amendment announced in *Miranda v. Arizona* (1966)[8] that sharply circumscribes custodial interrogation of criminal suspects by police.

The statute has slumbered, however, for many years without any attempt at implementation by the executive.[9] As a consequence, the constructive and constitutional legislative effort to obtain a reconsideration of the *Miranda* ruling by the Supreme Court has been frustrated.

The executive should give life to the anti-*Miranda* statute for at least three reasons. The *Miranda* strictures on police interrogations deprive the government and factfinder in criminal prosecutions of reliable evidence elicited from the accused without coercion or compulsion. In addition, several Supreme Court decisions postdating *Miranda* suggest a substantial probability of obtaining an overruling. Finally, congressional and executive questioning of Supreme Court decrees should be encouraged to safeguard against judicial errors or usurpations.

CONGRESS AND THE *MIRANDA* DECISION

In *Miranda v. Arizona*, a divided Supreme Court delimited the authority of law enforcement officers to interrogate criminal suspects held in custody. Writing for a 5–4 majority, Chief Justice Earl Warren noted that the Fifth Amendment provides: "No person... shall be compelled in any criminal case to be a witness against himself." Drawing from this succinct injunction, the Chief Justice extrapolated the following detailed constitutional code to regulate police interrogations:

> The prosecution may not use statements, whether exculpatory or inculpatory, stemming from custodial interrogation of the defendant unless it demonstrates the use of procedural safeguards effective to secure the privilege against self-incrimination. By custodial interrogation, we mean questioning initiated by law enforcement officers after a person has been taken into custody or otherwise deprived of his freedom of action in any significant way. As for the procedural safeguards to be employed, unless other fully effective means are devised to inform accused persons of their right of silence and to assure a continuous opportunity to exercise it, the following measures are required. Prior to any questioning, the person must be warned that he has a right to remain silent, that any statement he does make may be used as evidence against him, and that he has a right to the presence of an attorney, either retained or appointed. The defendant may waive effectuation of these rights, provided the waiver is made voluntarily, knowingly and intelligently. If, however, he indicates in any manner and at any stage of the process that he wishes to consult with an attorney before speaking there can be no questioning. Likewise, if the individual is alone and indicates in any manner that he does not wish to be interrogated, the police may not question him. The

mere fact that he may have answered some questions or volunteered some statements on his own does not deprive him of the right to refrain from answering any further inquiries until he has consulted with an attorney and thereafter consents to be questioned.[10]

The need for these constitutional rules, Warren asserted, stemmed in part from incidents of physical brutality[11] and the employment of shrewd or tricky psychology[12] by police to elicit confessions from suspects. Even absent brutality or psychological strategems, the Chief Justice worried, "the very fact of custodial interrogation exacts a heavy toll on individual liberty and trades on the weakness of individuals."[13] The atmosphere of custodial interrogation, the Chief insisted, intimidates, is destructive of human dignity, and induces confessions that are not "truly the product of free choice."[14] Moreover, the Fifth Amendment privilege against compulsory self-incrimination symbolizes a concern for requiring government to accord dignity to its citizens.[15] In addition, practices of the Federal Bureau of Investigation and experience in foreign countries indicated that a constitutional insistence on *Miranda* warnings as a prerequisite to police interrogations would not unduly hamper law enforcement.[16]

Accordingly, Warren concluded, the Fifth Amendment privilege against compulsory self-incrimination prohibits the use in criminal trials of inculpatory or exculpatory statements made in response to police questioning unless the accused was earlier informed that he possessed a right to remain silent; that any statements made would be used against him; and that he had a right to the presence of an attorney, either retained or paid by government. Congress and the states might constitutionally replace these warnings, the Chief Justice maintained, only with substitute procedures that are at least equally effective in safeguarding the right of an accused to remain silent.[17] No guides were offered to determine whether substitute procedures would satisfy the equally effective test.

The reasoning of the *Miranda* decision seems flawed. No evidence was proffered to demonstrate that the High Court's strictures against custodial interrogation were intended by the architects of the Fifth Amendment.[18] In addition, the Court's *ipse dixit* that no custodial confession can be the product of free will and thus is unconstitutionally coerced unless preceded by *Miranda* warnings informing the suspect of legal rights is unpersuasive. In contract law, for example, statements are binding and are not treated as coerced or involuntary simply because the utterer lacked knowledge of the legal implications of his assertions.[19]

The *Miranda* opinion notes that voluntariness was the previous Fifth Amendment test for adjudicating the admissibility of confessions. Furthermore, the decision concedes that an accused may voluntarily decide to waive the exercise of his constitutional rights to silence and to an attorney while detained by the police. If detention does not by itself destroy free will, then why cannot an accused speak voluntarily in response to questioning in a custodial setting without information regarding legal rights? Notably, the absence of legal knowledge in noncustodial settings does not, *simpliciter*, make statements by a suspect involuntary.[20]

The Court trumpeted only unedifying rhapsodies extolling human dignity to support the conclusion that the combination of detention plus ignorance of legal rights uniquely forecloses the exercise of free will by an accused subject to interrogation. No psychological apercus were expounded that might substantiate the Court's unprecedented claim of knowledge regarding free will. Intuition suggests that an individual's capacity to resist psychological pressure to speak inadvisedly is at its zenith when life or liberty is at stake, and certainly stronger than when only contract rights could be affected. As the pithy sage Sam Johnson remarked, the knowledge that a man will be hung in a fortnight concentrates his mind wonderfully.

Congress voiced disagreement with *Miranda* in enacting a provision of the Crime Control Act of 1968.[21] That statute (18 U.S. Code 3501) provides that "voluntary" confessions of an accused are admissible in federal criminal trials, notwithstanding a failue to administer *Miranda* warnings. In making the voluntariness determination, the trial judge is instructed to examine all circumstances of the confession, including:

(1) The time elapsing between arrest and arraignment of the defendant making the confession, if it was made after arrest and before arraignment.

(2) Whether such defendant knew the nature of the offense with which he was charged or of which he was suspected at the time of making the confession.

(3) Whether or not such defendant was advised or knew that he was not required to make any statement and that any such statement could be used against him.

(4) Whether or not such defendant had been advised prior to questioning of his right to the assistance of counsel.

(5) Whether or not such defendant was without the assistance of counsel when questioned and when giving such confession.[22]

The reasons for enactment of Section 3501 were several. Congress found that the *Miranda* decision occasioned the release of criminals whose guilt was unquestioned,[23] and substantially diminished the number of statements or confessions from suspects useful in solving crimes.[24] In addition, *Miranda* excluded from jury consideration voluntary confessions, traditionally considered the very highest type of evidence, and the most convincing evidence of guilt.[25] Finally, Congress believed that the 5-4 majority opinion in *Miranda* misconstrued the Constitution. A Senate Committee Report expressed agreement with the *Miranda* dissenters,[26] and defended the propriety of the legislation despite constitutional doubts:

> No one can predict with any assurance what the Supreme Court might at some future date decide if these provisions are enacted. The committee has concluded that this approach to the balancing of the rights of society and the rights of individuals served us well over the years, that it is constitutional and that Congress should adopt it. After all, the *Miranda* decision itself was by a bare majority of one, and with increasing frequency the Supreme Court has reversed itself. The committee feels that by the time the issue of constitutionality would reach the Supreme Court, the probability rather is that this legislation would be upheld.[27]

THE HIGH COURT AND *MIRANDA*

An impressive tableaux of Supreme Court decisions postdating the enactment of Section 3501 strengthens the congressional conviction that the Supreme Court would uphold the constitutionality of the statutory voluntariness standard to govern the admissibility of confessions in federal prosecutions. In *Harris v. New York* (1970),[28] at issue was whether statements elicited in violation of *Miranda* could be employed to impeach the credibility of the accused who chose to testify at trial. By a 5-4 vote, the Court ruled in the affirmative. Writing for the majority, Chief Justice Warren Burger observed that although the questioned statements were obtained without warning the suspect of his right to appointed counsel, no claim of coercion or involuntariness was made. Moreover, the strong public policy against perjurious testimony militated against disabling the government from impeachment use of statements made without *Miranda* warnings. Additionally, such circumscribed trial use would not impermissibly encourage *Miranda* violations, the Chief Justice maintained. Accordingly, the Court concluded:

[t]he shield provided by *Miranda* cannot be perverted into a license to use perjury by way of defense, free from the risk of confrontation with prior inconsistent utterances.[29]

The question in *Michigan v. Tucker* (1974)[30] was whether the testimony of a witness identified by exploitation of a *Miranda* violation (failure to advise of right to free counsel) must be suppressed when the deficient interrogation antedated the *Miranda* decision. By an 8-1 vote, the Court answered in the negative. Justice William Rehnquist, speaking for the majority, explained that the Fifth Amendment privilege against compulsory self-incrimination does not require *Miranda* warnings before police interrogation commences; that Amendment only proscribes coerced or involuntary confessions. Thus, *Miranda* warnings are merely supplemental safeguards to protect the Fifth Amendment privilege, but not constitutional injunctions. Accordingly, Rehnquist concluded, police interrogations tainted under *Miranda* are not necessarily constitutional infractions.

Rehnquist further noted that excluding the witness testimony would not deter police misconduct because the failure to provide complete *Miranda* warnings occurred before the *Miranda* decision was announced.[31] In addition, there was no claim that the third-party witness testimony was involuntary or unreliable. And nothing in the adversary criminal justice system ordained by the Constitution denies the government use of any evidence derived from an accused.[32] Thus, the Court held, neither the Fifth Amendment nor *Miranda* required suppression of the third-party witness testimony.

The Court further frowned on *Miranda* in *Oregon v. Haas* (1975).[33] There an accused requested to speak to an attorney after receiving full *Miranda* warnings. In contravention of *Miranda*, police interrogation continued, and elicited incriminating evidence from the suspect. The evidence was employed by the government for impeachment purposes when the suspect testified during his prosecution. By a 6-2 vote, the Court held that the impeachment use of the evidence was irreproachable.

Justice Harry Blackmun, writing for the majority, stressed that the questioned statements were neither coerced nor involuntary, and advanced the transcendent truth-seeking purpose of a criminal trial.[34] Moreover, any incentive to continue improper police interrogation of a suspect after an attorney is requested in the hope of uncovering impeachment material is insubstantial.[35] Accordingly, Blackmun reasoned, the rationale of *Harris v. New York* compelled the conclusion that use of the challenged evidence to impeach the testimony of the accused was legally unassailable.

In *United States v. Mandujano* (1976),[36] the target of an investigation urged a constitutional right to *Miranda* warnings prior to questioning before a grand jury. It was additionally urged that failure to provide such warnings justified suppressing perjurious statements made to the grand jury. The Court unanimously rejected the latter contention, while four Justices opined that *Miranda* had no application outside the hostile and unfriendly environment of police custody. Speaking for a plurality, Chief Justice Burger declared that judicial supervision of grand jury inquiries safeguards against the types of interrogation abuses—violence, physical brutality, and sustained incommunicado questioning—that *Miranda* was designed to deter.[37] Burger expostulated:

> To extend these concepts to questioning before a grand jury inquiring into criminal activity under the guidance of a judge is an extravagant expansion never remotely contemplated by this Court in *Miranda*.[38]

In *New York v. Quarles* (1984),[39] the Court unequivocally declared that *Miranda* warnings were not a constitutional injunction of the Fifth Amendment privilege against compulsory self-incrimination. In that case, police officers arrested an accused rapist believed to have discarded a gun. Before informing the arrestee of *Miranda* rights, an officer inquired as to the location of the gun and elicited an incriminating answer. A majority of the Court concluded that the interrogation neither violated *Miranda* nor the Fifth Amendment.

Speaking for five members, Justice Rehnquist explained that the Fifth Amendment denounces only coerced self-accusations.[40] The *Miranda* decision was not compelled by that Amendment, but was issued as a prophylactic to reinforce the privilege against self-incrimination.[41] Because the interrogation at issue did not coerce a response from the suspect, no constitutional violation attached to the failure to provide *Miranda* warnings.

Rehnquist also found the police questioning legally irreproachable by fashioning a "public safety" exception to *Miranda*. He denied that "doctrinal underpinnings of *Miranda* require that it be applied in all its rigor to a situation in which police officers ask questions reasonably prompted by a concern for the public safety."[42] In these circumstances, *Miranda* warnings might deter suspects from yielding information necessary to forestall public danger, as well as to obtaining a criminal conviction.[43] Such social costs are too steep to justify the prophylactic edicts of *Miranda*. Those edicts were found tolerable only if the social consequences were restricted to less convictions of guilty persons, and did not imperil broader social concerns.[44]

A jaundiced eye was again cast on *Miranda* in *Berkemer v. McCarty* (1984).[45] In that case, highway patrol officers stopped a motorist suspected of a traffic offense and commenced roadside questioning regarding the use of intoxicants. The driver was neither provided *Miranda* warnings nor formally arrested when the roadside interrogation was initiated. Eight justices held that in these circumstances the interrogation did not offend the *Miranda* decision.

Justice Thurgood Marshall, speaking for the Court, maintained that *Miranda* governs questioning that occurs under pressures that substantially impair exercise of the privilege against self-incrimination.[46] But an ordinary traffic stop is presumptively temporary and brief, unlike stationhouse interrogation which is typically prolonged and accompanied by tricky psychological strategems.[47] In addition, roadside questioning is public and ordinarily performed by at most two policemen, which reduces the likelihood of police abuse or any sense of vulnerability by the motorist.[48] Thus, Marshall concluded:

[t]he noncoercive aspect of ordinary traffic stops prompts us to hold that persons temporarily detained pursuant to such stops are not 'in custody' for the purposes of Miranda.[49]

Any other result would unacceptably obstruct

enforcement of the nation's traffic laws—by compelling the police either to take the time to warn all detained motorists of their constitutional rights or to forgo use of self-incriminating statements made by those motorists—while doing little to protect citizens' Fifth Amendment rights.[50]

The Court also displayed chilly aloofness towards *Miranda* in *Oregon v. Elstad* (1985).[51] A 6–3 majority held that confessions obtained in contravention of *Miranda* do not taint subsequent admissions made after *Miranda* warnings were administered.

Justice Sandra Day O'Connor, speaking for the Court, emphasized that the constitutional privilege against self-incrimination is unconcerned with moral or psychological pressures to confess emanating from sources other than official coercion. Voluntary statements are not only a proper element of law enforcement, but inherently desirable, O'Connor explained. Thus, voluntary admissions elicited without *Miranda* warnings are constitutionally unassailable; only the preventive medicine of the *Miranda* decision requires the exclusion of the admissions to prove the prosecutor's case in chief. Accordingly, Justice O'Connor declared:

> [i]f errors are made by law enforcement officers in administering the prophylactic *Miranda* procedures, they should not breed the same irremediable consequences as police infringement of the Fifth Amendment itself. It is an unwarranted extension of *Miranda* to hold that a simple failure to administer the warnings, unaccompanied by any actual coercion or other circumstances calculated to undermine the suspect's ability to exercise his free will so taints the investigatory process that a subsequent voluntary and informed waiver is ineffective for some indefinite period.[52]

Waiving a Fifth Amendment banner of voluntariness, the Court concluded that confessions obtained in violation of *Miranda* but in conformity with the Constitution do not, without more, exert such a psychological compulsion on an accused as to taint subsequent admissions made after receipt of *Miranda* warnings.

A CHALLENGE TO *MIRANDA*

Despite the several Supreme Court avowals that *Miranda* warnings are not a Fifth Amendment imperative, the Federal Bureau of Investigation of the Department of Justice has declined to test that understanding by aiding implementation of Section 3501. The FBI instructs its agents to comply with *Miranda*, thereby foreclosing the opportunity to test the constitutionality of the statutory voluntariness standard to govern the admissibility of confessions in federal criminal prosecutions. To both effectuate Section 3501 and enhance criminal law enforcement, the following strategy should be considered.

The FBI should videotape custodial interrogation of a federal criminal suspect without administering *Miranda* warnings. The suspect should be informed, however, that questioning will cease if he affirmatively declares that he feels coerced or compelled to answer.

If incriminating evidence is obtained from the suspect through this procedure, federal prosecutors should seek its admissibility in a subsequent criminal trial under the voluntariness standard delineated in Section 3501. Introduction of the videotape as evidence will bolster proof that the incriminating statements were the product of free will despite the absence of *Miranda* warnings. In this fashion, the FBI and the Department of Justice can precipitate a judicial ruling on the constitutionality of Section 3501. A favorable decision is probable in light of the recent Supreme Court precedents that address the scope and meaning of *Miranda*.

CONCLUSION

Enlightened evolution of constitutional jurisprudence is advanced by congressional or executive challenges to Supreme Court precedents. As Justice Louis Brandeis lectured in *Burnet v. Coronado Oil & Gas* (1932)[53] with regard to precedent,

> The Court bows to the lessons of experience and the force of better reasoning, recognizing that the process of trial and error, so fruitful in the physical sciences, is appropriate also in the judicial function.[54]

The healthy process of judicial trial and error languishes, however, unless Congress and the President exercise independent judgement in evaluating the soundness of constitutional doctrines pronounced by the Supreme Court. The legislature and executive too often entrust sole responsibility for constitutional interpretations to the federal judiciary. As a consequence, the intellectual foundations of Supreme Court rulings are frequently flawed or flabby, and misuse of judicial authority is frequently unchecked.

The trenchant words of Congressman Cordell Hull and President Abraham Lincoln illuminate the constitutional necessity for active legislative and executive challenge to perceived errors of the Supreme Court. Elaborating on the role of congressmen in the evolution of constitutional law, Hull explained:

> I agree that Members of Congress are under oath to support the Constitution, and that it is the duty of the Supreme Court, under proper circumstances, to construe and expound the instrument; but I submit that where, in the judgement of Members of Congress, a palpably erroneous decision has been rendered by the Supreme Court, stripping the coordinate legislative branch of the Government of one of its strong arms of power and

duty...every Member of Congress owes to himself and to the country the duty of exhausting every reasonable and legitimate means to secure a review by the Court of the questions erroneously decided.[55]

President Lincoln similarly admonished against robotic submission to every Supreme Court precedent:

[T]he candid citizen must confess that if the policy of the Government upon vital questions affecting the whole people is to be irrevocably fixed by decisions of the Supreme Court the instant they are made in ordinary litigation between parties in personal actions, the people will have ceased to be their own rulers, having to that extent practically resigned their Government into the hands of that eminent tribunal.[56]

In sum, seeking judicial vindication of Section 3501 and an eclipse or overruling of *Miranda* will both advance legitimate law enforcement objectives and reestablish the Congress and the Executive as constructive limited partners with the Supreme Court in expounding constitutional doctrines.

REFERENCES

Congressional and Executive Challenge of Miranda v. Arizona: *A Strategy for Correcting Error or Excesses in the Supreme Court* by Bruce E. Fein

1. *The Federalist*, Nos. 48, 51.
2. U.S. Constitution, Article V provides: The Congress, whenever two-thirds of both Houses shall deem it necessary, shall propose Amendments to this Constitution, or, on the Application of the Legislatures of two-thirds of the several States, shall call a Convention for proposing Amendments, which, in either Case, shall be valid to all Intents and Purposes, as part of this Constitution, when ratified, by the Legislatures of three-fourths of the several States, or by conventions in three-fourths thereof, as the one or the other Mode of Ratification may be proposed by the Congress...Amendments 11, 13, 14, 16, and 26 were adopted to overturn Supreme Court decisions in *Chisolm v. Georgia*, 2 U.S. 419 (1793), *Dred Scott v. Sanford*, 60 U.S. (19 How.) 393 (1856), *Pollock v. Farmers' Loan & Trust Co.*, 157 U.S. 429 (1895), and *Oregon v. Mitchell*, 400 U.S. 112 (1970).
3. See, e.g., the Norris-LaGuardia Act, Ch. 90, 47 Stat. 70 (March 23, 1932). The Act circumscribed, in cases involving labor disputes, the issuance by the federal courts of restraining orders and temporary or permanent injunctions. It also made all yellow-dog contracts unenforceable in federal court. Before the Act was passed, the Supreme Court had held that state legislation which similarly restricted the legal remedies of employers was a denial of due process [*Truax v. Corrigan*, 257 U.S. 312 (1921)], and that legislative restrictions of yellow-dog contracts also violated the due process clause, whether enacted by a state [*Coppage v. Kansas*, 236 U.S. 1 (1915)] or by Congress [*Adair v. United States*, 208 U.S. 161 (1908)]. It is also noteworthy that the Emancipation Proclamation would never have been issued, and the network of New Deal legislation would never have been enacted, if Congress and the President had been unwilling to challenge Supreme Court precedents. See Ch. CXI, 12 Stat. 432 (1862); Tennessee Valley Authority Act of 1933, Ch. 32, 48 Stat. 58 (May 18, 1933); National Labor Relations Act, Ch. 372, 49 Stat. 449 (July 5, 1935); Social Security Act, Ch. 531, 49 Stat. 620 (August 14, 1935); Public Utility Holding Company Act, Ch. 687, 49 Stat. 803 (August 26, 1935); Railroad Retirement Act of 1935

and 1937, Ch. 812, 49 Stat. 967 (August 29, 1935) and Ch. 382, 50 Stat. 307 (June 24, 1937); Guffey-Snyder Coal Act, Ch. 824, 49 Stat. 991 (August 30, 1935); Agriculture Adjustment Act of 1937 and 1938, Ch. 296, 50 Stat. 246 (June 3, 1937) and Ch. 30, 52 Stat. 31 (February 16, 1938); Fair Labor Standards Act, Ch. 676, 52 Stat. 1060 (June 25, 1938).

4. 344 U.S. 443, 540 (1953) (concurring opinion).

5. *See* Congressional Research Service, Library of Congress, *The Constitution of the United States of America, Analysis and Interpretaiton* at 1789–97 (and Supp. 1982).

6. Oliver Wendell Holmes, *Law and the Court,* Occasional Speeches, p. 172 (Howe ed. 1962).

7. 18 U.S.C. §3501 (1982).

8. 1968 *U.S. Code Cong. & Adm. News* 2112, 2126, 2127.

9. *Compare* 63 *G.E.O. L.J.* 305, 307, 308 (1974).

10. 384 U.S. 436,444, 445 (1965) (hereinafter *Miranda* rules).

11. *Miranda* rules at 446.

12. *Id.* at 448, 453.

13. *Id.* at 455.

14. *Id.* at 458.

15. *Id.* at 460.

16. *Id.* at 483–490.

17. *Id.* at 467.

18. *Id.* The custodial confession at issue in *Miranda* was obtained and utilized by state officials in a state prosecution. In *Malloy v. Hogan,* 378 U.S. 1 (1964), the Court held that the due process clause of the Fourteenth Amendment applicable to state action incorporates limits on the federal government imposed by the Fifth Amendment privilege against compulsory self-incrimination.

19. *See, Restatement (Second) of Contracts* §§ 174–175 (1981).

20. *Miranda* rules at 478.

21. 18 U.S.C. § 3501 (1982).

22. 18 U.S.C. § 3501.

23. 1968 *U.S. Code Cong. & Adm. News* 2127.

24. *Id.* at 2128.

25. *Id.* at 2136.

26. *Id.* at 2134–2138.

27. *Id.* at 2138.

28. *Harris v. New York,* 401 U.S. 222 (1970).

29. *Id.* at 226.

30. *Michigan v. Tucker,* 417 U.S. 433 (1974).

31. *Id.* at 447–448.

32. *Id.* at 449–450.

33. *Oregon v. Haas,* 420 U.S. 714 (1975).

34. *Id.* at 722.

35. *Id.*

36. *U.S. v. Mandujano,* 425 U.S. 564 (1976).

37. *Id.* at 579–580.

38. *Id.* at 580.

39. *New York v. Quarles,* U.S., _____, 104 S.Ct. 2626 (1984).

40. *Id.* at 2630–2631.

41. *Id.* at 2631.

42. *Id.* at 2632.

43. *Id.* at 2632–633.

44. *Id.*

45. *Berkemer v. McCarty*, U.S. _____, 104 S.Ct. 3138 (1984).

46. *Id.* at 3149.

47. *Id.* at 3149–3150.

48. *Id.* at 3150.

49. *Id.* at 3151.

50. *Id.*

51. *Oregon v. Elstad*, U.S. _____, _____ S.Ct. _____ (1985).

52. *Id.*

53. 285 U.S. 393 (1932).

54. *Id.* at 407–408.

55. *The Memoirs of Cordell Hull*, Vol. 1, p. 59 (New York 1948).

56. *The Inaugural Addresses of the American Presidents* 238 (D. Lott ed. 1961). [Editor's note: Here are the legal citations for three of the cases covered in this essay: *New York v. Quarles*, 467 U.S. 649 (1984); *Berkemer v. McCarty*, 468 U.S. 420 (1984); and *Oregon v. Elstad*, 470 U.S. _____, *or* 105 S.Ct. 1285 (1985).]

11

LET'S ESTOP CRIMINALS:
The Collateral Estoppel Effect of a Criminal Conviction in a Subsequent Civil Trial
by Kurt W. Wolfgang

The doctrine of collateral estoppal has existed, in parallel, in both criminal and civil proceedings for many decades. Relatively recent developments in the law have cleared the way for the next logical step: crossover.[1] Crossover is the phenomenon of granting collateral estoppel effect to the findings of a criminal proceeding in a subsequent civil proceeding or, in rare occasions, the reverse. This essay offers a brief history of collateral estoppel, how the modern developments added to the development of crossover, how crossover can be asserted by those injured by a criminal act, a survey of the status of the crossover phenomenon in various jurisdictions, and some recommendations favoring crossover.[2]

COLLATERAL ESTOPPEL: ITS ELEMENTS

Collateral Estoppel is a judicial doctrine calling for the preclusion from determination of issues that have already been fully and fairly decided by a valid, final judgment of the merits.[3] While the elements necessary to the assertion of this doctrine naturally vary between jurisdictions, the following requirements are commonly found:[4]

- The party against whom collateral estoppel is asserted must be a privy or a party to the earlier litigation. The roots of this requirement are in the due process clause. Briefly stated, one whose interests are not represented in a trial cannot be bound by the outcome of the trial.[5]

- The issue precluded in the subsequent litigation must correlate precisely to an issue that was essential to the adjudication of the first trial. The issue must have not only been determined in the former trial, but it must have been an essential element of the verdict, rather than dicta or surplusage.[6] This correlation is often difficult to determine. Only those issues which are necessary to the existence of the prior judgment are subject to collateral estoppel. In a trial by the court, the findings of fact may firmly establish certain issues, because judges often verbalize the elements of their decisions. Likewise, special verdicts by juries make the determination of issues fairly simple because their verdict is in the form of answers to specific questions comprising the elements of the decision. In contrast, a general verdict affords far less information. If the case is simple, the issues necessarily decided by the verdict will probably be evident. In a more complex case, divining the issues determined in a general verdict may present a greater task. Because all jury verdicts in criminal cases are general in nature, as opposed to special verdicts, this problem takes on added significance in the context of crossover.

• The party against whom collateral estoppel is asserted must have actually litigated the issue in the former adjudication, or at least the party must have had the incentive and the full and fair opportunity to litigate the issue.[7] This requirement is discussed in more detail below.

• Finally, there is also a requirement that the prior judgment be "final." Generally this element is satisfied by an enrolled judgment. While there must exist an avenue of appeal from the first judgment in order to assert collateral estoppel, the jurisdictions seem to split on the question of whether an issue arising from a case pending appeal can be the basis for collateral estoppel.[8] There is an exception to the rules requiring collateral estoppel in the event of a reversal on appeal of the original case.[9]

SOME HISTORICAL DEVELOPMENTS

Until 1942 a requirement prevailed that collateral estoppel could only be asserted against a participant in the first litigation by an adverse party to that same initial litigation. This so-called mutuality requirement disallowed the use of collateral estoppel except between adverse parties to the original action.[10]

Historically, judgments rendered in criminal trials were not admissible in subsequent civil proceedings.[11]

Among the reasons cited for this policy were:

• The fact that technically the evidence of the prior conviction was hearsay.[12]

• The possibility that the defendant lacked the motive or opportunity to defend the issue adequately in the criminal trial, especially in the case of a minor criminal offense such as a traffic violation.[13]

- The likelihood that the issues involved in the subsequent civil litigation would not be identical to those in the criminal litigation.[14]
- The fear that criminal defendants might "manufacture" evidence in the criminal trial in order to benefit in the subsequent civil proceeding.[15]
- The possibility of jury confusion as to whether the evidence of a conviction is decisive or merely persuasive on the issue of liability.[16]
- The lack of mutuality of the parties.[17]

As early as 1931 the federal courts allowed collateral estoppel effect to cross over into subsequent civil litigation.[18] However, the federal courts clung to the mutuality doctrine for quite some time after 1931. Only the United States or its privies could benefit from estoppel in a subsequent civil case.[19]

Stated briefly, the reason that usually only the United States could benefit from estoppel in a subsequent criminal trial is that an acquittal is almost unanimously held to have no estoppel effect in a subsequent civil trial. This is due to the difference of the degree and allocation of the burden of proof. All that is proven by an acquittal is that the state has failed to meet the "beyond a reasonable doubt" standard. That proof which the state rendered in the criminal trial may well have met the "preponderance of the evidence" standard, the norm in civil suits, and thus further civil litigation of the issues is allowed. Other permutations are possible, although not prevalent, such as civil litigation followed by criminal litigation.[20] The dearth of cases of this type is probably caused by the archaic requirement that the party against whom collateral estoppel is asserted must have been a party or a privy to the earlier litigation. In other words, the criminal defendant could not assert collateral estoppel of a favorable judgment against the government, unless the government was a party to the original suit. Furthermore, no one has argued seriously that civil determinations adverse to the subsequent criminal defendant should collaterally estop an issue, because of the lower burden of proof in the prior civil case, and the extra safeguards mandated in a criminal case.[21]

The next development in the crossover effect was the abatement of mutuality. The *Bernhard* doctrine[22] allowed litigants not involved in the prior litigation to assert collateral estoppel. Initially, the courts recognized defensive collateral estoppel, that is, estoppel raised as a defense to a claim. The strongest arguments for dismantling mutuality arise from defensive use of collateral estoppel. The most obvious rationale is the judicial economy of denying relitigation of an issue which was once determined.[23]

Equally important is the goal of removing from the litigant asserting collateral estoppel the burden of proving that which has already been established. Also, courts recognized the unfairness of allowing relitigation of an issue against subsequent parties in the hope that the fortune of the gaming table would produce a decision favorable to the party who could afford relitigation until exhausting opposing parties.

The next historical development was the notion that a stranger to the original suit could assert collateral estoppel in furtherance of his or her claim against a party to the original suit: offensive collateral estoppel. It almost seems as though originally the courts failed to recognize the fact that at least some of the policy reasons listed above supporting defensive collateral estoppel do not necessarily apply to offensive assertion of collateral estoppel. For instance, in some cases, offensive collateral estoppel will encourage litigation by strangers to the original suit whose chances of prevailing increase because of an issue decided in their favor in the original suit. Secondly, offensive collateral estoppel encourages multiple plaintiffs to refrain from joining the original action, and even subsequent actions, until finally a similarly situated plaintiff prevails upon the common issue in question. Then the prudent plaintiff may sue, asserting collateral estoppel of the favorable judgment. In a case involving one hundred plaintiffs, it is conceivable that the courts would deal with one hundred suits, rather than just one. By this time, these shortcomings of offensive collateral have certainly become apparent and are considered an acceptable price for the benefits of its use.

It comes as no surprise that the first case to combine the demise of mutuality with the notion of crossover estoppel came from the same jurisdiction as the landmark crossover decision. In *Teitelbaum Furs, Inc. v. Dominion Insurance Company* (1962), Justice Traynor reasoned that because collateral estoppel applies to successive criminal trials, estoppel in a subsequent civil trial would be even more appropriate. Traynor felt that crossover collateral estoppel would be less severe than collateral estoppel in sucessive civil suits, because the party against whom estoppel would be asserted is entitled to far greater safeguards in a criminal trial than in a civil trial. His statements imply that a criminal conviction is more reliable than a civil judgment.[24]

While the *Teitelbaum* decision has been followed by the Federal Courts[25] and a number of other jurisdictions, the majority of jurisdictions have yet to address the issue of crossover, since abandoning mutuality. Indeed, there are still some jurisdictions that cling to the mutuality requirement. Some of those states have made exceptions allowing the admission as evidence of a conviction as persuasive but not preclusive of the issues for which it is offered.[26] Another permutation is to allow such evidence only as a defense when a convicted criminal seeks to profit in the subsequent civil suit.[27]

One of the more lively subtopics in recent law review articles, if any discussion of collateral estoppel can be called lively, is whether courts should allow preclusive effect to pleas of guilty.[28] The common law approach was (or is) to allow guilty pleas as evidence in the subsequent civil trial, because the plea or admission of guilt is a declaration against interest, and, therefore, not excluded as hearsay.[29] The *Teitelbaum* decision itself called for the preservation of the common law approach to pleas of guilty.[30] Most opponents of the use of guilty pleas in subsequent civil trials argue that such pleas are inherently unreliable.[31] Professor Vestal and others have (accurately) stated that because no issue has been litigated by a guilty plea such a plea fails the requirement that the issue to be precluded is one which was determined in the previous trial.[32]

The states that have ruled in favor of preclusive effect, have altered this requirement so that all that is required is that the party had a full and fair opportunity to litigate the issue.[33] This so-called "day in court" rationale has also been applied occasionally to consent judgments and other judgments not based upon actual litigation.[34]

Curiously lacking from the arguments in favor of preclusive effect is a discussion of the *nolo contendere* plea. Decisions unanimously hold that a nolo plea has no preclusive effect in a subsequent civil trial.[35] In a jurisdiction such as Maryland, which allows such pleas, a defendant who wishes to avoid subsequent civil liability may try for a nolo plea. In fact, this seems to be the primary reason for such a plea. The argument would probably arise that judges can reject a nolo plea. Perhaps the principal reason that judges hold this power is to avoid the injustice of allowing the defendant to escape preclusive judgments.

COLLATERAL ESTOPPEL IN MARYLAND: A CASE STUDY

The Maryland development of collateral estoppel seems to closely parallel the general body of law. Maryland recognizes that the rules of collateral estoppel are identical in civil and criminal law.[36] Maryland embraces the *Bernhard* doctrine[37] and also requires the standard elements in order to claim estoppel.[38] Maryland also recognizes offensive collateral estoppel.[39] On the issue of guilty pleas, Maryland allows their use as evidence, but affords them no collateral estoppel effect.[40]

Apparently the issue of crossover collateral estoppel of a conviction not based upon a guilty plea had not come to the appellate courts in Maryland through 1984. This author postulates that attorneys fail to raise the issue of estoppel by criminal judgment in the subsequent civil proceeding. Because Maryland law follows the general trends in this area of collateral estoppel so closely, there is every reason to believe that an attempt to use crossover collateral estoppel would prevail.

Lest some overzealous attorney attempt to create a crossover situation, there is some authority for the position that pursuing criminal prosecution solely to obtain advantage in a civil matter violates ethical considerations.[41] The Model Code of Professional Responsibility states: "A lawyer shall not present, participate in presenting, or threaten to present criminal charges solely to obtain an advantage in a civil matter."[42]

While it is doubtful that this provision has ever been applied in the novel area of crossover collateral estoppel, caution and prudence should govern the attorney's approach to the situation of pursuing criminal charges. There are, of course, many legitimate reasons for advocating criminal charges, such as dissuading personal retribution, promoting justice, protecting one's client from repeated victimization and so forth. The code restriction does not apply to these actions.

HOW COLLATERAL ESTOPPEL COULD BE ASSERTED IN MARYLAND

This section originated in an attempt to foster the use of crossover collateral estoppel in the Maryland courts. While the concepts might apply generally to the courts of other jurisdictions, the information contained herein may not suit other jurisdictions.

One of the issues involved in asserting preclusion in non-crossover cases virtually dissolves in a crossover situation. In a civil-to-civil court preclusion attempt the party claiming preclusion may have the option of claiming *res judicata*, or claim preclusion, when the parties in both actions are the same, or essentially the same.[43] Even in the circumstance where the state becomes a party in a criminal action subsequent to a civil action, or vice versa, *res judicata* could have no place in a crossover situation because by definition *res judicata* requires identical actions as well as identical parties, and the subsequent civil action, by definition, is never identical to the prior criminal action.

Issue preclusion may be offensive or defensive in nature regardless of the party's posture as plaintiff or defendant. Generally, a plaintiff desires to avoid the burden of producing or proving evidence of an element of plaintiff's case. A defendant, by raising collateral estoppel, attempts to destroy an element of the plaintiff's case by proving that the essence of that element has already been judicially negated. While various procedural methods exist to accomplish these goals, it is important to point out that attempting to submit evidence of a judicial proceeding, as in the matter of admissibility of guilty pleas, is governed by the rules of evidence, and is discussed here because of its inextricable relationship with the subject of crossover.

The issue of collateral estoppel may be established in the pleadings by merely stating the relevant facts, then alleging that the issue is precluded by the previous judgment. Some jurisdictions, including Maryland, require that collateral estoppel as a defense to a claim be raised as an affirmative defense.[44] Perhaps because of the novelty of offensive collateral estoppel, no such requirement is imposed for estoppel offensively asserted.

As a result, it would appear that defensive collateral estoppel must appear in the *defendant's* pleading, under the revised rules, but offensive collateral estoppel may appear in the alternative through the procedural vehicles discussed below.

Summary judgment seems tailor-made for asserting collateral estoppel.[45] Offensively, if the matters precluded by the previous conviction establish the elements of the civil claim, then summary judgment would be appropriate. Defensively, when the previous adjudication establishes an affirmative defense to the claim, or where the previous judgment invalidates an element of the plaintiff's claim, then summary judgment could be rendered. Caution must again prevail for unless the defendant in Maryland submits an answer asserting collateral estoppel, the defendant may run into serious problems.

Similarly, a motion for directed verdict would certainly be an appropriate method to effectuate collateral estoppel,[46] as would a motion for judgment N.O.V.[47] These two motions should not be the first to raise the issue of collateral estoppel, however. They are better suited to dispose of the case after raising collateral estoppel through the pleadings. Offensively, the estoppel could be introduced as evidence at trial or at the pre-trial conference, and defensively, it could be raised as an objection to the admission of evidence already proffered.

In Maryland, it would constitute a gamble to raise collateral estoppel at trial through an attempt to produce evidence of conviction. Maryland only recently reaffirmed the almost forgotten concept that a conviction not based on a guilty plea cannot be admitted as proof of the facts supporting the conviction. While this ruling would seem to conflict with the concept of crossover collateral estoppel, the issue was neither raised nor addressed in the recent case of *Aetna Casualty and Surety Company v. Kuhl* (1983).[48] Indeed, the Court of Appeals founded its decision on the moldy cases of the forties, thirties, and even earlier, without the slightest mention of collateral estoppel. While the *Aetna v. Kuhl* case does not seem to conflict with the crossover concept, the case certainly bodes ill for the attorney who attempts to present a prior conviction not based upon a guilty plea as evidence of the facts upon which the conviction is based. Technically, if the attorney asserts collateral estoppel, the court should hear this information in order to rule on the issue. However, given the highly technical nature of this relatively new concept of crossover, the attorney who relies on the court's ability to divine the difference between offering the conviction as evidence and offering the conviction in order to assert collateral estoppel is tempting the Fates.

A motion to strike[49] may not present a proper manner in which a defendant could raise collateral estoppel. The Maryland courts have ruled *res judicata* may not be properly raised in a motion *ne re* (or to strike).[50] Because the courts still have trouble distinguishing between collateral estoppel and *res judicata*, one of the other alternatives presented herein should provide a safer, if not a better course.

There is a possibility that collateral estoppel may be raised by demurrer or motion to dismiss.[51] At least one federal court has found that *res judicata* would be properly raised in a 12(b)(6) motion under the Federal Rules of Civil Procedure. The language of 12(b)(6) reads "failure to state a claim upon which relief can be granted." If the issue to be estopped negates the claim stated, then presumably collateral estoppel would be as appropriately raised by a 12(b)(6)—as would *res judicata*. The Maryland courts would, of course, be free to adopt or reject this reasoning as applied to a 1–322 (a)(6) motion[52] to dismiss under the revised rules.

To summarize, the safest approach to collateral estoppel is to raise the matter in the pleadings. For defensive collateral estoppel under the revised Maryland rules, this will generally be a requirement. Offensively, the issue could be properly raised at a pre-trial conference, but probably not during trial as evidence. The matter could also be properly initially raised in a motion for summary judgment, or motion for directed verdict.

BURDEN OF PROOF

The burden of proving the existence of the prior judgment naturally rests on the party asserting collateral estoppel. Probably due to the relative ease in producing evidence of a prior conviction, there is a dearth of case law in this area. Those cases that exist require that the asserting party introduce the record of conviction.[53] That record should include, as a minimum, the charging document, (indictment or information) the court judgment or jury verdict (or guilty plea in those states extending crossover collateral estoppel to guilty pleas), the judgment and sentence of the court, and any decision, order or judgment of any appellate court.[54] It is also incumbent upon the party asserting estoppel to prove the remaining elements of collateral estoppel discussed above. The asserting party may also resort to the use of the record transcript of the prior trial, parol (unwritten) evidence in the form of testimony by the judge, jurors, attorneys, witnesses, etc., the jury instructions, the appellate record, or admissions and stipulations, in order to prove the requisites of collateral estoppel.

TURNABOUT IS NOT FAIR PLAY

The question naturally arises that if the convicted criminal can be bound by the findings of the criminal proceeding in a subsequent civil trial, then can the party injured by the criminal act also be bound by the determination? The general answer at this stage in the development of crossover collateral estoppel is: no. As noted earlier, the party against whom collateral estoppel is asserted must have been a party or privy to the previous action in order to satisfy the requirements of due process. Because the victim of the crime is not a party, then the requirement imposed by due process considerations would bar estoppel against the victim, unless the victim was considered to be in privity with the criminal.[55] Furthermore, even if there was no such requirement that the party against whom collateral estoppel is asserted must have been a party to the prior litigation, a judgment of acquittal would not allow him (or her) to use his (or her) acquittal in a subsequent civil trial, because no factual matter is "necessarily determined" by a judgment of acquittal, save that the state failed to prove its case beyond a reasonable doubt.[56] In a subsequent *criminal trial*, under the correct circumstances, the state may be estopped from raising issues determined in the acquittal, even over and above double jeopardy considerations,[57] but the subject here is crossover to subsequent civil litigation, not collateral estoppel within criminal courts.

A REASONABLE EXCEPTION

Some commentators have called for an exception to the use of both crossover collateral estoppel and the use of a guilty plea as evidence in the case of criminal offenses which are so trivial in nature that the criminal defendant may not have dedicated a great deal of resources or effort into his defense.[58] Indeed, in some states, courts have imposed such a limitation.[59] Those commentators would add this element of "reliability" to the list of requirements already enumerated as prerequisites to collateral estoppel, in both crossover and non-crossover forms.

This would seem to be a reasonable precaution against allowing a rational, reasonable doctrine to extend to the absurd. Someone, for example, who receives a speeding ticket (which he pays through the mail or fights pro se in court) for an accident involving injury to another party may find that his ticket cost him $300,030 rather than $30. While the party may or may not have been speeding, most reasonable people would agree that this determination is not reliable enough to support the enormity of its consequences. Had the defendant and even the court foreseen the possibility of the grave consequences of the subsequent suit, they would have undoubtedly exerted more effort in the initial trial.

At the federal level, the Supreme Court has held that granting

194

collateral estoppel effect to a non-jury proceeding does not deny a party the right to a jury trial guaranteed in the Seventh Amendment.[60] This seems to clear the way for minor criminal convictions in which the defendant was not entitled to a jury, to collaterally estop issues in a subsequent civil proceeding where the party would normally be entitled to a jury determination of the issue. Because the Seventh Amendment does not apply to the states, and because, absent constitutional considerations, the states are free to develop their own law concerning collateral estoppel, this Supreme Court determination holds only persuasive value. However, it does point out one of the inequities of allowing preclusive effect to issues arising from relatively minor cases.

CONCLUSION

The primary purpose of collateral estoppel is to bar unnecessary relitigation. The most important justification for the *Bernhard* doctrine of non-mutuality is to relieve the asserting party of the unnecessary burden of litigation of a previously determined issue. The requirements of collateral estoppel guard against undue unfairness by assuming that the party to be bound by the previous judgment had a full and fair opportunity to litigate the matter in the first adjudication. The additional safeguards of a criminal prosecution result in a more reliable determination of factual issues, at least in a trial and conviction, than in a civil adjudication. One commentator states:

> When criminal convictions stem from trials, collateral estoppel in subsequent civil proceedings is unquestionably sound. A criminal defendant that proceeds to trial benefits from a vast array of procedural protections that should inspire confidence in the reliability of the outcomes.[61]

Because of these safeguards, because of the higher standard of proof in criminal cases, and because it ameliorates the welfare of those wronged by the acts of convicted criminals, Maryland and other states should adopt crossover collateral estoppel.

Convictions based upon guilty pleas are also reliable. Unless a guilty plea is a rare "Alford" plea[62] in which the defendant denies commission of the offense, then the defendant has accepted, in court, his responsibility for the crime. Because those who are not guilty but wish to plead guilty have the alternatives of *nolo contendere* and "Alford" pleas, those convicted of more serious offenses based on guilty pleas should also be subject to collateral estoppel. There is no manifest injustice in binding a wrongdoer to that which he or she has freely admitted in open court. Guilty pleas, and even convictions, in crimes involving relatively inconsequential penalties should be excepted from crossover. Delineating between inconsequential and significant penalties is a subject worthy of its own article, but one suggestion would be that a significant penalty would be one in which jail term was possible or probable.

REFERENCES

Let's Estop Criminals: The Collateral Estoppel Effect of a Criminal Conviction in a Subsequent Civil Trial by Kurt W. Wolfgang

1. There is a need for a term that denotes the use of a criminal judgment in a subsequent civil proceeding for collateral estoppel purposes. At least for the purposes of this article, the term "crossover" has been selected to reflect this relatively new phenomenon of collateral estoppel.

2. Preliminary determinations which would not be traditionally considered as "on the merits" can also be afforded collateral estoppel *res judicata* effect. *See, Baldwin v. Iowa State Traveling Men's Association*, 283 U.S. 522, 51 S.Ct. 571 (1931).

3. Collateral estoppel can apply to preliminary issues as well as trial issues settled by a judgment on the merits. *See, Baldwin v. Iowa, supra* n. 2.

4. Due to the nature of collateral estoppel as a common law doctrine, each jurisdiction is free (subject to constitutional limitations) to develop its own rules of law in this area and, therefore, choice of law and "Erie" doctrine questions come into play. These questions I leave for treatment by wiser scholars than myself.

5. Collateral estoppel itself evolved from the doctrine of *res judicata*, and most of the core requirements for collateral estoppel derive from the requirements of that doctrine. No scholarly work on collateral estoppel could be complete without briefly describing the troubles in distinguishing between these two separate doctrines. *Res judicata*, sometimes known as claims preclusion, precludes identical claims between identical parties in a subsequent adjudication. Collateral estoppel precludes the use of issues that have been adjudicated rather than claims or causes of action, and in most jurisdictions collateral estoppel is not limited to use between identical parties. While the scholars seem finally to stand in agreement upon the use of the terms collateral estoppel and *res judicata* to represent the respective doctrines, the courts seem still to confuse and interchange these terms and, indeed, the doctrines themselves. For a complete treatment of the differences and similarities of the two doctrines, *see generally* Alan Vestal, *Res Judicata/Preclusion* (Matthew Bender, publishers, 1969).

6. *Blonder-Tongue Laboratories, Inc., v. University of Illinois Foundation*, 402 U.S. 313, 329 (1971); *Montana v. United States*, 440 U.S. 147, 153 (1979); *Allen v. McCurry*, 449 U.S. 90, 95 (1980).

7. *Emich Motors Corporation v. General Motors Corporation*, 340 U.S. 558, 568 (1951); *Tomlinson v. Lefkowitz*, 334 F. 2d, 262 (5th Cir. 1964); Vestal, *supra* n. 5, pp. v-190.

8. Vestal, *supra* n. 5, p. 233.

9. *Ibid.*, p. 235.

10. *Montana v. U.S.*, 440 U.S. at 153; *Blonder-Tongue*, 402 U.S. at 328.

11. *Triplett v. Lowell*, 297 U.S. 638, 644 (1936); *Bigelow v. Old Dominion Copper Company*, 225 U.S. 111, 127 (1912). *See also* James F. Flanagan, "Offensive Collateral Estoppel: Inefficiency and Foolish Inconsistency," *Arizona State Law Journal* 45 (1982).

12. *Teitelbaum v. Dominion Insurance Company*, 58 Cal. 2d, 601, 603, 561, 375 P.2d. 439, 441,

Annot. (1962); 18 *ALR* 2d, 1287, 1289; *Brooks v. Daley*, 242 MD 185, 218, A. 2d 184, 190 (1966).

13. Note, "Use of Record of Criminal Conviction in Subsequent Action Arising From the Same Facts as the Prosecution," 64 *Michigan Law Review* 702, 703 (1966).

14. McCormick on Evidence, Sec. 318, p. 739 (2d. ed. 1972).

15. *Id.*

16. John J. Keilbach, Comment, "Admissibility of a Criminal Conviction as Proof of its Facts in a Subsequent Civil Action," 10 *St. Louis Law Journal* 393, 402 (1966).

17. McCormick, *supra* n. 14, Sec. 318, p. 739; RJR, Note, "Admissibility and Weight of a Criminal Conviction in a Subsequent Civil action," 39 *Virginia Law Review* 995, 996 (1953); *Schindler v. Royal Insurance Company*, 258 NY 310, 179 NE 711 (1932); *Fidelity-Phoenix Fire Insurance Company v. Murphy*, 226 Ala. 226, 146 So. 387 (1933); *Eagle, Star and British Dominion Insurance Company v. Heller*, 149 Va. 82, 140 S.E. 314, 323 (1927).

18. *United States v. Greater New York Live Poultry Chamber of Commerce*, 53 F. 2d. 518 (S.D.N.Y., 1931) aff'd sub nom. *Local 167 v. United States*, 291 U.S. 293 (1934).

19. *Emich Motors*, *supra* n. 7 at 568; *Frank v. Mangum*, 237 U.S. 309 (1915).

20. Vestal, *supra* n. 5, pp. 368–390.

21. *Ibid.*, p. 366.

22. *Bernhard v. Bank of America*, 19 Cal. 2d. 807, 122 P. 2d. 892 (1942).

23. Jonathan C. Thau, "Collateral Estoppel and the Reliability of Criminal Determinations: Theoretical, Practical and Strategic Implications for Criminal and Civil Litigation," 70 *Geo. L. J.* 1085 (1982).

24. *Teitelbaum*, *supra* n. 12 at 603.

25. *Haring v. Prosise*, 1 U.S. (1983); *Allen v. McCurry*, 449 U.S. 90 (1980); *Wolfson v. Baker*, 623 F. 2d 1974 (5th Cir. 1980), cert. den. 450 U.S. 966 (1981); *Cardillo v. Zyla*, 486 F. 2d. 473 (1st Cir. 1973).

26. *Aetna Casualty and Surety Co. v. Dichtl*, 78 Ill. App. 3d 970, 398 NE 2d 582; *Harlow v. Dick*, 245 S.W. 2d 616 (Ky. App. 1952).

27. *Eagle, Star and British Dominion*, 149 Va. 82.; *Lipman Bros. v. Hartford Accident and Indemnity Co.*, 149 Me. 199, 207, 100 A. 2d 246, 251 (1953).

28. *Brohawn v. Transamerica Co.*, 276 Md. 396, 347 A. 2d 842 (1975); Thau, *supra* n. 23, p. 1079. See also "Preclusive Effect Extended to Guilty Pleas in Subsequent Civil Ligitation—*Ideal Mutual Insurance Co. v. Winkler*," 68 *Iowa L. Rev.* 1331 (1983).

29. Thau, *supra* n. 23, p. 1089.

30. *Teitelbaum*, *supra* n. 12 at 603.

31. Thau, *supra* n. 23, p. 1104.

32. *Id.*, p. 1109.

33. *Scott v. Robertson*, 581 P. 2d 188 (Ak., 1975).

34. *Id.*

35. The matter of *nolo* pleas is discussed, generally in Vestal, *supra* n. 5, p. 386, but not as a rationale for applying crossover to guilty pleas. In those states which refuse to allow the use of a guilty plea in a subsequent civil proceeding, it would seem that the existence of a *nolo contendere* plea is superfluous, other than for obvious social considerations. For a compilation of cases, see Annotation, "Conviction or Acquittal as Evidence," 18 *American Law Reporter* 2d 1287 (1955).

36. *State v. Coblentz*, 169 Md. 159, 180 A. 266, motion ovrrld., 169 Md. 159 (1931).

37. *Pat Perusse Realty v. Lingo*, 249 Md. 33, 43, 238 A. 2d 100 (1968).

38. *M.P.C. v. Kenny*, 279 Md. 29, 486 A. 2d 367 (1977).

39. *Gelblum v. Bloom*, 21 Md. App. 406, 319 A. 2d 546 (1974).

40. *Brohawn v. Transamerica Ins. Co.*, 276 Md. 396, 347 A. 2d 842 (1975).

41. Judson W. Calkins, "Pursuit of Criminal Matter to Expedite a Civil Matter," 38 *J. Mo. B.* 369 (July–August 1982).

42. Model Code of Professional Responsibility, DR 7-105, also EC 7-21 (1979).

43. Vestal, *supra* n. 5, p. 528.

44. Tentative Draft, Revised Maryland Rules of Procedure, Rule 2-323 F.

45. Md. R. 610, *supra* n. 44 r. 2-501. *See also* Vestal, *supra* no. 5.

46. Md. R. 552, or *supra* n. 44 R. 2-519.

47. Md. R. 563, *supra* n. 44 R. 2-532.

48. *Sur. and Casualty Co. v. Kuhl*, 296 Md. 446, 463 A. 2d 822 (1983).

49. Md. R. 322.

50. *Doug-Dun Corp. v. Simms*, 31 Md. App. 350, 357 A. 2d 392 (1976).

51. *Parklane Hosiery Co. v. Shore*, 439 U.S. 322 (1979).

52. Although the term is no longer used in Maryland, this is commonly known as a demurrer motion.

53. *Moore Drug Co. v. Schaneman*, 10 Ariz. App. 587, 461 P. 2d 95 (1969), *In Re Kravitz' Estate*, 418 P. 2d 319, 211 A. 2d 443 (1965).

54. *Moore Drug Co.* at 589.

,55. Amazingly, there is such a case. *See, Clemmer v. Hartford Ins. Co.*, 587 P. 2d 1098 (Wa. 1978).

56. *Carbaugh v. State*, 294 Md. 323, 449 A. 2d 1153 (1982).

57. *Id.*

58. Thau, *supra* n. 23, p. 1101; Vestal, *supra* n. 5, p. 391.

59. *Keebler v. Willard*, 91 Ga. App. 551, 86 S.E. 2d 379, 380 (1955).

60. *Parklane Hosiery Company, supra* n. 51.

61. Thau, *supra* n. 5, p. 1099.

62. An "Alford" plea is a guilty plea in which the defendant is allowed to plead guilty for the purpose of trial and punishment, but the defendant admits no guilt. *See, North Carolina v. Alford*, 400 U.S. 25 (1970).

12

THE A.P.A. INSANITY RULE–CASE STUDIES OF A METAPHYSICAL SUBTLETY

by Abraham L. Halpern

"Laws are made for men of ordinary understanding and should, therefore, be construed by the ordinary rules of common sense. Their meaning is not to be sought for in metaphysical subtleties, which may make anything mean everything or nothing at pleasure."

—Thomas Jefferson[1]

The acquittal of John W. Hinckley, Jr., by reason of insanity in June 1982, although it aroused a public outcry against the exculpatory insanity rule and provoked widespread criticism of the psychiatric profession, did not further the drive for abolition of the insanity defense. On the contrary, the Hinckley verdict served as a stimulus for organizations and individuals favoring retention of the defense to conjoin the concept to state and federal laws more firmly than ever before.

Prior to Hinckley's attempt to assassinate the President of the United States on March 30, 1981, the movement to abolish the insanity defense, although not notably successful, was advancing with deliberate speed. A bill,[2] providing for the total elimination of the insanity plea yet permitting psychiatric testimony on the issue of criminal intent (*mens rea*), was the result of extensive study by the staff of the attorney-general of Idaho.[3] The state of Montana had severely narrowed the insanity rule, virtually abolishing the plea.[4] Articles in popular magazines argued strongly for abolition.[5] Legislation had been introduced in New York State to repeal the insanity defense statute.[6] The New York State Department of Mental Hygiene had submitted a report to the Governor recommending abandonment of the insanity defense and its substitution with a comprehensive diminished capacity rule.[7] A "Great Debate" on the abolition of the insanity defense was a featured event at the Ninth Annual Meeting of the American Academy of Psychiatry and the Law in October 1978, and a "Scientific Debate" was scheduled for the 134th Annual Meeting of the American Psychiatric Association in May 1981. Finally, just before the assassination attempt, a bill[8] was introduced in the United States by Senator Orrin G. Hatch which would have severely limited the insanity defense by permitting exculpation of a mentally disordered defendant only if he lacked the state of mind required as an element of the offense charged. Like the Idaho law, in the unlikely event that a still dangerous mentally ill individual were acquitted, this legislation, since it did not provide for a federal post-acquittal confinement system, would have looked to state commitment statutes to hospitalize such a person. In other words, the Hatch bill would not have created "an insanity defense industry within the Federal Government,"[9] in contradistinction to all the post-Hinckley insanity bills introduced in the Congress, including the Insanity Defense Reform Act of 1984 signed into law by President Reagan on October 12, 1984.[10]

With the acquittal of John Hinckley, advocates of the insanity defense mounted a powerful, coordinated and highly publicized campaign[11] to preserve the defense in some form. A spate of articles[12] appeared in the professional literature in the ensuing two years, proclaiming the moral basis to the existence of the insanity defense over the centuries, even equating abolition of the insanity defense with holding a two-year-old child criminally responsible for its misconduct.[13] Several states avoided the issue of elimination of the insanity defense by enacting legislation[14] patterned after laws previously passed in Michigan,[15] Illinois[16] and Indiana,[17] adopting an additional verdict of "Guilty but mentally ill" while retaining the insanity defense, indeed requiring that the insanity plea be asserted before the "Guilty but mentally ill" plea could be considered. Opposition to abolition reached its zenith when the APA in a personal communication[18] to every member of Congress, attacked the *mens rea* approach, represented by the Hatch bill mentioned above, warning that such legislation could "result in less protection for the general public." The reasoning of the APA in this regard[19] is incomprehensible in view of the fact that conviction, not acquittal, is the almost inevitable outcome when the *mens rea* standard is used in cases of mentally disordered offenders charged with violent crime. It should be noted, moreover, that the *mens rea* approach, found by legal scholars[20] to be rooted in sound legal principles, has been endorsed by the American Medical Association[21] and, in a recent case decided by the Supreme Court of Montana,[22] declared to be in accord with constitutional requirements.

CHANGING THE INSANITY RULE: A DISTINCTION WITHOUT A DIFFERENCE

Prior to promulgation of the "American Psychiatric Association Statement on the Insanity Defense" in December 1982,[23] I had demonstrated in several articles that nothing short of abolition of the insanity defense could permit a rational approach to the handling of mentally disordered offenders who come to trial. I pointed out that regardless of the legal standard to be followed, actual practice proved that the most liberal rule could be contracted (resulting in conviction) and the narrowest rule expanded (resulting in acquittal) depending on the whim or conscience of the factfinder. The use of the insanity defense in many jurisdictions over the years, no matter what the language of the insanity test might be, substantiates my view that no insanity rule is amenable to construction by the ordinary rules of common sense. At a hearing before the Committee on the Judiciary of the United States Senate on August 2, 1982, I testified[25] that there is no place to go in the quest for a new insanity formulation, no matter how narrow; that every insanity definition is irrelevant and essentially meaningless; and that abolition of the insanity defense is the only rational path. I now assert even more strongly that the exculpatory insanity concept is inapplicable to a rational administration of criminal justice. To illustrate the validity of my position I will offer examples of how the insanity rule is employed by psychiatrists and psychologists presenting expert testimony on behalf of criminal defendants pleading insanity. First, however, let me stress that the most ardent proponents of the insanity defense will acknowledge that the wording of the test is irrelevant. Let us examine, for example, the statements of several representatives of the American Psychiatric Association who testified at a hearing before the Subcommittee on Criminal Law on June 30, 1982 a few weeks before I addressed the Senate Judiciary Committee.

Dr. Loren H. Roth, Chairperson of the APA Commission on Judicial Action, a member of the APA Insanity Defense Work Group and principal author of the APA Statement on the Insanity Defense, told the Subcommittee: "Senator Specter, there is no difference between the various legal standards. Now, most legal scholars believe—for example, Mr. Goldstein was opposed to the ALI formulation, believing that all testimony which can be introduced under ALI can also be introduced under M'Naghten, and that as a practical

201

matter it does not matter. I think that this is the experience of most forensic psychiatrists."[26]

Dr. Seymour Halleck, one of America's most distinguished forensic psychiatrists and 1983 winner of the APA's Isaac Ray Award explained, "The jury will probably come to similar conclusions, whatever the standard is."[27] Dr. Roth agreed, saying, "I think one standard in practice in the great majority of cases will translate into the other standard."[28]

Dr. Allan Beigel, Chairperson of the APA Joint Commission on Government Relations, and a member of the Insanity Defense Work Group, maintained: "I think it is my personal opinion that changing the standard will not change either the extent or limits of our expertise."[29]

For his part, Dr. Roth noted, "I believe that the idea to infinitely refine the standard, while satisfying to us as rational types who want neat categories, does not necessarily come to the final solution."[30]

At the Subcommittee hearing, Dr. Alan A. Stone (Chairperson of the APA Council on Governmental Policy and Law, and ex-officio member of the Insanity Defense Work Group) proposed an insanity standard that would abolish the insanity defense if fact-finders were to follow it literally:

> I make this not as my perfect solution: I just bring it to you as a consideration. One could simply alter the ALI by changing two words. "A person is not responsible for criminal conduct if at the time of such conduct, as a result of 'severe'—I have added 'severe'—mental disease or defect, he lacks entirely the capacity either to appreciate," et cetera.
>
> So, all I have done is put in "severe" and say "lacks entirely." Now, it seems to me that comes close to what you have been reaching for, Senator, although I think you want to move in the direction of totally different language. I think what I have done captures the sentiments you have been expressing, if not the exact words.[31]

The futility of changing the wording of the insanity rule was made clear in the following verbal exchange at the Subcomittee hearing:

> Sen. Arlen Specter: "Well the issue that we have to decide is not what the jury is going to find, but what the judge is going to say the law is. Would it be adequate, in your judgment, if the judge said 'If you find that the mother knew she was killing her child and intended to kill her child, then you may convict; if on the other hand, you find that the mother thought she was killing the devil, then you may acquit by reason of insanity?' "

202

Dr. Halleck: "My guess is that what would happen is what happened before the American Law Institute ruling became more prevalent, and that is that people played games with the word 'know' intellectually or 'know' emotionally, and good attorneys and good psychiatrists were able to convince juries that she did not really know that she was killing the child."[32]

Notwithstanding the above, the Insanity Defense Work Group recommended, and the American Psychiatric Association adopted, the following standard in the belief that it permits "relevant psychiatric testimony to be brought to bear in the great majority of cases where criminal responsibility is at issue":

A person charged with a criminal offense should be found not guilty by reason of insanity if it is shown that as a result of mental disease or mental retardation he was unable to appreciate the wrongfulness of his conduct at the time of the offense. As used in this standard, the terms mental disease or mental retardation include only those severely abnormal mental conditions that grossly and demonstrably impair a person's perception or understanding of reality and that are not attributable primarily to the voluntary ingestion of alcohol or other psychoactive substances.[33]

The insanity standard employed in the Hinckley trial was the American Law Institute formulation which includes the so-called volitional rule: "A person is not responsible for criminal conduct if at the time of such conduct as a result of mental disease or defect he lacks substantial capacity to appreciate the wrongfulness of his conduct, or to *conform his conduct* to the requirements of law."[34] The APA formulation purports to eliminate this prong, but, as the Statement itself indicates:

In practice there is considerable overlap between a psychotic person's defective understanding or appreciation and his ability to control his behavior. Most psychotic persons who fail a volitional test for insanity will also fail a cognitive-type test when such a test is applied to their behavior, thus rendering the volitional test superfluous in judging them.[35]

Thus, the claimed narrowing of the insanity rule is without substance. The APA standard, presumably designed to make it extremely difficult for defendants such as Hinckley to escape a guilty verdict, would in no way have altered the testimony nor the result had that standard been applied at this trial. The same Washington psychiatrist would have testified that Hinckley had a serious mental illness (schizotypal personality disorder with psychosis) that drove him to shoot the President and deprived him of the ability to obey the law or to appreciate the wrongfulness of his conduct.[36] The same Harvard Medical School radiologist would have said that brain scans show Hinckley's brain is slightly shrunken and has "more folds and ventricles [sic] than is usual in people his age," and that this suggests organic brain disease.[37] The same Yale Medical School psychologist would have pointed out that Hinckley knew "in his head" that he was doing wrong when he shot President Reagan but was "too insane to appreciate this emotionally," and would have testified that standard psychological tests had shown that Hinckley was plagued by extreme, longstanding depression that was part of a serious mental illness; according to the psychologist, in addition to major depressive disorder, he had borderline schizophrenia and paranoid personality disorder.[38] The same University of Maryland professor of psychiatry would have told the jury that Hinckley suffered from process schizophrenia at least since 1976, an illness that becomes increasingly severe with age, and involved, in this case, gradual withdrawal from social contacts into an inner world dominated by delusions that had no basis in fact, eccentric or bizarre thoughts, and irrational impulses to commit violent acts.[39]

THE PSYCHIATRIC WITNESS TESTIFIES

The psychiatrist testifying on behalf of a patient-defendant charged with serious crime will invariably see his mental disorder as "severe," rendering the defendant not responsible, from a psychiatric standpoint, for his conduct. The words "know," "appreciate," "as a result of," and "at the time of" are no bar to the defense psychiatrist's seeking to explain the defendant's entitlement to exculpation. Every insanity trial, before and after Hinckley, shows this to be true. Nor will legislative changes[40] designed to prohibit an expert witness from testifying "as to whether the defendant did or did not have the mental state or condition constituting an element of the crime charged or of a defense thereto," as urged by the APA,[41] the National Mental Health Association,[42] and the American Bar Association,[43] significantly interfere with psychiatrists and psychologists presenting their testimony in their customary fashion. As stated by the New York Times,[44] "In the last 30 years, doctors and lawyers have given juries their views about the entire personality and won't easily return to a legal straitjacket."

A striking example of testimony offered by a psychiatrist with genuine concern for his seriously mentally ill patient–defendant is that of Dr. Robert L. Custer, a member of the DSM-III Advisory Committee on Impulse Control Disorders and this country's most highly recognized expert in the treatment of pathological gambling. The following colloquy took place in a jury trial in which the defendant asserted an insanity plea under the M'Naghten rule:

> Q. Doctor, is he by virtue of the condition under which he labors at the time that he drew the specific checks before you incapable or capable of distinguishing right from wrong as regard that check?
>
> A. Well, here's a man who was a law enforcement officer, who knows the law well, who knows about right and wrong but a man who is in a desperate strait. He is under tremendous amount of stress at that point, does not even consider right and wrong. I don't think that becomes part of his thinking process. His process then is to survive. He's losing his job, his family, his children, his reputation, everything is going down. So he functions this way, in an irrational way to which his judgment is that impaired.
>
> Q. You say, Doctor, that he does not consider right from wrong. Can he consider the distinction between right and wrong at that juncture?
>
> A. I think he's on automatic at that point. I don't think thinking becomes a process. This man is acting only on impulse. His impulse control is totally gone. He functions. He reacts. He does not use the thinking process to enter into it so a value judgment is not placed at that point.
>
> Q. Is he capable of making a value judgment at this point?
>
> A. No.
>
> Q. Doctor, does Michael accord with the classic pattern of compulsive gambling as has been defined by the Board of American Psychiatric Association in this regard?
>
> A. Yes, he does. He meets all the criteria.[45]

In another case, in a jurisdiction adhering to the American Law Institute rule, Dr. Custer testified as follows:

> Q. Dr. Custer, in your opinion, is pathological gambling a mental disease or defect?
>
> A. Yes, I certainly feel that it is.
>
> Q. Which of those is it?
>
> A. I beg your pardon?
>
> Q. Which of those is pathological gambling? Would you call it a mental disease or a defect?
>
> A. I would call it a disease. I don't feel it is a defect, which I consider more something within the central nervous system that isn't present or has been damaged.

Q. Do you believe that a person who is a pathological gambler can be rendered incapable of substantially conforming their conduct to the requirements of law?

A. Since they cannot conform their conduct to standards of law.

Q. At least in some cases?

A. In the vast majority of them.

Q. Okay.

A. It depends upon the stage at which they are in. If it is in the early stage, I think they still can. Certainly in the late stage, they have lost that control.

Q. All right. Do you think that persons who are pathological gamblers and incapable of conforming their conduct are equally incapable of resisting activity like embezzlement or fraud?

A. No, I don't feel they can resist it because they have to gamble and they have to obtain money in order to do that.

Q. Dr. Custer, in the DSM-III, the term mental disorder is used. Do you agree with the statement that mental disorder, as used in DSM-III, is the legal equivalent of mental disease or defect?

A. Yes, I feel it is equivalent to disease, not to defect.

Q. You have stated your opinion that some pathological gamblers are incapable of conforming their conduct substantially to the requirements of law, is that correct?

A. That's correct.

Q. Has that always been your opinion?

A. No, it wasn't my opinion when I first started treating them about ten years ago. I certainly didn't know what it was at that point, and I had never given it that much consideration, but it was only after I had probably treated about 25 of them that I realized that I was dealing with people that actually began to think in a delusional way. Then I realized that they weren't able to control it, but it takes a while to understand this problem.[46]

BATTLE OF THE "EXPERTS": Case Studies

In my view, the logical inconsistencies and the distortions that are part and parcel of every insanity rule, and the damage to the psychiatric profession, are best exemplified not by the ordinary "Not guilty by reason of insanity" case, but by the 90 percent of insanity trials that result in a guilty verdict, by the rare case of feigned insanity and by the increasingly common "split verdict" case.

The following cases in which the insanity plea was unsuccessful are representative of what appears from time to time in newspapers throughout the country, papers not given to sensationalistic reporting. The expert witnesses involved are in the private practice of psychiatry, some of them on medical school faculties, and are generally held in high regard in the psychiatric community.

206

Case #1. "Man convicted in headless bartender murder":

Charles Dingle, age 25, was convicted of second-degree murder, first-degree rape, second-degree kidnapping and first-degree robbery. He had been accused of shooting a bartender, raping a topless dancer and forcing a woman to cut the bartender's head off. After a month-long, non-jury trial, the judge took about 20 minutes to deliberate before rendering the verdict. Defense attorneys had presented psychiatric testimony that Dingle didn't know what he was doing when he shot Anthony Cummings, a bar owner who had asked him to leave Herbie's Bar on Jamaica Avenue in Queens. After shooting Cummings, he handcuffed the bartender's wife, Paula, bound a barmaid and raped a topless dancer. Later, when the bar manager arrived for work, he learned that she was a licensed mortician and ordered her to remove the bullet from Cummings' head. When that failed, he ordered her to remove the head, which she did with a kitchen knife and two steak knives. Dingle later released the barmaid and dancer, called a cab and tied up the driver. He then drove into Manhattan with Mrs. Cummings, the bar manager and a box containing the bartender's head. The two women sought help after Dingle fell asleep and he was arrested a short time later inside the cab.[47]

Case #2. "Suspect in Texas now says he killed 360 people nationwide":

Henry Lee Lucas was on trial for the rape and murder of an unidentified young hitchhiker whose body was found near Georgetown in Central Texas. He had pleaded guilty of one Texas slaying and was convicted of another. His lawyers insist he is not guilty by reason of insanity and also contend he was at work in Jacksonville, Florida, when the Georgetown murder occurred. With the jurors out of the courtroom, the prosecutors played a video-taped interview showing Lucas puffing on a cigarette, calmly relating that he had shot, stabbed, burned, beaten, strangled, hung and "crucified" his victims, and that some had been "fileted like fish." Mr. Lucas said he had killed 360 people in the United States, more than 60 of them in Texas.[48]

Case #3. "Jury rejects 'fumes' defense":

A Massachusetts jury rendered a guilty verdict in a first-degree murder trial of a gardener who claimed he was driven insane by lawn chemicals. The defendant maintained that exposure to organophosphate pesticides had clouded his ability to tell right from wrong. He did not deny that he had become angry and choked the woman when she discovered him urinating in her yard. His insanity claim was supported by a psychiatrist's testimony, but a physician testifying for the prosecutor introduced blood tests that showed no evidence of chemical intoxication.[49]

Case #4. "Ohio physician's lawyer concedes 22 rapes":

Dr. Edward F. Jackson Jr. pleaded not guilty and not guilty by reason of insanity to 96 charges, including forced sex with 22 women, one of them a nun, and 38 other felonious acts. "We acknowledge to you that Dr. Jackson committed the acts for which he has been charged," the defense lawyer, John Bowen, told prospective jurors. "Very frankly, I would describe him as a Dr.

Jekyll–Mr. Hyde. I contend he is a sick man." Dr. Jackson's indictment the previous summer freed another man, a look-alike with the same last name, William Bernard Jackson, who has served five years in Ohio prisons for rapes now ascribed to the doctor.[50]

Case #5. "Ex-resident appealing kidnapping charges":

Christine Gladstone was convicted by a county jury of second-degree kidnapping, first-degree criminal use of a firearm, and third-degree criminal possession of a deadly weapon. The defense attorney is basing an appeal, in part, on the fact that the prosecution failed to counter testimony by two psychiatrists who said that the defendant was not responsible for her actions. Dr. X, a Syracuse psychiatrist, called to the witness stand by the defense, testified that Mrs. Gladstone suffered from an "atypical psychosis." He said the mental disorder would affect her capacity to understand and appreciate the nature and consequences of her actions. The prosecutor considered the testimony by the defense psychiatrists to be so absurd and outrageous that he did not bother to waste the taxpayer's money in employing his own experts, relying instead on cross-examination to controvert the defense psychiatrist's testimony. In his summation, he commented as follows: "I think the only thing they have proved is that witchcraft is alive and well in the 20th century." He asked the jury at one point, referring to the psychiatrist's testimony: "Does anybody believe this slop? You'd do a hell of a lot better to bring in some tribal warrior and have him rip open and read the entrails of a sheep."[51]

Case #6. "Killer who cited Vietnam Trauma Convicted":

A Vietnam veteran who contended that delayed stress from his war experiences had caused him to strangle and stab his fiancée to death was convicted of first-degree murder by a New Hampshire jury. The jury heard three weeks of testimony which included defense experts who said post-traumatic stress disorder had caused the murder and a prosecution expert who said the disorder was not involved in the killing. The prosecution argued that while the defendant was troubled, he knew what he was doing when he strangled the woman by hand, then used an extension cord, and later stabbed her seven times in the heart. Defense witnesses said the smell of rice from a nearby Chinese restaurant might have reminded the defendant of being at Khe Sanh in Vietnam. Another veteran of the battle testified that the smell of rice cooking wafted into the camp just before enemy attacks. "He was so brittle and so fragile that all he needed was the stimulus of the environment, the smells," said Dr. Y, one of the defense experts. "I believe that if it was not for the post-traumatic stress disorder, this would not have happened."[52]

FAKED INSANITY: A Case Study

On occasion (all too frequently) publicity is given to a case of faked insanity, invariably making a laughingstock of both the legal system and the psychiatric profession. Here is an example:

208

Case #7. "Insanity plea upheld although illness was faked":

A New York State appeals court ruled that a man who escaped prosecution for 16 Brooklyn robberies by faking a mental disorder can keep the rewards of his fiction because prosecutors failed to detect it until after they consented to his insanity plea. Samuel Lockett had contended that he was not criminally responsible due to his inability to appreciate the wrongfulness of his acts because of a post-traumatic stress disorder resulting from his experiences in Vietnam as a member of the United States Air Force. Based on extensive psychiatric reports which showed that he was in fact suffering from a post-traumatic stress disorder due to his service in Vietnam (at least six different psychiatrists examined him), he was adjudicated not guilty by reason of mental disease or defect. Subsequently, his military records were obtained; they showed that he had been an accounting clerk at an Air Force base in Texas during the entire time he was supposedly in combat in Indochina from 1972 to 1974. The appellate court ruled that although acceptance of Lockett's plea of "Not responsible by reason of mental disease or defect" may have been based on erroneous information given to the psychiatrists by Lockett himself, no legal authorization exists to vacate the plea and Lockett's subsequent commitment to a secure psychiatric facility. The state's highest court, however, eventually overturned the lower appeals court ruling and ordered a new trial on the grounds that he had never been subjected to the risk of conviction. "An accused must first suffer jeopardy before he can suffer double jeopardy."[53]

SPLIT VERDICT: Case Studies

Legally elegant but fundamentally hypocritical, the "split verdict" concept pertains to cases in which the defendant is found guilty of a crime and not guilty by reason of insanity of another crime, the crimes having been committed during the same period of time. The defendant receives the worst of all alternatives, for now he is pronounced both *insane and a criminal.*[54] In such cases (multiple-offense cases), the prosecution attempts to show that some of the crimes are not the result of mental disease or defect, at the same time allowing the insanity issue to stand for other crimes. The defendant, after he is released from a hospital for the criminally insane, is sent to prison to serve the sentence for the crime of which he was found guilty.

Case #8. "Convicted killer of 4 faces death penalty."

The trial of Steven J. Wood in West Hartford, Connecticut, lasted over 14 weeks, after 20 weeks was spent in selecting a jury. The judge instructed the jury that the crux of its deliberations had to be determining the defendant's mental state on the day of the murders. The defendant had handcuffed and then shot his former wife and her male companion, before traveling to her home and killing her daughter and mother. After 54 hours of deliberations, the six men and six women on the jury decided that the defendant was not guilty by reason of insanity for killing his former wife and guilty of murder in each of the other three deaths.[55]

Case #9. The Court of Special Appeals of Maryland affirmed the split verdict in the case of Joy Ann Robey who was charged with homicide in the death of her baby. The Court reasoned as follows: The psychiatrists for the prosecution diagnosed reactive depression and found the defendant to be responsible for the beatings, but the defense psychiatrist found that the defendant also suffered from an atypical impulse disorder and a dependent personality disorder. As a result of these disorders, the baby's cries triggered an intermittent explosive disorder, during which the defendant would lose control and beat the child until its cries subsided. Immediately after each beating episode, the defendant would regain her self-control and feel remorse. Consequently, she could not be held responsible for beating the baby and was acquitted of murder by reason of insanity, but could be held responsible for failing to seek medical care for the battered child after regaining self-control and was found guilty of involuntary manslaughter and child abuse. She was sentenced to a ten-year term in the custody of the Division of Correction.[56]

NEW FEDERAL INSANITY RULE

The Comprehensive Crime Control Act of 1984 containing the new insanity defense legislation was the result, in part, of an intense lobbying effort[57] by staff members of the APA's Division of Government Relations and by the Chairperson of the APA Commission on Judicial Action. The insanity standard adopted by Congress, the first such statute to be enacted for all federal jurisdictions, is patterned closely after the formulation recommended in the APA Statement on the Insanity Defense, and passage of the legislation was hailed by the APA as a "victory."[58] The new rule, replacing the more "liberal" American Law Institute standard, which in one form or another had been adopted over the years by the federal circuit courts, reads as follows:

> It is an affirmative defense to a prosecution under any Federal statute that, at the time of the commission of the acts constituting the offense, the defendant, as a result of a severe mental disease or defect, was unable to appreciate the nature and quality or the wrongfulness of his acts. Mental disease or defect does not otherwise constitute a defense.[59]

My argument (that the various definitions of legal insanity are distinctions without a difference) necessarily compels the conclusion

210

that there will be no reduction in the number of cases in which the insanity plea is asserted. Already, under new rule, we are seeing felony trials of defendants whose "severe" mental condition is presented as justification for acquittal by reason of insanity.

"Case #10. "Clinic bomb trial told of disorders":

A defense psychiatrist testified in Federal district court in Pensacola, Florida, that three of four young defendants on trial in the bombings of three abortion clinics suffer "severe" mental disorder. The psychiatrist said that James T. Simmons, age 21; his wife, Kathren, 18; and Matthew J. Goldsby, 21, were "borderline personalities" capable of slipping into psychotic behavior. According to the psychiatrist, a fourth defendant, Kaye Wiggins, 18, suffered periodic depression but was less troubled than the others. The defense made no effort to deny that Mr. Goldsby and Mr. Simmons plotted and carried out the bombings for the stated purpose of ending what was depicted as "the murders of unborn children." Nor did they deny that Mrs. Simmons and Miss Wiggins had been enlisted to buy explosive powder for the bombs at local gun shops. The defense attempted to portray the defendants as deeply religious individuals torn by a conflicting view in American society of the human fetus as a living human being, on the one hand, and as "tissue in a minor medical procedure," on the other. At one point in the cross-examination of a prosecution witness, one of the defense attorneys described God as an "unindicted coconspirator" in the case. Psychiatrists were called to rebut the defense's psychiatric testimony concerning the symptoms of "severe" mental disorder. The two men were convicted on all counts and the women were found guilty of conspiracy.[60]

The Insanity Defense Reform Act of 1984 contains detailed provisions relating to post-acquittal confinement and release.[61] While analysis of these provisions is beyond the scope of this discussion, I must point out that establishing, for the first time in the federal justice system, formal procedures for confining persons acquitted of violent acts by reason of insanity, and that placing on such acquittees the burden of proving by clear and convincing evidence that their release "would not create a substantial risk of bodily injury to another person or serious damage of property of another due to a present mental disease or defect," lead me to predict that there will be a considerable increase in acquittals by reason of insanity in the federal courts. This is particularly bound to occur in light of the fact that the vast majority of successful insanity cases are decided without a jury; indeed, resolved by acceptance of an insanity plea without a trial.

CONCLUSION

In this chapter I have attempted to show how the insanity defense militates against rationality in the handling of mentally disordered lawbreakers. I have elsewhere[62] argued that the use of the insanity plea, rather than uplifting the law's moral character, makes a mockery of the criminal justice system; that its practical application is hurtful to the population it is intended to benefit; that it undermines the processes of the law; that it tarnishes the public sense of justice; and that it results in the involuntary hospitalization (in overcrowded and chronically understaffed institutions for the criminally insane) of substantial numbers of individuals who are not mentally ill and may not have been mentally ill in the first place. Moreover, as a matter of particular concern to the psychiatric profession, the insanity defense in every phase of its administration fosters the extensive and systematic abuse of psychiatry. It is my view that if it were not possible to misuse psychiatry in the period of post-acquittal confinement, the insanity defense would be statutorily abolished in every jurisdiction in this country.

Let me now outline briefly my alternative to the exculpatory insanity rule. I would include in statutes abolishing the special defense of insanity, a provision for acquittal when the defendant as a result of mental illness lacked the state of mind required as an element of the offense charged. The following features would be added:

- The presentation of psychiatric and psychological testimony in the courtroom when appropriate;

- Comprehensive pre-sentence evaluation (including psychiatric evaluation where indicated) of *all* persons convicted of serious crime (This is already the law in a number of jurisdictions);

- Application of regular civil commitment laws in those few cases of acquittal where the defendant is so severely mentally ill as not to satisfy the mental state required for conviction (yet still adjudged mentally competent to stand trial), such a person having had his own expert witnesses present convincing evidence of his serious mental illness and thus in all likelihood having demonstrated his need for mental hospitalization; and

- Disposition of the case decided by the sentencing authority on the basis of the community's need for protection and retribution carefully balanced against the convicted person's need for treatment and rehabilitation. (Thus, a non-dangerous mentally ill convicted felon might be placed on probation and required to receive in-

212

hospital treatment if found suitable for such treatment by hospital personnel; while a dangerous personality-disordered individual, who may not appreciate wrongfulness as a result of his severe mental disorder, yet whose condition is not suitable for hospital treatment, or who might indeed not be treatable, would be sentenced to a correctional facility.)

In conclusion, the exculpatory insanity rule, however it is worded, is a metaphysical subtlety, a spurious attempt to soften the harshness of the criminal law. There are more humane, more ethical, and more effective alternatives. The insanity defense, in the words used 27 years ago by APA President Harry Solomon[63] in describing the large state hospitals, is antiquated, outmoded and obsolete.

REFERENCES

The A.P.A. Insanity Rule: Case Studies of a Metaphysical Subtlety by Abraham L. Halpern

1. T. Jefferson, Letter to William Johnson, June 12, 1823. Cited in 2 *J. Leg. Med.* 10 (1974).
2. Idaho Senate Bill No. 1396, signed by Governor John B. Evans on April 2, 1982.
3. Landmark legislation eliminates "insanity defense" in Idaho. *Newsletter Am. Legisl. Exch. Council,* 8/5: 1, 1982.
4. 1979 Mont. Laws ch. 713.
5. *See,* for example, R. Gambino, "The murderous mind: insanity vs. the law," *Saturday Review,* March 18, 1978, pp. 10–13.
6. Senate Bill No. 9345 and Senate Bill No. 4910 introduced on April 13, 1978 and April 2, 1979, respectively.
7. *The Insanity Defense in New York—A Report to Governor Hugh L. Carey,* New York State Department of Mental Hygiene, February 11, 1978.
8. Senate Bill S. 818, dated March 26, 1981.
9. W.A. Carnahan, Hearings Before the Committee on the Judiciary, United States Senate, July 19 and 28, August 2 and 4, 1982. Serial No. J-97-126 (Washington, D.C.: Government Printing Office, 1982), p. 422.
10. P.L. 98-473.
11. "Psychiatric Group urges stiffer rules for insanity plea," New York *Times,* January 20, 1983, p. 18a; "Changes endorsed on insanity pleas," New York *Times,* February 10, 1983, p. 18a; "APA release statement calling for reform of insanity defense," *Clin. Psychiat. News,* February 1983, p. 1; and "APA calls for tightening of insanity defense criteria," *Psychiat. News,* February 4, 1983, p. 1.
12. J. Robitscher and A.K. Haynes, "In defense of the insanity defense," 31 *Emory Law J.* 9–60 (1982); R. Bonnie, "The moral basis of the insanity defense," 69 *Am. Bar Assoc. J.* 194–197 (1983); D.H.J. Hermann, "Assault on the insanity defense: limitations on the effectiveness and effect of the defense of insanity," 14 *Rutgers Law J.* 241–371 (1983); and R. Slovenko, "The meaning of mental illness in criminal responsibility," 5 *J. Leg. Med.* 1–61 (1984).
13. E. Prelinger, "Dilemmas of the expert witness: reflections on the insanity defense," 13 *Psychiat. Annals* 237–241 (1983).
14. 1982 Alaska Sess. Laws ch. 143; 1982 Ga. Laws 143, 1982 Ky. Rev. Stat. & R. Serv. ch. 113 (Baldwin); N.M. Stat. Ann. §§ 31-9-3, 31-9-4 (1982); and Del. House Bill No. 567 (1982).
15. Mich. Comp. Laws Ann. § 768.36 (West 1982).
16. 1981 Ill. Legis. Serv. 82-553 (West).

17. Ind. Code Ann. §§ 35-5-2-3, 35-5-2-6 (Burns Supp. 1980).

18. *Psychiat. News*, August 17, 1984, p. 5.

19. J.J. McGrath, "Analysis of the AMA-APA insanity defense," presented to the American Medical Association, December 6, 1983. *See also*, L.H. Roth, "Tighten but do not discard," 251 JAMA 2949-2950 (1984).

20. J. Goldstein and J. Katz, "Abolish the insanity defense—why not? 72 *Yale Law J.* 853-876 (1963); N. Morris, "Psychiatry and the dangerous criminal," 41 *S. Cal. Law R.* 514-547 (1968); N. Morris and G. Hawkins, *The Honest Politician's Guide to Crime Control* (Chicago: University of Chicago Press, 1969); and A. Brooks, "The merits of abolishing the insanity defense," 477 *Annals Amer. Acad. Pol. and Soc. Science* 125-136 (1985).

21. "Insanity defense in criminal trials and limitations of psychiatric testimony: Report of the AMA board of trustees," 251 JAMA 2967-2981 (1984).

22. *State v. Korell* 690 P. 2d 992 (Mont. 1984).

23. Insanity Defense Work Group: American Psychiatric Association statement on the insanity defense, 140 *Am. J. Psychiat.* 681-688 (1983).

24. A.L. Halpern, "The insanity defense: a juridical anachronism," 7 *Psychiat. Annals* 398-409 (1977); A.L. Halpern, "The fiction of legal insanity and the misuse of psychiatry," 2 *J. Leg. Med.* 18-74 (1980); A.L. Halpern, "Uncloseting the Conscience of the jury: a justly acquitted doctrine," 52 *Psychiat. Quart.* 144-157 (1980); and A.L. Halpern and R.B. Sussman, "The psychotic mother charged with infanticide: new dispositional developments," 80 *N.Y. State J. Med.* 1553-1556 (1980).

25. A.L. Halpern in Hearings Before the Committee on the Judiciary, *supra* n. 9, p. 286.

26. Hearings before the Subcommittee on Criminal Law of the Committee on the Judiciary, U.S. Senate, June 24, 30 and July 14, 1982. Serial No. J-97-122 (Washington, D.C.: Government Printing Office, 1983), p. 260. [Editor's note: Senator Edward Zorinsky (D-NE) explains the M'Naghten rule this way: "In an attempt to assassinate the Prime Minister, M'Naghten mistakenly killed the Minister's secretary. M'Naghten was found not guilty by reason of insanity when the defense showed that he was under the delusion he was being persecuted by the Prime Minister. The public reaction to this verdict was similar to that of the Hinckley verdict in this country, and there was a cry for reform. As a result of this review, the standard articulated in M'Naghten's acquittal was declared void by fourteen of the fifteen common law judges and the old right-wrong test was re-instituted: and as Judge Irving Kaufman pointed out, it was ironically known as the M'Naghten Rule." *See*, Edward Zorinsky, "The Insanity Defense: Recommendations for Reform," in McGuigan and Rader, eds., *Criminal Justice Reform: A Blueprint* (Washington, D.C.: Free Congress Foundation, 1983). *See also*, *M'Naghten's Case*, 8 Eng. Rep. 718 (1843).]

27. *Ibid.*, p. 270.

28. *Ibid.*, P. 275.

29. *Ibid.*, p. 277.

30. *Ibid.*, p. 261.

31. *Ibid.*, p. 255.

32. *Ibid.*, p. 271.

33. *Supra* n. 23, p. 685.

34. Model Penal Code § 4.01 (1), Proposed Official Draft, (Philadelphia, Pennsylvania: American Law Institute, 1962). (Emphasis added.)

35. *Supra* n. 23, p. 685.

36. "Witness says Hinckley trailed actress with gun," New York *Times*, May 26, 1982, p. 19a.

37. "Witness talks of Hinckley's brain scans," Elmira (NY) *Star-Gazette*, June 2, 1982, p. 5a.

38. "Psychologist sees split in Hinckley mind and emotions in shootings," New York *Times*, May 22, 1982, p. 16.

39. "Hinckley witness pressed on stand," New York *Times*, May 18, 1982, p. 16a.

40. *See*, for example, *Federal Rules of Evidence*, Rule 704 (amended October 12, 1984).

41. *Supra* n. 19 (Roth) and n. 23.

42. *Myths & Realities: A Report of the National Commission on the Insanity Defense* (Arlington, Virginia: National Mental Health Association, 1983).

43. ABA Standing Committee on Association Standards for Criminal Justice, *First Tentative Draft, Criminal Justice Mental Health Standards* (Washington D.C.: American Bar Association, 1983), Standard 7-6.6.

44. "Double reverse," New York *Times*, June 4, 1985 (editorial), p. 28a.

45. *State of New Jersey v. Michael Campanaro*, Superior Court of New Jersey, Criminal Division. Union County Indictment Nos. 632–79; 1309–79, 1317–79, 514–80, 707–80; May 5, 1981, transcript, pp. 19–20.

46. *U.S. v. Gary Lewellyn*, U.S. District Court, Southern District of Iowa, Central Division, Cr. No. 82–43, August 16, 1982, transcript, pp. 199–200.

47. Mamaroneck (NY) *Daily Times*, March 27, 1984, p. 9a.

48. New York *Times*, April 12, 1984, p. 19a.

49. *American Medical News*, February 24, 1984, p. 41.

50. New York *Times*, August 23, 1983, p. 12a.

51. Mamaroneck (NY) *Daily Times*, April 27, 1984, p. 1a.

52. New York *Times*, May 24, 1984, p. 14a.

53. New York *Times*, June 24, 1984, p. 28; *In the Matter of Samuel Lockett, petitioner v. Michael R. Juviler et al., Respondents*, 102 App. Div. 2d 869 (1984). *See also*, "New trial ordered for a man feigning Vietnam syndrome," New York *Times*, June 7, 1985, p. 2b.

54. C.R. Jeffery, *Criminal Responsibility and Mental Disease* (Springfield, Illinois: Charles C. Thomas, 1967), p. 89.

55. Mamaroneck (NY) *Daily Times*, June 29, 1984, p. 7a.

56. *Robey v. State* 456 A.2d 953 (Md. App. 1983).

57. *Psychiat. News*, May 18, 1984, p. 4; and *Clin. Psychiat. News*, November 1984, p. 3.

58. *Psychiat. News*, November 16, 1984, p. 1.

59. United States Code, Title 18, Chap. 1, § 20.

60. New York *Times*, April 21, 1985, p. 32; and *American Medical News*, May 20, 1985, p. 27.

61. United States Code, Title 18, Chap. 313, § 4243.

62. A.L. Halpern, "Reconsideration of the insanity defense and related issues in the aftermath of the Hinckley trial," 54 *Psychiat. Quart.* 260–264 (1982); A.L. Halpern, "Elimination of the exculpatory insanity rule: a modern societal need," 6 *Psychiat. Clinics of N. Am.* 611–627 (1983); A.L. Halpern, "Paltering with the insanity defense: the drive to narrow the rule and to expand the legal abuse of psychiatry," Report to the Assembly of the American Psychiatric Association, February 5, 1984; A.L. Halpern, "Further comments on the insanity defense in the aftermath of the Hinckley trial," 56 *Psychiat. Quart.* 62–69 (1984); A.L. Halpern, "Toward rationality in the handling of the violent mentally disordered offender," 52 *Westchester Medical Bulletin* 11–12 (1984); and A.L. Halpern, "The AMA report on the insanity defense in criminal trials," 56 *Psychiat. Quart.* 236–238 (1984).

63. H. Solomon, "The American Psychiatric Association in relation to American psychiatry," *Am. J. Psychiat.* 115/7: 1–9 (1958).

13

ENACTING A CONSTITUTIONAL PROCEDURE FOR FEDERAL CAPITAL CRIMES

by Strom Thurmond

Few issues regarding crime and punishment in America in modern times have been debated as long or as vigorously as capital punishment. This debate has taken place at all levels: the public at large, in every State, and in the Congress of the United States. I have confronted this penalty as a state legislator, a state circuit judge, a state governor, and finally, as a United States Senator. Grappling with appropriate public policy responses to inhuman brutal behavior directed at some of the most vulnerable and innocent members of society—or conduct aimed at fundamental security interests of a nation—is a sobering responsibility for a public servant; but it is a responsibility that cannot be avoided.

I approach this responsibility from a simple perspective. The first duty of government, as the operating arm of organized society, is the protection of individuals within the society from lawless predators, whether foreign or domestic, so that the law abiding citizen may go about his pursuits in peace and safety. In the context of this fundamental principle, one must resolve whether a person may act so brutally, so viciously, so contrary to the value placed on innocent human life or so contrary to the well-being of the country as a sovereign nation as to justify the ultimate punishment of death. For the reasons set forth herein, I have concluded that the death penalty is necessary for certain aggravated offenses: those involving the taking of human life or the wanton jeopardizing of the survival of the nation and that the Congress should promptly act to provide constitutional procedures for imposition of the death penalty in federal cases for murder, attempted assassination of the President, treason, and espionage.

A BRIEF HISTORICAL PERSPECTIVE

The United States Supreme Court has been the governmental institution setting the framework for consideration of the death penalty in this country for some fourteen years.[1] In 1972, the Court, by a five to four vote involving a combination of nine concurring and dissenting opinions, rejected the argument that the death penalty was unconstitutional *per se*; instead, the Court began the process of attempting to narrow and discipline the mechanism for determining those cases in which death would actually be imposed.[2] The Court concluded—or, more accurately, Justice Potter Stewart, as the apparent swing vote in the five to four decision, concluded—that unlimited and unguided discretion given to the judge and jury in the sentencing process had resulted in such arbitrary and capricious application of the sentence of death as to constitute cruel and unusual punishment under the Eighth Amendment to the Constitution. The effect was to make the then existing federal and state death penalty statutes inoperative pending legislative disciplining of the capital sentencing process.[3]

It is fair to observe that the combination of opinions in *Furman* did not provide a "bright line principle" to guide the inevitable legislative reaction. Instead, legislatures were compelled to attempt to satisfy the constitutional concerns expressed by Justice Stewart, who seemed to hinge constitutional acceptance, in the first instance, upon a demonstrated frustration of the legislative will if the penalty is not imposed[4] and, in the second instance, upon eliminating or minimizing the unfettered discretion that had resulted in permitting this unique penalty to be wantonly and actually imposed.[5]

The States reacted quickly to the challenge. Within four years of the *Furman* decision, at least thirty-five states had enacted new statutes providing for the death penalty in at least some homicides.[6] In addition, in 1974 the United States Congress enacted a procedure designed to meet the concerns of Justice Stewart for the imposition of the death penalty for aircraft hijacking resulting in death.[7]

These new statutes dealt with the problems addressed in *Furman* primarily (1) by specifying aggravating and mitigating factors to be weighed and procedures to be followed in deciding when to impose a capital sentence in a particular case, or (2) by making the death penalty mandatory for specific crimes.[8] In a series of landmark cases in 1976, the Supreme Court validated the more flexible approach in the first category[9] and struck down mandatory death penalty statutes.[10] While there have ensued other Supreme Court decisions to refine the application of the death penalty,[11] the "guided discretion" approach illustrated by the Georgia statute

218

upheld in *Gregg v. Georgia* remains the basic model for a constitutional capital punishment statute for crimes for which the death penalty is constitutional.

Finally, the Supreme Court by narrow majorities has applied a "grossly disproportionate and excessive punishment" rationale to hold unconstitutional the imposition of the death penalty for the nonfatal rape of an adult woman[12] and for a murder perpetrated by an accomplice in which the defendant had little or no culpable responsibility for the death of the victim.[13] Some have suggested that these cases cast doubt on the constitutionality of a death penalty for federal treason and espionage where death does not result, as well as a dangerously close attempt to assassinate the President of the United States.[14] In my judgment, the death penalty is a constitutionally appropriate punishment for these crimes, and Congress should act to pass legislation that would establish such a penalty.[15]

INTOLERABLE CRIMINAL CONDUCT WARRANTING THE DEATH PENALTY

Within the bounds of the Constitution,[16] it is the legislator who must, in the first instance, determine the conduct a society deems so violative of its fundamental norms as to merit the death penalty. While civilized society does not, and should not, favor the unjustified or indiscriminate use of capital punishment, instances arise where the penalty is appropriate or, indeed, demanded.

The most obvious first place to focus is the application of appropriate and just penalties for the taking of human life. Some human beings so far depart from even the outer limit of civilized tolerance that a sense of justice, a compelling need to deter others, and an absolute insistence upon incapacitating this individual from inflicting further terror demand the death penalty. In presenting the case for capital punishment, it is helpful to keep in mind an accurate picture of the type of conduct involved with respect to homicide. A number of famous cases come to mind, but a few examples will illustrate the point.[17]

Everyone over thirty years old will remember the Chicago student nurse massacre of 1966. On a hot July night in 1966, a man named Richard Speck broke into the dormitory bedroom of a Chicago student nurse. Armed with a pistol and butcher knife, Speck led her into the bedrooms of numerous student nurses, finally abducting and restraining nine victims. Then, individually, Speck forced each girl, bound and gagged, into an adjoining room, where he committed unspeakable horrors. By rolling under a bed undetected, one was able to escape the resultant tragedies. The others were not so lucky. They were strangled, stabbed repeatedly, and mutilated. Speck received a life sentence.

Another case involved a Robert Allen Bailey. In October 1973, Bailey and two accomplices abducted two 16-year-old high school sweethearts at a pizza parlor. The victims were forced at gunpoint to drive to a secluded wooded area beyond the Roanoke, Virginia, city limits. While forcing the boy to watch, Bailey raped and sodomized the young girl. He then robbed the boy of his wallet and shot him in the head. Meanwhile, Bailey's companions again sodomized the young girl, who was then shot twice in the head. Finding the boy still alive, Bailey attempted to shoot him again, slit his throat, and repeatedly cut his body. For these unbelievable, grotesque acts, Bailey received a sentence of imprisonment.

A third case involved the routine use of a van named the "Murder Mack" as the site of brutal premeditated murders. In 1979, two friends and former California prisoners, Lawrence Sigmond Bittaker and Roy Lewis Norris, began a gruesome murder spree. The first victim, a 16-year-old, was kidnapped while returning from church, forced into the van and taken to a prearranged mountain location. There she was repeatedly raped and forced to listen to detailed plans for her killing. While she was pleading to be allowed to engage in a final prayer, one of the perpetrators began to strangle her with his hands, finishing the job with a coat hanger. The second and third victims, 18 and 15 years old, were taken to the same location, strangled, and killed with an icepick. A fourth was also raped and strangled. The last known victim, a 16-year-old, experienced further horrifying forms of torture, rape, and sodomy. Upon arrest, Bittaker bragged of these acts and numerous additional murders. Plans for more victims and other forms of torture and death were unveiled in courtroom testimony. In exchange for testimony against Bittaker and a guilty plea, Norris received a lengthy prison sentence. Bittaker was sentenced to die.

A fourth case in which the death penalty was imposed and carried out was described by *Washington Post* columnist George F. Will as follows:

> Judy, who was executed March 9 by Indiana, committed his first rape when he was 13. Pretending to be selling Boy Scout raffle tickets, he forced his way

into a woman's house, raped her, stabbed her more than 40 times (hard enough to break his knife), smashed her on the head several times with a hatchet and cut off her thumb. Miraculously, she survived.

Such is the criminal incompetence of America's criminal justice system. Judy was on parole in Illinois (he had served just 20 months for viciously beating a stranger—a woman) and was free on bond in Indiana (the offense was armed robbery; the bond was just $750, in spite of his lurid record) when he committed what he says was his 13th rape. It certainly was his last.

Pretending that his car was disabled, he got a passing motorist to stop. He raped her, killed her, then drowned her three small children in a creek. He never expressed remorse, and advised the jury to impose the death sentence, lest he someday be released and kill again.[18]

Often, the victims are public servants carrying out official duties. Just a few years ago, two corrections officers were savagely murdered by stabbing in two separate incidents by two inmates in the maximum security federal prison at Marion, Illinois. Two other officers suffered serious injuries. The violence perpetrated by these inmates was, to them, a game. They were each serving life sentences and had nothing to lose. In combination, they had already killed six other individuals since being locked behind bars.[19]

Murder is not the only crime that jeopardizes a societal or national interest so fundamental that the death penalty may be appropriate. Traditionally, the laws of the United States have provided the death penalty for treason and espionage. No one knows, for example, the damage that has been done to the national defense of this country—or the effect this course of conduct has had or will have in armed conflicts involving the United States—by the outrageous espionage activities of Arthur Walker from 1968 until his recent arrest and conviction. These offenses concern the very survival of the nation itself. Those who engage in such conduct under aggravated circumstances presenting a grave risk of substantial danger to the security of the nation, or a significant defense component (such as disclosure of technological breakthroughs in major weapons systems to a potential enemy) merit being at risk for the death penalty. Indeed, while direct connection may be difficult, relatively minor acts of treason or espionage might in particular circumstances so endanger the successful pursuit of strategic and tactical defense activities, particularly in time of war, as to lead to extensive loss of life or drastically affect the outcome of a military engagement. The death penalty should be available for individuals who commit these egregious crimes against the nation.

Similarly, a serious and dangerously close attempt to assassinate the President of the United States merits the availability of the death penalty for a crime jeopardizing both human life and the life of the nation. As noted by the Office of Legal Counsel in the Department of Justice in concluding that the death penalty would be constitutional under these circumstances:

> As the most powerful and visible of the nation's leaders, the President maintains a unique position within the Federal Government. As Commander-in-Chief of the armed forces, he discharges unique responsibilities for the security of the country. As head of the Executive Branch, he is entrusted with the authority of coordinating and executing all laws of the United States. For these reasons, an assault on the President threatens the national security in a distinctive fashion.[20]

The Department of Justice goes on to distinguish such an attempt from an attempt on a private citizen and further states, "we believe that the unique nature of the office of the President of the United States furnishes support for the view that an attempted assassination of the President can be subjected to the death penalty."

Finally, wanton acts of terrorism against innocent civilians, without even sympathy or respect for women, children, the elderly, or crippled, cry out for a penalty that matches the brutality and inhumanity of such acts.

SOUND POLICY DEMANDS THE DEATH PENALTY IN CERTAIN CASES

Capital punishment as a potential sentence in the most aggravated cases of murder, attempted assassination of the President, treason, and espionage is demanded by the importance of the interest of society threatened by the conduct. If, as I believe to be true, the primary responsibility of government is the protection of its citizens so that the law abiding person may go about his pursuits in peace and safety, the criminal law must promote respect for the lives and property of others through appropriate punishment. The severity of the penalty a society assigns to a breach of one of its norms is a direct measure of the value the society attaches to that particular norm. Walter Berns has aptly observed:

> . . . [T]he purpose of the criminal law is not merely to control behavior—a tyrant can do that—but also to promote respect for that which should be respected, especially the lives, the moral integrity, and even the property of

others. In a country whose principles forbid it to preach, the criminal law is one of the few available institutions through which it can make a moral statement and, thereby, hope to promote this respect. To be successful, what it says—and it makes this moral statement when it punishes—must be appropriate to the offense and, therefore, to what has been offended. If human life is to be held in awe, the law forbidding the taking of it must be held in awe; and the only way it can be made to be awful or awe inspiring is to entitle it to inflict the penalty of death.[21]

The crimes noted in the preceding section involve societal interests so fundamental as to suggest the death penalty as a necessary vehicle to promote the appropriate respect for the interest involved.

In addition to promoting an appropriate general respect for a fundamental interest, there are other sound reasons for imposition of the death penalty in these classes of cases.

First, and perhaps most important, is the potential deterrent effect of capital punishment. True, the issue of deterrence has been debated with vigor by both proponents and opponents of the death penalty.[22] It may be, as the Supreme Court has observed, that the empirical evidence with respect to the deterrent effect of capital punishment over some other penalty is largely inconclusive.[23] It is *unarguably* a *specific* deterrent; it also is a *general* deterrent. Common sense, however, dictates that capital punishment imposed with some consistency for specific crimes will deter the commission of those crimes. Indeed, I have heard over the years in discussions with law enforcement officials of instances in which a violent criminal faced with a strong reason to kill, such as the ability of a victim to identify the perpetrator of a serious crime, has admitted the choice not to kill was based on a fear of the "chair." Moreover, most law enforcement and corrections officers who are routinely exposed to confrontations with potentially dangerous persons strongly support capital punishment for murder largely because they sincerely believe that the death penalty in such cases will save some officers' lives.[24] In my judgment, capital punishment might well supply that margin for survival of the innocent in cases in which the violent criminal either has nothing to lose, such as the prison inmate serving a life term without parole, or has a great deal to lose by survival of the victim, such as a robber who may think twice about killing an identifying victim or witness. As observed by the Supreme Court in *Gregg*:

. . .[Notwithstanding the absence of empirical evidence] . . .We may nevertheless assume safely that there are murderers such as those who act in

223

passion, for whom the threat of death has little or no deterrent effect. But for many others, the death penalty undoubtedly is a significant deterrent. There are carefully contemplated murders, such as murder for hire, where the possible penalty of death may well enter into the cold calculus that precedes the decision to act. And there are some categories of murder, such as murder by a life prisoner, where other sanctions may not be adequate.[25]

While not everyone will be deterred, I firmly believe many will. If so, it would be unconscionable to fail to provide this protection for innocent human life or other comparable interest of society.

Second, capital punishment serves a legitimate retributive function—a sense that justice was done. As modern nations have developed, the individual has forfeited his ancient right for personal vengence, relying instead upon the state to vindicate personal grievances through the criminal law and the courts. The state has an obligation to those who look to it for protection and safety to respond to violations of lawful interests in a manner reasonably related to the harm inflicted. Justice Stewart ably explained the retributive basis for the death penalty in *Gregg*:

> In part, capital punishment is an expression of society's moral outrage at particularly offensive conduct. This function may be unappealing to many, but it is essential in an ordered society that asks its citizens to rely on legal processes rather than self-help to vindicate their wrongs.
>
> "The instinct for retribution is part of the nature of man, and channeling that instinct in the administration of criminal justice serves an important purpose in promoting the stability of a free society governed by law. When people begin to believe that organized society is unwilling or unable to impose upon criminal offenders the punishment they 'deserve,' then there are sown the seeds of anarchy—of self-help, vigilante justice, and lynch law," *Furman v. Georgia, supra* at 308 (Stewart J., concurring).
>
> "Retribution is no longer the dominant objective of the criminal law," *Williams v. New York*, 337 U.S. 241, 248 (1949), but neither is it a forbidden objective nor one inconsistent with our respect for the dignity of men. *Furman v. Georgia*, 408 U.S. at 394-5 (Burger, J., dissenting): *id.* at 452-4 (Powell, J., dissenting); *Powell v. Texas*, 392 U.S. at 531, 535-6. Indeed, the decision that capital punishment may be the appropriate sanction in extreme cases is an expression of the community's belief that certain crimes are themselves so grievous an affront to humanity that the only adequate response may be the penalty of death.[26]

Public sentiment concerning appropriate punishment for the most serious offenses is relevant to the inquiry whether a particular punishment resonably satisfies the public sense of justice. Evidence

224

that the people of the United States feel that the death penalty is a justified sentence in aggravated murders was demonstrated between 1972 and 1976 when over two-thirds of the state legislatures enacted capital punishment statutes in response to the *Furman* decision.[27] I suspect that the magnitude and swiftness of the legislative response to cure the constitutional concerns reflected in the *Furman* decision—and thereby attempt to provide effective capital punishment statutes—has seldom been exceeded. In addition, public opinion polls in the decade following *Furman* show a consistent rise in the number of Americans in favor of the death penalty—from about 49 percent in 1971 to 66 percent in 1981. A Gallup Poll in March 1985 found that the figure had risen to 72 percent—a six percent increase since the last Gallup poll on the subject in 1981 and the highest favorable percentage since 1936.[28]

Finally, capital punishment may be compelled for some crimes committed under special circumstances by the overwhelming need to eliminate the dangers posed by the individual even under the most stringent maximum security imprisonment condition.[29] The Senate Committee on the Judiciary evaluated this basis for the death penalty in the following terms:

> In some cases, imprisonment is simply not a sufficient safeguard against the future actions of criminals. Some criminals are incorrigibly anti-social and will remain potentially dangerous to society for the rest of their lives. Mere imprisonment offers these people the possibility of escape or, in some cases, release on parole. Even if they are successfully imprisoned for life, prison itself is an environment presenting dangers to guards, inmates, and others. In each of these cases, society is the victim. Basically, there is no satisfactory alternative sentence for these individuals. Life imprisonment without parole, although at first appearing to be a reasonable answer, is in reality highly unsatisfactory. Such a sentence greatly increases the danger to guards and to other prisoners who come into contact with those who have been so sentenced.[30]

Some of the most brutal assaults on human life come from these patently incorrigible individuals. Exposure of the innocent to such danger is unjustifiable.

FEDERAL LEGISLATION ON CAPITAL PUNISHMENT

The current bill on capital punishment which was approved by the United States Senate Committee on the Judiciary on February 20, 1986 (S. 239) would create a constitutional procedure to be used by the federal courts to determine the relatively small number of aggravated crimes within the categories herein discussed that warrant imposition of the death penalty[31] and is patterned after the Georgia statute upheld by the Supreme Court in 1976.[32] The federal crimes to which the procedure would apply are murder, an attempt to assassinate the President, treason, and espionage. All of these crimes, except an attempt to kill the President and certain homicide statutes proposed or enacted after 1972, are already Federal capital offenses, but simply lack valid procedure.

The bill would provide that, after a conviction for an offense for which a penalty of death is authorized and sought by the government, the court must hold a separate hearing on whether to impose the death penalty. With respect to imposition of the death penalty for a homicide, the jury must find that the defendant committed an offense whereby he (1) intentionally killed the victim; (2) intentionally inflicted serious bodily injury that resulted in the death of the victim; or (3) intentionally participated in an act, contemplating that the life of a person would be taken or intending that lethal force would be used in connection with a person, other than one of the participants in the offense, and that person dies as a direct result of the act. If the offense is an attempt to kill the President, the jury must find that the defendant attempted to engage in conduct punishable under 18 U.S.C. 1751(c) that resulted in bodily injury to the President or otherwise came dangerously close to causing the death of the President.

The separate hearing would normally be before the same jury which sat for trial, or, if both parties agree, before the judge. After both sides have an opportunity to present all relevant information, the jury would be asked to make special findings as to whether any of a list of statutory mitigating or aggravating factors exist. The statutory mitigating factors include such things as the extent of the defendant's involvement in the offense; his mental problems; any unusual and substantial duress; and the unforeseen nature of a resulting death. The bill, as introduced, included the fact that the defendant was less than eighteen years of age at the time of the offense as a mitigating factor. This was deleted, however, when the Committee adopted an amendment prohibiting the imposition of a sentence of death upon such a person.

The aggravating factors vary depending on the nature of the offense. Aggravating factors relating to espionage and treason include a past conviction for an offense involving espionage or treason; whether the defendant knowingly created a grave risk of substantial danger to the national security; and whether the defendant knowingly created a grave risk of death to another person. Aggravating factors for homicides and attempted assassination of the President include the existence of repeated serious violent crimes by the defendant; the commission of the offense in an especially heinous, cruel, or depraved manner, or for hire, or against certain United States or foreign officials and law enforcement officers; and whether the death occurred during the commission of another serious offense. The jury or judge could also consider whether nonstatutory aggravating factors exist.

The jury would be required to determine whether any statutory aggravating factors relied upon by the government to support its request for the death penalty exist. If the jury agrees that at least one such factor exists, the jury would then determine, in light of all the evidence, whether the aggravating factor or factors sufficiently outweigh the mitigating factors to justify the death penalty, or, in the absence of mitigating factors, whether the aggravating factors are themselves sufficient to justify a sentence of death. The jury must be specifically instructed not to consider the race, color, national origin, creed, or sex of the defendant in considering whether a sentence of death is justified. In order to impose a sentence of death the jury must find by unanimous vote that the death penalty is justified. However, even if the jury unanimously determines that such a sentence is justified, it has the discretion not to impose that sentence. If no statutory aggravating factor relied upon by the government is found to exist, or if for any other reason the jury finds that the death penalty is not justified, the court must impose a sentence, other than death, authorized by law. If the maximum term of imprisonment is life, the court may impose a life sentence without eligibility for parole.

The bill further provides that the defendant shall have a right to appeal the sentence and that such review shall have priority over all other cases. In order to affirm the sentence, the appellate court must determine that the sentence of death was not imposed under the influence of passion, prejudice, or other arbitrary factors and that the evidence supports the special finding.

This legislative scheme could cure the procedural problems identified by the Supreme Court with respect to imposition of the death penalty under the Constitution. It is a carefully balanced measure designed to meet the interests of society in adequate punishment for intolerable heinous conduct, as well as the legitimate rights of the defendant.

CONCLUSION

There are some crimes so contrary to the value placed on human life and the well-being of the country as to justify the death penalty in aggravated cases. Murder, attempts to assassinate the President, treason, and espionage fall in this category. The Supreme Court has held that the imposition of the death penalty is constitutional for aggravated murder so long as the process is governed by legislative guidance designed to eliminate the "wanton and freakish" nature of the current system. Analysis of the interests protected by statutes prohibiting treason, espionage, and attempts to kill the President supports imposition of the death penalty for aggravated forms of these offenses. The death penalty is an appropriate penalty not only to identify and vindicate the norms of society with respect to intolerable conduct, but to deter, justly punish, and incapacitate those who would violate such norms.[33]

REFERENCES

Enacting a Constitutional Procedure for Federal Capital Crimes by Strom Thurmond

1. Prior to the historic decisions of the Supreme Court in the early and mid-1970s, the primary focus on capital punishment took the form of political efforts to abolish the death penalty through the legislative process. See generally, *To Abolish the Death Penalty*, Hearings before the Subcommittee on Criminal Laws and Procedures of the Committee on the Judiciary, United States Senate, 90th Cong., 2d Sess. (1968).

2. *Furman v. Georgia*, 408 U.S. 238 (1972).

3. *Furman* effectively eliminated the availability of the death penalty in the six categories of federal offenses then authorizing the penalty—treason, espionage, first degree murder, felony-murder, rape, and certain kidnapping offenses. See 18 U.S.C. 32-34 (destruction of aircraft or aircraft facilities and motor vehicles or motor vehicle facilities where death results); 18 U.S.C. 351(a) (murder of a Member of Congress, a Member of Congress-elect, a Supreme Court justice, or certain high executive branch officials); 18 U.S.C. 351(b) (kidnaping a Member of Congress, Member of Congress-elect, a Supreme Court Justice, or certain high executive branch officials, where death results); 18 U.S.C. 794 (espionage); 18 U.S.C. 844 (d), (f), and (i) (explosive offenses where death results); 18 U.S.C. 1111 (murder in the special maritime and territorial jurisdiction of the United States); 18 U.S.C. 1114 (murder of specified Federal officials and employees); 18 U.S.C. 1201 (kidnaping where the victim was not liberated unharmed); 18 U.S.C. 1716 (injurious articles as nonmailable where death results); 18 U.S.C. 1751(a) (murder of the President, President-elect, Vice President, the officer next in order of succession to the President, or certain high White House officials); 18 U.S.C. 1751(b) (kidnaping of President, Vice President, the officer next in order in succession to the Presidency, or certain high White House officials, where death results); 18 U.S.C. 2031 (rape in the special maritime and territorial jurisdiction of the United States); 18 U.S.C. 2381 (treason); 18 U.S.C. 1992 (destruction of trains or train

facilities where death results); 18 U.S.C. 2113(e) (murder or kidnaping in the course of a bank robbery); and 49 U.S.C. 1472 (aircraft hijacking where death results). When the kidnaping section was revised in other respects in 1972 (Public Law 92-539), the death penalty language was dropped as superfluous in light of the *Furman* decision.

4. *Supra* n. 2 at 306–309. This concept encouraged the idea that the more mandatory the death penalty, the more likely its constitutionality. See statement of Robert Dixon for the Department of Justice, *Reform of the Federal Criminal Laws*, Hearings before the Subcommittee on Criminal Laws and Procedures of the Committee on the Judiciary, United States Senate, 93d Cong., 1st Sess., Part V, pp. 5224–5246 (1973).

5. *Id.* at 310.

6. *Gregg v. Georgia*, 428 U.S. 153, 179–180 and n. 23 (1976).

7. 49 U.S.C. 1472(i) and (n). Beginning with S. 1401, an Administration bill introduced by Senator Hruska in the 93rd Congress, the United States Senate has actively considered enactment of a constitutional procedure to impose the death penalty for *all* Federal capital offenses directed at aggravated homicide (including an attempt to kill the President in later bills), treason, and espionage. Such bills passed the Senate twice by wide margins— S. 1401 on March 13, 1974, by a vote of 54 to 33; S. 1765 on February 22, 1984, by a vote of 63 to 32—only to die in the House. For a summary of the history of federal death penalty legislation, *see*, *Establishing Constitutional Procedures for the Imposition of Capital Punishment*, Committee Report to Accompany S. 1765, United States Senate, Committee on the Judiciary, S. Rept. No. 98-251, 98th Cong., 1st Sess., pp. 1–4 (1983). *See also, Imposition of Capital Punishment*, Hearings before the Subcommittee on Criminal Laws and Procedures of the Committee on the Judiciary, United States Senate, 93d Cong. 1st Sess. (1973); *To Establish Constitutional Procedures for the Imposition of Capital Punishment*, Hearing before the Committee on the Judiciary, United States Senate, 95th Cong., 2d Sess. (1978); *Capital Punishment*, Hearings before the Committee on the Judiciary, United States Senate, 97th Cong., 1st Sess. (1981).

8. *Gregg v. Georgia, supra* n. 6 at 180.

9. *Gregg v. Georgia, supra* n. 6; *Proffitt v. Florida*, 428 U.S. 242 (1976); *Jurek v. Texas*, 428 U.S. 262 (1976).

10. *Woodson v. North Carolina*, 428 U.S. 280 (1976); *Roberts v. Louisiana*, 428 U.S. 325 (1976).

11. *See, e.g., Lockett v. Ohio*, 438 U.S. 586 (1978) (legislature may not limit the mitigating circumstances to be considered).

12. *Coker v. Georgia*, 433 U.S. 584 (1977).

13. *Enmund v. Florida*, 458 U.S. 782 (1982). *See also, Cabana v. Bullock*, 106 S. Ct. 689 (1986), in which the Supreme Court affirmed its holding in *Enmund.*

14. *See, e.g., Comprehensive Crime Control Act of 1983*, Hearings on S. 829 before the Subcommittee on Criminal Law of the Committee on the Judiciary, 98th Cong., 1st Sess., pp. 345, 367 (1983) (statement of the American Civil Liberties Union).

15. *See* discussion, *Establishing Constitutional Procedures For the Imposition of Capital Punishment*, S. Rept. No. 98-251, *supra* n. 7, pp. 7–9.

16. As noted, the Supreme Court has held that the death penalty for the non-fatal rape of an adult woman and accomplice liability for murder under certain circumstances is an unconstitutionally disproportionate sentence. *Coker v. Georgia, supra* n. 12; *Enmund v. Florida*, and *Cabana v. Bullock, supra* n. 13.

17. Most of these examples, and others, were recounted as a part of the debate on S. 1765, a bill to create constitutional procedures for imposition of the death penalty in Federal capital cases, considered and passed by the Senate in February 1984 (see, e.g., 130 Cong. Rec. S1203-1205, S1214, S1468-S1471 (February 9, 22, 1984 [daily ed.]).

18. Reproduced in 130 Cong. Rec. S1471 (February 22, 1984 [daily ed.]).

19. *Id.* at S1203-S1204; *See also, Prison Violence and Capital Punishment*, Hearings before the Subcommittee on Criminal Law of the Committee on the Judiciary, United States Senate, 98th Cong., 1st Sess. (1983).

20. *Capital Punishment, supra* n. 7 at 64–65.

21. Walter Berns, Resident Scholar, The American Enterprise Institute for Foreign Policy Research, Defending the Death Penalty, *Crime and Delinquency*, October 1980, reprinted in *Capital Punishment*, *supra* n. 7 at 220.. See also, *Gregg v. Georgia*, *supra* n. 6 at 184 and n. 30.

22. *See* sources cited in *Gregg v. Georgia*, *supra* n. 6 at 184 note 31.

23. *Id.* at 184–185.

24. See, e.g., *Capital Punishment*, *supra* n. 7 at 114, 119; *Prison Violence and Capital Punishment*, *supra* n. 19.

25. *Gregg v. Georgia*, *supra* n. 6 at 185–186.

26. *Id.* at 183–184.

27. *See*, S. Rept. No. 98-251, *supra* n. 15 at 15.

28. *See* Lauren Rubenstein Reskin, "Majority of Lawyers Support Capital Punishment," *ABA Journal*, (April 1985) p. 44.

29. *See*, *Prison Violence and Capital Punishment*, *supra* n. 19.

30. S. Rept. No. 98-251, *supra* n. 15 at 12.

31. *See* discussion *supra* n. 7. The same bill was reported by the Senate Committee on the Judiciary in the 98th Congress as S. 1765 (S. Rept. No. 98-251) and passed the Senate by a vote of 63 to 32.

32. *Gregg v. Georgia*, *supra* n. 6.

33. [Editor's note: As this book went to print in the fall of 1986, the U.S. Senate was considering Senator Thurmond's death penalty legislation.]

14

THE SIDEWALK AND STREET PEACE:
Safeguarding America's Finest
by David A. Jones and L. Stephen Jennings

The first thing to understand is that the public peace—the sidewalk and street peace—of cities is not kept primarily by the police, necessary as police are. It is kept primarily by an intricate, almost unconscious, network of voluntary controls and standards among the people themselves.

> Jane Jacobs,
> The Death And Life Of Great American Cities (1961)

Today, there are more than forty thousand separate law enforcement agencies in the United States at the federal, state and local levels of government. Some fifty of these agencies are at the federal level, another two hundred are at the state level, but the balance are local law enforcement agencies, responding to peace-keeping and service needs of our counties and municipalities. This is as it should be in a free country: the police represent the people because, in the ultimate analysis, the people are the police.

American law enforcement agencies employ more than 420,000 full- and part-time sworn police officers and civilians, of whom over 300,000 provide police manpower at the local level of government.[1] This chapter will focus on one particular kind of peace keeper—the policeman on the beat, known as the street cop. Of all the workers in the criminal justice system, he is the person who is the most visible and, perhaps, the most valuable to the nation. The street cop provides front line law enforcement because, for the average American, as well as for typical foreign visitors, the street cop is the primary contact not only with law enforcement but also with government generally. He is, in one sense, is representative of America itself.

How the street cop performs his duty, multifold as that duty has become, shapes public attitudes toward justice and, indeed, toward the entire political system.[2] The American policeman has worked quietly and in relative obscurity for many years. Going largely unpraised, he went largely unappreciated for over 150 years. Now, at least in some circles, the American police officer has become the scapegoat for social unrest, blamed for problems that were not of his making, expected to correct inequities—accurate or imaginary— that he is powerless to redress. In one sense, the policeman's plight serves to reinforce the fact that, in the public's eyes, he *is* the nation. In his own eyes, however, he is just a person trying to earn a living to support a family. He seems larger than life, but he has only one life. To those who fail to see beyond his uniform, each police officer seems to be 300,000 persons wrapped in one. To himself, sometimes he is one man standing alone against the vagaries of his world.

Virtually everyone benefits from police services and from a strong and visible police presence on the streets, particularly in our major cities, yet those who have not witnessed the police in action helping *them* personally may not comprehend exactly what the police are called upon to do in the line of duty. Consequently, a typical person ignores issues that are of critical importance to the police, not necessarily because the public bears any animosity toward the police, but out of ignorance and apathy. As people in general tend to blame the messenger for the message, some citizens blame the police for enforcing our laws, particularly when those laws are enforced against them individually. Therefore, when someone is stopped by the police for a routine matter, such as a traffic violation (which will happen to nearly every motorist who drives enough miles), such a person may become hostile to the police officer who detains him and, possibly, to police as a class, as a convenient alternative to accepting his own blame for failing to obey the law in the first place. This kind of an encounter with the police heightens frustration on the part of citizens and police alike. Police exist to serve the public, to help people, yet occasionally the police must discipline the very persons they are mandated to serve.[3] This paradox fosters confusion.

An ever-changing America has contributed, also, to a negative public image of the street cop, who came into the spotlight during the civil rights movement of the 1960s. Then, particularly, but on occasion since then as well, the news media focused on reports of police misconduct and sometimes embellished those accounts into what seemed to constitute brutality. In some instances, a few police were wrongdoers, but the national publicity they received tarnished the reputations of all police generally. In most instances, news reports of violence among police were inaccurate, highlighted unnecessarily, and utilized by irresponsible journalists to portray police and the system of justice in a bad light. For example, during some urban protests kept peaceful by the police, the national television networks hounded police day in and day out. Most police behaved well and rose to the difficult occasion, but accounts of these officers were edited out before they appeared on the morning or evening news. Some of those pushed beyond their limits received substantial news coverage causing police to appear abusive in the eyes of those Americans who saw police only in their living room television sets. The image of the police officer sunk to its lowest ebb during the 1968 Democratic National Convention, held in Chicago, where Mayor Richard J. Daley ordered police to arrest delegates and demonstrators alike, provoking a frightful onslaught. Agitation for immediate changes in law enforcement policies reached a new peak.

But already in the wake of the assassinations of Martin Luther King and Robert F. Kennedy in the spring of 1968, President Lyndon B. Johnson had created the National Commission on the Causes and Prevention of Violence, with Milton S. Eisenhower as chairman. President Richard M. Nixon extended the Commission's life in 1969, but the Final Report[4] and a variety of task force reports, actually said very little:

> We wish we could promise solutions to all of the problems of illegitimate violence. We can not. There is no simple answer to the problem of illegitimate violence: no single explanation of its causes, and no single prescription for its control.[5]

One of the commission task forces[6] issued a report that seemed to blame violence in American streets on "strife," both domestic and international, reflected in the "J-Curve of Rising and Declining Satisfactions."[7]

Beyond this activity, the Johnson Administration had created The President's Commission on Law Enforcement and Administration of Justice, headed by former Attorney General Nicholas Katzenbach. Subsequently, the Nixon Administration formed the National Advisory Commission on Criminal Justice Standards and Goals, headed by Delaware governor Russell W. Peterson. Both the Katzenbach and Peterson Commissions published major reports[8] oriented toward improving America's police. In one sense, both succeeded, as in another sense, both failed. Each commission reawakened citizens to the basic needs of police. Each recommended an assortment of changes, only a few of which were implementable, and most of which have never become operational.[9] Both commissions created task forces focusing on the police as well as among other areas of our criminal justice system.[10] The Katzenbach Commission's Task Force on the Police was led informally by Chicago police chief Orlando W. Wilson, whereas The Peterson Commission appointed Los Angeles police chief Edward M. Davis as chairman of its Task Force on Police. The two police task forces were influenced, if not dominated, by the two men who may fairly be said to have contributed more to Twentieth Century American police management than any other persons.

Superficially, the Peterson Commission's Task Force on Police would appear to have been the more prescriptive in its recommendations, having set forth 107 separate standards for "police service in America"[11] as well as sixteen specific recommendations for changes in police operations.[12] In some sense, this might seem paradoxical, in that the Katzenbach Commission reflected America of the 1960s, searching for a set of uniform *national* truths, rather in the mold of the modern Democratic Party; whereas the Peterson Commission reflected America of the 1970s and early 1980s, desirous of *community* standards that might vary from one locale to another, in the mold of the modern Republican Party. What paradox exists is but superficial indeed. In the Peterson Commission's Task Force Report, *Police* offered simple guidelines in the form of its standards and recommendations, with which communities were encouraged to comply in their own way.[13] In the Katzenbach Commission's Task Force Report, *Police* mandated particular courses of action, almost always to be taken at the state level or above.[14]

The Katzenbach Commission's Task Force on the Police seemingly grimaced at the thought of retaining control of police policies at the municipal and county levels of government, the traditional pattern in this country. In one example in point from the Report:

> A State Commission on Police Standards can do much to improve local law enforcement. . . . In most states, the existing Commissions do not have the power either to establish mandatory standards or to give financial assistance to local departments. This lack of authority limits their impact. If properly constituted and empowered, however, State Commissions on Police Standards could play a significant role in the process of upgrading police effectiveness.[15]

A more pointed example:

> [T]he majority of the American public favors reasonable firearms control legislation. Since laws, as they now stand, do not effectively control the supply

of firearms, legislative bodies at Federal, State, and local levels should act to strengthen controls. . . . [16]

Finally, prevention of crime and apprehension of criminals would be enhanced if each firearm were registered with a governmental jurisdiction. A record of ownership would aid the police in tracing and locating those who have committed or who threaten to commit violent crime. Law enforcement officers should know where each gun is and who owns it. [17]

Why should "law enforcement officers" know where each gun is and who owns it? How would they, anyway, when a weapon has been stolen? Who says the "majority" of the American public favors firearms control legislation? Unhappily, the Katzenbach Commission's Task Force Report, *The Police*, is replete with such shibboleths.

On the contrary, the Peterson Commission's Task Force on Police identified issues to be resolved by the populace, rather than declaring in advance what the population wants, as the Katzenbach Commission seemed to do. For instance, the Peterson Commission targeted "Crime Problem Identification and Resource Development" as an area worthy of joint citizen–police efforts:

Every police agency should insure that patrolmen and members of the public are brought together to solve crime problems on a local basis. Police agencies with more than 75 personnel should immediately adopt a program to insure joint participation in crime problem identification.

1. Every police agency should, consistent with local police needs and its internal organization, adopt geographic policing programs which insure stability of assignment for individual officers who are operationally deployed.

2. Every patrol officer assigned to a geographic policing program should be responsible for the control of crime in his area and, consistent with agency priorities and policies and subject to normal approval, should be granted authority to determine the immediate means he will use in fulfilling that responsibility.

3. Every police agency should arrange for officers assigned to geographic policing programs to meet regularly with persons who live or work in their area to discuss the identification of crime problems and the cooperative development of solutions to these problems. [18]

The Commentary to Standard 3.1 declared that the "emphasis of this standard is on the police-community relations aspect of team policing." The Peterson Commission predicated much of its team policing emphasis upon recommendations offered by Dean Richard A. Myren in 1972:

...That support of the citizens living and working in the many discrete neighborhoods of our metropolitan areas, which is absolutely necessary for successfully policing, can best be achieved by having a police subunit permanently assigned to each neighborhood; that the personnel of these subunits must get to know the people in the neighborhood through positive efforts to promote continuous dialog in both formal and informal settings; and that assistance to the people, both in handling their crime problems and in helping them to make contact with the proper agencies to handle the myriad of other problems of big city living, is the best means of achieving respect for and support of police operations.[19]

Underlying much of the Peterson Commission's thought, consequently, is the honest belief that citizens themselves are the real police, the only really effective support for what is usually called the police force.

From the Peterson Commission and its reports emerged the two major criminal justice task forces of the 1980s, each created by President Ronald Reagan: The Attorney General's Task Force on Violent Crime, co-chaired by former attorney general Griffin B. Bell and Illinois governor James R. Thompson; and The President's Task Force on Victims of Crime, chaired by former Alameda County (California) prosecutor Lois Haight Herrington.[20] These two recent task forces went directly to the people by conducting hearings in an aggregate of thirteen American cities[21] as part of a widespread effort at gathering *citizen* evaluations of how police were doing, and at the same time listening to citizen recommendations for improvements in police operations. The Violent Crime Task Force reported to the attorney general in August 1981,[22] while the Victims' Task Force reported to The President in December 1982.[23] These two task forces recognized that much crime in America, particularly in the major cities, is the product of foreign criminal syndicalism that can be interdicted best by the federal government, frequently working outside of the United States. Among the most poignant recommendations of the Violent Crime Task Force were:

• Use of Navy aircraft to assist in interdicting narcotic traffic;

• Development of a comprehensive narcotics control program that includes (a) source control in the country of origin; (b) border interdiction; and (c) a domestic legislative program to enhance the government's ability to prosecute drug-related cases;

• Allowing federal law enforcement officers access to income tax return information in drug trafficking and organized crime cases; and

236

- Mandatory prison sentences for the *use* of a firearm in the commission of a federal felony.

Both the Violent Crime Task Force and the Victims' Task Force recommended the following:

- Denial of bail to dangerous criminal offenders.

- Abolition of parole and reduction of judicial discretion over sentencing.

- A feasibility study to determine whether parole board members should be liable for negligence in the release of prisoners who victimize again.

- Modification of the exclusionary rule by creating, at a minimum, a good faith exception.

Without much doubt, most recommendations of these two task forces reflect the sentiments of the vast majority of Americans in the 1980s.[24] To understand possible methods to improve and safeguard our police, the history of policing as a profession should be addressed so that then contemporary issues can be discussed in context.

HISTORY OF POLICING

The first modern police force emerged in England in 1829 when Sir Robert Peel, then Home Secretary, introduced into Parliament "An Act for Improving the Police In and Near the Metropolis" of London. The proposal took effect on July 19, 1829 as the Metropolitan Police Act. With that legislation, England created a single metropolitan police district across a seven mile radius from the center of London, and staffed it with one thousand "Bobbies," as they would come to be known affectionately in honor of Sir Robert Peel, their founder. Army colonel Charles Rowan was appointed as the first chief superintendent of the new metropolitan police force, which soon would take its name from that of an old fortress where its headquarters would be housed: Scotland Yard. The force was divided into seventeen police divisions, each manned by 165 officers. Each division was commanded by a superintendent, under whom four inspectors supervised sixteen sergeants, each of whom watched over nine constables.[25] Peel declared that "the chief prerequisite of an efficient police" was "unity of design and responsibility of its agents."[26]

Actually the notion of a centralized police department under command of a well-trained management team did not begin with Peel in 1829, but anteceded that date by at least thirty-five years. As early as 1795, Patrick Colquhoun published the first systematic survey of police pratices to be conducted anywhere, and noted the ineffectiveness of the "Charlies," an unpaid group of watchmen who patrolled the London streets at night looking for fires:

> The watchmen destined to guard the lives and properties of the inhabitants residing in and near eight thousand streets, lanes, courts, and alleys, and about 162,000 houses...are under the direction of no less than above seventy different Trusts; regulated by perhaps double the number of local acts of Parliament...under which the directors, guardians, governors, trustees, or vestries according to the title they assume are authorized to act, each attending only to their own particular Ward, Parish, Hamlet, Liberty, or Precinct.[27]

With the creation of Scotland Yard in London, the movement toward centralized policing spread rapidly throughout England and America. By 1856, England enacted the County and Borough Police Act, under which 226 police forces emerged across the British Isles. Borough constables were given county-wide jurisdiction, and county constables were permitted to perform official acts inside of boroughs. In the early Nineteenth Century, American cities were inundated with crime:

> New York City was alleged to be the most crime-ridden city in the world, with Philadelphia, Baltimore and Cincinnati not far behind....Gangs of youthful rowdies in the larger cities...threatened to destroy the American reputation for respect for law....Before their boisterous demonstrations the crude police forces of the day were often helpless.[28]

In 1833, a wealthy philanthropist left a will containing a legacy to finance a competent police force in Philadelphia, which in turn prompted the city council to pass an ordinance creating a 24-man police force by day and 120 watchmen to patrol the city at night.[29] Other cities followed. Boston created a daytime police to supplement its nightwatch in 1838. New York City created the first unified day and night police in America in 1844, followed by Boston in 1848. By 1875, virtually every American city had a full-time police force on patrol day and night. Almost all of these forces were corrupt.[30] The public came to view the police with scorn and contempt, so much so that by 1900, one observer noted:

> Rotation in office enjoyed so much popular favor that police posts of both high and low degree were constantly changing hands, with political fixers determining the price and conditions of each change.
>
> . . .The whole police question simply churned about in the public mind and eventually became identified with the corruption and degradation of the city politics and local governments of the period.[31]

The more centralized urban police forces became during the Nineteenth Century, the more corrupt they seemed.

One reason for corruption among early American police was the fact that recruits, having been hired largely by politicians, received training on the job chiefly from older officers who were seldom qualified by training or character to educate their successors.[32] In 1931, President Herbert Hoover convened the National Commission on Law Observance and Enforcement, and recalled from retirement former attorney general George W. Wickersham to serve as chairman. The Wickersham Commission concluded that the average police chief's term of office was too short to render him truly effective; that police departments were influenced too closely by corrupt politicians; that no effort was being made to educate, train or discipline rank-and-file police officers; and that almost all police departments lacked adequate communications systems and other equipment necessary to enforce the laws effectively.[33] Changes were forthcoming. In 1931, Detroit initiated a merit selection system for police, then Cincinatti created an improved retirement system, and the Tucson police department was placed under jurisdiction of the civil service.[34]

By 1934, at least eight states had created state police academies within which to train municipal police, and the Federal Bureau of Investigation created the National Academy in 1935.[35] In 1931, the first complete college major in police administration was created at San Jose State College. In 1932, August Vollmer, who authored the Wickersham Commission's *Report on the Police*, was appointed professor of police administration at the University of California, Berkeley. Other college-level education programs flourished at Northwestern University, University of Wichita, and Michigan State College.

Yet, although the image of the American police officer has fluctuated over the half-century since 1935, it has not risen measurably.[36] Nor has the role of the peace officer become safer; in fact, it has become far more dangerous.

In 1965, Congress enacted the Law Enforcement Assistance Act, creating the Law Enforcement Assistance Administration (LEAA), and followed this with the Omnibus Crime Control and Safe Streets Act of 1968, which mandated each state to establish a state planning agency (SPA) in order to receive federal funds through LEAA. The Peterson Commission identified one major problem with SPAs in many states, although it spoke too gently in its condemnation:

> When planners are not responsible for actual implementation or for financing the implementation of their plans, the plans sometimes lack practicality or financial feasibility....
>
> Every police agency should participate in this type of planning to increase the agency's effectiveness and efficiency and to contribute to the effectiveness and efficiency of the police system and the criminal justice system within which it operates.[37]

In fact, the vast proportion of the millions of dollars allocated by the Congress to LEAA and distributed to police agencies through SPAs never benefitted the street cop and provided but minimal upgrading of his image and his safety.[38] What proportion was not siphoned-off by the "planners" themselves went to purchase useless equipment or to decorate the offices of police managers. Perhaps the singular value of LEAA monies to some American police officers was to provide an opportunity for officers to begin and, in an increasing number of instances, to finish college educations. This, unfortunately, has not contributed significantly to the safety of police on the sidewalk or the street.

CONTEMPORARY PROBLEMS: THE COURT, DRUGS, TERRORISM, ET AL.

Much has been written about the changing role of the American police officer. James Q. Wilson and others have described his role as at least three-fold: enforcer of our laws, guardian of the public order, and provider of a multiplicity of services.[39] In fact, the police may be providing too many services, or devoting too much time to their service function, possibly at the expense of maintaining the public order and/or law enforcement.[40] To a street cop, law enforcement and apprehension of the criminal, with protection of the public as the ultimate result of his effort, must be his main function. Yet, a typical street cop does not object to fulfilling a wider public service role, provided that not all of his valuable time becomes expended on "garbage" calls—responses to citizen requests that require no law enforcement expertise.[41] When the citizens of a given community demand too many public services from the local police, the police may become confused particularly when forced to choose between conflicting roles,[42] and police management will find it necessary to call for greater manpower and, consequently, a larger budget. The alternative to greater manpower and a larger budget may be, necessarily, lessened enforcement of the laws, an alternative that can result in an increase in the rate of certain crimes when potential criminals interpret this election of peace-keeping activities.

The life of a street cop is a hard one, unappreciated even by most right-thinking citizens, made very dangerous and difficult by that small criminal element that terrorizes our country. The average cop wants to do a good job, whatever his role may be, but he is unhappy because not only does he not know what the role is, but also he does not feel supported in many of his conflicting roles by the rest of our society, especially by the courts. The street cop bears the brunt of constant criticism of his performance as violent crime rates continue to escalate. Yet, in some respects, the courts have handcuffed our police, limiting the ability of the police fully to enforce the laws, by applying a number of "constitutional" standards invented magically by the Federal courts, mostly by the Supreme Court over the past twenty-five years. The *ex cathedra* manner the Supreme Court has chosen to rule on constitutional issues has permeated to the off-the-bench utterances some Supreme Court justices have made recently. Consider, as but two examples, the recent contentions of Justices William J. Brennan and John Paul Stevens. Brennan averred: "We current Justices read the Constitution in the only way that we can: as 20th century Americans. . . . [It is] little more than arrogance [to believe that anyone can] gauge accurately the intent of the [F]ramers" of the Constitution.[43] Stevens remarked that for the Supreme Court to focus rigidly upon the intent of the Framers would be near-sighted because doing so "overlooks the importance of subsequent events in the development of our law."[44]

What subsequent events? Most "subsequent events" on which the Supreme Court has relied in recent years in interpreting criminal law and procedure have been events set into motion by the Court itself, sometimes mischievously, over the years, such as the "incorporation"[45] of the Bill of Rights, quite selectively,[46] into the Fourteenth Amendment, in order to make certain procedures ob-

241

ligatory upon the states in state criminal prosecutions. In fact, another of these "subsequent events" is the authority of the Supreme Court to review state criminal convictions at all, an authority the Court gave to itself in the Nineteenth Century,[47] as it groped for power.

The average street cop, perhaps to the chagrin of the Supreme Court, enjoys the same opportunity as other Americans: to read the Constitution for himself. The Constitution, written of course by the Framers, clearly envisioned a Supreme Court with rather more limited powers than that of the present court. Section 1 of Article III vests the judicial power of the United States "in one supreme Court, and in such inferior Courts as the Congress may from time to time ordain and establish." Section 2 of Article III extends the judicial power of the United States and, by implication, the power of the Supreme Court, to resolve a *limited* set of controversies, not all those imaginable. Most such controversies bear no relation at all to the criminal law.[48] Some might bear a limited relation to *federal* criminal laws.[49] Only a very few could possibly bear any relation to *state* criminal matters.[50] Inasmuch as criminal issues, Federal or state in scope, could not possibly come within the Supreme Court's original jurisdiction,[51] they must come within its appellate jurisdiction if they should concern the Court at all. In fact, horrifying as this may seem to some justices of the Supreme Court, Congress has the power under Article III to enact "exceptions" and "regulations" to further limit the Supreme Court's appellate jurisdiction.[52] The policeman and his sympathizers ask: Why has the Congress not exercised this power? Why does the Supreme Court "review" so many criminal convictions?

There are many vital efforts the Congress might make that it has seen fit not to do, to the resulting detriment of the street cop. Local law enforcement issues should be left to the discretion of the local police, to be sure, but not all law enforcement issues are purely of a local nature. One major example: international drug trafficking, facilitated daily by the "greenwashing" activities of several major American and foreign banks. The role of large banks as drug-money laundromats, an enterprise known as "greenwashing," has soared in the last decade to at least a $100 billion a year practice, according to recent reports.[53] What this means is that no matter what the street cop does to combat the sale and distribution of contraband drugs—particularly cocaine and heroin, but also amphetamines and even marijuana—he will be doomed to failure. Interdicting international drug trafficking is a mammoth task that can be accomplished effectively only by the federal government, with the aggressive assistance of local police. To the local police officer, frequently, falls the duty to arrest street dealers, addicts, and user novitiates. Seldom does the street cop encounter the big drug dealers; even less frequently will he recognize them even if contact is made. Yet, the sordid need for "junkies" to steal and rob rampantly to generate the cash flow sufficient to support cocaine habits endangers the typical police officer more so than most other hazards that will befall him while on or off duty.

Morale among drug enforcement officers sunk to its lowest level in February of 1985 with the torture-murder in Mexico of special agent Enrique Camarena-Salazar of the United States Enforcement Administration. Naturally, this triggered a decline in morale among the street police officers as well, particularly among street cops who patrol the big "drug cities" and counties of Florida and Texas.[54] The continued existence of outlaw towns and counties—safe havens for smugglers and other dangerous criminals—is an incentive for drug lords and their cohorts to take control of more cities and counties, which by some accounts they seem to be doing.[55] Drug trafficking is a form of terrorism, but not the only form to confront and confound American police on our sidewalks and in our streets.

Another form of domestic terrorism is being waged against the American police officer today by the armed criminal who prowls our streets by day and night, intent upon robbing and murdering any victim he can find. Studies have shown that the armed criminal can haunt most easily the cities and towns where honest citizens cannot be armed[56] because even they would become branded as "criminals" for merely possessing a firearm. One study, funded by the Department of Justice, has shown that up to 71 percent of criminals operating in Massachusetts—a "strict gun control" state—typically prowl the streets armed, whereas only perhaps 35–45 percent of criminals go armed in Georgia and Oklahoma, two states where right-thinking citizens may go about their daily business while armed, and many do so.[57] Clearly, gun "controls," through which the honest citizen is deprived of the right to protect himself via possession of firearms against the criminal elements, are not helpful to the street cop.[58]

A less violent but even more ominous form of terrorism is being waged across America today by a smaller number of criminals who kidnap and sometimes kill children. Dozens of American children disappear, particularly from the outskirts of our major cities, every year, either never to be heard from again or to be discovered mutilated and dead months or years afterwards.[59] Although the victims of these depredations are fewer in number than victims of most other crimes, they are more helpless and such crimes against children are totally inexcusable. Many citizens find inexcusable the inability of local police to find children who have disappeared, also, although within hours, such kidnappers may be far from the jurisdiction of the police who patrol the area where a kidnapping occurred. The federal government response has been to create national clearinghouses to assemble and to screen vital information pertaining to the disappearances of children.[60] The typical street cop realizes that much more federal and even international involvement will be needed to restore public confidence in the safety of our children.

Gradually, foreign terrorists are infiltrating America itself, sometimes functioning as "sleeper" operatives for the moment, preparing to strike directly against our local police by means of automatic weapons and explosives. The American street cop knows that what happened at the Leonardo da Vinci International Airport[61] in Rome can happen at virtually any American airport or bus terminal at any time, unless the international community takes steps to neutralize those foreign governments, notably Libya, that plan terrorism against Americans and train terrorists in techniques that will enable them to count on some margin of success. What is more, why should foreign terrorists recoil at the thought of waging war within the United States: they are but criminals, and the track record of convicting and punishing armed assailants in America has been shaky at best, thanks in part to the ineptitude of trial and appellate courts. Why, then, should foreign terrorists fear American law enforcement? America has difficulty controlling its own criminal population, which is much less trained and much less dedicated than the cadre of foreign terrorists who seem bent on invading America.

OPTIONS FOR REFORM

More Visible Police Presence. The first option for improving the sidewalk and street peace as well as safeguarding our police is for nearly every community to increase quite substantially the *visible* police presence on the street. Undoubtedly, this means that more police need to be hired and trained, perhaps as many as 300,000 new police should be recruited, to nearly double the strength of existing police forces nationally. What is needed is not merely more police riding about the streets in automobiles, aloof from the population.[62]

There is no reason why any police officer should patrol our streets alone; all police should be deployed in pairs. There is no reason why any municipal police should patrol miles of geographic area; all police should be thoroughly familiar with an area of the city within which they are known on a first-name basis to most of the citizens residing there.[63] Although mobile units can be helpful to police in emergency situations and must be available to every police officer on the basis of need, the primary tool the police officer has is not machinery any more than it is firepower: his primary tool is his individual personality. To make his personality work to keep the sidewalk and street peace, the police officer must stand and walk along the sidewalks, talk with the people, be constantly on view as a reminder to potential criminals to think twice. The police officer must assume a leadership role, the role of a magnate, in promoting the obeyance of our laws and the maintenance of public order. Thus, what is being proposed is for the police officer to become leader of the streets, proactive instead of merely reactive to crises, and readily available for immediate response before sidewalk or street problems have any opportunity to escalate.

Judicial Support of Local Police. The people cannot be blamed totally for their lack of enough support for local police when our judiciary mocks the image and the role of the police officer daily within court decisions that release dangerous criminal offenders back onto the streets on technicalities. In recent years, federal courts have been more guilty of this practice than most state courts. The leadership for this denigration of our police came largely from the Supreme Court of the United States in decisions within which the Court gave to the American public the impression that "the criminal must go free because the constable has blundered."[64] Of course, in many Supreme Court decisions reversing criminal convictions, the police did not "blunder" at all, because the "laws" the Court created had never been enacted previously by a legislative body.[65] The Court enacted judge-made laws, then predicated the same on alleged police misconduct to justify judicial intervention in violation of the separation of powers principle.

The Supreme Court has taken a few steps in the right direction over the course of its past several terms, such as by adding a "good faith" exception to what once seemed to be a mandatory "exclusionary rule,"[66] a rule created by the Court itself. Under a good faith exception, a trier of fact (judge or jury) is permitted at least to hear and consider evidence obtained by police which shows a defendant's guilt, notwithstanding the fact that this evidence may be technically "tainted," where the police did not intentionally set-out to violate the legal rights of the accused. Yet, the Court could do much more to promote the safety of the American police officer, such as by abstaining from intervention in state criminal cases altogether, except where there is clear evidence that a state has contravened an express provision of the Constitution or a federal law. The Court should stop the practice of interpreting our Constitution in the light of "subsequent events," in Justice Stevens' words, many if not most of which the Court itself precipitated earlier. Individual justices of the Supreme Court and other Federal judges should refrain from making inflammatory speeches that afford the public the misimpression that our police do their duty properly only when under strict scrutiny by the courts. Among the qualifications to be considered of candidates for future federal judgeships should be some measurable sensitivity to the feelings of the police and to the feelings of the citizenry toward the crime problem.

Citizen Participation in Policing. The police officer cannot be expected, as he is currently, to enforce all of our laws by himself. Just as the individual police officer must call for a "back-up" before confronting a criminal offender known to be dangerous, so also must local police officers as a group be able to count upon the active participation as well as moral support of right-thinking members of the public-at-large whenever such a back-up is needed to safeguard the police. The *posse comitatus*, a group of private citizens temporarily deputized by sworn law enforcement personnel in times of crisis both in feudal England and on the American frontier during the Nineteenth Century, has a vital place in America today. It goes without saying that the citizen who has not abused his right to keep and bear arms should do so in his own home or place of business at all times, and that laws frustrating our Second Amendment privileges should be repealed. But more than this is necessary. . . Americans might benefit from the example set by the Swiss:[67] Every American community could organize, together with the local police, into small groups of citizens who will stand ready, willing and able to provide armed reinforcements for their police upon short notice.

What is suggested here is different from, and intended to be in addition to, the National Guard. This force of citizen–soldiers is available to back-up our professional military in case of war or domestic insurrection. However, most national guardsmen are trained to work in larger teams—squads, platoons, companies—and to man defensive (along with some offensive) army equipment such as mortar, hardly useful in neighborhoods against guerilla terrorists. The principle behind the National Guard can be adapted for a separate force of citizen-police, trained to work in small teams within given neighborhoods, and skilled in the use of small arms firepower commonly adopted by the police. Unless such a plan is implemented soon in this era of rising terrorism, American neighborhoods face a mounting danger that existing police will be numerically insufficient to protect citizens.

Crackdown on Drug Producers—and on "Greenwashing." The American police officer provides front-line protection to the American public, much the same as would a rifleman within an infantry unit of the United States Army. Just as the rifleman requires air support, artillery support, and similar reinforcement on occasion, so the American police officer requires kinds of support. The soldier receives such support from the United States Air Force or Navy. The municipal police officer looks to the state and federal governments for such support—but only when absolutely necessary. America does not need a national police force, and does not need the federal government to underwrite each local police officer's paycheck. But substantial federal assistance is required if local police are to win the war against drug dealing, today's number one threat to the safety and effectiveness of the American police officer.

The federal government can interdict drug traffickers in one or more of several ways. The Drug Enforcement Administration makes periodic seizures of large quantities of contraband drugs, usually from airplanes or boats used by smugglers as the contraband enters the United States. Our government could launch military or paramilitary assaults, overt or covert, against drug facilities in nations within which contraband drugs are harvested.

Undoubtedly, federal officers should continue to seize contraband whenever law enforcement agencies locate it, but it may be time to destroy these execrable substances before they reach this country. To

247

date, however, we have concentrated exclusively on seizing the contraband substances, and have ignored the plain and obvious fact that drug traffickers must have money with which to purchase new supplies.

The street dealer sells drugs to users, usually in exchange for cash, which the dealer "banks," eventually by depositing the cash in a bank account, or by exchanging the cash in turn for bank paper (a check, a money order, or some other negotiable instrument). In other words, dealers in contraband substances need to "launder" their profits—to make the filthy profits they have generated appear to have been obtained from a clean source. Investigations have estimated that as much as $100 billion in such dirty money may be "laundered" by American banks annually.[68] Naturally, some banks are exploited and become the innocent victims of criminal depositors. Many banks appear to be willing participants in this type of a criminal enterprise. After all, money is money, and banks are in the business of trading in currency.

The average American does not walk into his local bank daily or even monthly to deposit $10,000 to $100,000 in cash! This is true whether the depositor is a wage-earner, a salaried executive or professional, or independently wealthy. Indeed, for anyone to roam our dangerous streets, replete with muggers, carrying large sums of cash is an invitation to be robbed and murdered.

Most persons who deposit these astonishingly large sums of cash into banks are criminals and, when the practice is repeated periodically, these banks know or should know these customers are criminals. What, if anything, can our criminal justice system do about banks that conspire to "launder" drug money?

Acting upon probable cause, pursuant to warrant whenever feasible, the Federal Bureau of Investigation and other federal law enforcement agencies can trace assets deposited into our banks under suspicious circumstances easily and with minimal invasion of the privacy owed to honest depositors. Once a pattern of "laundering" is discovered at a bank, our government should move immediately to seize the drug-money deposits and cause the same to be forfeited to the government, just as would happen to an airplane, automobile or boat used in drug smuggling. Thus, banks that issue commercial paper in exchange for such dirty cash would lose the cash and, perhaps, become obliged to make good the commercial paper from their own funds—a practice that will cause virtually any bank either to terminate its "laundry" or go out of business.[69] Stiff penalties may be imposed against repeat offender banks, also. As assistant treasury secretary John Walker, Jr. has warned: "To force a bank to pay a penalty of more than $1 billion would wake up even the sleepiest of chief executive officers."[70]

ANOTHER IDEA: UNITED STATES COURT OF CRIMINAL APPEALS

The Congress should consider carefully the wisdom and value of eliminating entirely all criminal appeals from the jurisdiction of the Supreme Court of the United States, by exercising authority contained within Article III, section 2, Constitution of the United States of America.[71] Doing so would sharply reduce the unmanageable caseload of the Supreme Court and eliminate its temptation to police the police, hardly among its constitutional duties. The Court could, and undoubtedly should, retain jurisdiction to hear and determine *true* constitutional controversies, whether they involve criminal or civil issues, but only after the criminal controversies have been more properly screened by courts below. In other words, following the examples set by several states such as Oklahoma and Texas, the Congress should re-route criminal appeals away from the Supreme Court and into another court more fully prepared to provide a limited review intended by the Congress.

This nation could benefit from the creation of a United States Court of Criminal Appeals, and such a court stands ready-made for operationalization at the discretion of the Congress, in the form of the current United States Court of Military Appeals (COMA). There is no doubt that the Congress may, in its exclusive discretion, both terminate the existence of COMA and substitute for it a Court of Criminal Appeals (COCA), pursuant to its authority under Article I, section 1, Constitution of the United States of America.[72] Although COMA has served this Nation well in wartime, the size of our military forces has shrunk in peacetime and with it has shrunk, also, the caseload of COMA.[73] In fact, all cases presently heard and determined by COMA are criminal in nature, arising under the Uniform Code of Military Justice (UCMJ), civil controversies involving our military having been transferred, and properly so, to the Claims Court and other federal courts. The present COMA building, situated near Judiciary Square in Washington,

D.C., could be adapted easily to accommodate the headquarters of COCA, nothwithstanding the need for COCA to house a larger staff than works presently at COMA.

Undoubtedly, the Court of Criminal Appeals should retain some characteristics of the Court of Military Appeals. For instance, its judges could be appointed for lengthy terms of, say, ten years, instead of for life, to permit substitution of judges periodically to conform to the changing posture of the citizenry toward criminal justice. In addition, COCA could parallel the circuit courts of appeals and meet periodically in panels of three judges at various locations throughout the nation, all COCA judges returning to Washington on occasion for *en banc* sittings, such as to hear capital cases argued.

In support of this proposal, the following more specific points may be considered: First, in eliminating all criminal appeals from the jurisdiction of the Supreme Court, the Congress may opt to eliminate criminal appeals also from the jurisdiction of the federal circuit courts of appeals, and to eliminate federal habeas corpus jurisdiction from both the federal district courts and courts of appeals.[74] In this way, the crowded dockets of our courts of appeals could become unclogged. Federal criminal defendants would have *one* right of automatic appeal directly to COCA from conviction in the federal district court. State criminal defendants would have *one* right of appeal or review[75] of federal issues, from the highest applicable state court directly to COCA. Second, COCA would require more than the three judges who sit currently on COMA. The COMA judges might serve out their terms on COCA, and the Congress might decide to add at least six additional seats for COCA, bringing the new court to a full complement of nine jurists. Third, COCA could be structured to meet in three panels, each panel constituting a division, and each division overlaping the jurisdictions served presently by four circuit courts of appeals. COCA judges could occupy circuit court chambers, courtrooms, and some existing support facilities at nominal or no increase in cost to the government. Fourth, the additional six judgeships COCA might require do not have to cost the government a penny; a corresponding reduction in judgeships may be achieved through attrition on the circuits the criminal caseloads of which would be diverted to COCA.

Creation of a United States Court of Criminal Appeals could become the greatest possible boost to the morale of our police and to citizens who are tired of the way our Supreme Court has been "reviewing" criminal convictions and sentences on an *ad hoc* basis. No longer would thirteen different federal circuit courts of appeals be rendering conflicting rulings, such as on *habeas corpus* matters. No longer could the Supreme Court provide a sweeping review of all aspects of a criminal case in the guise of interpreting our Constitution. To be sure, Democrats might perceive this plan as one of "court packing," because President Reagan would appoint the first COCA judges. To be sure, also, the proposed Court of Criminal Appeals eventually could become a surrogate Supreme Court, and even parallel its mistakes. Yet, the Congress could grant to COCA a much more limited jurisdiction to review criminal cases. COCA could be limited to reviewing cases for patent unfairness or obvious lack of compliance with *existing* laws. COCA could be prohibited from rendering any "new" constitutional interpretations, such as the Supreme Court has done to disguise its "judge-made laws." The Congress may even require COCA to hear and determine cases on an individual basis, and not make its decisions *stare decisis* (binding precedent) in state or lower federal courts. The *obiter dicta* ramblings of COCA judges, presumably, would count for less than the similar utterances of Supreme Court justices, which would avoid much of the confusion the Supreme Court has prompted in the minds of citizens and police alike. Finally, COCA could be given authority only to *remand* criminal cases to the trial level courts below, such as for sentencing review or to determine whether an error was "harmless." The Court of Criminal Appeals would not have to be granted authority to order retrials or even to vacate convictions, much less the authority to "supervise" the lower federal courts and, in that guise, to police the police as the Supreme Court has tried to do, very unsuccessfully and very detrimentally to the American police officer.

CONCLUSION

The Supreme Court of the United States cannot continue to sit as a super-legislature, usurping the functions of the Congress and state legislative bodies in its efforts to police the police. For the immediate future, the Congress should revoke from the Supreme Court its jurisdiction to hear and determine criminal appeals and to review criminal cases via writ of *certiorari*, and vest such jurisdiction in a new United States Court of Criminal Appeals, to be reconstituted from the current United States Court of Military Appeals.

In addition to reducing judicial interference in policing America, as a Nation we must take immediate measures to shore-up our local police, such as by increasing the numbers of professional police officers and by adding to those numbers groups of right-thinking Americans within every neighborhood in each city and town who have been trained as citizen-police and who stand ready, willing, and able to defend their neighborhoods whenever the need arises by providing armed reinforcement to the police. Uniformed police should be more visible on our streets, patrol in pairs, and interact much more directly and on foot with the citizenry. The federal government must act now to support local police further by hitting the drug traffickers where it will really hurt—at the bank. We must act swiftly to dry-up the supply of drugs, which pose a clear and present danger not only to police but also to the American way of life.

Making life better for the street cop—and for all Americans—will require innovative, dynamic new approaches. Whether or not the foregoing proposals are the correct blueprint, there is little doubt of the need for policy makers to pursue such innovations in order to sustain the recent progress made in reducing the rate of crime.

REFERENCES

The Sidewalk and Street Peace by David A. Jones and L. Stephen Jennings.

1. See the President's Commission on Law Enforcement and Administration of Justice, Task Force Report: *The Police*, July 1967, pp. 7–8.

2. For a more comprehensive discussion of life as a street cop, see J. Norman Swatan and Loren Morgan, *Administration of Justice: An Introduction* (New York; D. van Nortrand Co., 1980), pp. 113–14.

3. See William A. Westley, "The Police: A Sociological Study of Law, Custom and Morality" (unpublished Ph.D. dissertation, University of Chicago, Department of Sociology, 1951), cited in William J. Chambliss, *Crime and the Legal Process* (New York; McGraw-Hill Book Co. 1961), p. 156.

4. *To Establish Justice, To Insure Domestic Tranquility*, Final Report of the National Commission on the Causes and Prevention of Violence, December 10, 1969.

5. *Id.*, p. 288.

6. *Id.* p. 310–12. Task Force on Historical and Comparative Perspectives.

7. *Id.* p. 312. See *Violence in America: Historical and Comparative Perspectives*, Report of the Task Force on Historical and Comparative Perspectives (Washington: U.S. Government Printing Office, 1969).

8. See, *The Challenge of Crime in a Free Society*, General Report of the President's Commission on Law Enforcement and Administration of Justice February 1967; and Task Force Report: *The Police*, July 1967. See also *A National Strategy to Reduce Crime* and *Criminal Justice System*, Reports of the National Advisory Commission on Criminal Justice Standards and Goals, 1972, and Task Force Report: *Police*, January 1973.

9. See, for instance, "The Need to Recognize the Police as an Administrative Agency with Important Policymaking Responsibility," in The President's Commission on Law Enforce-

ment and Administration of Justice, Task Force Report: *The Police*, (July 1967) p. 18; and a recommendation "that a national study be undertaken to determine methods to evaluate and measure the effectiveness of individual police agencies in performing their crime control functions" contained in the National Commission on Criminal Justice Standards and Goals, Task Force Report: *Police*, January 1973, p. 151.

10. Both commissions issued task force reports on Police, Courts, and Corrections. The Katzenbach Commission also issued task force reports on Juvenile Delinquency and Youth Crime, on Organized Crime, Science and Technology, Assessment of Crime, Narcotics and Drugs, and on Drunkeness. The Peterson Commission also issued a task force report on Community Crime Prevention.

11. The National Commission on Criminal Justice Standards and Goals, Task Force Report; *Police*, January, 1973, pp. xiii–xvii.

12. *Id.* These recommendations pertained to alcohol and drug abuse centers, telephonic search warrants, court supervised electronic surveillance, interrelationship of public and private police agencies, the National Institute of Law Enforcement and Criminal Justice Advisory Committee, measures of effectiveness, certification of crime laboratories, job-related ability and personality inventory tests for police applicants, development and validation of a (police) selection scoring system, identification of police educational needs, study in police corruption, police officer benefits for duty-connected injury, disease, and death; transportation testing, digital communications system, standardized radio equipment, and frequency congestion. *Id., passim.*

13. As one example: "Standard 5.2. Combined Police Services. Every State and local government and every police agency should provide police services by the most effective and efficient organizational means available to it. In determining this means, each should acknowledge that the police organization (and any functional unit within it) should be large enough to be effective but small enough to be responsive to the people. If the most effective and efficient police service can be provided through mutual agreement or joint participation with other criminal justice agencies, the governmental entity or the police agency immediately should enter into the appropriate agreement or joint operation. . . . 1. Every State should enact legislation enabling local governments and police and criminal justice agencies, with the concurrence of their governing bodies, to enter into interagency agreements to permit total or partial police services. . . . *Id.* at 108.

14. The President's Commission on Law Enforcement and Administration of Justice Task Force Report: *The Police*, July, 1967, *passim.*

15. *Id.* p. 216.

16. *Id.* p. 227.

17. *Id.* p. 228.

18. *Id.* p. 63.

19. Richard A Myren, "Decentralization and Citizen Participation in Criminal Justice Systems," *The Public Administration Review*, October 1972. This passage is quoted in the National Commission on Criminal Justice Standards and Goals, Task Force Report: *Police*, January 1973, p. 64. At that time, Myren was dean of the School of Criminal Justice, State University of New York at Albany.

20. One person, Frank Carrington, served on both task forces. He is executive director of the Victims' Assistance Legal Organization, and he was chairman of the Advisory Task Force on Victims created by Ronald Reagan as governor of California.

21. The Violent Crime Task Force held hearings in Washington, D.C., Atlanta, Chicago, Detroit, Los Angeles, Miami and New York City. The Victims' Task Force held hearings in Washington, D.C., Boston, Denver, Houston, St. Louis, and San Francisco.

22. Report: Attorney General's Task Force on Violent Crime, August 1981.

23. Report: The President's Task Force on Victims of Crime, December 1982.

24. For a worthy expression of the views of most Americans on criminal justice issues, *see* both the introduction and the conclusion of this book.

25. *See* David A. Jones, *History of Criminology: A Philosophical Perspective* (Westport, Connecticut: Greenwood Press, 1986), Chapter Four, *passim.*

26. See Thomas Critchley, *A History of Police in England and Wales* (London: Routledge and Kegan, Paul, 1967) p. 50, quoting from Parliamentary Debates, volume 21, pp. 872–77, April 15, 1829.

27. Patrick Colquhoun, *A Treatise on the Police of the Metropolis*, 1795, preface. The watchmen took the nickname "Charlies" from King Charles II, during whose reign they were established.

28. Arthur Charles Cole, "The Irrepressible Conflict, 1859–1865," in Arthur M. Schlessinger, Sr. and Dixon Ryan Fox, editors: *A History of American Life in 12 Volumes*, volume 8 (New York: The MacMillan Company, 1934), pp. 154–55.

29. Harry W. Moore, Jr., *The American Police* (St. Paul, Minnesota: West Publishing Company, 1976), pp. 6–7.

30. See Raymond B. Fosdick, *American Police Systems* (New York: The Century Company, 1920).

31. Bruce Smith, Sr., *Police Systems in the United States* (New York: Harper and Brothers, 2d revised edition 1960), pp. 105–06.

32. See Elmer D. Graper, *American Police Administration* (New York: The MacMillan Company, 1921), pp. 109–110.

33. National Commission on Law Observance and Enforcement, *Report on the Police* (Washington: U.S. Government Printing Office, 1931; reprinted Montclair, New Jersey, Patterson Smith Publishing Corporation, 1968), pp. 5–7.

34. See William J. Bopp and Donald O. Schultz, *A Short History of American Law Enforcement* (Springfield, Illinois: Charles C. Thomas, 1972), pp. 109–10.

35. *Id.* at 111. The first state police academy was established in New York, followed shortly thereafter in Pennsylvania, Michigan, New Jersey, Connecticut, Oregon, Washington and Texas. See also, Allen Z. Gammage, *Police Training in the United States* (Springfield, Illinois: Charles C. Thomas, 1963)), pp. 10–16.

36. "At one moment the policemen is hero, the next, monster." Arthur Neiderhoffer, *Behind the Shield: The Police in Urban Society* (Garden City, New York: Doubleday and Company, Inc., 1967), p. 1. See also, Gene E. Carte, " Changes in Public Attitudes Toward the Police: A Comparison of 1938 and 1971 Surveys," *Journal of Police Science and Administration*, volume 1, number 2, 1973, pp. 1973, pp. 182–200.

37. *Supra*, n. 11, at 125–26.

38. See National Opinion Research Center Library (Chicago, Illinois): Amalgam Studies SRC-4050, April 1968 and SRS-4100, Spring 1970. See also Nelson Watson, *The Police and Their Opinions* (Washington: IACP, 1969). *See also*, Harry W. More, Jr., "The Police Function" in *The American Police* (St. Paul, Minnesota: West Publishing Company, 1976), pp. 51–58.

39. James Q. Wilson, *Varieties of Police Behavior* (Cambridge, Massachusetts: Harvard University Press, 1968).

40. *See, inter alia*, Daniel Cruse and Jesse Rubin, *Determinants of Police Behavior, A Summary* (Washington: U.S. Government Printing Office, June, 1973), pp. ii, 2–9. See also, Elmer H. Johnson, *Crime, Correction and Society* (Homewood, Illinois: The Dorsey Press, 1978), pp. 284–85 and David P. Stang, " The Police and Their Problems," in *Law and Order Reconsidered* (Washington, U.S. Government Printing Office, 1969), pp. 290–91.

41. "Garbage" calls might include, for instance, citizen requests for the police to search for a stray cat, to ask a next-door neighbor to turn-down the radio, to find an emergency source of gasoline for a stranded motorist, and then to fill the tank! Obviously, these tasks could be performed better by the S.P.C.A., the citizen himself, or an automobile club.

42. The policeman as law enforcer may pose a conflict for the policeman as social worker. One example: when one spouse calls for the police to intercede in a domestic dispute; the officer may witness the husband assaulting the wife, but detect that the wife prefers to avoid formal prosecution. The officer is left in the middle, holding the bag.

43. See "Judges with their Minds Right," *Time*, November 4, 1985, p. 77. Justice Brennan delivered his speech at Georgetown University, Washington, D.C.

44. *Id.* Justice Stevens delivered his speech to lawyers in Chicago.

45. For a discussion of the "selective incorporation" doctrine, see Justice Hugo L. Black's dissenting opinion to *Adamson v. California*, 332 U.S. 46, 68–112 (1947). For a discussion of what this author has termed "selective disincorporation" of the Bill of Rights, see David A. Jones, *The Law of Criminal Procedure: An Analysis and Critique* (Boston: Little, Brown and Company, 1981), Chapter 20. The author has suggested that by refusing to "incorporate" the Second Amendment along with most other provisions of the Bill of Rights, the Supreme Court castrated the Second Amendment and with it the right of Americans "to keep and bear arms" totally in denigration of the wishes of the Framers of the Constitution and the Founders of the Republic. *Id.* at 139, n. 61.

46. For instance, the Supreme Court has determined on several occasions that the Second Amendment, "the right of the people to keep and bear Arms," is not obligatory upon the states. *See, United States v. Cruikshank*, 92 U.S. 542 (1875) and *United States v. Miller*, 307 U.S. 174 (1939). *See also*, David A. Jones, *The Law of Criminal Procedure: An Analysis and Critique* (Boston: Little, Brown and Company, 1981), pp. 130, 139, n. 61. Nor has the Court made the Bail Clause of the Eighth Amendment obligatory upon the states. Perhaps, in this respect only, we should thank Heaven for small wonders. Of course, the Fourteenth Amendment never was intended by its draftsmen to facilitate anything more than racial equality. The Supreme Court has abused the Fourteenth as much as it has the Second Amendment, or even more so.

47. The Supreme Court ruled that it possessed the power to exercise appellate jurisdiction over state courts and that it and other federal courts may, "without question, revise the proceedings of the executive and legislative authorities of the states, and if they are found to be contrary to the constitution, may declare them to be of no legal validity." *Martin v. Hunter's Lessee*, 14 U.S. (1 Wheat.) 304, 344 (1816). Then, the Supreme Court ruled that, under section 25 of the Judiciary Act of 1789, it possessed authority to review state court judgments in *criminal* as well as civil proceedings. *Cohens v. Virginia*, 19 U.S. (6 Wheat.) 264 (1821). So far, attempts in the Congress to repeal section 25 of the Judiciary Act have been unsuccessful. *See, inter alia*, H.R. No. 43, 21st Congress, 2nd session, 1831. *See also*, Warren, "Legislative and Judicial Attacks on the Supreme Court of the United States—A History of the Twenty-fifth Section of the Judiciary Act," *American Law Review*, volume 47, pp. 1, 161, (1913).

48. Included here would be "Cases affecting Ambassadors, other public Ministers and Consuls;" "Controversies between two or more States;—between a State and Citizen of another State;—between Citizens of different States,—between Citizens of the saame State claiming Lands under Grants of different States, and between a State, or the Citizens thereof, and foreign States, Citizens or Subjects." See Article III, section 2, Constitution of the United States of America.

49. Included here might be "Cases, in Law and Equity, arising under this Constitution, the Laws of the United States, and Treaties made, or which shall be made, under their Authority;" and "Controversies to which the United States shall be a Party." *Id.*

50. To bear relation to a state criminal matter a controversy might involve the attempt of a state to disregard an express prohibition of the federal constitution, such as by granting a Letter of Marque or Reprisal, or by enacting an *ex post facto* law or a Bill of Attainder, all in contravention of Article I, section 10. Other examples might arise, including some effort by a state to violate the "Laws" of the United States, such as by purporting to decriminalize conduct where the very conduct has been proscribed by an Act of Congress and, consequently, pre-empted by operation of the Supremacy Clause. Example: a state trying to nullify the Taft-Hartley Law, in an effort to perpetuate a union strike.

51. "In all Cases affecting Ambassadors, other public Ministers and Consuls, and those in which a State shall be a Party, the Supreme Court shall have original jurisdiction." *Supra* n. 48.

52. "In all other Cases *before mentioned*, the supreme Court shall have appellate Jurisdiction, both as to Law and Fact, with such Exceptions, and under such Regulations as the Congress shall make." (Emphasis added) *Id.* What about controversies besides those "before mentioned" within section 2 of Article III? Did our Framers intend, by adding the words "before mentioned," to foreclose the Supreme Court from considering other controversies even with the tacit approval of the Congress?

53. See, *inter alia,* "Crackdown on 'Greenwashing,' " *Time,* March 25, 1985, p. 56.

54. For a description of drug smuggling, in Starr County, Texas, see "Secluded Texas County is Smuggler's Paradise, and Others Profit Too." *The Wall Street Journal,* October 23, 1985, p. 1. col. 1.

55. See, *inter alia,* "Fighting the Cocaine Wars," *Time,* February 25, 1985, pp. 26–35. *See also* "Miami Virtue, Miami Vice," *Time,* November 4, 1985, p. 33.

56. In Massachusetts, for instance, it is difficult to obtain a permit to own or possess a firearm and the penalty for possessing one without a permit is a mandatory one year jail sentence.

57. The study was conducted by James W. Wright and Peter H. Rossi, both of the University of Massachusetts. See Paul H. Blackman, "The Armed Criminal in America," *American Rifleman,* August 1985, pp. 34–35, 78. *See also,* David Hardy, "Gun Control, Crime and Freedom," in Patrick B. McGuigan and Randall R. Raders, eds., *Criminal Justice Reform* (Washington: Free Congress Research and Education Foundation, 1983) pp. 69–81.

58. Yet, some that purport to "document" police opposition to reform of the Gun Control Act, such as through S.1030 or H.R. 3300, seem not to have their facts straight. *Id.* at 75, citing as one example *The Charleston Gazette,* July 8, 1982, p. 4A. *See also,* David Warner, "Police Support Protection Act, Oppose Gun Control, Says Union Leader," *The Monitor,* January 31, 1986. This is an interview with Robert Kliesmet, President of the International Union of Police Associations (IUPA, AFL-CIO).

59. Examine such cases as the disappearances of Sarah Pryor from Woburn, Massachusetts and Cherry Mehan from Butler, Pennsylvania, during 1985.

60. "Childfind" is such a project—operated by the National Center for Missing and Exploited Children—which opened on June 13, 1984. It maintains a twenty-four hour "hotline" (800/843-5678). We have not taken sufficient steps to train local police in techniques of *immediate* response necessary to secure the area surrounding a reported kidnapping of a child by a stranger.

61. At least five Americans were killed in the twin Rome-Vienna terrorist attacks on airports early December 27, 1985, including a young man and a twelve-year-old girl. One of the Arab murderers possessed a note addressed to all Americans: "As you have violated our land, our honor, our people, we in exchange will violate everything, *even your children. . . .* The war has started from this moment." See *The Sunday Boston Herald,* December 29, 1985, pp. 1 and 4. (Emphasis added).

62. One has only to recall the civil guard in Spain during the time General Francisco Franco served as its *caudillo* to understand what really *visible* police presence means: two uniformed police officers on every corner of every street. This may raise some eyebrows, but the authors never felt so safe as when walking along the streets of Franco Spain, the green-uniformed police in their three-point hats standing at ease, hands behind their backs, fully armed but with smiling faces, graciously assisting passers-by as need be. A similar system was effective in Portugal under the late president Antonio Salazar. Of course, left-wingers will criticize such a police presence as exerting a "chilling effect" upon freedom of interaction. Do such critics prefer secret police, hidden from the population, but constantly watching from peepholes?

63. State police officers must continue to patrol our highways within automobiles, of course, but even they should ride in pairs, much as most Texas Ranger units have done for years. The single police officer alone on the freeway, particularly at night, is in grave danger and unjustifiably so.

64. Justice Benjamin Cardozo wrote this some fifty years ago. *See also* Frank Carrington, *Crime and Justice: A Conservative Strategy* (Washington: The Heritage Foundation, 1983), p. 20.

65. *Mapp v. Ohio,* 367 U.S. 643 (1961), the original case within which the Supreme Court made the Fourth Amendment obligatory upon the states in state criminal prosecutions, is such an example. Mapp had no reason to believe evidence seized against her by Ohio law enforcement authorities should be suppressed; police who did the searching and the seizing had every reason to believe such evidence would not be suppressed. Police were acting according to the standard of the day. The Supreme Court changed the rules in the middle of the game, then accused the police of cheating.

66. *Illinois v. Gates*, 462 U.S. 213 (1984). Another pro-police decision by the Supreme Court came in *United States v. Ross*, 456 U.S. 798 (1982), giving the police leeway to conduct a warrantless search of anything contained within an automobile, provided this search is predicated upon probable cause.

67. *See, inter alia*, John J. Putman, "Switzerland: The Clockwork Country," *National Geographic*, January 1986, pp. 96–127. Switzerland's 625,000-member Militia can mobilize in forty-eight hours or less. Members house their state's military equipment even within their own homes, for ready access in case of emergency.

68. *Supra* n. 53.

69. Naturally, the Federal Deposit Insurance Corporation should not idemnify a bank or its stockholders or its depositors for "losses" incurred through criminal enterprises. In practice, however, the F.D.I.C. may have to indemnify depositors up to $100,000 deposited within a given bank, but the cost may be offset by funds forfeited by such banks that could be made available to the F.D.I.C.

70. *Supra* n. 53.

71. *Supra* n. 52.

72. Article III, section 1 vests the judicial power of the United States "in one supreme Court, and in such inferior Courts as the Congress may from time to time ordain and establish."

73. The United States Court of Military Appeals (COMA) reached a disposition in 3,296 cases out of the 4,038 cases filed during 1984, according to its Annual Report.

74. Congress might decide to eliminate the federal Writ of Habeas Corpus entirely for state prisoners, as recommended by former Attorney General William French Smith. See William French Smith, "Proposals for Habeas Corpus Reform," in Patrick B. McGuigan and Randall R. Rader, eds., *Criminal Justice Reform* (Washington: Free Congress Research and Education Foundation, 1983), pp. 137–54.

75. COCA should not be granted authority to issue writs of *certiorari*, and appeals to COCA should be limited to one per appellant, under an *omnibus* motion model. However, perhaps COCA should have jurisdiction to review matters on appeal even if not designated as being on appeal by the appellant, in the interests of justice, *sua sponte*, as most intermediate-level appellate courts can do presently.

15

THE CHRISTIAN AND THE PROBLEM OF CRIME:
What We Can Do About It
by Daniel W. Van Ness

It was late afternoon one day in November when I received a tele-phone call from the woman who lived below us in our two-flat apartment building.

"I just got home," she said. "Our apartments have been broken into. You had better come."

The burglars had been there sometime in the early afternoon. They had rung both doorbells to make sure no one was home, then jimmied the front door of the building. Both apartments were un-locked, but our door had a catch in it which apparently led the bur-glars to believe it was locked. They kicked the door in, destroying the jamb.

They had ransacked both apartments. Drawers were pulled out and their contents disturbed; closet doors stood open with clothes pushed around. Our brand new clock-radio was gone, as was a cam-era, an old watch and a beautiful alarm clock my wife had purchased on a trip to Switzerland. The people downstairs were missing similar valuables. Apparently the intruders had taken only small items they could hide easily.

The police arrived more than an hour after we called them. They didn't bother to come upstairs to see our door or apartment; they just filled out a report so we could file insurance claims. They said it was unlikely the burglars would be caught and, warning us that they might come back for larger items, suggested we install better locks. They also recommended that we move to a safer neighborhood.

We slept two nights with a door that would not lock. We came home each day apprehensive that the "return visit" the police had predicted might have happened already. I spent a day and a half repairing our door. We never filed an insurance claim for fear that the raised premiums would be too expensive.

Our experience was not unique. According to the United States

Census Bureau, one out of four households experienced some kind of crime last year.[1] While this is a decrease over previous years, it suggests that victimization and fear are pervasive in this country. One public opinion survey, for example, found that half of the American people were afraid to walk the streets within one mile of their houses.[2]

As a result, crime becomes not only a public policy issue, but also a political one. Law and order speeches have become a basic part of American political life. Of course, no one would argue against law or order. But the criminal justice system can become the fall guy in the political process. As elections approach, the temptation is to "talk tough" about crime. This translates into longer prison sentences, mandatory imprisonment laws and the like. The dilemma of what to do about crime is made painfully real by the stories of those caught in crime as well as victimized by it.

A TRUE STORY, AND A REVIEW OF THE ISSUES

The 18-year-old stood before the judge for sentencing. He was part of a ring of boys his age who had burglarized houses all over town. They had stolen an estimated $150,000 worth of goods.

The judge faced considerable community pressure to do something forceful, to send a message to high school students that crime does not pay. The victims were frustrated, angry and resentful. Police had discovered that the teenagers were committing the crimes because they wanted to buy cars and maintain a high standard of living. It was easier and faster to break into people's houses than it was to get a job.

What should the judge do? How should Christians respond? Ought we to agree with the law-and-order rhetoric? Does Scripture have something to say about how our criminal justice system could become more equitable and effective?

Let's first review some crime-related issues that are being debated today and then consider a biblical framework with which to examine these issues. After that we will return to the rest of this story and what the judge decided.

Issue 1: Crime Rates. During the 1970s the number of crimes reported to the police increased dramatically. The FBI compiles these statistics into one of two major indexes of criminal activity in the United States. The other index is the Census Bureau survey conducted every six months which determines how many households have experienced a crime during the past half year. Interestingly, the Census Bureau index did not show an increase during the 1970s, but did reveal that a staggering one out of three households were affected by crime each year. This figure remained constant throughout the decade.[3]

Perhaps the best explanation for the difference between the two is that while crime remained constant during the 1970s, more victims of those crimes began reporting those incidents to the police. Because crime reported to the police is what the FBI tabulates, its figures may have simply reflected an increasingly complete view of the extent of crime, rather than indicating that crime was rising.

In any event, the 1980s have produced a dramatic drop in both reports. The 1981 FBI statistics showed no increase in crime; in 1982 it dropped 3.4 percent, in 1983, 6.7 percent, and in 1984, another 3 percent.[4]

And the Census Bureau study agreed. Their 1983 survey showed a decline in victimization to one out of every four households.[5]

Several explanations have been given for this phenomenon. For one thing, the number of people in the 15–25 age group is declining.[6] These appear to be the "crime prone" years, and a smaller population within that age-group means less crime. If this is true, then the drop in crime is likely to continue throughout the 1980s.

Another plausible explanation is that neighborhood crime prevention programs are working. Studies have shown that crime goes down in neighborhoods with such programs (and up in the surrounding neighborhoods).[7]

Issue 2: Victims' Rights. Crime involves four parties: the victim, the offender, the surrounding community and the state. But the criminal justice process focuses on only two of the parties: the offender and the state (e.g., *State of Illinois versus John Smith*).

This was not always the case. In the Old Testament, all four parties were involved in fixing responsibility for a criminal act and in bringing restoration to the victim. For example, thieves and other property offenders were required to pay restitution to the victim. The community was to help the offender and victim work out a fair payment. If they had difficulty in doing this, the case was taken to priests or judges for final determination.

Over time, however, the state's role increased, in part to curb vigilante justice, but also to facilitate the growing powers of centralized government. The result was that increasingly the victim was excluded from the criminal justice process. As the state became more powerful, protections were established to protect defendants from arbitrary or unfairly intrusive government actions in investigations and prosecutions.[8]

Growth of the victim assistance movement has resulted in increased public and private resources to help victims deal with the impact of crime. It has also produced a variety of recommendations for reforming the criminal justice process. Many proposals are excellent and much-needed. Others, however, have nothing to do with victims. Instead they restrict the rights of defendants or mandate long prison sentences. Such measures should be discussed on their own merits. The true value of "victims'-rights" proposals should be gauged by asking how the reform will benefit victims.

Issue 3: The Purpose of Prisons. The use of prisons to punish offenders is an uniquely American innovation. In 1790, Philadelphia converted its jail from a place to hold defendants prior to trial, to a place of penitence—a penitentiary—for those convicted of crimes. The offender was placed in solitary confinement and given a Bible and regular visits by the warden and a minister. The reformers hoped that offenders would be rehabilitated when they were separated from bad moral influences and given biblical training.[9]

However, there were problems from the outset. Many early "penitents," locked in their solitary cells, went mad, and there was little evidence that this treatment produced rehabilitation. But the idea had caught on, and by the 1850s all states had adopted imprisonment to punish crimes.[10]

Four reasons have been given to justify imprisonment to offenders:

• *Incapacitation.* A person locked up in prison cannot commit new crimes outside of prison.

• *Deterrence.* The knowledge that criminals are punished will keep potential criminals from breaking the law.

• *Rehabilitation.* Services can be provided to rehabilitate the offender.

• *Punishment.* Society must provide sanctions to be used against those who violate the law.

The one function unique to prisons is incapacitation. Prison provides a place where dangerous offenders can be physically restrained from committing new crimes in society. It is interesting to note, however, that only about half of the nation's prisoners are convicted of violent offenses. The other purposes can be served as well or better through other, less costly sanctions.

262

First, law enforcement experts generally agree that what deters people from committing a crime is the expectation of being caught and punished, not the severity of the punishment. This is why drivers do not speed when they see a police car behind them; they know they will be pulled over.

Because fewer than 7 crimes out of 100 even result in an *arrest*,[11] the deterrent value of any punishment is slim. Increasing the potential punishment will do less to deter crime than increasing the likelihood that the offender will be apprehended. This is why neighborhood crime watch programs have been successful. Criminals know they are more likely to be caught in these neighborhoods.

Second, few criminal justice professionals believe that prison rehabilitates. Norman Carlson, director of the Federal Bureau of Prisons, has said, "I've given up hope for rehabilitation, because there's nothing we can do to force change on offenders. Change has got to come from the heart."[12] To put an offender in prison with other criminal offenders, hoping he leaves the abnormal society of the prison a healthy and law-abiding person, is a curious strategy. Far too often the opposite occurs, and the offender is released a potentially more dangerous person than when he went to prison.

Third and finally, prison's purpose is punishment. Punishment, in the scriptural view, serves justice. Those who violate the law must face an appropriate sanction, or else law becomes simply an expression of hoped-for behavior.

In the United States, prison and punishment have become almost synonymous. But this is a recent development. Until 200 years ago, prisons were used only to hold people prior to trial or punishment. Genesis tells us that Joseph was thrown into prison. But as we know from what happened to his fellow prisoners, the baker and the cupbearer, that prison was used to hold people until they were tried or punished.[13] And there were a whole array of punishments.

The predominant punishment in the Old Testament was restitution. The offender was required to repay the victim according to a formula set down in the Law. Zacchaeus referred to this in the New Testament when he came down from the sycamore tree and had lunch with Jesus. He promised to pay back four-fold anyone that he had defrauded in his tax collection.[14] That was what Jewish law required.

There were even provisions in the Old Testament to cover situations where the offender had no money to repay the victim. The offender had to work off the debt by performing free service for the victim.[15]

So while the particular punishment of prison serves several purposes, other punishments do as well. The unique role of prisons is to incapacitate violent and dangerous offenders.

Issue 4: Prison Overcrowding. America's prison population is growing dramatically. The number of prisoners has more than doubled in the last decade, going from 218,205 in 1974 to 463,866 at the end of 1984.[16] What do these figures mean? Simply that our prison population is now growing 15 times faster than the general population.

We use prisons more than any country in the world, other than South Africa and the Soviet Union.[17] In fact, our prison population itself is now larger than the population of 20 member countries of the United Nations, larger than Alaska and roughly the size of Atlanta and Pittsburgh.[18]

With such explosive growth, state and federal officials have been struggling to find room for all the prisoners. Virtually every state has exceeded its prison capacity. In several, chapels have been converted into dormitories to hold the overflow.

Thirty-two states and the District of Columbia are under court order.[19] Conditions in one or more of their prisons are so bad, a judge has ruled that it is actually "cruel and unusual punishment" to send someone there. Why? Because of the marked increase in violence, disease, suicide, disciplinary violations and deaths that result from overcrowding.

Overcrowding affects the general public as well. Attorney General William French Smith's Task Force on Violent Crime stated in its 1981 report that overcrowding was the number one problem facing corrections authorities. It found a substantial number of cases where serious offenders who should have been incarcerated received probation because there was no prison space.[20]

A simple answer to prison overcrowding is to build more prisons. But states are discovering they cannot build their way out of this crisis. Prisons are just too expensive.

States spend an average of $60,000 to $80,000 per bed to construct a typical prison.[21] That's just under the median cost of a new home in the United States. And construction costs are only the beginning. A prison will cost 12.5 times more to run for 30 years than to build. This means that a prison costing $80,000 per bed to build will cost an additional $1,000,000 per bed to run over the next 30 years![22]

It takes an average of $16,245 to keep one person in prison for a year.[23] That cost is more than room, board and tuition charges for a year at Harvard or Yale.

In other words, prison overcrowding has become an economic as well as a criminal justice issue, one that the courts are requiring public officials to resolve.

Issue 5: Sentencing innovations. Faced with the prohibitive cost of building new prisons and the realization that for some offenders other punishments may be more useful in serving the purposes of the criminal justice system, many states have begun to implement alternative punishments.

In most states, the correction authorities have begun by identifying the nondangerous offenders who are being sent to prison. These offenders are then either diverted to other forms of punishment or released from prison early and placed under intensive parole supervision.

For example, a number of states have established restitution and community service programs for property offenders. These offenders are required to repay their victims and to perform free work for a charity or a government agency in their community. In properly run programs the success rate is high, because the offender knows that, if he fails to perform adequately, the judge will order him to serve the rest of his time in prison.

Georgia, Texas, and several other states have supplemented this program with intensive probation. An offender subjected to intensive probation is required to set a daily schedule with his probation officers. One officer makes three surprise visits throughout the week to make sure the probationer is keeping to his schedule. The other officer meets with him twice a week for counseling and other assistance.

These states have discovered that they can enforce appropriate behavior at a fraction of the cost of prison. Georgia has saved $5.4 million per year.[24] Texas saved $8 million a year in the early 1980s.[25] And repeat offender rates are lower. Alabama has experienced a failure rate only 17–18 percent for people in intensive probation.[26]

Other states have released prisoners early to alleviate overcrowding. In 1984, over 17,000 inmates nationwide had sentences shortened to make room for new inmates.[27] Some states used a formula to identify those least likely to commit a new crime. In others the legislature has reduced all sentences by 60- to 90-day intervals.

As would be expected, some of these released prisoners have committed new crimes, a few of which have received a great deal of publicity. But overall the recidivism rates for people released early has been about the same as for those serving full sentences.

A FRAMEWORK FOR DISCUSSION OF THE ISSUES

While we must consider economics as we evaluate our criminal justice system, no one wants to settle for a second-rate criminal justice system simply because that's all we can afford. Fortunately, we have alternatives.

The Old Testament justice system was built on restitution. The advantage of such an approach is that it blends two ideas; we must hold an offender *responsible* for his conduct, and we must do so in a way that promotes *restoration* of the victim.

Responsibility is a major theme in Judeo-Christian thought. Individuals are responsible for their own acts and therefore are obligated to accept the punishments that result.

But restoration is an equally important concept which should help shape the form of that punishment. The offender must not only accept responsibility for his acts, he must also be required to take appropriate steps to restore the victim.

Such an approach answers the concerns being voiced by many victims today. Instead of being excluded from the criminal justice process, a restitution-based approach recognizes and enforces the most fundamental right of the victim: the right to be made whole.

Although violent and serious offenders—that 50 percent who pose an ongoing danger to society—must be locked up for our protection, the other 50 percent of the prison population could be punished in ways, such as intensive supervision coupled with restitution and community service, that promote restoration of the victim. This would have the additional benefit of lowering the prison population and avoiding costly prison expansion.

Restitution-based reform would require three changes:

• Create a variety of criminal punishments for judges to use, including restitution and community service.

• Reserve imprisonment for dangerous offenders who must be incapacitated.

• Punish the other offenders—the non-dangerous ones—in ways

266

that require them to accept responsibility for restoring the victim. Courts around the country are using this approach with success.

THE REST OF THE STORY

What happened to our teenage burglar, introduced at the beginning of this article? In his case, the judge concluded that the defendant was not likely to ever burglarize houses again. "You have been caught," he said. "I think you will find it easier and safer to work for your income rather than steal it. But you broke the law, and I must see that you face the consequences. So I am sentencing you to do three things. First of all, I order you to perform community service."

And every Saturday (because he was still going to school), the young man did free work for the city. He painted buildings and cleaned up the park and that sort of thing. It was conspicuous punishment.

"Second, I order you to pay restitution to the victims." This meant repaying the market value of the items stolen. That amounted to much more than what the teenager got when he fenced the goods.

The judge gave him time to get a job and then took most of his paycheck for restitution payments. And because the judge wanted the defendant to know what it is like to be burglarized and lose everything he owned, part of the restitution order was to sell all of his property and put the proceeds into the restitution fund.

Initially the young man thought that meant only his car, which he had purchased with the proceeds of the crime. And it did mean his car, but it also meant everything else he owned, except for his clothes and his bed. It meant the trophy he had won at a track meet. It meant his baseball bat. He had to sell everything that he owned so he would understand that, to their owner, personal belongings have a value greater than their monetary worth.

"Third, the victims want to talk to you about the crime. They have questions they want to ask you and things they want to tell you. So I want you to sit down and talk to them about it."

As it turned out, that was the toughest part of the sentence. The defendant said later that he would rather have done almost anything else. But he met with them.

The victims were very angry. They had been collectors of antique oriental furniture for years. So what they lost in the burglary was very valuable. But the couple had lost more than valuable furniture and art. They had lost memories. Their custom had been to purchase the antiques as souvenirs of trips and other memorable events. For example, one of the stolen items was a Ming vase they had purchased 10 years earlier at the end of a month-long vacation in Europe.

"Do you understand what you took from us?" they asked. "It was more than a beautiful, expensive vase. It was a memento of our trip. When guests admired it, we could talk to them not only about the vase, but also about our trip to Europe."

The young man was genuinely remorseful. He was beginning to understand what it was like to be victimized and to experience loss. And he wanted to make it up to them. The couple proposed a fascinating idea.

They told him that as a down payment on his restitution he should go to an antique store and find something he thought they would like. If they agreed then he would buy it.

So he went to several stores and finally found a beautiful oriental coffee table painted with black lacquer with a delicate flower design. He was giving them something that fit them as individuals, and they received something from him that showed he was a sensitive young man, not simply a burglar.

Although the couple lost one memento, they gained another. Now when visitors put down their coffee cups and comment on the beautiful table, one of them says, "There is an interesting story about this coffee table..."

STRATEGY FOR ACTION

The judge in this story was able to impose a restitution-based sentence. His decision benefited the victims, saved the state thousands of dollars, and held the defendant responsible without subjecting him to the violence, idleness and destructive influences of an overcrowded prison.

It is easy to see how judges, legislators and other public officials bring about reform. But what can private citizens do? Can an average Christian really help accomplish change in the criminal justice system?

The answer is yes. Right now around the country people like you are taking effective steps to accomplish reform. The most successful ones follow a plan of action.

First: Get the Facts. You now know more about the criminal justice system than most people. But do a little more investigating.

Are the prisons in your state overcrowded? What would it cost to build new ones? How many of your state's prisoners are nonviolent offenders who could be punished through restitution or community service instead? Are these programs available in your state?

The best way to get this information is to contact your state corrections department or your state legislators. But reform organizations can also help you. Just about every state has a local group working on reform, or you can contact a national organization such as Justice Fellowship which monitors what is happening in each state.

Collecting this information is only part of the process. There are several ways you can get first-hand knowledge of how the criminal justice system works.

Visit a nearby prison. As a taxpayer you have the right to see what is happening with your money. Prisons do have security reasons for screening visitors, so call ahead to ask how you can tour the facility.

Get involved with a prison ministry. This will help you understand more about the kinds of people who are in prison, and will give you an opportunity to serve.

Sit in a courtroom for an afternoon and watch how cases are handled.

Talk to the police about crime prevention programs that are working in your state.

Second: Know The Arguments for Reform. Review the issues and the framework for solutions discussed earlier in this chapter. How do these fit with what you have learned about your state? What would be the most compelling argument you could make to your friends for criminal justice reform?

Often the cost of imprisonment gets people's attention. How much does it cost to keep a prisoner for a year compared to a year at your state university?

Follow up by thinking about and discussing the principles of responsibility, restoration and restitution.

Third: Let Other People Know What You Have Found. Everyone has a group of people he or she influences. Who are the people who pay attention to your ideas? They probably have not thought much about these issues, and they will be curious about what you are learning. Let them know what you have found and ask them to help.

Although most people do not think so, you can have a real influence on state and federal representatives. These people do read their mail, and most of them get very little about criminal justice. A brief, polite letter explaining your view that nonviolent, non-dangerous offenders should be punished through restitution and community service will be effective.

Fourth: Find Other People to Work With. It is much easier to work on a project like this with other people. Have a friend help you lead a discussion on criminal justice in a Bible study at church. Find out whether your denomination has a staff person or committee working on criminal justice issues.

Ask your state legislators to suggest a local reform organization working for these changes. Contact national organizations as well. Justice Fellowship, for example, helps people around the country work for reform and provide materials, ideas and information on helpful steps being taken around the country.

Fifth: Be Specific. Identify for the people you are working with the specific changes that need to be made in the criminal justice and punishment system in your state. These should not be trivial changes. There should be some possibility for change and success. There may be legislation that should be supported or a new report that should get attention. Be ready to make specific recommendations when people ask what should be done.

If you know what you want done, do your research and let people know. Change will happen. It did in Indiana. In that state, Justice Fellowship worked with a group of Christians who were concerned about the problems in the state's criminal justice system. They first checked with state officials and discovered that Indiana was under court order to improve its prisons. The state was considering a $200 million prison construction program to ease overcrowding, even though officials felt there were a substantial number of prisoners who would pose no danger to society if they were punished outside of prison.

Their next action was to form a task force to raise support in the Christian community for reform. They agreed on those agruments that would best aid passage of a bill to set up local restitution and community service programs.

This group of dedicated believers also spoke in churches, civic clubs, professional meetings and on radio shows. They wrote letters to friends and business associates. They identified hundreds of people who agreed on the need for change. And ultimately they succeeded.

As a result of their activities and those of other concerned people throughout the state, Indiana's legislature appropriated $6 million to develop those local programs. (A subsequent study found that for every dollar spent in this way, the state saved $23.)[28]

The hard work and perseverance of committed Christians paid off. And they found out that other people were also ready to support changes that were appropriate.

Yes, Christians can be salt and light, even in the criminal justice system. If enough of us work together, we can see similar change take place in every state.[29]

REFERENCES

The Christian and the Problem of Crime by Daniel W. Van Ness

1. *Households Touched By Crime, 1983*, Bureau of Justice Statistics, May 1984 (Washington, D.C.: U.S. Department of Justice).
2. *Newsweek*, March 23, 1981.
3. "Households Touched by Crime, 1983," *supra* n. 1.
4. "Statistics Show Crime Drop," *Washington Post*, April 21, 1984.
5. "Households Touched by Crime, 1983," *supra* n. 1.
6. "Good News About Crime," Editorial, *The Washington Post*, April 23, 1983. See also: "Estimates of the Population of States by Age: July 1, 1981–1983," United States Bureau of the Census, Washington, D.C., May 1984; "Population Estimates and Projections: Estimates of the Population of the United States by Age, Sex and Race 1970–1977," United States Bureau of the Census, Washington, D.C., April 1978; "Statistical Abstracts of the United States—1984," United States Bureau of the Census, Washington, D.C. 1983.
7. Thomas Gabor, "The Crime Displacement Hypothesis: An Empirical Examination," *Crime and Delinquency*, July 1981, p. 390.
8. Jacobs, "The Concept of Restitution: An Historical Overview," in Joe Hudson and Burt Galaway, eds., *Restitution in Criminal Justice: A Critical Assessment of Sanctions* (Lexington, Massachusetts: Lexington Books, 1977), pp. 45ff.
9. Thorston Sellin, "The Origin of the Pennsylvania System of Prison Discipline," in George Killinger and Paul Cromwell, Jr., eds., *Penology: The Evolution of Corrections in America* (St. Paul, Minn.: West Publishing, 1973), pp. 13ff.
10. The first public institution built in the territory that would, fourteen years later, become the state of Oregon was a prison.
11. According to the Bureau of Justice Statistics, only one-third of all crimes are reported to the police. Of every five crimes which are reported, one crime results in an arrest. *Report to the Nation on Crime and Justice*, Bureau of Justice Statistics (Washington, D.C.: U.S. Department of Justice, 1983), pp. 24, 52–53.
12. Mr. Carlson made this remark in a speech at the Prison Fellowship National Leadership Conference in Washington, D.C., September 19, 1980.
13. See Genesis, 40.
14. See Luke, 19:1–10.
15. Exodus 22:3.
16. These statistics are derived from "Sentenced Prisoners in State and Federal Institutions, 1974," Bureau of Justice Statistics (1975), and "Prisoner Count Reaches Record High," *USA Today*, April 22, 1985. [Editor's note: The increase continued in 1985. Preliminary data found 505,037 prisoners in 1985. BJS, June 1986.]
17. "International Rates of Imprisonment" (mimeo), National Council on Crime and Delinquency, 1981.

271

18. These statistics derived from comparison with city, state and country populations recorded in *Reader's Digest Almanac.*

19. *Prisoners in 1984,* Bureau of Justice Statistics, May 1985 (Washington, D.C.: U.S. Department of Justice).

20. Griffin Bell and James Thompson, *Attorney General's Task Force on Violent Crime Final Report* (Washington, D.C.: U.S. Department of Justice, 1981), p. 10.

21. These figures cited by Norman Carlson, Director of the Federal Bureau of Prisons, in remarks at a conference sponsored by Ethics and Public Policy, Washington, D.C., March 30, 1984.

22. "Estimated 30-year Life Cycle Cost for a Correctional Facility," Chicago: Moyer Associates, Inc., 1981.

23. *The Corrections Yearbook, 1984,* Criminal Justice Institute, Inc., p. 26.

24. Steve Gettinger, "Intensive Supervision: Can it Rehabilitate Probation?," *Corrections Magazine,* April 1983, p. 8.

25. Ibid.

26. Telephone conversation with Al Dodd, Administrative Assistant to the Director of S.I.R., Alabama Dept. of Corrections, May 16, 1985.

27. "Prisoners in 1984," *supra* n. 19.

28. Mark S. Umbreit, "Reducing Prison Overcrowding Through Community Corrections," PACT: Prisoner and Community Together, Inc., January 1981.

29. This article is copyright by Daniel W. Van Ness.

16

THE RESTITUTIONARY PURPOSE OF THE CRIMINAL LAW

by Herbert W. Titus

In the May 1985 issue of the American Bar Association Journal J.S. Bainbridge, Jr., a Baltimore lawyer, made the startling claim that "[r]etribution has returned to criminal justice." Documenting the failure of the criminal law to rehabilitate offenders, Mr. Bainbridge supported his claim on the grounds that legislators, judges, and scholars had lately discovered the shortcomings of the rehabilitative ideal: "Rehabilitation is being passed over like a dish that didn't digest well."[1]

But the demise of rehabilitation in the criminal law will not guarantee that retribution will return to center-stage. Legal scholars, especially, have been reluctant to embrace a philosophy of punishment linked closely to retribution; indeed they greatly fear any penal philosophy based upon retribution. Overwhelmingly they favor the widely embraced utilitarian philosophy of deterrence. They endorse a criminal penalty only if it is likely to restrain convicted offenders from committing other crimes or to deter others from engaging in crime. They believe that the role of retribution is a limited one to be applied only when their utilitarian purpose infringes unreasonably upon individual autonomy.[2]

In their popular criminal law textbook, law professors Wayne La Fave and the late Austin Scott, Jr., have summarized this conventional wisdom:

> The broad aim of the criminal law is. . .to prevent harm to society. . . .This is accomplished by punishing those who have done harm, and by threatening with punishment those who would do harm. . . .[3]

Having maintained that no criminal penalty, whether retributive or rehabilitative in effect, may be justified unless it deters criminal behavior, America's law teachers and scholars both within the classroom and in the public marketplace have directed the debate about criminal law penalties to one issue: Do they work?

Ironically, law teachers and scholars prefer their utilitarian theories even though it has been proved that penalties imposed upon people after they have been convicted of criminal activity do not work very well. Criminology experts have conducted studies that question whether anyone is deterred by the conviction of another person and whether even the convicted criminal, himself, is deterred except during the period of time of incarceration.[4] Some social scientists have even suggested that a much more efficient and effective system would provide "treatment" to "cure" actual and potential criminal offenders whose behavior is, in their opinion, determined not chosen.[5]

Almost all law teachers and scholars, lawyers and judges, legislators and ordinary people have refused this invitation. But on what grounds? In their recently published casebook on criminal law three University of Virginia law professors have summarized the most popular reason:

> The underlying premise of the criminal law is that it is morally right to treat people as responsible moral agents, whatever the fact of the matter, because any other view would be inconsistent with the values of individual autonomy and freedom that the law should reflect and with the perceptions of each other on which people at least think they are governing their daily lives.[6]

Law students who are taught by these three professors and by most of their colleagues learn that, while the social scientists may have accurately described the real world and the reality of man's condition in it, the law must ignore that reality to achieve other more important goals. In the words of the three Virginia law professors quoted above:

> Determinism is rejected by the criminal law, in other words, not because it is a false scientific theory but because it should be rejected in light of the proper normative premises on which the criminal law should function.[7]

By divorcing the criminal law from "scientific reality" law teachers and scholars have freed themselves to keep their favored deterrence rationale for the criminal law without having to account for its failures. By embracing the criminal law's traditional requirements that a man may be punished for conduct only if he may be blamed for making a wrong choice and that his punishment must be proportionate to the seriousness of his offense, they are able to preserve liberty. But they are free to sacrifice that liberty if such principles interfere with the overriding utilitarian objective to deter crime. By refusing to decide whether or not man is a free moral agent, the typical law teacher and scholar may pick and choose according to his own hidden agenda. Consequently, he has held the criminal law captive to a series of uneasy compromises between "two contending philosophical views regarding the ultimate purpose of punishment...: to prevent or minimize criminal behavior...[or] to impose upon the criminal his just deserts."[8]

Not only have law students suffered at the hands of their double-minded teachers, the American public has suffered as well. In the 1960s, for example, legal experts championed new programs to finance employment and educational opportunities for convicted felons so that they will not return to their previous lives of crime. Taxpayers found themselves paying for such programs; yet they had to pay for their own children's education or training for employment. Later, they discovered that such expensive rehabilitative programs have not "deterred" those who have benefited from them.[9]

In the 1980s ordinary citizens watch in dismay expensive appeals and long delays as lawyers and courts review and rereview for legal errors the trial records of convicted murderers sentenced to death. Why? Partly, because the experts cannot agree that the death penalty deters crime and, also, because they are frightened by the imposition of such a "final penalty" when they are not sure if convicted murderers are really morally responsible for the deaths of their victims.

Such examples, and they could be multiplied without great effort, establish with certainty that the deterrent rationale cannot support any system of criminal law that, in fact, administers true justice. On the one hand, failures will never be discovered until after the programs have been implemented at great cost to liberty and to security. On the other hand, the lives of human beings and the well-being of human society cannot be subjected to scientific experimentation without treating men as mice in a psychological maze.

Notwithstanding this irrefutable dilemma, leaders of America's legal community have been unwilling to jettison the utilitarian concept of deterrence which justifies punishment in preventive terms. At the heart of their refusal is a misunderstanding of the true purpose of criminal punishment as given by God to man and revealed to the nation of Israel through their prophet, Moses.

EYE FOR EYE, TOOTH FOR TOOTH:
RESTITUTION NOT RETRIBUTION

Many legal scholars cite the Old Testament passages calling for an "eye for eye, tooth for tooth" as the foundation for the "retributive view" of criminal punishment.[10] The late Herbert Packer attacked these Old Testament verses, known as the *lex talionis*, as calling for the satisfaction of "what is essentially a community blood lust." He claimed that the only purpose of the *lex talionis* was to achieve revenge against the wrongdoer: The criminal must be "paid back" for his crime and he must "pay back" society. On those grounds Packer dismissed the *lex talionis* as having "no useful place in a theory of justification for punishment, because what it expresses is nothing more than dogma, unverifiable and on its face implausible."[11]

What has made the *lex talionis* so implausible to Packer and to his fellow colleagues has been twofold: 1) Their aversion to any truth based upon the Christian faith in God's revelation to man and 2) their dogmatic faith in the scientific method as the only source of knowledge. As a consequence of these prejudices Packer and his fellow law teachers and scholars have mistaken the true purpose and meaning of the *lex talionis*.

They have assumed that the Old Testament standard requiring an "eye for eye" and a "tooth for tooth" is to be *literally* applied. They have made this assumption for one simple reason: They have not carefully studied the *lex talionis* in the context in which it appears in three of the books of Moses—Exodus, Leviticus, and Deuteronomy. In each of the three passages it is clear that the rule of "eye for eye" and "tooth for tooth" was never intended to be applied literally. Rather, it was intended to be a principled guide for tailoring all remedies, civil and criminal, to restore a person injured in accordance with the blameworthiness of the wrongdoer and the seriousness of the injury of the person wronged.

In Deuteronomy, chapter 19, God revealed to Moses the crime of perjury and specified the penalty to be imposed in those instances where the perjurer has accused another of having committed a crime. Upon conviction of such an offense, God commanded that the offender suffer the same penalty that the one against whom he had falsely testified would have suffered if his testimony had been true.[12] For example, if the perjurer had falsely testified that another had stolen and destroyed one of his oxen, then the perjurer would

276

have been required to pay to the one against whom he had falsely testified five oxen according to the rule of Exodus 22:1. Or if the perjurer had testified falsely that another had committed murder, then the perjurer would pay with his life as if he, the false witness, had committed murder.

These penalties were justified in this passage as conforming with the Biblical command of an "eye for eye, tooth for tooth."[13] Yet, if Packer was correct that the *lex talionis* called for retaliation, an equivalent "pay back" for the wrong done, the penalty should have been literally applied, a "lie for a lie." But that was not the case; rather, the penalty was to fit according to the blameworthiness of the offender and to the harm suffered by the one wronged. By this passage alone, then, it is clear that the "eye for eye/tooth for tooth" rule stated a general principle, not a specific command to be literally applied in every case.

Another passage, this one from Leviticus chapter 24, confirms this reading of the *lex talionis*. In verses 17 through 21, God revealed to Moses the penalties for murder, assault and battery, and destruction of property, specifically the killing of another's animal. Each of the prescribed penalties was linked specifically to the *lex talionis* principle in verse 20: "Breach for breach, eye for eye, tooth for tooth...." At first glance, it appears that the penalty is to be literally applied: "[H]e that killeth any man shall be put to death...[H]e that killeth a beast shall make it good; beast for beast...[I]f a man cause a blemish in his neighbor; as he hath done, so shall it be done to him."[14] But careful study of these verses in context reveals otherwise. Following verse 20, containing the recitation of the "eye for eye/tooth for tooth" principle is verse 21, which reads, as follows:

And he that killeth a beast, he shall restore it; and he that killeth a man, he shall be put to death.

A literal application of the *lex talionis* would have required the killer of the beast to allow the owner of that beast to kill one of the killer's beasts. Instead, as Exodus 22:1 prescribes, the convicted beast killer was required to provide four live sheep in exchange for the one sheep that he killed, or five live oxen in exchange for the one ox that he killed. Again, this passage from Leviticus confirms that the *lex talionis* principle is not to be literally applied.

In fact, the Leviticus passage leads the careful Bible reader to Exodus chapter 21 where "eye for eye/tooth for tooth" was first revealed to Moses just after he received the Ten Commandments. In that chapter, God revealed the remedy for assault and battery not to be a returned blow of the same magnitude and to the same part of the guilty party's body as the one that had been delivered; instead, the one guilty of assault was to pay damages resulting from lost wages and medical expenses. This remedy appears with a host of others beginning with the death penalty for murder and ending with an exchange of a live ox for a dead one,[15] all of which are sandwiched around the "eye for eye/tooth for tooth" principle. Anyone, other than the already prejudiced reader, would see clearly that God never intended that man literally apply that principle. Because it was not to be taken literally, it was never intended to embody the revenge or retaliation purpose that has been attributed to it by its critics. To the contrary, as Dr. R. J. Rushdoony, has stated:

> The principle of restitution is basic to Biblical law; it appears with especial prominence in laws under the sixth and eighth commandments, but it is basic to the purpose of the whole law. The "eye for eye, tooth for tooth" concept is not retaliation, but restitution.[16]

As a restitutionary principle, the "eye for eye, tooth for tooth" principle serves as a safeguard *against* revenge and retaliation. It limits the available remedies to those proportionate to the blame of the offender and to the harm caused. Moreover, it directs the attention of the judge or other minister of justice to ascertain the specific restitutionary purpose and its primary recipient. Relevant scripture reveals that the victim of crime is often the primary beneficiary of a correct application of the "eye for eye, tooth for tooth" rule. And where the victim is not the primary beneficiary, the purpose of the *lex talionis* is to restore the offender or society.

RESTITUTION AND VICTIMS

One of the great scandals of Twentieth Century America has been its prison system. In recent years almost no one has come to its defense. Certainly few take seriously any longer the original purpose of a penitentiary, a place to which a convicted criminal is sent to repent, to do penance, and to come out morally regenerated. Instead, the state and federal prisons have become moral cesspools rampant with violence, sexual perversion, and corruption. Moreover, they have served for years as "graduate schools of crime" especially for young offenders who, during their time of incarceration have learned a variety of new skills from their elders.[17]

If incarceration makes little sense generally, then it makes even less sense as appropriate punishment for those whose crimes are offenses against property, such as theft. In a recent article in the *Detroit College of Law Review* Charles Colson, founder and director of Prison Fellowship, and Daniel Benson, professor of law at Texas Tech University, have called for the implementation of "restitution programs" designed to compensate victims for losses resulting from crimes against property. As the authors have ably demonstrated, a criminal justice system without any mechanism for compensating victims for losses suffered cannot properly be called a system of justice. In America, victims of crime have been "virtually ignored. . . . not compensated in most cases, . . . given little or no help in recovering losses, . . . and left entirely to their own resources in picking up their lives and adjusting to what has befallen them."[18] To aggravate this sad state of affairs, these same victims, as taxpayers, must pay higher taxes to house, clothe, and feed the very ones who have injured them.

To support their proposal to establish programs of restitution, Colson and Benson have cited data suggesting that restitution programs, already begun on a trial basis in the United States, have been effective deterrents to criminal behavior as well as sources of substantial financial assistance for their victims.[19] More significantly, they have relied upon the Biblical law requiring restitution to the victims, especially in those instances of crimes against property. In Exodus, chapter 22, the word "restitution" (or one of its derivatives) appears six times in the first twelve verses. For a stolen and destroyed ox, the thief was required to "restore" to its owner five oxen; for a stolen and destroyed sheep, the thief was liable to "restore" to its owner four sheep. If the sheep or ox was found alive, then the thief was required to "restore double." For an act of trespass, the trespasser was required to "make restitution" and in some circumstances to pay double. For acts of embezzlement, the guilty one was to pay double or otherwise to make restitution.[20]

These Biblical commands to pay a greater sum than the exact monetary value of the property stolen or destroyed were necessary to pay for the "pain and suffering" that follows whenever anyone has been wronged by another person. Indeed, as Justice Oliver Wendell Holmes, Jr., once said: "Even a dog distinguishes between being stumbled over and being kicked."[21] Moreover, the value of

"Old Bessie" to her owner often exceeds the dollar amount that he might receive by selling her. The Biblical requirements of five-fold, four-fold, and double money damages reflected the reality of the pain and suffering that the wrongdoer had inflicted.

Such a measure of damages has long been used in America's civil justice system to compensate for injuries caused by negligent driving of an automobile or other like wrongs. While a few legal scholars have called compensation for "pain and suffering" a camouflage for excessive lawyer's fees, most have conceded that such money damages above and beyond the out-of-pocket loss are legitimate. Thus, standard jury instructions in civil tort cases include directions to award a victorious plaintiff with an amount to make restitution for the plaintiff's pain and suffering.

Such restitutionary remedies were designed to make the victim whole, to do all that was humanly possible to place him in as good a position as he was before the commission of the crime. Because man, unlike God, was unable to restore an animal back to life and to heal the victim of the pain and suffering experienced, money damages or other substitutes were required. The greater the loss and the more serious the offense, the greater the amount of damages or other substitute property was required in conformity with the "eye to eye, tooth to tooth" principle. Thus, if an ox were stolen and killed, five oxen were required; but if the ox were merely stolen, that plus another were required.[22]

As Colson and Benson have pointed out, the criminal penalties for theft in America do not reflect these Biblical commands. Instead of paying restitution to their victims, thiefs may be required to pay a fine to the state and to serve time in prison. A system of restitutionary remedies designed to repay the victims for their losses would be like the one that already exists in the civil tort system that provides compensation for out-of-pocket expenses and for pain and suffering.

Some may object, however, to this proposal because most convicted thieves are financially unable to pay their victims anything. God has provided that in the event that the thief has "nothing, then he shall be sold for his theft."[23] Under the "eye for eye/tooth for tooth" principle the offender would be set free as soon as he made restitution to the victim. If the victim preferred, he could sell the offender rather than hold him in servitude.

Such a system could be instituted today. The Thirteenth Amendment of the United States Constitution allows for "involuntary servitude" upon conviction of a crime.[24] In fact, such servitude limited to making restitution to the victim is not as enslaving as the current system of incarceration with its "prolonged imprisonment, with all the deterioration, corruption, destruction of family, impairment of earning ability and the bitterness that goes along with it." Moreover, "the basic principle being applied in the rendering and enforcement of a civil judgment in a tort suit is substantially the same: a civil defendant is forced by the legal system to pay for the loss or injury that he caused."[25]

Restitution to the victim need not be limited to crimes against property. For example, one guilty of an assault and battery on the person of another ought to pay for the loss of wages and for expenses for medical treatment. Even a male guilty of "statutory rape" ought to pay recompense for the damage caused to the young lady. While money cannot completely restore anyone who suffers personal injury wrongfully inflicted, it is the best restitutionary remedy that man has to offer. Because money damages in civil tort actions for personal injury have always been available, it would not be difficult to allow for them in a criminal action. And as was the case with property loss, the damage award should include compensation for "pain and suffering" as well as for out-of-pocket losses such as medical expenses and earnings lost. Such compensation could exceed five times the actual expenses without violating the "eye for eye/tooth for tooth" principle, because injury to a human being is more serious than injury to one's ox.[26]

At one time in the history of the administration of criminal justice in America, restitutionary payments to victims measured by the Biblical "eye for eye/tooth for tooth" standard were authorized. For example, in 1790 the First Congress enacted a law against theft that provided that any offender, "on conviction, be fined not exceeding the fourfold value of the property so stolen." One-half of this fine was to be paid to the owner of the goods and the half as a reward to the informer and prosecutor.[27] Restitution to the victim through criminal fines is not, therefore, unprecedented in America.

In recent years state legislatures have begun to respond to pleas on behalf of crime victims by enacting laws providing for restitution for victims. For example, on July 10, 1985, the Governor of Michigan signed into law a bill authorizing the sentencing judge to order a convicted criminal to make restitution for losses to property or for injuries to person caused by his criminal conduct. While the restitution provided may not exceed the market value of the property lost or the cost of medical expenses and loss of wages, the new Michigan statute does authorize the judge to "require that the defendant make restitution in services in lieu of money." Moreover, the new law prohibits the convicted defendant from profiting from any sales of a book or other recollection regarding his criminal activity until restitution to his victim is paid in full and until reimbursement to the state for the cost of room and board in prison is made.[28] Steps such as this are certainly significant ones towards reinstituting Biblical principles of restitution for victims in the administration of criminal justice in America.

RESTITUTION AND OFFENDERS

A criminal justice system that incorporated restitution for the victim of crime would, in turn, provide for restitution for the criminal offender. In the New Testament a man named Zacchaeus encountered Jesus Christ. In that eventful meeting Zacchaeus promised the Lord that if he had "taken anything from any man by false accusation" he would "restore him four fold." Christ's response to Zacchaeus was immediate: "This day is salvation come to this house forsomuch as he also is a son of Abraham."[29]

Compliance with God's command to restore a person wronged, if accompanied by true repentance as in the case of Zacchaeus, brings reconciliation between the wrongdoer and his Creator and between the wrongdoer and his victim.[30] As Colson and Benson have noted, pilot victim restitution programs in the United States have brought rehabilitation to offenders and deterrence from further criminal activities. This dual restitutionary role of the proper application of the Biblical sanctions for recompensing the crime victim was revealed to Moses in Leviticus, chapter 6, where God commanded that an offender who volunteers to make restitution must present an offering to the Lord for atonement for the sin committed and make restitutionary payment to his victim.[31]

But in many cases criminal offenders will not exhibit the kind of repentant attitude evidenced by Zacchaeus and reflected in Leviticus. In the Old Testament such offenders faced corporal punishment:

> If there be a controversy between men...the judges...shall justify the righteous, and condemn the wicked. And it shall be, if the wicked man be worthy to be beaten, that the judge shall cause him to lie down, and to be beaten before his face, according to his fault, by a certain number.[32]

The severity of the beating administered was subjected to the "eye for eye/tooth for tooth" principle. Thus, a convicted man, deserving of physical punishment "according to his fault," could not be beaten beyond forty times lest the offender "seem vile unto thee."[33]

For what purpose did the Bible prescribe such physical punishment for certain wrongdoers? Again, the answer is restitution, but this time restitution for the offender.

The Book of Proverbs documents that physical punishment administered according to the Law of God restores the offender's soul, that is, it relieves him from the burden of his guilt:

> The blueness of a wound cleanseth away evil; so do stripes the inwards parts of the belly.

> Withhold not correction from the child: for if thou beatest him with the rod, he shall not die. Thou shalt beat him with the rod, he shall not die.[34]

Moreover, physical punishment has been designed by God to restore the offender to true knowledge and wisdom. Again, according to the writer of Proverbs:

> ...(A) rod is for the back of him that is void of understanding.

> Foolishness is bound in the heart of the child; but the rod of correction shall drive it far from him.

> The rod and reproof give wisdom...[35]

Almost all penological experts in Twentieth Century America have, however, rejected these truths in God's word. Indeed, most Americans without hesitation would reject physical punishment of convicted criminals. Indeed, the outcry against corporal punishment has become so intense that some have already attempted to discourage and ultimately to prohibit parents from spanking their children.[36] Indeed, in Europe the Swedish parliament has already outlawed corporal punishment as a means of disciplining children.[37]

Such opposition to corporal punishment of convicted felons and of rebellious children has been reinforced by judicial opinions such as one written by Judge Harry Blackmun before he became a justice of the United States Supreme Court. In *Jackson v. Bishop*,[38] Judge Blackmun ruled that the Arkansas practice of whipping prisoners with the strap, despite all safeguards, violated the United States

Constitution's Eighth Amendment that prohibits "cruel and unusual punishment." The Arkansas authorities maintained that whipping was necessary to maintain discipline. Under an earlier court order the Board that supervised the Arkansas prison system had adopted rules that limited the use of physical punishment, in part, as follows:

- Proof of a "major offense";
- No more than ten lashes, the exact number to be determined by a four-man board of inquiry; and
- An opportunity for the inmate to be heard.

In the trial court, penology experts and inmates testified that "corporal punishment generates hate...[and] frustrates correctional and rehabilatative goals." At the appellate level Judge Blackmun concluded, in addition, that no matter what safeguards were employed, there would always be abuses of the authority to inflict physical punishment and that, in light of "contemporary concepts of decency and human dignity" any corporal punishment violated the constitutional prohibition against cruel and unusual punishment. In drawing this conclusion Judge Blackmun followed earlier United States Supreme Court opinions that declared that the meaning of "cruel and unusual" depended upon "the evolving standards of decency that mark the progress of a maturing society."[39]

Judge Blackmun's ruling was possible only if one agreed with the Supreme Court's assumption that it had the power to change the original meaning of the constitutional text. Unquestionably, the framers did not intend to outlaw corporal punishment because the same Congress that had adopted the constitutional prohibition against cruel and unusual punishment had enacted a law that required certain convicted thiefs to "be publicly whipped, not exceeding thirty-nine stripes."[40] Indeed, corporal punishment for certain offenders was not uncommon in America in colonial times. For example, Section 43 of the Massachusetts Body of Liberties provided for such punishment as prescribed by Biblical principles:

No man shall be beaten with above 40 stripes, nor shall any true gentleman, nor any man equal to a gentleman be punished with whipping, unless his crime be very shameful, and his course of life vicious and profligate.[41]

And Section 46 of that same document proved that such corporal punishments did not, per se, violate any prohibition against "cruel and unusual" punishments:

For bodily punishments we allow amongst us none that are inhumane Barbarous or cruel.[42]

While provisions for corporal punishment of certain convicted criminals remained on the books as late as 1972,[43] such practice has long been discontinued. Perhaps, this occurred because obvious abuses had taken place in England and America[44] just as they had in Israel when Jesus Christ, Himself, was beaten[45] and when the early church's apostles had likewise suffered for preaching the Gospel.[46] Perhaps, this practice discontinued because civil authorities began to listen to penology experts and to convicted felons, as had Judge Blackmun in the *Jackson* case, and concluded that, even with carefully enforced safeguards, physical punishment was counter productive.

Whatever the reason, God has reminded a nation's leaders through the Book of Proverbs that "there is a way which seemeth right to a man, but the end thereof are the ways of death."[47] Moreover, He has warned those leaders that if they seek the best for their nation they will follow God's laws for nations: "Righteousness exalteth a nation: but sin is a reproach to any people."[48] The Holy Spirit through the Apostle Paul repeated this warning in the form of a command to the civil rulers:

For rulers are not a terror to good works, but to the evil . . . for he is the minister [servant] of God, a revenger to execute wrath upon him that doeth evil.[49]

The remedy for abuse of power is not to disregard God's clear command that in appropriate cases convicted criminals should be physically punished, but to see that the civil rulers abide by the "eye for eye/tooth for tooth" principle of proportionality. By completely abandoning such punishment in the criminal justice system and by threatening to stop the practice of such punishment in the home, America's leaders have not only robbed its law-abiding citizenry of the protection that God affords them, but it has stolen from the offenders themselves opportunities for spiritual and intellectual restoration, the divinely guaranteed benefits of corporal punishment.

In a recent book on dealing with the problem of depression, authors Don Baker and Emery Nester have dramatically documented the therapeutic effect of corporal punishment properly administered according to Biblical standards.

One young man had returned from Vietnam a psychological cripple. His mood swings would take him from the extremes of deep depression to acts of insane violence.

He had accidentally killed some Vietnamese children.

The counselor had been working with him for months, trying to help him gain release from the overpowering sense of guilt that bound him. David finally persuaded him to verbally relive those tragic moments in "Nam." We listened spellbound as he painted a grim work picture of the scene that smoldered in his mind.

When finally he had said it all and had left us mentally staring at the lifeless corpses of innocent children, he began to cry. The convulsive sobs that followed wracked his entire body.

No one moved to comfort him. No attempt was made to quiet him; we all sat mute and still.

Finally, as his crying began to subside, David said quietly, "And you feel that you need to be punished for what you did?" The young veteran began nodding his head and saying, "Yes, yes...I need to be punished. Yes, yes."

To my utter amazement, David moved from his chair, picked up a wooden ruler, and said, "Hold out your hands." As the ex-soldier obeyed, the therapist began beating his hands and his forearms mercilessly.

I expected just token punishment—a symbolic beating. But David didn't stop, and we recoiled as we saw that ruler come down again and again on hands that began reddening and swelling with each successive blow.

After what seemed an eternity, the beating ended. The tears gone, the look of pain had eased. Our counselor took that grown man in his arms and held him close as a father would his son, all the time repeating, "It's all right. It's all right. It's over. It's over."

The rest of us then crowded close and held that Vietnam veteran until he began to relax. He looked at the therapist and then at the rest of us and began to sob in relief, uttering over and over again. "Thank you, thank you."[50]

In addition to this contemporary testimony of the restorative effect of corporal punishment, others are beginning to question the almost universal assumption that corporal punishment of convicted criminals is "cruel and unusual." In 1983 Graeme Newman, professor of criminology and dean of the School of Criminal Justice, State University of New York, Albany, published *Just and Painful, A Case for the Corporal Punishment of Criminals*. In this short but well-documented study, Dean Newman demonstrated that "none of the research substantiates" the claim "that corporal punishment causes humiliation and terror." To the contrary, Dean Newman pointed out, "it is well established that prison rests on a platform of humiliation and terror."[51]

At the conclusion of his study the dean issued "A Punishment Manifesto" that included the following two proposals:

286

(1) Acute corporal punishment should be introduced to fill the gap between severe punishment of prison and non-punishment of probation....
(2) For violent crimes in which the victim was terrified and humiliated...a violent corporal punishment should be considered, such as whipping....

In part, Dean Newman's endorsement of corporal punishment was based upon this concurrence with the proposition that through suffering pain "the offender can come to understand the evil of his offense.[52]

RESTITUTION AND SOCIETY

In his book on the limitations of the criminal sanction, Herbert Packer cited the death penalty for murder as the most "conspicuous example" of the revenge theory underpinning the *lex talionis*. At first glance it appears that Packer is right. Capital punishment imposed upon a murderer prevents any possible remedy that would restore the victim or that would make restitution to the victim's family. And only those with a preference for the macabre would argue that killing the offender would be good for his soul or for his mind. Careful examination of the Biblical provisions commanding the death penalty for murder, however, reveals that it, too, has a restitutionary purpose, namely, to restore the nation or society in which the murder occurred.

From the time of the first murder, when Cain killed Abel, the unlawful taking of innocent blood has literally "defiled" the land where the murder took place. This "law of the land" was first revealed by God in His encounter with Cain after he had murdered his brother: "And He [God] said, what hast thou done? The voice of thy brother's blood crieth unto me from the ground."[53]

God elaborated upon this law in His instructions to the nation of Israel through the prophet, Moses:

Whoso killeth any person, the murderer shall be put to death by the mouth of the witnesses...Moreover, ye shall take no satisfaction for the life of a murderer...but he shall be surely put to death...So ye shall not pollute the land wherein ye are: for blood it defileth the land: and the land cannot be cleansed of the blood that is shed therein, but the blood of him that shed it.[54]

Finally, God announced through the Psalmist that the nation of Israel had been destroyed and its people scattered, in part, because

287

of its failure to enforce the law of murder and to impose the death penalty upon those guilty of shedding innocent blood:

> Yea, they...shed innocent blood, even the blood of their sons and of their daughters, whom they sacrificed unto the idols of Canaan: and the land was polluted with blood...Therefore was the wrath of the Lord kindled against his people...And he gave them into the hand of the heathen.[55]

The prophet Isaiah has made clear that this "law of the land" has not been limited by God to the geographical boundaries of Israel or to the historical period of the Old Testament. In a timeless prophecy concerning the history of nations past, present, and future Isaiah proclaimed that "the earth...is defiled under the inhabitants thereof; because they have transgressed the laws, changed the ordinances, broken the everlasting covenant."[56] Part of the covenant referred to in this passage undoubtedly includes the covenant that God made with all nations through the patriarch, Noah: "Whoso sheddeth man's blood, by man shall his blood be shed: For in the image of God made he man."[57] That covenant has bound all nations ever since. The prophet, Habakkuk, warned that God still brings judgment upon any nation that habitually violates "the law of the land."[58]

Notwithstanding this consistent Old Testament record, G. Aiken Taylor, editor of the *Presbyterian Journal*, has recently observed:

> Within the Christian community...it is widely believed that the Christian "ethic" demands the abolition of capital punishment. Some Christian leaders declare that the New Testament modifies the Old Testament in this respect and that Jesus Christ would have rejected capital punishment.[59]

For example, the Southern Presbyterian Assembly's Christian Relations Committee reported in 1961 "that the New Testament 'ethics of love' effectively forbids capital punishment and that the process of rehabilitation which is 'God's redemption' should not be denied any man."[60] But does capital punishment deny to the man executed an opportunity to come to a saving knowledge of Jesus Christ? To this speculation C. S. Lewis has replied: "I do not know whether a murderer is more likely to repent and make a good end on the gallows a few weeks after his trial or in the prison infirmary thirty years later."[61]

Lewis's comment certainly fits the picture that Jesus Christ, Himself, painted for Nicodemus in their conversation about the Christian, born again salvation experience:

> The wind bloweth where it listeth, and thou hearest the sound thereof, but canst not tell whence it cometh, and whither it goeth: So is everyone that is born of the Spirit.[62]

In fact, the Bible record gives assurance that the death penalty, even if erroneously imposed, cannot possibly deny anyone the opportunity to be saved. For as Christ has promised all mankind, the Father's will cannot be thwarted by any created thing, including the death penalty:

> All that the Father giveth me shall come to me. . . And this is the Father's will which hath sent me, that of all which he hath given me I should lose nothing, but should raise it up again at the last day.[63]

Another argument made by some Christians is actually based upon one of the Ten Commandments, "Thou shalt not kill." Does the sixth commandment prohibit capital punishment? Those who make that claim inevitably place God in contradiction to Himself. The God who wrote the Ten Commandments on the two tablets of stone and who gave them to Moses, was the same God who commanded the people of Israel through the same Moses to take the life of anyone who was found guilty of murder.[64] As God has witnessed of Himself, He cannot lie[65] and, therefore, cannot give two contradictory commandments. His Word is one harmonious whole, as the writer of Proverbs has reminded us:

> Every word of God is pure [tested]; He is a shield unto them that put their trust in Him. Add thou not unto His words, lest He reprove thee, and thou be found a liar.[66]

Finally, some have argued against capital punishment on the basis of two events in the life of Jesus Christ, the Sermon on the Mount and the defense of the adulteress. The passage most often cited from the Sermon has been the one, as follows:

> Ye have heard that it hath been said, An eye for an eye and a tooth for a tooth: But I say unto you, that ye resist not evil: But whosoever shall smite thee on the right cheek, turn to him the other also.[67]

If this statement dictates the repeal of capital punishment on the ground that Jesus rejected the "eye for eye/tooth for tooth" rule of the Old Testament, then for the same reason it requires abolition of all forms of punishment, including the discipline of children. How else could one live and not violate the command "to turn the other cheek." But that was not Christ's message here. The New Testament affirms the right of civil authorities to punish evil doers[68] and the right of fathers to discipline their children.[69] Christ, Himself, reminded His followers to "render therefore unto Caesar the things which be Caesar's."[70] Clearly, then, Christ in His Sermon did not call for an anarchical society governed solely by the law of love.

What He did teach, however, is that those who desired to live in the Kingdom of God could not do so simply by conforming their outward behavior to the rules of civil society. Thus, He told His listeners that hating a man in one's heart is murder and lusting after a woman in one's heart is adultery.[71] While civil authorities had no jurisdiction over a man's heart,[72] God did. Therefore, if a man desired to enter God's kingdom his righteousness must exceed that of the law-abiding citizen of a nation on earth.[73]

In light of this analysis Christ did not even address the question of civil authority in His sermon on the Mount. He limited His remarks to the responsibilities and duties of those who desired to be right with God. His reference to the "eye for eye/tooth for tooth" principle simply meant that one may be entitled in a human court to a favorable judgment, but that alone would not give that person favor in God's court. The "turn the other cheek" principle applicable in God's system of justice required that even when one has been wronged by another, the one wronged must forgive the wrongdoer and reach out to him in love.[74]

As Christ did not modify or change the authority of civil rulers in His Sermon on the Mount, He did not do so in His defense of the adulteress. In that case Christ contended that only those "without sin" could execute judgment upon the adulterous woman. Of course, not one sitting in judgment qualified.[75] If this passage dictated the demise of capital punishment,[76] because Jesus required those in judgment to be sinless, then for the same reason it would require the elimination of all punishment, including the discipline of children. But that was not Christ's message. As has been stated above in the analysis of the Sermon on the Mount, the New Testament affirms the right of civil rulers to wield the sword against evil doers and of fathers to discipline their children.

What was Christ's message then? It was a message for the church. The Pharisees and Scribes, the religious leaders of the Jewish community at the time of Christ, sought to continue to exercise the authority that God had given them when Israel was an independent nation and still fulfilling the purposes and plan of God. They had overlooked two things: 1) That Israel had failed to obey God and God had now instituted a new plan to reach all nations with His salvation message;[77] and 2) they had the power to stone the adulteress not from God, but from the Roman Empire.[78] Christ taught in this encounter that the Church had no authority to judge or to condemn, but only to bring the message of salvation to the lost. After all, Christ came to save the world, not to judge it.[79] His disciples could do no more than what Christ authorized them to do. Therefore, He rebuked James and John who desired to bring down the fire of judgment upon a village of Samaritans who had rejected the gospel:

> Ye know not what manner of spirit ye are of. For the Son of man is not come to destroy men's lives, but to save them.[80]

In summary, the New Testament, especially Christ's teachings, has not repealed capital punishment. Civil rulers still have the authority, indeed the duty under the Noahic covenant, to impose the death penalty upon any one duly convicted of murder.[81] That was certainly the teaching of the common law at the time of the founding of the United States of America. Indeed, Sir William Blackstone in his *Commentaries* taught that murder was an unpardonable offense. He supported his view by explicit reference to the Bible:

> We are next to consider the crime of deliberate and wilful murder; a crime...which is I believe punished almost universally throughout the world with death. The words of the mosaical law (over and above the general precept to Noah, that "whoso sheddeth man's blood, by man shall his blood be shed") are very emphatical in prohibiting the pardon of murderers.[82]

Quoting from Numbers chapter 35, Blackstone reminded his readers of "the law of the land:"

> ...(Y)e shall take no satisfaction for the life of a murderer, who is guilty of death, but he shall surely be put to death; for the land cannot be cleansed of the blood that is shed therein, but by the blood of him that shed it.[83]

Finally, Blackstone hailed the common law that prohibited the king from pardoning a murderer, and criticized the Polish monarch. . . who thought proper to remit the penalties of murder to all the nobility, in an edict with this arrogant preamble, "*nos, divini juris rigonem moderantes, Etc.*"[84]

This Latin phrase, "we, moderating the rigors of divine justice," could very well be inserted as the introduction to many twentieth century court opinions and legislative enactments that have modified God's law governing the death penalty. For example, in 1976 the United States Supreme Court found North Carolina's mandatory death penalty for murder unconstitutional under the cruel-and-unusual punishment prohibition of the Eighth Amendment.[85] The Court objected to the statute's "withdrawing all sentencing discretion from juries in capital cases" on two principal grounds: First, that juries would simply disregard their legal duty to impose the death penalty by haphazard refusals to convict of the capital offense; and second, that a mandatory death penalty statute fails "to allow the particularized consideration of relevant aspects of the character and record of each convicted defendant before the imposition upon him of a sentence of death."

As for the first point, if all laws were subject to constitutional infirmity on account of speculations that those with a duty to enforce them would do so only haphazardly, few laws would survive. Probable disobedience of civil duty should never be grounds for the unconstitutionality of any law.

On the second point, the Court has adopted as constitutionally-mandated a system of sentencing that directly contradicts the Biblical principle that "the penalty must fit the crime." By requiring the sentencing authority to examine the character of a convicted murderer, and the particular circumstances of the murder, the Court has not only disregarded the Biblical norm that all convicted murderers deserve the death penalty, but it has multiplied opportunities for unfairness in the administration of that penalty.

Moses instructed the judges of Israel to show no "respect" of "persons in judgment."[86] The writer of Proverbs echoed the Mosaic law:

These things also belong to the wise. It is not good to have respect of persons in judgment.[87]

By requiring the death penalty to be tailored to the individual, the Court has virtually invited the civil authorities to favor the "great" over the "small,"[88] the "mighty" over the "powerless"[89] and the "rich" over the "poor."[90] Yet "the law of the land" is violated by anyone who commits murder whether it is his first and only offense after an otherwise exemplary life or the last in a series of offenses by one "trapped" in a lifestyle of crime. In disregard of this law requiring death of one who has spilled innocent blood, the Court has ordained that "a just and appropriate sentence" must take into account "both the offender and the offense" in order to comply with the "progressive and humanizing development...[of] enlightened policy" of the last half of the twentieth century.[91] The Polish monarch to whom Blackstone referred in his *Commentaries* would undoubtedly have concurred with this opinion as the best way to protect the "noble class" without having to say so.

Because of a growing public opinion favoring the death penalty for murder, executions have begun to appear more frequently in several states in America. But capital punishment should not depend upon the ebb and flow of public opinion as if it were subject to a popularity contest. The "law of the land" does not change whether by public referendum or initiative or by legislative enactment or judicial fiat. Nor should the Noahic covenant commanding all nations to protect innocent blood by putting to death convicted murderers depend upon who wins the philosophical debate whether capital punishment "denies the executed person's humanity" or "affirms the murdered victim's humanity." That was settled by God, Himself, when He disclosed to Noah the reason for capital punishment for murder: "For in the image of God made he man."[92]

CONCLUSION

If a society follows the "eye for eye/tooth for tooth" principle and if it adheres to the restitutionary purposes of that principle, then the criminal law will have the deterrent effect that the experts claim to desire. That is the promise of God's word as revealed to Moses in Deuteronomy.[93] So long as those experts seek their utilitarian goals of deterrence they will find those goals always eluding them as they, themselves, have acknowledged:

> The utilitarian concept of deterrence...justifies punishment in preventive terms and as such makes an assertion that in principle is subject to empirical verification. We should be able to find out, in other words, whether criminal punishment in fact deters people from committing crimes and more precisely, which sanctions and in what amounts provide the most effective

deterrents. Yet to date, we have been unable to do so in a manner that can claim general recognition and acceptance in the scientific community.[94]

More importantly, these experts will be tempted to tamper and to experiment with men's freedom and dignity in order to achieve their higher goals, as Oliver Wendell Holmes, Jr., was willing to do:

> If I were having a philosophical talk with a man I was going to have hanged (or electrocuted) I should say, "I don't doubt that your act was inevitable for you but to make it more avoidable by others we propose to sacrifice you to the common good. You may regard yourself as a soldier dying for your country if you like. But the law must keep its promises."[95]

Holmes' view that punishment may be justified for the "common good," even though the individual punished did not deserve it was not at all novel. Caiaphas, the Jewish high priest, advocated the same thing when he called for the crucifixion of Jesus: ". . .[I]t is expedient for you that one man should die for the people, and that the whole nation should not perish."[96] As Dean Newman of the State University of New York, Albany, has pointed out, the lesson to be learned from this passage of Scripture is the one taught by Dante who "reserved the 8th circle of Hell for the utilitarians of history:"

> This was the punishment for Caiaphas. . .[He] was to be crucified to the ground across the road where people could not help stepping on his body as they passed through. The logic of the punishment is indeed satisfying: the body is used by others as a means to go somewhere. . . .This punitive expression of the crime lays bare the basic injustice of the utilitarian philosophy: it treats men as means rather than ends.[97]

C. S. Lewis was absolutely right when he urged England to turn away from the so-called modern theories that justified criminal punishment for the purpose of deterring others by example. He called for a return to the traditional common law justification of deserved punishment "not solely, not even primarily, in the interests of society, but in the interests of liberty:"

> If the justification of exemplary punishment is not based upon desert but solely on its efficacy as a deterrent, it is not absolutely necessary that the man we punish should even have committed the crime.[98]

America, too, ought to be called back to its original Judeo-Christian roots and be recommitted to a system of restitutionary justice that will restore both liberty and order to a society that has suffered long enough from the "best" that its "brightest" have had to offer.[99]

REFERENCES

The Restitutionary Purpose of The Criminal Law by Herbert W. Titus

1. John S. Bainbridge, Jr., "The Return of Retribution," 71 *A.B. A.J.* 61 (1985).

2. *See, e.g.*, Herbert L. Packer, *The Limits of the Criminal Sanction* (Stanford: Stanford University Press, 1968), pp.19–70.

3. Wayne R. LaFave and Austin W. Scott, Jr., *Criminal Law* (St. Paul: West Publishing Company, 1978), p. 9.

4. *See, e.g.*, Daniel Nagin, "General Deterrence: A Review of the Empirical Evidence," in *Deterrence and Incapacitation: Estimating the Effects of Criminal Sanctions on Crime Rates* (Washington: National Academy of Sciences, 1978), pp. 95, 135–136, and Daniel Glaser, *The Effectiveness of a Prison and Parole System* (Indianapolis: Bobbs-Merrill, 1964, 1969).

5. *See, e.g.*, Karl Menninger, *The Crime of Punishment* (N.Y.: Penguin Books, 1968), pp. 264–270.

6. Peter W. Low, John Calvin Jeffries, Jr., Richard J. Bonnie, *Criminal Law: Cases and Materials* (Mineola, N.Y.: The Foundation Press, Inc., 1982), p. 7.

7. *Id.*

8. *Id.*, pp. 1–2.

9. *See*, for example, James Q. Wilson, ed., *Crime and Public Policy* (San Francisco: ICS Press, 1983), pp. 220–223, 253.

10. *See, e.g.*, John Kaplan, *Criminal Justice* (Mineola, N.Y.: Foundation Press, 1973), p. 9.

11. H. Packer, *The Limits of the Criminal Sanction, supra* n. 2, pp. 37, 38–39 (1968).

12. Deuteronomy 19:15–18; 19:19.

13. Deueronomy 19:20–21.

14. Leviticus 24:17–19.

15. Exodus 21:19; 21:12, 36.

16. Rousas J. Rushdoony, *The Institutes of Biblical Law* (Philisburg, N.J.: Presbyterian and Reformed Publishing Co., 1973) p. 272.

17. *See, e.g.*, Peter W. Greenwood, "Controlling the Crime Rate through Imprisonment," in James Q. Wilson, *Crime and Public Policy* (San Francisco: ICS Press, 1983), pp. 252–253.

18. Charles W. Colson and Daniel H. Benson, "Restitution as an Alternative to Imprisonment," 77 *Detroit College of Law Review* 523, 525–26 (1980). (Hereinafter Colson and Benson, "Reinstitution".)

19. *Id.*, pp. 565–76.

20. Exodus 22:1, 4, 6, 9; 22:7, 10–12.

21. Oliver W. Holmes, *The Common Law* (Birmingham: The Legal Classics Library, 1982, c. 1881), p. 3.

22. Exodus 22:1, 4.

23. Exodus 22:3.

24. "Neither slavery nor involuntary servitude, except as punishment for crime whereof the party shall have been duly convicted, shall exist within the United States..."

25. Colson and Benson, "Restitution," *supra* n. 18, p. 555.

26. Exodus 21:19; 22:17; 22:1 and Genesis 9:6.

27. An Act For the Punishment of Certain Crimes Against the United States, Section 16, 1 Stat. 116 (1790).

28. Act No. 87, Public Acts of 1985, State of Michigan.

29. Luke 19:8, 9.

30. I Timothy 2:5.

31. Leviticus 6:1–7.

32. Deuteronomy 25:1–2, 3.

33. Deuteronomy 25:3.

34. Proverbs 20:30; 23:13–14.

35. Proverbs 10:13; 22:15; 29:15.

36. *Battered Women: Issues of Public Policy* (U.S. Commission on Civil Rights, 1978) pp. 479–480.

37. Ronald F. Docksai, *You Won't Get Spanked in Sweden* (Institute of American Relations, Washington, D.C.)

38. *Jackson v. Bishop*, 404 F.2d 571 (8th Cir. 1968).

39. *Trop v. Dulles*, 356 U.S. 86, 102, 78 S.Ct. 590, 598 (1958).

40. An Act For the Punishment of Certain Crimes Against the United States, Section 16 1 Stat. 116 (1790).

41. Richard L. Perry, ed., *Sources of Our Liberties* (Chicago: American Bar Association, 1978), p. 153.

42. *Id.*

43. See 11 Dela. Code, Section 631, 811, 3905, 3906, 3907, and 3908 and Gaeme R. Newman, *Just and Painful: A Case for the Corporal Punishment of Criminals* (N.Y.: MacMillan, 1983) p. 129.

44. G. Newman, *Just and Painful, supra* n. 43, pp. 28–35.

45. Matthew 27:26.

46. Acts 5:40; 16:23 and II Corinthians 11:24.

47. Proverbs 14:12 and 16:25.

48. Proverbs 14:34.

49. Romans 13:3–4.

50. Don Baker and Emery Nester, *Depression*, (Portland: Multnomah Press, 1983), p. 60.

51. *Supra* n. 43, p. 8.

52. *Id.*, pp. 139, 100.

53. Genesis 4:10.

54. Numbers 35:30–31, 33.

55. Psalms 106:38–41.

56. Isaiah 24:5.

57. Genesis 9:6.

58. Habakkuk 2:1–17.

59. G. Aiken Taylor, "Capital Punishment—Right and Necessary," in T. Robert Ingram, ed., *Essays on the Death Penalty* (Houston: St. Thomas Press, 1963), p. 47.

60. *Id.*

61. C. S. Lewis, "The Humanitarian Theory of Punishment," in *God in the Dock* (Grand Rapids, Eerdmans, 1970), p. 287.

62. John 3:8.

63. John 6:37, 39.

64. Exodus 20:13; 31:18; 21:12, 14; Leviticus 24:17; Numbers 35:30–34; Deuteronomy 19:11–12.

65. Numbers 23:19; Titus 1:2.

66. Proverbs 30:5–6.

67. Matthew 5:38–39.

68. Romans 13:1–4; I Peter 2:13–14.

69. Ephesians 6:4.

70. Luke 20:25.

71. Matthew 5:22, 28.

72. Matthew 5:21.

73. Matthew 5:20.

74. Matthew 5:42–45.

75. John 8:7; 9–10.

76. Anyone committing adultery in Israel deserved death. Leviticus 10:20.

77. Romans 9:24–33.

78. John 11:48.

79. John 12:47.

80. Luke 9:55–56.

81. Whether or not there is authority to impose the death penalty for offenses beyond murder is beyond the scope of this essay. See, for example, Deuteronomy 22:25–26.

82. William Blackstone, *Commentaries on the Laws of England* (Chicago: University of Chicago Press, 1979, c. 1769), vol. 4, p. 194.

83. *Id.,* p. 194.

84. *Id.,* p. 94.

85. *Woodsen v. North Carolina,* 428 U.S. 280 (1976).

86. Deuteronomy 1:17 and 16:19.

87. Proverbs 24:24. *Cf.* Proverbs 28:21.

88. Deuteronomy 1:17.

89. Leviticus 19:15.

90. James 2:3–4.

91. *Supra* n. 85, 428 U.S. at 304.

92. Genesis 9:6.

93. Deuteronomy 17:13 and 19:20.

94. P. Low, J. Jeffries, and R. Bonnie, *Criminal Law* 17–18 (1982).

95. Mark DeWolfe Howe, ed., *Holmes-Laski Letters* (Cambridge: Harvard University Press, 1953), p. 806.

96. John 11:50.

97. *Supra* n. 43, pp. 98–99.

98. Lewis, "The Humanitarian Theory of Punishment," reprinted in *God in the Dock, supra* n. 61, p. 291.

99. This article is copyright, August 1985, by Herbert W. Titus. All rights reserved.

17

THE IMPETUS
FOR SENTENCING REFORM
IN THE CRIMINAL JUSTICE SYSTEM

by Kenneth W. Starr

Few principles are more firmly entrenched in our system of government than the concept of equal justice—that similarly situated individuals should be treated equally before the law. Another bedrock principle of our democracy is that institutions and individuals vested with the authority and power of government should be held accountable for the exercise of that authority. Those basic principles of our Republic seem ill-served, however, by the traditional system of sentencing in this country.[1]

The principle of equal justice is implicated by a pervasive characteristic of the system of sentencing prevailing in most of the nation—gross disparities in the sentences imposed upon individuals convicted of crimes. That wide disparities in sentencing exist across the country is too firmly established at this late date to be disputed. Research carried out during the past decade produced dramatic evidence in sentencing—both from one judge to another, and from one court to another. The groundbreaking *1972 Sentencing Study for the Southern District of New York* graphically characterized the extremes in sentencing among 28 federal district judges who tried "inside" postal theft cases in 1967–71:

> [A postal theft] defendant assigned to Judge T stood a 50-50 chance of going to prison, while if he was assigned to Judge AA his chances were only 1 in 25.[2]

An equally diverse set of outcomes faced individuals convicted of selective service offenses during 1970–72. Of the 26 judges studied, eight *never* imposed a prison term in such cases, while one judge imposed prison sentences upon each of the ten selective service defendants who were convicted in his court.

This seminal study also highlighted the sentencing variations from court to court. Thus, within the Second Circuit (New York, Connecticut and Vermont), the average sentence imposed in robbery cases during fiscal year 1970 ranged dramatically—from 66 months in the Western District of New York, to 142.3 months in the District of Connecticut and 152.3 months in the Eastern District of New York. That year, the Second Circuit's overall average sentence for robbery convictions was 122.2 months. Among all the federal circuits, the stiffest average penalty for robbery during FY 1970 was meted out in the District of Columbia Circuit (333 months), while the lightest average sentence was to be found in the First Circuit (106.3 months) (Massachusetts, Maine, Rhode Island, New Hampshire and Puerto Rico). The overall national average was 148.2 months.

The real-world disparities which exist in sentencing, as demonstrated by the Southern District study and other studies, have been confirmed in experiments conducted with the help of sitting federal judges. In *The Second Circuit Sentencing Study*, conducted in 1974, fifty district court judges were furnished twenty identical files drawn from actual cases and asked to specify the sentence they would impose on each defendant. Not surprisingly, a very wide range of sentences were meted out in the context of this experiment. For example, the sentence imposed by the fifty judges in one bank robbery case ranged from 18 years in prison and a $5,000 fine down to five years in prison with no fine. In another case involving interstate transportation of stolen securities, the sentences varied among the judges from three years in prison to one year's probation, with no prison term.

The results of the 1974 Second Circuit study have been buttressed by a study conducted for the Justice Department, in which 208 federal judges indicated the sentences they would impose in 16 hypothetical cases—eight bank robbery and eight fraud convictions. Here is what happened:

> In only 3 of the 16 cases was there a unanimous agreement to impose a prison term. Even when most judges agreed that a prison term was appropriate, there was a substantial variation in the lengths of prison terms recommended. In one fraud case in which the mean prison term was 8.5 years, the longest term was life in prison. In another case the mean prison term was 1.1 years, yet the longest prison term recommended was 15 years.[3]

JUDICIAL DISCRETION: PLUSSES AND MINUSES

A citizen examining our criminal justice system is thus confronted with overwhelming empirical and experimental evidence of sentencing disparities. These disparities are the result in no small part of the current system of sentencing in the ninety-four federal judicial districts across the Nation, as well as in the 50 States. In a word, judges in this country are typically endowed with extraordinarily wide latitude in imposing sentences.[4] The limitations and constraints placed on that discretion are, moreover, quite modest in nature. Generally, Congress will have prescribed a statutory maximum sentence, but provided no further guidelines for the imposition of sentences.[5] If the sentence imposed by the judge is within that statutory maximum and is not based on improper considerations, the sentence is permissible, and will not likely be overturned on review by an appellate court.[6]

This sort of discretion, which so directly affects individual liberty, would be viewed with great suspicion if vested in another branch of government. The notion of a government official whose acts are circumscribed by few legal restraints and who answers only to his or her own conscience is inconsistent with the very principle of accountability. In a government of limited and enumerated powers, the vision of an official clothed with governmental authority acting with unfettered discretion should in the main engender considerable discomfort.

To shift ground for a moment, a comparison of the sentencing process in the criminal justice system with the federal administrative process illustrates the uniqueness of the wide discretion possessed by judges in sentencing. Congress has, over the years, created numerous administrative agencies with varying missions. But in creating those agencies, Congress has limited the discretion of agency officials in several ways. First, congressional enactments establishing administrative agencies specify broad policy guidelines and impose express requirements. Second, the Administrative Procedure Act governs most agency actions and provides procedural and substantive constraints on administrative actions not present in the sentencing process. Third, Congress exercises continuing supervisory oversight over the agencies. Finally, agency actions are subject, with various exceptions, to the scrutiny of the federal judiciary. Congress, therefore, has not seen fit in most respects to vest unbridled discretion in administrative agencies.

The nature of judicial review of agency action is instructive when compared with the setting of sentencing. While the standard is articulated in varying ways, the basic purposes of judicial review of administrative action is to ensure that all requisite procedures were

301

followed by the agency and that the substantive result is neither "arbitrary or capricious." This judicial inquiry requires the courts, in a word, to ascertain whether the agency considered all relevant factors and engaged in reasoned decision-making.

The elaborate system of review of agency action is designed to ensure that the agency conducts itself consistently with applicable statutory requirements and, beyond that, to ensure that the substantive result reached by the agency is neither arbitrary nor capricious. In theory, therefore, judicial review of agency decisions cabins the discretion and power of agencies. And in practice, courts routinely review and at times invalidate administrative agency actions under this standard.

The process of sentencing individuals convicted of crimes poses a striking contrast to the reasoned process of decision-making required of administrative agencies. As we have seen, similarly situated defendants may be given drastically different sentences by judges within the same judicial district. So, too, when presented with the identical hypothetical defendant, judges prescribe widely variant sentences. The law, however, generally does not require the sentencing judge even to explain why a particular sentence is being meted out.[7] Unless there is some evidence that the judge considered an impermissible factor, such as the race or national origin of the defendant, or that the court failed to follow prescribed procedures, the sentence will typically not be disturbed by a reviewing court.[8] Thus, the general rule is simple: if the sentence is within the maximum prescribed by Congress, the sentence will stand.

Despite the criticism of the sentencing model suggested by the comparison with the administrative law model, it can be argued with some force that the delicate process of depriving an individual of liberty for a particular period of time is an inherently judgmental enterprise. Thus, the argument goes, sentencing, unlike regulation of the environment or the railroads, requires consideration of numerous individual factors that are not amenable to appellate review. Under this view, the wisdom and good sense of sentencing judges is the ultimate check on unwise or arbitrary sentencing. So long as the will of Congress as set forth in the maximum sentence is obeyed, the process of imposing an individual sentence is best left to the sound judgment and common sense of judges. Sentencing, in this view, is a process that cannot lend itself to mechanical rules and rigid charts or guidelines. Because every individual is different and the circumstances of each crime are unique, different factors must be considered in imposing sentence.

Despite the appeal of this humanistic vision of sentencing, it fails to confront the hard evidence showing that the differences among judges, not just the differences among defendants, play a large role in widely variant sentences.[9] Just as every criminal case is distinct, so too 540 federal district judges across the country (and literally thousands of state judges) are simply not likely to act in a uniform manner.

Variations among judges have always been with us, as some judges have eloquently pointed out. Few have spoken more directly to the vagaries of sentencing than former United States District Judge Marvin Frankel, whose book, *Criminal Sentences: Law Without Order*,[10] caused a stir upon its publication over a decade ago. But in the intervening thirteen years since Judge Frankel's book appeared, a pivotal development has occurred in the federal judiciary. The judiciary has expanded dramatically in size, with almost a forty percent increase as a result of the 1978 legislation creating at one stroke almost 160 new federal judgeships. Then again, in 1984, Congress passed a measure creating some 85 additional judgeships, all of which are badly needed in an overburdened system.

In short, the federal judiciary is not, if it ever was, a small elite of individuals sharing the same perspectives and values. The variety among federal judges is reflective of the variety of the nation itself and its people. It is thus highly unrealistic to rely upon the image of the judiciary marching to the tune of the same drummer. Federal judges (and their more numerous counterparts in the several states) simply cannot be compared to the hypothetical rational actor, armed with full information and acting in a predictable manner.

Even if the traditional vision of the judiciary ever enjoyed broad currency, another and more appealing rationale for the broad discretion possessed by sentencing judges has undergirded the sentencing process. That theory is the much debated theory of rehabilitation.[11] Under this theory, of course, the primary purpose of incarceration is to rehabilitate a person convicted of crime and return that individual to society as a law-abiding citizen.

The theory of rehabilitation has long informed American corrections policy. This fact is eloquently reflected in an early name for prisons—penitentiaries. Under earlier notions of corrections policy, prisons were places of secular redemption and repentance, where

303

the convict would repair until rehabilitated and ready to return to productive life in the community. Sentencing under a system premised on broad discretion fitted comfortably within this theory of corrections. Because it was impossible to predict how long the rehabilitation process might take in a specific case, individuals were given an indeterminate sentence with a maximum limit. The inmate sentenced to an indeterminate sentence might face a period of incarceration ranging from, say, 3 to 5 years, depending of course upon the time actually needed for rehabilitation to take place.

According to this once predominant theory, parole authorities are in the best position both to determine when release is appropriate and to reduce disparities generated by the broad discretion accorded judges under the substantive criminal statutes.[12] The rationale was that the time needed for rehabilitation cannot be ascertained inside the courtroom at the time of sentencing, but can be determined only by observation of the individual behind prison walls. Under the rehabilitative theory, the Parole Commission picks up where sentencing judges leave off and, in consultation with corrections officials, determine the moment when the prisoner is ready to be reintroduced into civilian life—that is to say, when the inmate has been rehabilitated.

Not surprisingly, this theory is now widely regarded as ill conceived. Through various studies, it has been powerfully demonstrated that rehabilitation within prison is, at best, an uncertain process with dubious results. Experience in this country as well as others belies the efficacy of the rehabilitation model of sentencing. Those countries with prison systems universally viewed as enlightened, progressive, and humane still experience recidivism rates comparable to those prevailing in the United States and elsewhere.

Moreover, quite apart from the rehabilitation theory, the present system of parole *in practice* does not comport with the rehabilitation model. The Parole Commission does not conduct a decisive review of a prisoner's rehabilitation after a substantial portion of the sentence has been served. Rather, Parole Commission representatives set a presumptive parole date within weeks of the inmate's arrival at prison, when no rational prediction as to the inmate's rehabilitation is either practically or theoretically possible. In fact, the presumptive parole date is determined by reference to standard, nationally applicable guidelines which reflect a number of factors, but not including the predicted length of time necessary for the "rehabilitation" of the inmate.[13]

Although rehabilitation within prison walls obviously should remain a hope, it cannot reasonably rise to the level of an expectancy. And no rational system of criminal justice can be based upon hopes sadly belied both by practical experience and, more recently, by thoughtful study and research. Entrusting broad discretion to federal judges to impose indeterminate sentences, which will then actually be determined by parole authorities, thus appears to be a system built upon a faulty foundation. Our experience with parole suggests that we simply do not know when or if an individual inmate will, upon release, lead a law-abiding life.

Now in those limited instances when the goal of rehabilitation is already expressly foregone, there exists a much greater interest in guiding the exercise of sentencing judges' discretion. For if there is one sentence that by definition jettisons completely the rehabilitation model, it is the ultimate sanction of capital punishment. It cannot, of course, be gainsaid that the penalty of death is different, and that a rational society electing to impose the maximum punishment on one of its own would likely and appropriately seek to erect safeguards to avoid the evils of arbitrariness and caprice in the imposition of its ultimate sanction. References in Supreme Court decisions in capital cases going back to the Nineteenth Century, when it could not or at least was not seriously maintained that capital punishment violated the Eighth Amendment, can be seen as evidencing the especial care of appellate courts in reviewing capital cases. In short, where life itself is at stake, there has traditionally been discomfort with leaving the choice of the death penalty to the unfettered discretion of a single sentencing judge.

Indeed, one overriding concern regarding the death penalty has been the specter of disparity. Proportionality, the principle that the punishment should fit the crime, applies with enormous force to the ultimate penalty of death. This principle also suggests that a sentencing system should be purged to the fullest possible extent of disparities. An individual convicted of first-degree murder should not be given the death penalty except in accordance with the specific demands of law, elaborately articulated to eliminate as fully as possible the human elements of arbitrariness and caprice. A civilized society should not tolerate a situation in which a hypothetical Judge Smith uniformly sentences first-degree murderers to death, while in the same courthouse, Judge Jones openly refuses to impose the death penalty in such cases and uniformly imposes a life sentence instead. Where the stakes are sufficiently high, and with temporal authority there is plainly no higher stake than human life itself, we as a people should simply not tolerate a system in which such decisions are left to the individual propensities of particular judges.

VICTIMS AND SENTENCING

Another principle at work in the contemporary impetus for nationwide sentencing reform is that the system should seek justice for the *victims* of crime. Under this view, justice must be done as between the victim and the accused as well as between society and the accused. A healthy outpouring of interest and concern about victims and "victims' rights" have been evidenced in recent years. The President's Task Force on Victims of Crime, chaired by Assistant Attorney General Lois Haight Herrington, helped rivet national attention on the forgotten people in the criminal justice system. Congress in 1982 passed highly important, ground-breaking legislation that expressly imposes certain requirements with respect to the treatment of victims in the federal justice system.

Some of the essential proposals of sentencing reform, such as the elimination of broad, unfettered discretion among sentencing judges, are entirely consonant with the reawakened concern for the rights of victims. A fundamental justification for prohibiting private retribution and reserving to government the exclusive authority to punish criminal acts is to bring order, rationality and fairness to bear in determining guilt and imposing a just punishment. Under the current system, with the exception of civil remedies, which are all too often illusory, the victim of crime must look for justice to the criminal justice system. The victim of a crime deserves to know, as a matter of basic fairness, what penalty is actually being imposed upon the convicted defendant.

Under the system of sentencing prevailing in most of the nation, the victim as well as the public is badly misled. Generally, only those steeped in the intricacies of the criminal justice process realize that when the judge imposes a sentence of ten years, the convicted defendant in federal court may actually serve only one-third of the sentence.[14] The victim and the public are greatly disserved by this illusory sentence when the judge appears to impose one sentence, while all the *cognoscenti* in the courtroom realize that the judge is really imposing another sentence of only one-third the announced length. Thus, a frequent and powerful theme of the movement for sentencing reform is to restore "truth in sentencing," so that both the victim and the public are truthfully informed about the actual sentence to be served.

DETERRENCE, INCAPACITATION AND SENTENCING REFORM

Another principle undergirds the current sentencing reform effort. As recognition of the practical limitations of the rehabilitation model of sentencing increases, other values traditionally embodied in the criminal justice system, such as deterrence and incapacitation, come to the fore. Law enforcement personnel now almost uniformly subscribe to the view that the goal of incarceration should be to punish and incapacitate through incarceration those engaged in criminal conduct in order to prevent the repetition of criminal activity. The development of "career criminal" units in both state and federal prosecutors' offices across the country dramatically reflects the implementation of this view. Armed with the recognition that even a single individual can quite literally constitute a continuing one-man crime wave, law enforcement and prosecutorial personnel in various communities are working to identify and bring such persons to justice.

Similarly, a growing consensus of those involved with law enforcement strongly advocate the view that the purpose of deterrence is best served by sure and certain punishment. Under this view, deterrence is served not so much by the length of sentence imposed by the judge, but by the certainty that actual incarceration for a reasonable, determinate period will inexorably follow a lawful conviction.

These related but distinct purposes of deterrence and incapacitation would be more effectively served by a system of sentencing founded upon specific, determinate sentences imposed within a more limited range of permissible sentences, rather than a system of judicial discretion resulting in enormous disparities. The certainty that incarceration for a determinate period will be visited upon an individual convicted of a specific crime theoretically provides most potential criminals with a clearer reason not to engage in that activity. Under this approach, deterrence is achieved only by reintroducing certainty of incarceration, so the criminal cannot hope to escape justice by coming before a lenient judge ever willing to give criminal defendants the benefit of the doubt.

Although the goal of deterrence may remain a matter of theory, incapacitation by means of incarceration is quite a different matter.

Incapacitation through incarceration implicates the paramount interests of society in security and order. Incapacitation is plainly more effectively achieved when the determination of the length of a sentence is not left principally to the discretion of judges. Because, as we have already seen, the length and nature of sentences to be imposed varies widely depending upon the individual judge, the goal of incapacitation may be defeated by the discretion accorded judges, who are able to observe the defendant only in the context of a formal judicial proceeding. The very orderliness, decorum, and rationality of the criminal justice system minimizes the impact of the actual crime. The sentencing judge during the course of the trial observes the defendant on his or her best behavior, with character witnesses attesting to the defendant's better qualities, with family members present in the courtroom solemnly keeping watch for a loved one in a time of need, and counsel seeking to sow seeds of reasonable doubt as to guilt. These incidents of trial and sentencing operate to shape a sentencing judge's view as to the proper sentence. Such factors can and undoubtedly at times do lead to the perception that there is a basis for giving the individual a "second chance," through a less stringent sentence that may provide for no incarceration at all, or for minimal incarceration followed by an extended period of supervised parole.

HOPES FOR THE NEW SENTENCING PROVISIONS

The varying themes of the debate on sentencing reform touched upon here have produced a consensus that sentencing reform is necessary,[15] a consensus that eventually led Congress to enact the Sentencing Reform Act of 1984 as part of the Comprehensive Crime Control Act. The principal characteristic of that Act, not surprisingly, is to curtail the substantial disparities in the sentencing process and to bring greater certainty to that process. The goal is achieved by reducing the permissible range of discretion afforded to the sentencing judge and eliminating the role of the parole officer.

The new federal law contains three key elements that start taking effect in November 1986. First, it establishes a Federal Sentencing Commission, whose members were not appointed until the fall of 1985, and charges it with the task of formulating a new set of sentencing "guidelines." Second, the law provides for appellate review of sentences which fall outside the range suggested by the new sentencing guidelines. Third, it would abolish parole, and instead require that prisoners be released only after serving a full sentence, minus a maximum of fifty-four days of "good time" credit per year.[16]

Clearly the most important feature of the law is the Sentencing Commission. Its appointed task is to bring coherence to the federal criminal code by ranking categories of offenses and offenders in light of whatever factors it deems relevant.[17] The Commission will also establish a sentencing range for each category of offense involving each category of defendant.

The point of this reform is not to "strip" the sentencing judge of all discretion.[18] Rather, it is to offer guidance in the exercise of sound judicial judgement, and to provide a coherent, consistent sentencing philosophy and policy, framed by the Congress, for the federal judiciary.

A further spur to greater consistency in sentencing is sought from the provision for appellate review of sentences above or below that suggested by the guidelines. Under the new system, a judge will state the reasons for the sentence imposed in each criminal case.[19] If the sentence imposed falls within the guidelines, the judge would be required to explain why he chose the particular sentence within the acceptable range. If the sentence is outside the range set by the guidelines, the judge must explain the reasons he chose to impose an extraordinary sentence in that case. If the sentence is below the range, the Government may appeal; if the sentence is above the range, the defendant may appeal.[20]

The combination of the new sentencing guidelines and the introduction of appellate review should act to constrict the broad range now open to federal judges at the conclusion of criminal trials. By bringing more consistency and rationality into the sentencing process, this reform should in turn provide greater guidance for judges and a greater degree of public oversight in this vital area of the criminal justice system.

The predictable consequences of the restrictions soon to be placed on the discretion of federal judges will be enhanced by the law's straightforward answer to the problems posed by the parole system currently in place. By eliminating parole, the Sentencing Reform Act establishes, in effect, a system of "determinate sentencing," in which the sentence imposed by the judge would be the sentence actually served. The only exception will be the provision for allowing for a maximum fifteen percent adjustment in incarceration for an inmate's compliance with prison rules ("good time").

Eliminating parole will arguably serve several beneficial purposes, some of which were suggested above. First, a system of determinate sentencing would provide clear, truthful information to all concerned—victims, the general public, criminals and would-be criminals—of the punishments actually to be served by those convicted of crime. Thus, the modification of parole should go a long way toward eliminating the incorrect information now generated by the interrelated workings of sentencing and parole. Further, the abandonment of parole will free society from one more institutional manifestation of the less-accepted rehabilitation theory of penology. The judiciary would thus be able to go about its task in the criminal justice arena with a clearer view of the purposes of the system, and of its role in that system.

The curtailment of parole means, of course, that the judge, with the guidance of the Sentencing Commission's guidelines, must bear the lion's share of the sentencing burden. But this is as it should be. Should any particular judge fail adequately to discharge this heavier burden, appellate review would be available to rein in an exercise informed by poor judgement.

In short, the new sentencing system should work salutary changes in the way our criminal justice system operates. And it will have the beneficial side-effect of decreasing unbridled judicial discretion in a sensitive and vital part of the law. It deserves close watching in the next few years by the several states, where the vast majority of criminal defendants come face-to-face with our nation's criminal justice system.

REFERENCES

The Impetus for Sentencing Reform in the Criminal Justice System by Kenneth W. Starr

1. Although Congress has enacted a comprehensive reform of the sentencing system, *see* Sentencing Reform Act of 1984, Pub. L. No. 98-473, §§ 211-238, 98 Stat 1987-2040 (1984) (discussed *infra*), most of the old sentencing scheme will remain in force until Nov. 1, 1986. *Id.* § 235, 98 Stat at 2031-2033. This chapter seeks to elucidate the theoretical underpinnings of sentencing reform efforts and to encourage State legislatures to consider enactment of their own reform measures.

2. A. Partridge & W. Eldridge, *The Second Circuit Sentencing Study: A Report to Judges* (1974).

3. S. Rep. No. 98-225, 98th Cong., 1st Sess. 44 (1981) (describing findings of *Federal Sentencing: Toward a More Explicit Policy of Criminal Sanctions*).

4. *See, United States v. DiFrancesco*, 449 U.S. 117, 143 (1980) (observing that one of the basic problems is the unbridled power of judges to sentence in an arbitrary and discriminatory fashion).

5. *Cf. United States v. Schell*, 692 F.2d 672, 679 (10th Cir. 1982) (legislature primarily responsible for establishing rational sentencing structure).

6. *Dorsynski v. United States*, 418 U.S. 424, 431 (1974) (generally, if the sentence is within statutory requirements, reviewing courts will not overturn it).

7. *See, e.g., United States v. Vasquez*, 638 F.2d 507, 534 (2d Cir. 1980), *cert. denied*, 454 U.S. 847, 975 (1981) (judges ordinarily are not required to explain reasons for sentences).

8. *See, United States v. Grayson*, 438 U.S. 41, 47–52 (1978) (sentencing judge may consider numerous factors, including presentence report, potential for rehabilitation, participation in prior criminal acts, and evidence during trial).

9. Of course I do not mean to suggest that the sentencing process should be so inflexible that it bars judges from considering special mitigating or aggravating circumstances on a case-by-case basis.

10. Marvin Frankel, *Criminal Sentences: Law Without Order* (New York: Hill and Wang, 1973).

11. *See, United States v. Grayson*, 438 U.S. 41 (1978).

12. *Id.*

13. *See generally, United States v. Addonizio*, 442 U.S. 178 (1979).

14. Under the general parole provisions for federal crimes, a federal prisoner sentenced to a definite term must serve only one third of the sentence before being eligible for parole. 18 U.S.C. § 4205(a) (1982) (to be repealed as of Nov. 1, 1986, *see supra*, n. 1).

15. *United States v. DiFrancesco*, 449 U.S. 117, 142 (1980).

16. 18 U.S.C.A. § 3624 (West 1985). [Editor's note: "P.L. 99-217, signed by President Reagan on December 26, 1985, postponed for one year the Commission's reporting deadlines. The Commission's guidelines must now be submitted to Congress in April of 1987 and will, absent changes, go into effect in November of 1987." *See* essay by Randall R. Rader, forthcoming in late 1986 in the *Federal Bar Journal*.]

17. *See* 28 U.S.C.A. §§ 991, 994.

18. *See* 28 U.S.C. § 991(b)(1)(B) (West Supp. 1985) (calling for "sufficient flexibility" in sentencing guidelines "to permit individualized sentences").

19. 18 U.S.C.A. 3553(c).

20. 18 U.S.C.A. 3742(a)–(b).

18

A GOVERNOR'S PERSPECTIVE ON SENTENCING

by Pete du Pont

When I became Governor in 1977, Delaware was a state in trouble. Economic development was at a standstill, and a high-spending government had enacted tax increase after tax increase. Clearly part of the solution was to impose controls on state spending, and corrections was one of the most serious offenders when it came to demanding more and more of our revenue. We were pouring money into jails.

As we began to seek ways to slow the growth of the corrections budget, there was one reason to be optimistic about our chances of success: Just seven years earlier, Delaware had built the most modern prison facility in the nation, one designed to accommodate all of the State's projected incarceration needs until 1990. There would be no need, at least, to build more prisons.

Eight years later, we in Delaware have accomplished much: seven consecutive balanced budgets, two personal income tax cuts, a constitutional amendment limiting government spending, establishment of a "rainy day fund" for emergencies, and legislation which has made Delaware, long a haven for corporate enterprise, a national center for financial institutions. All of this has meant prosperity and jobs for the people of the State. Delaware's per capita income is the second highest in the nation, while its employment rate is the lowest.

But still we are pouring money into corrections! The prison that was to last until the end of the decade was filled to capacity before the decade even began.[1] To meet the rising tide of new inmates, we have converted our prison industries and vocational training facilities into cellblocks, while double- or triple-bunking every available cell. Despite these extraordinary (and counterproductive) measures, we have had to construct three major additions to the prison, and a fourth is in progress today. We have built a multi-purpose correctional facility in Wilmington, and have converted office space in our Sussex County correctional institution into jail cells. Yet our prisons remain filled to overflowing, and we are being told to begin thinking about constructing another minimum security facility in the next year or two.

THE HIGH COST OF CORRECTIONS

The pricetag for housing, feeding and guarding the offenders flooding into these prisons is appalling. It currently costs $17,000 a year for us to house one prisoner in a jail cell which costs $70,000 to build.[2] Given that the average Delawarean pays about $1,000 in State income taxes every year, it takes seventeen law-abiding citizens to support each criminal we incarcerate.

And these costs are escalating as our prison system eats up progressively bigger portions of our revenue. In Fiscal Year 1977 corrections accounted for 3.6 percent of the State budget; in 1985 the number was more than 6.0 percent.[3] Over the course of my two terms as Governor, Delaware's statewide corrections budget grew by more than 300 percent, by far the largest growth of any agency of State government. We may be punishing offenders in Delaware, but the taxpayers are taking a beating as well.

Part of the reason for this alarming growth in spending is that only two states put more people in jail, per capita, than Delaware—we have 274 prison inmates for every 100,000 people.[4] And we are putting them in prison for longer terms. Seven years ago for each inmate serving a term of ten years or more, there was roughly one prisoner serving a term of less than a year. Today long-termers outnumber prisoners serving terms of less than one year by four-to-one.[5]

These numbers might be different in some other state, but I believe that the difference is one only of degree. Despite its great cost, our present corrections system might be acceptable if it worked, but our crime and recidivism rates show it does not. The time clearly has come for us in Delaware, and I think for all of us in the United States, to take a long, hard look at corrections philosophy.

THE ESCALATING RACE TO BUILD MORE PRISONS

Consider this: We traditionally rely on incarceration as the primary method of punishing criminals, but there is no evidence that higher incarceration rates have any impact on the crime rate.[6] Yet we continue to finance expensive warehouses for criminals, barely keeping ahead of the burgeoning growth in our inmate population.

And not only is the cost of such warehousing skyrocketing, but prison overcrowding minimizes whatever chances exist for success in rehabilitative programs.

Yet we seem unable to influence the situation to any significant degree. In Delaware, as in other states, we are locked into a prison of tradition, faced with a complex system involving many agencies, each playing by its own rules, vaguely yet strongly influenced by a public outraged at the violence of a few and frustrated at their inability to comprehend the system. Buffeted by public pressure to "get tough," straining under the load of overcrowded prisons, and discouraged by a bureaucratic morass, we seem to have lost control over our criminal justice resources.

The response of public officials to all of this has been, by and large, to take the path of least resistance. Responding to public pressure, legislatures have enacted tough mandatory sentences for a host of specific crimes, magistrates have levied more onerous bail requirements, and, where they retain discretion, sentencing judges have imposed longer terms of imprisonment. These *ad hoc* policy choices have reined in ever-increasing numbers of new inmates, in response to which we have built more jails. We could continue in this vein, adding more and more resources to the present system. It would be the most expensive way to proceed, but it is a legitimate policy choice.

But even if we could afford to continue building prisons *ad infinitum*, which I submit we cannot afford to do, simply expanding the capacity of our jails will not end our overcrowding problems. If anything can be learned from Delaware's experiences over the past decade, it is that building more prisons simply frees legislators, sentencing judges, corrections officials, and, yes, governors, from the difficult job of looking for less costly, and perhaps more effective, ways of dealing with offenders. If we cannot get free of the mindset that building more prisons is the only answer to our overcrowding problem, then we can never hope to make the criminal justice system cost-effective, and thus truly accountable to the taxpayers.

ALTERNATIVES TO BUILDING MORE PRISONS

Several states have adopted prison population reduction strategies which require criminal justice decision-makers to take cell space into account in dealing with offenders. One approach, exemplified by Michigan's Emergency Powers Release Act, is to provide for the early

315

release of short-term inmates when prison capacities are exceeded. The Michigan statute requires the Corrections Commissioner to notify the Governor when the inmate population exceeds capacity for 30 consecutive days. The Governor then must declare a state of emergency, which automatically reduces all minimum sentences by 90 days, creating a pool of inmates eligible for early release. If this process does not reduce the prison population to 95 percent of capacity within 90 days, then minimum sentences again are reduced by an additional 90 days. The Governor must rescind the state of emergency whenever the Corrections Commissioner certifies that the prison population has been reduced to 95 percent of rated capacity.[7] Variations on the Michigan statute have been enacted in Connecticut, Georgia, Illinois, Iowa, Ohio, and Oklahoma.[8]

Early release of inmates is a legitimate policy choice, but in practice it has been controversial and difficult to administer. A state of emergency has been declared six times in Michigan since 1981, releasing over 2,500 inmates.[9] In testimony before the Congressional Crime Caucus, Michigan Governor James J. Blanchard stated that he was determined never to declare another "prison overcrowding emergency" because of the potential risk to public safety. Faced with continuing overcrowding problems, however, Governor Blanchard fell back on the most costly solution—building more prisons.[10]

Another approach to the prison overcrowding problem, which has been adopted in Minnesota, is to factor prison capacity into the sentencing decision. Under the Minnesota Sentencing Guidelines, presumptive sentences are determined according to the offender's criminal history and offense severity. Where an offender's presumptive sentence borders the jail/probation dividing line, the "in and out" decision is based on available cell space.[11] Judges can deviate from the presumptive sentence under the Minnesota guidelines, but at least the incarceration decision is made with an eye toward the limitations on prison resources.

The problem with the Michigan and Minnesota solutions to prison overcrowding is their appearance of arbitrariness. Public confidence in the criminal justice system is undermined when an offender who should go to jail is placed on probation because the prisons are too full, or when, for the same reason, an inmate is paroled who would not otherwise be released. To say that prison overcrowding forces compromises is not sufficient when other answers are available.

316

CHANGING OUR CORRECTIONS PHILOSOPHY: THE DELAWARE APPROACH

In my judgment, a fundamental reshaping of our approach to corrections is in order. We must begin this process with the recognition that the most significant factor causing prison overcrowding is not the crime rate or demographics but government policy. Prison population growth is the consequence of a series of poorly-coordinated policy determinations made on an *ad hoc* basis throughout the system by criminal justice decision-makers—legislators, prosecutors, judges, corrections officials, and parole boards.[12]

If we truly want to regain control over our corrections system, then we must change our concept of what the term "corrections" means. First, we must begin to view punishment in terms of certainty rather than severity. That a offender can count on *some* punishment for his crime is a far greater deterrent to him than the uncertain imposition of a very harsh sentence. Second, we must provide sentencing options between the extremes of probation and prison. Third, having provided intermediate sanction alternatives, we must make our corrections system more flexible in order to permit criminal justice agencies to regain control over the allocation of their resources.

With these principles in mind, the Delaware Sentencing Reform Commission proposed an entirely new approach to corrections, one that stresses accountability—accountability of the offender to the victim and to the state, and accountability of the corrections system to the public and to other criminal justice agencies. The Delaware approach would create an ordered yet flexible system of sentencing and corrections based on the belief that an offender should be sentenced to the least restrictive (and least costly) sanction available, consistent with public safety.[13] It would structure the movement of offenders into and out of the corrections system, making it fairer and more cost efficient. It would provide incentives for offenders to move into less restrictive (and less costly) levels of control. At the same time, this approach would strengthen existing safeguards against violent offenders and career criminals, who would be incarcerated as long as necessary to protect the public.

Today the sentencing judge is faced with conflicting goals of rehabilitation, incapacitation, deterrence and retribution, and generally he has no formal standards by which to consider a sentence in terms of achieving one or more of those goals. Moreover,

317

the judge must choose between probation, perhaps involving some form of treatment program, and jail. Flexibility exists only in terms of how long or how short a sentence is imposed, and the capacity to encourage compliance and discourage violations during probationary sentences is severely limited.

And if an offender fails to comply with the conditions of a less-restrictive sanction, such as probation, the judge has the same rigid choices: Assuming the probation officer even notifies the court of the violation, the judge may continue the offender on probation, or he may place him in jail.

There is no certainty of punishment in such a system.

The lack of flexibility in our corrections system is frustrating. Conventional probation is not an adequate answer for every offender whose crime is not serious enough to merit jail, but the sentencing options between the extremes of probation and jail rarely are in place. The accountability concept developed by Delaware's Sentencing Reform Commission addresses these concerns in a unique and imaginative way.

The chart on the following pages shows the framework of a sequential sentencing process. The proposed guidelines, which for us in Delaware would amount to nothing less than a complete overhaul of our sentencing and correction laws, establish a range of sanctions over ten "levels of accountability." Level I is unsupervised probation; Level X is maximum security imprisonment. In between is a full range of alternatives, each more restrictive than the last. Within each level there are degrees of control and accountability relating to mobility in the community, the amount of supervision, privileges withheld or special conditions, and any financial obligations imposed (including restitution to the victim), which can be tailored to the individual offender. By adding new methods and new elements of control, by structuring the offender's time and controlling his schedule, whereabouts and activities, we would control the offender's choice of a job, choice of residence, ability to drive, to drink, to travel, and even to make phone calls.

And to all of this we would add the probation fee concept. Successfully used in Georgia and Florida, the $10 to $50 per month fee is charged to probationers to offset the cost of supervision. Like the sanctions, the fee could be escalating, serving two purposes. First, the cost of increased supervision required at higher levels, which costs more, would be offset in part by the offender; and second, he or she would have an incentive to move to a lower and less expensive level of restriction.

Mixing all of these elements together in a comprehensive sentencing scheme, as Delaware's Sentencing Reform Commission proposed, will result in truly individualized, yet consistent sentencing. The range of alternatives within each accountability level enable refinement and minor adjustments tailored to the particular offender. But this flexibility in sentencing is permitted only within a predetermined range hinged to the offender's criminal history and current offense.

What is particularly attractive about the accountability level approach is that it applies not only to sentencing the offender, but to controlling him following sentencing as well, and the same ordered flexibility available to judges would be available to corrections officials. At the same time we undertake a comprehensive revision of our sentencing philosophy, we should seek to develop a comprehensive corrections philosophy—and that philosophy should be reflected in an objective and ordered process aimed at controlling the offender.

This is how it will work: a drug offender with a minimal record but unstable employment might be sentenced in Level II to supervised probation for two years, with restrictions on his place of residence and association with certain individuals and/or his right to visit high-drug crime locations, and with a $10 per month fee to offset the cost of keeping him straight. If he observes these conditions for the first year of his probation, he could move downscale to Level I—unsupervised probation. In this level no fee is imposed but perhaps certain restrictions in his mobility and associations might be ordered to minimize the chance of his slipping back into the drug scene and its associated crime. But the offender also could be moved into Level III, with heightened supervision, a curfew and an increased monthly fee, if he breaks the rules. Thus, the offender has clear incentives to comply with his sentence, and the sentencing judge has available options other than prison when probation is violated. Having and using these options will dramatically increase the certainty of punishment to be expected by offenders.

At the other end of the scale, a twice-convicted armed robber sentenced in Level X to 20 years of supervision, might, after serving 3 years in maximum security, and adhering to all the rules, be moved downscale to Level IX (medium security) where he might take ad-

Accountability Levels in The Delaware Sentencing Approach

Restrictions	I 0–100	II 101–200	II 201–300	IV 301–400	V 401–500
Mobility in the Community[1]	100% (unrestricted)	100% (unrestricted)	90% (restr. 0–10 hrs/wk)	80% (restr. 10–30 hrs/wk)	60% (restr. 30–40 hrs./wk)
Amount of Supervision	0:0	Written rpt/ monthly	1–2 face-to-face/ month 1–2 wkly phone cont.	3–6 face-to-face/ month Wkly phone contact	2–6 face-to-face/wk, dly phone, wrtn rpts/wkly
Priv. withheld or special conditions[2]	100%) same as prior offense convic.	(100%) same as prior convic.	1–2 priv withheld	1–4 priv withheld	1–7 priv. withheld
Financial Obligations[3]	Fine/cost may be applied (0–2 day fine)	Fine/costs/ rest./prob. supervis. fee may be applied (1–3 day fine)	Same (increase proba. fee by $5–10/mo) (2–4 dy/fine)	Same (increase proba. fee by $5–10/mo) (3–5 dy/fine)	Same (pay part. cost of food/lodg/supervis. fee) (4–7 dy/fine)
Examples (These are examp. only—many other scenarios could be constructed meeting the requir. of each level)	$50 fine/court cst; 6/mo unsupervised proba.	$50 fine, restitu., court costs; 6/mo superv. probation; $10/mo fee; wrtn report	Fine/costs/ restitu; 1 yr proba.; wkend comm. serv.; no drinking	Wkend comm. serv or mandatory treatm. 5 hrs/day; $30/mo. probat. fee no drinking; no out-of-st trips	Mandatory rehab. skills prog. 8 hrs/day; restitu.; probat. fee of $40/mo; no drinking; curfew

1. Restrictions on freedom essentially structures an offender's time, controlling his schedule, whereabouts, and activities for the designed amount of time. To the extent monitoring is not standard or consistent or to the extent that no sanctions for accountability accrues for failure on the part of the offender, the time is *not* structured. It could consist of residential, part-time residential, community service, or other specific methods for meeting the designated hours. The judge could order the hours be met daily (e.g. 2 hours/day) or in one period (e.g. weekend in jail).

vantage of expanded rehabilitative programs. Three years later, with continued good behavior, the offender again could move downscale, to a minimum security facility with even greater opportunities for rehabilitation. If everything goes well, this serious offender would continue to move downscale and perhaps spend the last several years of his sentence in a much less restrictive, and much less costly, environment than a maximum security prison. On the other hand, any slip-up along the way and he could be moved back into more secure levels of supervision.

Here, I suspect, might be part of the solution in looking for ways to encourage serious offenders, facing long prison sentences, to

Restrictions	VI 501–600	VII 601–700	VIII 701–800	IX 801–900	X 901–1,000
Mobility in the Community[1]	30% (restr. 50–100 hr/wk)	20% (restr. 100–140 hr/wk)	10% (90% of time restr.) incarcerated	0% Incarcerated	0% Incarcerated
Amount of Supervision	Daily phone dly face-to-face, wkly wrtn rpts	Dly on site supervis. 8–16 hrs/day	Dly on site supervis. 24 hours/day	Dly on site supervis. 24 hours/day	Daily on site supervis. 24 hours/day
Priv. withheld or special conditions[2]	1–10 withheld	1–12 withheld	5–15 withheld	15–19 withheld	20 or more withheld
Financial Obligations[3]	Same as V (8–10 day fine)	Same as V (11–12) day fine	Fine, costs restitu. payable upon release to VII or lower (12–15 day fine)	Same as VIII	Same as VIII
Examples (These are examp. only—many other scenarios could be constructed meeting the requir. of each level)	Work release; pay port. of rm/bd/restit; no kitchen priv. outside meal times; no drinking; no sex; wkends home	Resident. treatment prog; pay port. of program costs; limited privileges	Minimum security prison	Medium security prison	Maximum security prison

2. Privileges/Conditions: choice of job; choice of residence; mobility within setting; driving; drinking (possible use of Antabuse); out-of-state trips; phone calls; curfew; mail; urinalysis; associates; areas off limits.

3. As a more equiptable guide to appropriate fine, the amount would be measured in units equivalent daily income, such as 1 day's salary × 1 "day's fine."

abide by the rules and to attempt to rehabilitate themselves. Moreover, such a system could well enhance decision-making in the parole process. For example, once an inmate is eligible for parole under a statutory formula based on time served, the Parole Board might have the flexibility to reward a "good" inmate with placement in some appropriate pre-release program in Level VI, instead of simply releasing him prematurely to complete freedom on the streets or simply denying his application and thus discouraging his good behavior.

When the Delaware Sentencing Reform Commission analyzed the State's current offender population in terms of the accountability level scheme, it found that only 21 percent of the inmates were under Levels IX or X supervision, that is, medium or maximum security incarceration.[14] But medium and maximum security facilities account for 87 percent of the total corrections budget in Delaware, and I believe that there is a significant potential for savings if we provide the mechanism—consistent with the demands of public safety—for prisoners to move into less costly forms of custody.[15]

EXPANDING INTERMEDIATE SENTENCING OPTIONS

The Delaware Sentencing Reform Commission also found that roughly 70 percent of the State's offender population fell within Levels I through III, unsupervised and supervised probation, leaving less than 10 percent of Delaware offenders in the intermediate Levels IV through VIII, mostly in some outpatient drug or alcohol abuse treatment program.[16] Clearly this suggests the need for developing programs to handle a much larger segment of the offender population in the intermediate levels of supervision. This can be done within state government or by the private sector.

An example of Delaware's approach in this area is a new drug and alcohol treatment program about to start under private supervision. In 1983 a Bureau of Justice Statistics study found that almost a third of all state prisoners in 1979 were either intoxicated or under the influence of drugs at the time they committed their offenses.[17] In addition, 20 percent of all state prisoners drank heavily every day for the year prior to their crimes; more than half used drugs during the month prior to being arrested; and more than three-quarters used drugs sometime during their lives.[18] Yet despite these astounding statistics, only 16 percent of these prisoners ever had been in an alcohol treatment program and just 25 percent had been in a drug rehabilitation program.[19]

In the face of these statistics, the lack of treatment programs in this area is a yawning gap in Delaware's corrections system. Using vacant buildings on the grounds of a state hospital, the Bureau of Adult Corrections, in conjunction with the Bureau of Alcohol and Drug Abuse, has contracted with a private provider to run an inpatient and out-patient program for offenders. The private agency's specialized expertise in drug and alcohol abuse treatment will enable rapid start-up of the program, and using a private as opposed to government agency should result in greater flexibility in operation and easier elimination as the offender population falls. The key feature for sentencing reform, however, will be the additional flexibility this program's existence will provide to sentencing judges and to corrections officials.

This sort of drug and alcohol treatment program is but one example of the intermediate level sanctions which we need to develop to fill in the gaps between the extremes of probation and prison. Expanded vocational training programs, work release, supervised custody, intensive probation and parole units, halfway houses, part-time and weekend jails, and even such exotic methods as electronic monitoring of parolees and probationers, are all ways to deal with offenders in less restrictive (and much less costly) environments than secure incarceration. Importantly, they all are suited to private contracting with its added attraction of cost-effectiveness, a forgotten goal in criminal justice.

These are not particularly new ideas, but heretofore they have been viewed as the fringe elements, not the main body, of our corrections system. We need to begin to envision such intermediate level programs as the backbone of our management of offenders, because, in addition to cost avoidance, such programs offer our best hope for crime avoidance as well.

Whatever gains are made with offenders in institutional treatment, and I gauge them to be limited, such gains are rapidly lost with the offender's return to the community from which he came.[20] Because the offender's community network is the "most powerful predictor of recidivism," intensive institutional supervision most likely will be ineffective unless it is followed up by intensive community-based supervision and support.[21] Development of intermediate level programs will enable us to better handle the offender where it matters most—in the community where he lives with the rest of us.

A full range of sanctions, of course, will require a comprehensive set of guidelines to assure that offenders are assigned to proper accountability levels consistently. Whether these guidelines are voluntary or statutory, the result would be much greater consistency in tailoring sentences to the individual than provided by the system we now employ. Obviously, great care must be exercised because, absent that care, we risk repeating the inefficient resource allocation, erratic accounting for public safety concerns, and lack of certainty of punishment that exists today.

The Delaware Sentencing Accountability Commission, the permanent statutory successor to the gubernatorially-appointed Sentencing Reform Commission, has developed a sentencing guidelines matrix keyed to the offender's criminal history and the nature of his current offense. Adapted from the systems used in Minnesota and Washington, the guidelines matrix sets forth a presumptive sentence for the judge to follow. The presumptive sentence assigns the offender to a specific accountability level for a specific length of time. Built into the model is a presumptive time for the offender's moving downscale into less restrictive (and less costly) levels of supervision.

"Presumptive" does not mean mandatory. No structured sentencing scheme can account for all situations, and the judge will retain discretion to sentence outside the guidelines, although he must cite his reasons for doing so, and his decision is appealable by both the prosecution and defense.

It is important to underscore that the *offender's* needs will not determine his assignment to a level of punishment—that will be determined by the nature of his offense and his criminal history. But once the level of punishment is determined, the specific conditions attaching to the offender's sanction can be individualized as much as possible to his needs (such as drug or alcohol treatment) and to the needs of his victim (such as restitution). The sentencing guidelines define the first step, but a more sophisticated system of diagnosing and classifying will be required once the intermediate level programs are available.

These sequential sentencing and correction flow-down rules, adjusted by individualized needs assessments, will result in a consistently applied sentencing and corrections philosophy. The continuum of sanctions, and the offender's assignment and movement up and down the scale, will reflect the basic principle that our system will impose upon the criminal the least restrictive (and least costly) sanction consistent with public safety. Once in place, and administered with this philosophy in mind, accountability level sentencing should serve the best interests of the offender, the criminal justice system, and, most importantly, the taxpayer.

MAKING THE CORRECTIONS SYSTEM ACCOUNTABLE

In focusing on the development of alternative intermediate level programs and "least restrictive sanction" sentencing, we must not lose sight of what always should be the fundamental goals of our criminal justice system. In priority order the system should be striving

- to incapacitate the violent predator and career criminal,
- to restore the victim as nearly as possible to his or her pre-crime status, and
- to be cost-effective.

Rehabilitation of the offender, though obviously a goal of any corrections system, should follow all of these in priority and be seen as a by-product of accountability level sentencing, not its fundamental purpose.

These priorities must be clearly enunciated, for the biggest stumbling block to sentencing reform is the education effort which must precede it. Those within the criminal justice system, particularly prosecutors and judges, but more importantly those outside of it, particularly legislators and the public, must escape from the common belief that an offender who goes to jail gets punished while he who does not go to jail gets off. We must reject the "in" versus "out" dichotomy and simply acknowledge that there are more effective ways to hold the non-violent predator and career criminal accountable. "A new political consensus must emerge outside the criminal justice system in which the values of punishment and public safety are rationally balanced with fiscal constraints and competing claims for public revenue."[22]

It took us more than four years in Delaware to achieve this consensus and commit ourselves to the wholesale revision in our corrections philosophy which accountability level sentencing will entail. It also will entail a commitment of resources, to improve our diagnostic and classification systems, to develop intermediate level sanctions, to work with the private sector. But the fiscal hallmark of sentencing reform is cost avoidance—developing and using less costly alternatives in corrections. The more offenders handled in intermediate level programs, the longer we will be able to reserve our jails for violent offenders and avoid building costly new prisons.

As the Delaware experience has amply demonstrated, there are no quick fixes, or easy answers to the problem of prison overcrowding. One thing we have learned the hard way is that simply building more prisons is not the answer. Criminals can be punished without punishing the taxpayers as well. The prison overcrowding crisis presents an opportunity for a fundamental reshaping of our corrections philosophy which we cannot afford to pass up.

REFERENCES

A Governor's Perspective on Sentencing by Pete du Pont

1. When the Delaware Correctional Center opened for business in 1971, its design capacity was 475. By 1977, the inmate population reached over 700, leading to a civil rights action against corrections officials. *See, Anderson v. Redman*, 429 F. Supp. 1105 (D. Del. 1977). To compound my difficulties as a new Governor, I had to deal with the prison overcrowding problem under the scrutiny of a federal district judge.

2. *Delaware Sentencing Reform Comm'n — 1983 Report*, January 23, 1984, p. 5. These are average costs. The per-cell construction cost is even more alarming when one considers that the last two major additions to the Delaware Correctional Center were built entirely with inmate labor.

3. *Supra* n. 2, p. 5. This percentage growth reflects all appropriations to the Department of Corrections and to the Division of Youth Rehabilitation, which in 1983 was spun off from the Department of Corrections into the newly-formed Department of Services for Children, Youth and Their Families.

4. "Prisons at Mid-Year 1983," *Bureau of Justice Statistics Bulletin*, October 1983, (Washington, D.C., U.S. Department of Justice), p. 2.

5. This dramatic increase in the long-term population is ominous in terms of cost. A recent study of inmates serving life sentences (who account for almost 15 percent of Delaware's prison population) projects a full-term cost of $159,741,140 to maintain the 234 lifers already in our system, plus an additional $363,548,627 cost to maintain the 288 new lifers estimated to be admitted during the next decade. *Lifers in Delaware — Future Costs and Populations Through 1994* (Dover, Delaware: Statistical Analysis Center, July 1985).

6. *See, e.g., Biennium Report — Criminal Justice Research*, National Institute of Justice, April 1982 (Washington, D.C.: U.S. Department of Justice), p. 52; *supra* n. 2, p. 2; *Report to the House of Delegates*, American Bar Association Criminal Justice Section, Task Force on Crime, February 1983, p. 10. The lack of a verifiable correlation between incarceration rates and crime rates is demonstrated by states such as Oregon and Nevada, which both have high incarceration rates yet also have high (Nevada) and low (Oregon) crime rates, and by states such as Hawaii and Minnesota, which both have low incarceration rates yet also have high (Hawaii) and low (Minnesota) crimes rates. *Id.* To some, it appears that those states with the most severe criminal penalties tend to be those with the highest crime rates. M. Feeley, *Criminal Justice Policy: A View from the States* (National Governors Association, 1984), p. 3.

7. *See* E. Garry, *Options to Prison Overcrowding*, (Rockville, Maryland: National Institute of Justice, National Criminal Justice Reference Service, November 1984), p. 9; D. Steelman and R. Mathias, *Controlling Prison Population: An Assessment of Current Mechanisms* (Fort Lee, New Jersey: National Council on Crime and Delinquency, June 1983), p. 5.

8. *See* Garry, *supra* n. 7; "Setting Prison Terms," *Bureau of Justice Statistics Bulletin*, August 1983 (Washington, D.C.: U.S. Department of Justice), p. 5. The Oklahoma legislature in 1980 fixed a maximum capacity of the state's prison facilities. When capacity reaches the limits, the Pardon & Parole Board is required to consider for parole all nonviolent offenders within six months of their scheduled release. *See also* Prison and Jail Overcrowding in New York State (Voters Against Prison Construction Bond Budget, January 1982), p. 5.

9. *Supra* n. 7.

10. Testimony of the Honorable James J. Blanchard before the Congressional Crime Caucus, Washington, D.C., February 25, 1985.

11. *See* Garry, *supra* n. 7, pp. 13–14; *Minnesota Sentencing Guidelines and Commentary* (Sentencing Guidelines Commission, St. Paul, Minnesota).

12. G. Funke, "How Much Justice Can States Afford?," *State Legislatures* (July 1984), p. 1; Kay Knapp, *The Etiology of Prison Populations: Implications for Prison Population Projection Methodology* (Minnesota Sentencing Guideline Commission, 1983), p. 2; A. Blumstein, J. Cohen and H. Miller, "Demographically Disaggregated Projections of Prison Population," I *Research in Public Policy Analysis and Management* 3-37 (1981).

13. This standard already is incorporated in the American Bar Association's Standards for Criminal Justice. 3 A.B.A. *Standards for Criminal Justice*, Standard 18-2.2, "Sentencing Alternatives and Procedures." The National Criminal Justice Association Policy on prison overcrowding similarly favors this concept. *See, Delaware Sentencing Reform Comm'n – 1983 Report, supra* n. 2, p. 14.

14. *Supra* n. 2, pp. 29–30, Figure 12 and Attachment 7.

15. *Id.*, p. 31 and Figure 13.

16. *Id.*

17. *Bureau of Justice Statistics Bulletin*, January and March 1983, (Washington, D.C.: U.S. Department of Justice).

18. *Id.*

19. *Id.*

20. M. Feeley and L. Ollin, *Criminal Justice and Corrections* (Washington, D.C.: National Governors Association Center for Public Policy Research, 1982).

21. *Id.*

22. J. Austin and B. Krisberg, "The Unmet Promise of Alternatives to Incarceration," 28 *Crime and Delinquency* (No. 3, July 1982).

PAROLE BOARDS, VICTIMS AND SOCIETY
by Frank Carrington

Parole board members, and other custodial officials—wardens, superintendents, sheriffs who run jails, and so on—have difficult jobs. No questions about that. They deal with violent, evil people on a daily basis; they are usually underpaid, at least when one considers the demands that their jobs make of them; and, their decisions, particularly with reference to questions of whether to release a prisoner, can have a definite and dramatic impact on the safety of society. This is conceded. There is pressure on them.

The same thing can be said about law enforcement officers, the average "street cops." The only significant difference is that the law enforcement officer is called upon to make decisions in a matter of minutes, or even seconds, while the custodial official has months or even years to decide whether to release or not. Add to this the fact that the street cops almost invariably make their decisions on their own, that is, there is no lawyer with them to tell them whether an arrest or search is legal or illegal in a given situation; whereas, custodial officials will, in most cases, have a battery of counselors, psychologists, psychiatrists and the like, to advise on a particular decision.

Given this, it strains one's sense of fairness to think that, in almost every instance, the street police officer can be sued in state court for false arrest (or similar torts) or in federal district court for civil rights violations, while the custodial officials in many states are totally immune from the consequences of their actions. No matter how tragic the consequences may be—even the death of innocent people as a result of a killer's release—their decisions are immune to prosecution.

ABSOLUTE IMMUNITY?

Consider, for example, two cases from California in which that state's supreme court turned a blind eye to any rights claimed by survivors of the victims, even though the murderers in both cases had been released under circumstances which were grossly negligent.

Clearly, any reasonable person would have understood the probable outcome of the releases. For the victims the result was death; for the custodial officials the result was total and absolute immunity from the consequences of their negligence.

In *Martinez v. California*, a certain Richard June-Jordan Thomas was released from prison where he was serving a term for an aggravated sexual assault perpetrated in San Diego's Tecolote Canyon. The psychiatric report on June-Jordan Thomas indicated that he was a Mentally Disordered Sexual Offender (MDSO), unamenable to treatment. The judge who sentenced Thomas for his original crime endorsed on his case folder that he should not be paroled. Nevertheless, the California Adult Authority, in its wisdom, paroled June-Jordan Thomas after he had served only a small part of his sentence. Within months, he returned to the same Tecolote Canyon where he assaulted and murdered 14-year-old Mary Ellen Martinez.

The Martinez family sued the state of California for gross negligence by the Parole Board (Adult Authority) for releasing Thomas. Unfortunately for the family, California has a statute which provides that parole boards are absolutely immune from liability for a decision to release a prisoner, no matter how gross the negligence.

This resulted in the Martinez' suit being dismissed by the trial court, the California Court of Appeals[1] and the California Supreme Court. The Supreme Court of the United States accepted the case on appeal. It conceded the grossness of the negligence of the California authorities in one passage:

> [The members of the parole board] were fully informed about [Richard June-Jordan Thomas'] history, his propensities and the likelihood that he would commit another violent crime. We assume, as the complaint alleges, that the parole board knew that the release of Thomas created a clear and present danger that such an incident would occur.[2]

However, in a 9–0 decision (which will never go down in history as a humane ruling) the Supreme Court said that the California statute which makes the parole authorities immune was constitutional, and, in essence, the victims can go play in traffic.

One point should be made about what it is like to be a legal writer in victims cases. Just when it seems that the depths have been plumbed, that there is absolutely nothing more the legal system can do to denigrate victims rights, yet another case will come along, demonstrating once again how much contempt the system has for its victims.

Following *Martinez*, the Supreme Court of the state of California issued *Thompson v. County of Alameda*,[3] the facts of which make *Martinez* almost pale by comparison. *Thompson* involved the release of a vicious young criminal, James Fisher, by the Alameda County Probation authorities. Fisher, who was confined under court order for latent and extremely violent tendencies against young children, had an ongoing homosexual relationship with his "counselor," a psychologist. Not surprisingly, the counselor ordered Fisher released to go home for awhile. Fisher advised the probation authorities that if he was released he was going to go home and "...kill a kid in the neighborhood."

He was, and he did. Within six hours of his return to the neighborhood, Fisher had sexually molested and murdered a 5-year-old boy in the neighborhood. The victim's mother became a full-time mental patient because of the murder of her son. His father, a Deputy Attorney General of the State of California, sued the state for negligence in Fisher's release.

Was the state liable?

"Not at all," said the California Supreme Court. In an opinion that seems callous, at the very least, the Court threw the Thompsons out of court, based on the immunity provision which controlled in the *Martinez* case.

The California Supreme Court is considered the most liberal in the United States when it comes to the rights of the criminals. When the question of *victims* arises, however, it simply is not interested, witness *Martinez* and *Thompson*.

DEMOCRACY IMPLIES RESPONSIBILITY

On the other hand, the Supreme Court of Arizona is one of the most conservative on the crime issue. Criminals in Arizona do not get off lightly, and if they expect a kind of automatic "pass" from the highest court of that state, they are completely mistaken.

The Arizona Supreme Court has also taken a lead in the area of victims rights. Its decisions may signal a recognition of such rights by other courts in the future. The "watershed" case decided by Arizona's high court was *Grimm v. Arizona Board of Pardons and Paroles*.[4] The case is strikingly similar to *Martinez* and *Thompson*,

331

cited above, except for the fact that the *Grimm* court reached a totally opposite conclusion—ruling against blanket immunity for parole officials and in favor of those victimized by their gross negligence.

Mitchell Thomas Blazak had been confined in the Arizona penetentiary for a number of crimes. His record was not exemplary; it went back to 1961 when, as a minor, he served a term for burglary. In 1964, he received a second term for the same crime, and, in 1965, he was resentenced for parole violation. He was released in 1966 and rearrested three months later for marijuana possession. In April of 1967 he was again arrested for armed robbery and assault with intent to kill.

After the last arrest, while Blazak was still in prison, his psychiatric evaluation was:

> ...an extremely dangerous person who should not be free in society until some major psychological changes take place. He is a paranoid schizophrenic whose psychosis prevents him from controlling his conduct. He has never made an adjustment to society for any prolonged period and is unlikely to change. He has a definite potential for violence.[5]

Despite this clear-cut warning, Blazak was paroled after serving only one-third of his sentence. He promptly went out and murdered Mr. Grimm during the course of an armed robbery. Mrs. Grimm sued the parole board for gross negligence in releasing Blazak. The Arizona Supreme Court, in a major reversal of former law, held that Mrs. Grimm had indeed stated a cause of action.[6]

The state court's ruling looks back to the point made at the beginning of this chapter: if some government officials are going to be held liable for misconduct or gross negligence, then all should be. The court elaborated:

> We have come to this conclusion because of the increasing power of the bureaucracy—the administrators—in our society. The authority wielded by so-called faceless bureaucrats has often been criticized. Comparing the relatively small number of judges with the large number of administrators, the idea of fearless unbridled decision-making becomes less appealing. While society may want and need courageous, independent policy decisions among high-level government officials, there seems to be no benefit, and, indeed, great potential harm in allowing unbridled discretion without fear of being held to account for their actions for every single public official who exercises over our lives, the more we need some sort of responsibility to lie for their most outrageous conduct. There may even be some deterrent value in hold-

ing officials responsible for shocking, outrageous actions. In any case democracy by its very definition implies responsibility. In this day of increasing power wielded by governmental officials, absolute immunity for non-judicial, non-legislative officials is outmoded and even dangerous.[7]

LIABILITY FOR CUSTODIAL OFFICIALS?

The differences in philosophy, perhaps even ideology, demonstrated between the *Martinez* and *Thompson* courts on the one hand,[8] and the *Grimm* court on the other,[9] present, in microcosm, a fundamental question confronting our entire criminal justice system: isn't it time that we started raising the rights of crime victims to their proper stature within the system?

The idea of allowing victims or their survivors to sue parole boards for gross negligence in the release or handling of prisoners is repugnant to some. Various reasons have been given for making the victims fend for themselves. The first concern is understandable: enormous judgments against parole boards, and the states in which they serve, could literally bankrupt the government entity. It is true that jurors hearing cases such as *Martinez* and *Thompson* could react angrily and go overboard in awarding damages. However, it is also true that if the standard for liability is *gross* negligence, as was demonstrated in the three principal cases cited herein, then the number of cases which could, and should, be brought would be substantially reduced.

What is "gross" negligence? Former U.S. Supreme Court Justice Potter Stewart once said, with regard to obscenity, something to the effect that, "I can't define it, but I know it when I see it." The same applies in the context of this article. Any reading of *Martinez,* *Thompson* and *Grimm* demonstrates that the negligence in the release of prisoners in those cases was indeed "gross" by any objective standard.

The reason we have juries in civil trials is precisely to sort out such matters. Consider a hypothetical situation: X is in prison on a fifth-offense check forgery charge. He has never, to the knowledge of the authorities, committed a crime of violence, either in or out of prison. Now, assume in addition, that "X" is released, long before he should have been (probably to make room for someone who has been convicted of a truly violent offense) and that he then rapes and murders someone.

Was the release "grossly negligent?" Surely not. The crime was not foreseeable. Yet, just as surely, the crimes of Richard June-Jordan

333

Thomas in *Martinez*, James Fisher in *Thompson* and Mitchell Thomas Blazak in *Grimm* were eminently foreseeable. Psychiatrists had warned, and indeed, in *Thompson*, the perpetrator himself had warned, that future carnage was to occur. They were released, nevertheless, with the described results. If this is not "gross negligence," then nothing is. More to the point, if only cases of gross negligence, such as *Martinez*, *Thompson* and *Grimm* could cause liability, then the worry about "catastrophic" judgments is not nearly as "doom-sounding" as it appears on first impression. The Arizona Supreme Court emphasized this in *Grimm*: ". . .that no liability be imposed where the evidence is conflicting or contradictory, that is, when reasonable minds could differ."[10]

The second argument against parole board liability is more nebulous. It holds that imposing liability on correctional officials would "chill" them from making "courageous" decisions; hence, no one would serve on parole boards.

The answer to this concern is fairly simple: if it is a precondition to service for given individuals that they should *never* be held liable for their dispositions, no matter how grossly negligent and no matter how tragic the consequences, then they are precisely the kind of people we do *not* want in such important—even life threatening—positions.

Thus are the ideological lines drawn. The tension between the right of society to be reasonably free from harm at the hands of criminals who have already demonstrated that they are dangerous, and the presumed necessity to shield custodial officials from the consequences of their decisions, is perhaps best summed up by the Restatement (Second) of Torts, Section 319 (1965):

> One who takes charge of a dangerous individual whom he knows or should know to be likely to cause bodily harm to others if not controlled is under a duty to control the person to prevent him from doing such harm.

Under this provision there is little doubt that the custodial officials in *Martinez* and *Thompson*, who knew of the dangerous tendencies of the criminals, had a *duty* to control the conduct of June-Jordan Thomas and James Fisher by not releasing them—and that they failed in this duty. Nevertheless, they could not be held accountable because of the rigid concept of sovereign immunity.

There is, however, a burgeoning movement among high-level criminal justice and victims right authorities in this country to con-

334

front this apparent unfairness. For example, in 1981 Attorney General of the United States, William French Smith, appointed the Attorney General's Task Force on Violent Crime. The Task Force held hearings in seven cities and took testimony from criminal justice professionals on every aspect of violent crime in the United States. Among its recommendations was:

> The Attorney General should study the principle that would allow for suits against appropriate federal government agencies for gross negligence involved in allowing early release or failure to supervise obviously dangerous persons or for failure to warn expected victims of such dangerous persons.[11]

A year later, President Reagan established the President's Task Force on Victims of Crime, charged with examining every aspect of the plight of crime victims in this country and making recommendations to improve their situation. Again, the Task Force held hearings in six cities and took testimony from victims, victim advocates and other criminal justice professionals with an interest in victims. In striking similarity to the Attorney General's Task Force, the President's Task Force made the following recommendation:

> The Task Force endorses the principle of accountability for gross negligence of parole board officials in releasing into the community dangerous criminals who then injure others. A study should be commissioned at the federal level to determine how, and under what circumstances, this principle of accountability should be implemented.[12]

The Chairman of the President's Task Force on Victims of Crime was Lois Haight Herrington, a former prosecuting attorney in Alameda County (Oakland), California. In 1983, President Reagan appointed her to be an Assistant Attorney General of the United States in charge of the Office of Justice Assistance, Research and Statistics (OJARS), now the Office of Justice Programs (OJP). One of her tasks was to oversee implementation of the Recommendations of the Victims Task Force. Herrington set up a special Office on Victims at OJARS; and, with regard to the subject matter of this chapter, is currently in the process of implementing the Recommendation (Number 6), which calls for a study of the entire question of accountability, liability, and immunity of custodial officials. It is to be hoped that this study will shed enough legal and empirical light on this volatile issue to allow some specific changes in the system to take place.[13]

335

REFERENCES

Parole Boards, Victims and Society by Frank Carrington

1. *Martinez v. California*, 85 Cal. App. 3d 430, 149 Cal. Rptr. 519 (1978).
2. 444 U.S. at 279 (1980).
3. *Thomspon v. County of Alameda*, 27 Cal. 3d 741, 614 P.2d 728 (1980).
4. *Grimm v. Arizona Board of Pardons and Paroles*, 115 Ariz. 200; 564 P.2d 1227 (1977).
5. *Id.* at 263; 564 P.2d at 1230 (1977).
6. *Id.* at 266; 564 P.2d at 1233 (1977).
7. *Id.*
8. For cases following the *Martinez/Thompson* rationale, *see, e.g.*: *Payton v. United States*, 636 F. 2d 132 (5th Cir., *en banc*, 1981) (no liability for federal parole officials in deciding to release a homicidal psychopath who later murdered three women); *Pate v. Alabama Board of Pardons and Paroles*, 409 F.Supp. 478 (E.D. Ala. 1976) (no Civil Rights action for negligent release resulting in a rape-murder); *Lloyd v. State*, 251 N.W.2d 551 (Iowa, 1927) (no liability because of sovereign immunity for negligent release).
9. For cases adhering to the *Grimm* rationale, *see, e.g.*: *Semler v. Psychiatric Institute*, 538 F.2d 121 (4th Cir., 1976) (liability on the part of psychiatrist and state probation officer for releasing dangerous mental patient in violation of court order); *Robilotto v. State*, 104 Misc.2d 713, 429 N.Y.S.2d 362 (N.Y. 1980) (liability for negligent release from custody of dangerous juvenile who raped a woman); *Underwood v. United States*, 356 F.2d 92 (5th Cir. 1966) (liability for release of mentally disturbed person who subsequently murdered his wife).
10. 115 Ariz. at 267, 564 P.2d at 1234 (1977).
11. Final Report, Attorney General's Task Force on Violent Crime, United States Department of Justice, August 17, 1981, at 90.
12. Final Report, President's Task Force on Victims of Crime, The White House, December 1982, p. 54.
13. Regarding third-party liability generally, and liability of parole boards in particular, *see*: Carrington, "Victims Rights Litigation: A Wave of The Future?," 11 *U. Rich. L. Rev.* 447 (1976); *see also* Carrington and Duggan, "Restoring The Victims," in McGuigan and Rader, eds., *Criminal Justice Reform*, (Washington, D.C.: Free Congress Foundation, 1983).

20

ALTERNATIVES TO INCARCERATION:
The Sentencing Improvement Act
by William L. Armstrong and Sam Nunn

On July 20, 1983, we introduced Senate bill S. 1644, the Sentencing Improvement Act of 1983.[1] This bill directed federal judges to imprison those defendants who are convicted of violent and "dangerous" offenses as defined in the bill, while employing alternative sanctions such as community service and restitution for other defendants.[2]

In October 1984, the Comprehensive Crime Control Act was enacted into law. That legislation attempts a comprehensive reform of the federal criminal justice system, including sentencing procedures.[3] A resolution derived from S. 1644 was included in the new law requiring federal sentencing judges to consider the directives of S. 1644 in the period preceding adoption of formal sentencing guidelines by the U. S. Sentencing Commission. The resolution is scheduled to expire in October 1986. At this writing, there is no indication as to whether the Sentencing Commission will seek to promote similar guidelines for our federal judges.[4]

At first blush, one might argue that S. 1644 runs counter to conventional wisdom and to the prevailing public attitude toward criminals. To the contrary, however, it is clearly consistent with an emerging consensus of criminal justice professionals, political commentators, economists and public officials across the country.

PRISON OVERCROWDING/PRISON COSTS

Today the United States has a higher imprisonment rate (250 per 100,000 people) than any country in the world except the Soviet Union (391) and South Africa (400). Our rate of imprisonment is twice as high as Canada's, three times as high as Great Britain's, and four times as high as West Germany's.[5]

Moreover, our use of prisons is escalating. The U. S. prison population has doubled in the last decade, from 218,466 in 1974 to 463,866 at the close of 1984.[6] The prison population is increasing 10 times faster than the general population.[7] But prison capacity is not growing as fast. If these trends continue as expected, the future safety and well-being of all Americans will be gravely threatened by a prison system that will be physically unable to house those violent criminals who pose the greatest danger to society. Forty-one states, the District of Columbia, and the federal government report that their prison population exceeds their capacity.[8] Thirty-two states and the District of Columbia are currently under court order because of overcrowding and other prison conditions.[9] In eighteen of those states, inmates are sleeping on floors, in some cases in chapels and gymnasiums within the prison walls.[10]

A recent federal study reported that nearly two-thirds (65 percent) of state prisoners and over three-fifths (61 percent) of federal prisoners were living in overcrowded facilities (defined as less than 60 square feet of floor space).[11]

The Final Report of the Attorney General's Task Force on Violent Crime identified prison overcrowding as the number one problem facing corrections today. It cited a June 1977 survey which disclosed a nationwide deficit of 20,000 beds, and noted that since that time prison population has increased faster than prison construction.[12]

Even more impressive was its estimate that more than $10 billion in construction is needed to create sufficient space for just the *current* prison population.[13] By contrast, the total planned capital expenditures for both state and federal correctional systems in 1986 was $1.3 billion.[14]

Overcrowding, as one would expect, has well-documented adverse effects on prisoners. Illness complaints rise, death and suicide rates increase, and discipline declines under overcrowded conditions.[15] Inmate violence and other misconduct also increase. This has been true in England,[16] state prisons[17] and federal prisons.[18]

The general public suffers as well as a result of overcrowding. The Task Force on Violent Crime found that there are a substantial number of defendants who should be incarcerated who may receive probation because judges know there is no available prison space.[19] In fifteen states, a total of 21,420 prisoners had been granted early release due to overcrowding during 1983.[20] We have now reached the point where public safety is in fact being jeopardized because of prison overcrowding.

The federal prison system is overcrowded. Although conditions vary from prison to prison, the population exceeds the rated prison capacity of 26,131 by 46 percent.[21] And this figure rises monthly.

New prisons are now constructed to hold 450 to 500 persons. If the rate of increase in federal prisons remains constant (and new prosecution trends could send it even higher), the federal government will have to construct a new prison every two months to avoid the overcrowding crisis which the states now face. This could mean a prison *construction* budget of $1,800,000.00 per year, just to keep pace with increased population.[22] And construction costs are only the beginning.

The total costs of our corrections system are staggering. In 1970, the total corrections expenditures for state, federal and local governments was $1.7 billion. In 1986, it had jumped to $8.7 billion. This is over a 700 percent increase in sixteen years.[23]

For every dollar spent in constructing a prison, we spend an additional $12.50 in operation costs over the next 30 years.[24] This is because the average annual cost of maintaining an inmate is high. For example, in fiscal year 1984, the average cost per inmate was $17,324.[25] We today live in a country where the taxpayers spend more on the average per year to house a single prisoner than parents spend annually to send their child to the nation's most expensive colleges—$15,100 for tuition, room, and board at Harvard.[26] These costs of incarceration do not include related costs such as lost employment taxes and welfare payments to the families of prisoners.

THE SENTENCING IMPROVEMENT ACT

Senate bill S. 1644, the Sentencing Improvement Act of 1983, was introduced in response to a serious overcrowding problem in federal prisons.[27] The bill suggests that these scarce prison resources should be used only where violent and dangerous criminals are involved.[28] For nonviolent, nondangerous offenders, the bill proposes that society's interests are better served through the imposition of alternative sentences, such as restitution and community service.[29]

The basic principle underlying the Act is that penal imprisonment is not always an appropriate punishment for certain types of criminal offenses. It reflects dissatisfaction with American prisons, which are critically overcrowded, waste millions of tax dollars, and do little to rehabilitate the hundreds of thousands of prisoners currently incarcerated.

S. 1644 would have established a presumption that imprisonment is an inappropriate sanction for offenses which do not involve the threat or use of force, endanger national security, or threaten or cause serious physical harm to others.[30] The bill specifically removed the presumption in cases where: (1) the defendant's livelihood depends upon criminal conduct; (2) the defendant was paid or expected payment to commit the crime; (3) the offense involved narcotics trafficking; (4) the defendant was convicted of violating specified firearms or explosives laws; (5) the defendant was convicted of misusing his public office; or (6) "there are specified substantial and compelling reasons for imposing a sentence of imprisonment."[31]

For offenses not falling within the presumption, the court could impose a prison sentence. For example, under the last exception noted above, the judge could sentence to imprisonment a trusted pension official convicted of embezzling large amounts of money. Although such a crime would probably have involved no violence (thus, not creating a presumption of the appropriateness of imprisonment), the substantial economic injury to large numbers of people would justify imprisonment. In such a case, imprisonment may constitute the only appropriate punishment, particularly since restitution might be impossible.

S. 1644 further provided that a defendant who is convicted of conspiracy, attempt, or aiding and abetting, would be treated as a principal for sentencing purposes.[32] Thus, a party who aids a Presidential assassin would not escape imprisonment because he did not personally pull the trigger.

Pursuant to S. 1644, the U.S. probation service would be required to compile data on the defendant and recommend the appropriate sentence.[33] Thereafter, the prosecution and the defendant could contest the merits of these findings and recommendations.[34] If a fine, probation, or imprisonment were found to be inappropriate, the court could suspend imposition of sentence and order an alternative punishment.[35] Alternatives would include restitution or the performance of community service.[36] In its discretion, the court could impose a fine in addition to the primary sentence.[37]

Furthermore, the bill permitted a court to impose both imprisonment and alternative sanctions.[38] Thus, if special and compelling circumstances justifying imprisonment exist, the court could impose any prison sentence permitted by law, suspend execution of that portion of the sentence exceeding sixty days, and order restitution, community service, or both.[39]

S. 1644 also included flexible guidelines for courts to use in imprisoning or otherwise sentencing offenders. Again, the basic principle underlying the guidelines is that violent, habitual, or professional offenders deserve imprisonment, but that nonviolent and nondangerous offenders merit alternative forms of punishment.[40]

THE SEARCH FOR ALTERNATIVES

Faced with the prohibitive costs of prison construction, the questionable safety impact of indiscriminate incarceration, and the crisis in overcrowding, many commentators and criminal justice professionals have begun calling for the development and use of alternative sanctions for those defendants who are not dangerous to society.

For example, conservative commentator William F. Buckley has written on several occasions on the need to respond to prison overcrowding by sentencing nonviolent offenders to restitution and community service.[41]

In its report issued in May 1984, the national Advisory Commission on Intergovernmental Relations recommended that

> ...in punishing less serious felony and misdemeanor offenders, state governments encourage local governments to make increased use of community-based alternatives to incarceration such as community service and restitution.[42]

The Commission went on to state its belief that "alternative sentencing for less serious offenders may be more beneficial for the offenders, for the community, and for the victims."[43]

Political leaders have made similar calls for additional criminal sanctions as alternatives to prison. Former Attorney General William French Smith stated:

> Much can be done to improve correctional facilities. But while we move forward in our efforts to improve our Nation's prisons, we must recognize that we cannot continue to rely exclusively on incarceration and dismiss other forms of punishment....It is important that we examine alternatives to imprisonment that exact a punishment from the less serious offender without the exorbitant costs of incarceration.[44]

And correctional officials agree. Anthony Travisono, Executive Director of the American Correctional Association, has concluded:

> Prisons and jails should be viewed as scarce resources and used appropriately to confine only those offenders we can identify as dangerous. We must make greater use of alternatives to incarceration. Simply incarcerating greater

numbers of offenders in the interest of protecting society, without increasing the space or programs for inmates, works against the long-term goal of creating a safe society.

While prisons and jails across the country continue to be inundated with court suits alleging inhumane and overcrowded conditions, the corrections professional is caught in the middle. Without appropriate support and assistance, the correctional crisis in America will soon reach extremely dangerous levels. We don't have room in our institutions for those currently sentenced to imprisonment. With even a slight increase in the numbers of commitments to prisons and jails, some facilities will likely explode.[45]

These repeated calls to stop incarcerating non-dangerous offenders lead to a key question: how many of the current prison population must be confined for our protection? How many prisoners are actually dangerous? Although it is difficult to determine whether individual prisoners are dangerous, certain generalizations can be made.

First, in the nation as a whole, many individuals are incarcerated for non-violent crimes. A report from the Bureau of Justice Statistics found that violent offenders accounted for 37.5 percent of those admitted to prison and 35.9 percent of those released in 1982.[46]

Second, an examination of federal prisoners reveals disturbing patterns. Only a third of the prisoners (32.7 percent) were convicted of violent offenses. Another 20.4 percent were convicted of drug or firearms offenses. The remaining 36.9 percent were convicted of property and other nonviolent offenses.[47] In other words, around one out of every three federal prisoners was convicted of a non-dangerous offense.

In the context of the current prison problem, it is not surprising that many state and local governments have indeed begun developing alternative punishments for those who are not dangerous to society.[48]

Probation and fines are the most common alternatives. However, the public sometimes perceives these sanctions as inappropriate because they are not severe enough to respond appropriately to the seriousness of the offense. Therefore, other more restrictive alternative punishments are needed.

The principle of *restitution* requires an offender to repay the victim of his crime property lost or personal damages sustained as a result of the offender's acts.[49] Because of growing public concern for crime victims, the restitution concept holds great promise of gaining broad public support. This is especially true when one considers the total amount of economic loss suffered by victims of crime: $10.9

billion in 1981.[50] Recent surveys indicate that a great percentage of Americans would prefer to have the nonviolent offender repay his victim rather than serve time in prison at public expense.[51] Likewise, the surveys show that offender repayment is preferred over governmental compensation of crime victims.[52]

Restitution, however, is not a new phenomenon. In October 1982, Congress enacted the Victim and Witness Protection Act of 1982.[53] This Act provides that as a substitute or supplement to any penalty provided by law, the court may order a defendant convicted of specified offenses to make restitution to victims.[54] The court determines the amount of restitution to be made, which will then be offset by compensation which the victim received from third parties or through civil proceedings.[55]

The Sentencing Improvement Act would broaden the scope of the Victim and Witness Protection Act by extending that Act's coverage beyond specific Title XVIII offenses[56] and applying it to any offense if one of the previously discussed presumptions[57] is found to be present. The Sentencing Improvement Act incorporated by reference the appropriate provisions of the Victim and Witness Protection Act and specifies those offenses for which restitution is presumed applicable.[58]

As a sentencing alternative, restitution is often a more appropriate alternative than a prison sentence. For criminal, nonviolent offenders, society would logically be far better off to have the criminal "pay" for the crime committed rather than take up scarce prison space at taxpayer's expense. The Sentencing Improvement Act provided that in appropriate cases the court could, with due consideration of the defendant's resources, require him to pay the victim's medical expenses, repay the value of lost or damaged property, and/or return the property.[59] If the victim or victims are not ascertainable, the restitution would be paid into a special fund of the Treasury Department to be distributed quarterly on a per capita basis to a state victim compensation plan and help cover the costs of the growing demand of state restitution programs.[60]

This sentencing alternative, in combination with other non-prison sentencing alternatives, is intended to be as serious as a prison sentence. In its discretion, the court may impose a fine in addition to a sentence of restitution and/or community service. If an offender fails to adhere to the schedule of community service performance, this failure shall be treated as a violation of probation and possibly a full term of imprisonment.[61]

Community Service orders provide that instead of being sent to prison, offenders are required to work for a period of years, either at very modest pay or none at all, in ghettoes, hospitals, or other areas of public need. This alternative need not be limited to white collar offenders. Present community service programs provide work opportunities for skilled and unskilled workers alike. California is operating some 50 Community Service Alternatives for offenders.[62] Similar Community Service orders have been employed in England with dramatic success.[63]

Restitution and community service programs have gone past the theory stage in scores of communities across the country. A survey conducted in October and November, 1978, identified 289 such projects.[64] Some of these have been more successful than others in diverting non-dangerous offenders from prison to these other punishments.

Two key factors have been identified by observers of these programs, which increase the probability that they will truly be alternatives to imprisonment and not merely enhancements of probation.[65] One is that judges be presented with supervised programs of alternative punishments in which they can have confidence. The second is that the judges be prodded by the legislature into changing sentencing patterns.

Minnesota is an excellent example of both these factors.[66] It has developed a statewide community corrections program which gives money to the counties to establish restitution and community service programs. The counties are then charged for all petty felons who are sent to prison instead of diverted to Community Corrections.

While this fiscal incentive apparently failed to change judges' sentencing habits, a more drastic measure did. Minnesota became the first state to adopt sentencing guidelines which create presumed sentences from which judges can deviate only for reasonable cause. These presumptions range from probation or fine for certain property offenses to restitution or community service for more serious property offenders and less serious violent offenders, to imprisonment for most violent offenders and career property offenders. Since introduction of these guidelines Minnesota's prison population has remained under its capacity.

Oregon's experience has also been very instructive. The Community Corrections Act there was passed in 1977, and in 1979 received a $5 million appropriation to develop alternatives to imprisonment in punishing Class C felons.

A report issued in 1981 found that counties which participated fully in the program reduced their rate of commitment of Class C felons from 12 percent to 17 percent of all such felons. And burglars, which were a particular focus of the Act, were clearly diverted. In 1977, 40 percent of all convicted burglars went to prison. By 1979 this was reduced to 17 percent.

The net costs of Community Corrections (the direct costs offset by restitution and fines) were lower than the estimated costs in prisoner maintenance had the program not been implemented.[67]

SUMMARY

Federal criminal law does not prohibit the use of alternative sentences, but it does not encourage them either. An order of restitution may be imposed as an additional sentence for certain federal offenses under 18 U.S.C. 3556. Both restitution and community service are listed as possible conditions of probation in 18 U.S.C. 3563. But nowhere is there a stated presumption that certain types of offenders receive those sanctions as an alternative to prison.

There are, in our view, many sound arguments for clearly providing such sentencing options to federal judges and for creating a rebuttable presumption that they be used for non-violent and non-dangerous offenses.

First, such a sentencing policy will help insure that adequate prison space is available for violent and dangerous offenders. If the policy generated empty federal prison beds, additional state prisoners could be accommodated, particularly from those states where federal judges have found the state prison systems unconstitutional.

Second, in contrast to incarceration, restitution and community service sentences directly benefit both the victim and the community. Restitution provides the victim with something he would have been denied if the offender were incarcerated: monetary compensation for his loss. In Georgia, for example, in 1985 a residential restitution program resulted in $170,120 in payments to victims, $767,669 in state and federal taxes, $1,135,171 in room and board charges, and $420,806 in financial support to offenders' families.[68]

Community service also provides free labor for the local jurisdiction. The value of these services is substantial, particularly when compared to the alternative of subsidized idleness in prison. During 1983, the labor produced by the Georgia Community Service program had an estimated value of $1,046,547.[69] As tax revenues shrink, governments could find community service increasingly helpful to maintain services.

In sum, legislation such as S. 1644 which promotes the use of alternative sanctions for non-violent and non-dangerous offenders would accomplish many purposes:

• It would save money.

• It would ease the prison overcrowding problem immediately, thus helping to insure that there will be sufficient prison space for those offenders who are dangerous.

• It would result in punishments which are productive for the victim and the community, and are much less destructive to the offender.

• The prospects for the successful rehabilitation of offenders would be increased. Offenders serving alternative sentences have demonstrated lower recidivism rates than incarcerated offenders.

REFERENCES

Alternatives to Incarceration: The Sentencing Improvement Act by William L. Armstrong and Sam Nunn

1. 129 Cong. Rec. S10371-77 (daily ed., July 20, 1983). With minor changes the bill is identical to S. 3109, the Sentencing Improvement Act of 1982, which we introduced on December 17, 1982, in the 97th Congress. No action was taken on S. 3109 prior to adjournment later that month.

2. S. 1644, 98th Cong., 1st Sess., Sec. 3672 (1983).

3. The Act called for major reform of federal sentencing procedures: the establishment of a determinate sentencing system with no parole and limited good time credits; the promotion of uniform sentencing through a newly created U. S. Sentencing Commission to set narrow sentencing guidelines for federal offenses; and statutory authority for both the government and defendant to appeal sentences set beyond those guidelines.

4. The Act does require the Commission's guidelines to reflect "the general appropriateness of imposing a sentence other than imprisonment in cases in which the defendant is a first offender who has not been convicted of a crime of violence or an otherwise serious offense," 18 U.S.C. 994(j). By comparison, S. 1644 provides a clear presumption against imprisonment in certain categories of cases, specifically defining those violent or serious offenses which do not qualify for the presumption. In addition, S. 1644 includes an affirmative presumption for restitution and community service sentences in certain cases.

5. *See* Eugene Doleschal and Anne Newton, *International Rates of Imprisonment* (Hackensack, N.J.: National Council on Crime and Delinquency, 1979) memo.

6. "Prisoners 1925-1981," *Bureau of Justice Statistics Bulletin*, (December 1982) and "Prisoners in 1984," *Bureau of Justice Statistics Bulletin*, (April 1985) U. S. Department of Justice. [Editor's note: Preliminary BJS estimates for 1985 found 505,037 prisoners incarcerated.]

7. According to the United States Census Bureau, the United States population grew 11 percent from 215,973,000 on July 1, 1975 to 238,816,000 on July 1, 1985. Bureau of Justice data cited in note 6 show an increase of 113 percent in the prison population during that time.

8. "Prisoners in 1984," *supra. See also* "State Prisons Around Nation Scramble for Relief as Overcrowding Mounts," New York *Times,* September 29, 1983.

9. "Prisoners in 1984," *Bureau of Justice Statistics Bulletin,* U. S. Department of Justice, April 1985.

10. New York *Times, supra* n. 8.

11. *American Prisons and Jails* (Washington, D.C.: U.S. Department of Justice, 1980), p. 61.

12. Griffin Bell and James Thompson, *Attorney General's Task Force on Violent Crime Final Report* (Washington, D.C., Government Printing Office, 1981), p. 10.

13. *Ibid.*

14. *Juvenile and Adult Correctional Departments, Institutions, Agencies and Paroling Authorities,* (American Correctional Association, 1986).

15. *The Effect of Prison Crowding on Inmate Behavior* (Washington, D.C.: National Institute of Justice, 1980).

16. David Farrington, "Prison Size, Overcrowding, Prison Violence, and Recidivism," *Journal of Criminal Justice* (Pergamum Press, 1980).

17. Lee-Jan, "Overcrowding and Inmate Behavior," *Criminal Justice and Behavior* (American Association of Correctional Psychologists, 1980).

18. Nacci, Teitelbaum and Prather, "Population Density and Inmate Misconduct Rates in the Federal Prison System," *Federal Probation* (Washington, D.C.: U.S. Government Printing Office, 1977), p. 26.

19. *Task Force on Violent Crime, supra* n. 12, p. 10.

20. "Prisoners in 1983," *Bureau of Justice Statistics Bulletin,* Department of Justice, April 1984.

21. *Monday Morning Highlights,* Federal Prison System, U.S. Department of Justice, March 10, 1986.

22. This is based on a construction cost of $50,000 per bed (*See* "Prison Costs") multiplied by 450 beds per prison. At this rate of increase, eight new facilities would be needed each year.

23. Bureau of Justice Statistics press release, quoted in *Criminal Justice Newsletter,* November 22, 1982; *Juvenile and Adults Correctional Departments, Institutions, Agencies and Paroling Authorities,* (American Correctional Association, 1986).

24. "Estimated 30-Year Life Cycle Cost For A Correctional Facility," (Chicago: Moyer Associates, Inc., 1981).

25. *The Corrections Yearbook,* (Criminal Justice Institute, Inc., 1985), p. 26.

26. At Yale these same costs approximate $15,020. Andrea E. Lehmann, ed., *Guide to Four-Year Colleges: 1986* (Princeton: Peterson's Guides, 1985), pp. 1261; 2197.

27. S. 1644, *supra* n. 2, at sec. 2 (1983) (adding 18 U.S.C. sec. 3671(b)). The text of the bill states "[d]ue to the increasing problem of prison overcrowding, available Federal prison space must be treated as a scarce resource in the sentencing of criminal defendants."

28. *Ibid.*

29. *Ibid.*

30. *Ibid.*, sec. 2 (adding 18 U.S.C. sec. 3672(b)).

31. *Ibid.*

32. *Ibid.*, sec. 2 (adding 18 U.S.C. sec. 3672(d)).

33. *Ibid.*, sec. 2 (adding 18 U.S.C. sec. 3672(e)).

34. *Ibid.*

35. *Ibid.*, sec. 2 (adding 18 U.S.C. sec. 3672(f)).

36. *Ibid.*

37. *Ibid.*

38. *Ibid.*

39. *Ibid.*

40. *Ibid.*, sec. 2 (adding 18 U.S.C. sec. 3671(b)).

347

41. William F. Buckley, "Prisons: Radical Reforms Are Needed," Detroit *Free Press*, April 20, 1982; Buckley, "If Prisons Are Too Full, Why Jail The Nonviolent?," *Washington Star*, March 24, 1981.

42. "Jails: Intergovernmental Dimensions of a Local Problem, A Commission Report," (Washington, D.C., Advisory Commission on Intergovernmental Relations, 1984), p. 181.

43. *Ibid.*

44. In an address presented at Vanderbilt University School of Law, Nashville, Tenn., March 3, 1983.

45. Anthony Travisono, "There Are Time Bombs Ticking Away In Our Prisons And Jails," *Corrections Digest*, July 17, 1981.

46. "Prison Admissions and Releases, 1982," *Bureau of Justice Statistics Bulletins*, (July 1985), U.S. Department of Justice.

47. "Sentenced Prisoners (9/30/81)," unpublished computer print-out furnished by Federal Bureau of Prisons.

48. Charles W. Colson and Daniel Benson, "Restitution As An Alternative to Incarceration," 77 *Detroit College of Law Review*, 523–598 (No. 2, 1980).

49. Joe Hudson & Burt Galaway, *Offender Restitution in Theory and Action 1* (1978). *See generally* Note, "Where Offenders Pay for Their Crimes: Victim Restitution and Its Constitutionality," 59 *Notre Dame L. Rev.* 1401 (1984).

50. "The Economic Cost of Crime to Victims," Bureau of Justice Statistics, April 1984.

51. For example, a New York *Times* poll found 60 percent favoring alternative forms of punishment not involving incarceration for nonviolent offenders for relieving overcrowded prisons; New York *Times*, October 24, 1982.

52. Alan T. Harland, "Compensating the Victims of Crime," 14 *Criminal Law Bulletin* 203 (1978). *See also*, William Read, "How Restitution Works in Georgia," 60 *Judicature* 323 (1977).

53. Public Law 97-291, 96 Stat. 1284 (current version at 18 U.S.C. secs. 3579, 3580 (1982)).

54. Victim and Witness Protection Act of 1982, Public Law 97-291, sec. 5, 96 Stat. 1284, 1253.

55. *Ibid.*

56. *Ibid.*

57. *See supra* notes 31–32 and accompanying text. *See also* S. 1644, *supra* n. 2, sec. 2.

58. S. 1644, *supra* n. 2, sec. 2 (adding 18 U.S.C. secs. 3672, 3673).

59. *Ibid.*, sec. 2 (adding 18 U.S.C. sec. 3673(a), (c)).

60. *Ibid.*, sec. 2 (adding 18 U.S.C. sec. 3673(b)).

61. *Ibid.*

62. M. Kay Harris, *Community Service By Offenders*, (Washington, D.C.: National Institute of Corrections, U.S. Department of Justice, 1979).

63. *See* Howard Standish, "Community Service in England," *Federal Probation*, March 1975.

64. Joe Hudson, Burt Galaway and Steve Novack, *National Assessment of Adult Restitution Programs, Final Report*, 1980. This was funded by National Institute of Justice.

65. For an excellent development of this problem, and one solution, see Mark Umbreit, *Community Service Sentencing: Jail Alternative or Added Sanction?*, 1981. This report was funded by the National Institute of Corrections.

66. For comprehensive review of Minnesota's approach, see *Minnesota Community Corrections Act Evaluation*, 1981. The report was prepared by the Minnesota Department of Corrections, and was funded by the National Institute of Justice.

67. From a five-volume evaluation of the Community Corrections Act prepared by Applied Social Research, Inc., in 1981.

68. "Georgia Diversion Centers," a report issued by the Probation Division, Georgia Department of Corrections, July 1985.

69. Probation Division, Georgia Department of Offender Rehabilitation, "Sentencing Options State of Georgia," (November 1983).

21

PRISONS, PRIORITIES, AND JUDICIAL FIAT:
The Need for Constitutional Perspective
by Daniel J. Popeo and George C. Smith

There is a craziness in our society when you care more for the rights of those alleged to have committed crime than you do for the rights of society.

—Edward Koch
Mayor of New York City

[The criminal justice system] must deemphasize its concern with traditional crime because the emphasis is misplaced....The companies which knowingly manufacture unsafe products; the corporate executives who steal millions from the public by price-rigging and over-charging; the public officials who use their positions for personal gain; the industries that pollute our environment and the officials responsible for the My Lais and Cambodias are the criminals we need to be concerned about.

—Alvin J. Bronstein
Director of ACLU's
National Prison Project

On April 23, 1984, New York State's largest organization of state judges issued an extraordinary resolution which was the equivalent of the desperate outcry of the crazed TV news anchorman in the motion picture "Network": "I'm mad as hell, and I'm not gonna take it anymore!" The Federation of New York State Judges insisted that they were going to continue sending violent criminals to jail despite all the federal court decisions condemning overcrowded conditions in state prisons. As the judges said:[1]

When the safety of the people of this state cannot be assured except by the severe punishment of those who brutalize them, then the prisons to which such defendants should be sent should be built. Swift and severe punishment is the only defense against perpetrators.

The judges further stated that prison sentences must be imposed on violent criminals "regardless of the existence of prisons sufficient in size or number to receive such prisoners."[2]

The strong, public statement of these normally reticent sitting judges was made especially poignant because only five months earlier an interventionist federal judge had forced the release of 613 inmates awaiting trial because in his opinion the New York City jails were overcrowded. Only two days after the court-ordered release, one of the freed prisoners was accused in the brutal rape of a 21-year old woman. At least 65 of the released inmates were later reported rearrested for new crimes within several months of their release.[3] New York City paid dearly for running afoul of the views of a federal district judge regarding permissible conditions of confinement.

The disturbing events in New York are but one local manifestation of the problem which has come to be known as "prison overcrowding"—but which might be more aptly characterized as too many criminals.

• In Illinois, some 7,200 convicted inmates were given early or emergency release due to overcrowded conditions.

• In South Carolina, some 330 early releases were ordered because the state prisons had exceeded their "design capacity" by 15 percent.

• In Alabama, 277 inmates were released to ease crowded conditions under a sweeping federal court order condemning the entire state correctional system.

A total of 21,420 inmates in 15 states were released early in 1983 due to overcrowded conditions.[4]

As the incidence of violent crime has grown to staggering proportions,[5] existing prison facilities are no longer sufficient to house convicted criminals in a manner which meets the standards of the federal judiciary or the American Civil Liberties Union, which has become little more than a prisoners' lobby. The result has been a plethora of federal court orders declaring entire prison systems unconstitutional under the Eighth Amendment, prohibiting prison administrators from accommodating inmate increases by such measures as "double-celling," and in many cases appointing so-called "Special Masters" to supervise effectively the reform of entire prison systems. Although the numbers are continually changing, the American Civil Liberties Union's National Prison Project status report for December 1983, showed that 45 states were either under court order to relieve prison overcrowding or embroiled in litigation on that issue. Not surprisingly, the ACLU was the moving force in 24 of these cases and was busily collecting astronomical legal fees for its prison lawsuits—ultimately from the taxpayers' pocket[6]—even as thousands of dangerous felons are prematurely released as a result of ACLU's efforts. As shown in the statement from the Director of its Prison Project at the beginning of this essay the ACLU appears openly committed to undermining the basic legitimacy of imprisonment for violent crimes.

No responsible observer would dispute the fact that crowded prisons are a grave and difficult problem which demands the attention of government and citizens alike. But, the preemptory release of criminals has dangerous consequences for the rest of society, as demonstrated by the experiences in New York, Illinois and elsewhere. The usurpation of state power by activist federal judges has dangerously skewed governmental priorities in favor of the prisoner and at the expense of the law-abiding citizenry. Many lower federal court decisions have distorted the Eighth Amendment ban against cruel and unusual punishment beyond all recognition. As things now stand, the mere condition of incarceration has become constitutionally suspect simply because there are so many criminals that society's prisons can no longer comfortably accommodate them. Rather than limiting judicial redress to specific punishments which are genuinely cruel *and* genuinely *un*usual, the federal courts have extended their power to reforming prison conditions which often represent nothing worse than the national norm and which are caused solely by the limitations of state financial resources, rather than by any form of "cruelty."

The complicated and difficult choices demanded by crowded prisons should not—and constitutionally *can* not—be left to the arbitrary preferences of a remote federal judiciary which is answerable to no one. A constitutional and democratic solution demands the restoration of prison authority to the state legislatures and state authorities, who *are* answerable to the people if they fail to exercise it properly.

EVOLVING JUDICIAL STANDARDS

The problem of overcrowded prisons—specifically in relation to the Eighth Amendment ban against cruel and unusual punishment—is complicated by factors of subjectivity, semantics, and self-fulfilling prophecy.[7] At what point does a prison become legally "overcrowded?" And at what point does such overcrowding become unconstitutional and illegal?

351

Unhappily, the answer is the same as it is in so many of the critical issues of law and policy which dominate today's agenda: Whenever a federal district judge says it does.

The problem has become especially critical because the volume of violent crime in America has forced *most* prisons to accommodate inmate populations which exceed levels considered acceptable by the "experts." It has been estimated that some 65 percent of all prisoner housing units in the United States now provide less than the 60 square foot per inmate standard recommended as minimal by such groups as the American Correctional Association.[8] Yet in its most important decision on the issue of crowded prison conditions, the U.S. Supreme Court upheld the constitutionality of conditions in a prison where it was necessary for pairs of inmates to share a cell of only 63 square feet.[9] It is apparent, then, that the question of how much space is the minimum necessary for reasonably civilized confinement is a subjective, complex, and multi-faceted social issue—the kind of issue traditionally resolved by legislative and administrative judgments at the state or local level. But the power to make those critical social judgments is now all but monopolized by the federal judiciary.

Prison conditions which until the last decade or two were routine characteristics of felony incarceration are now just as routinely cited as conclusive evidence of unconstitutional confinement. Once the issue was effectively preempted by the federal judiciary, there was a remarkably rapid revolution in the conditions which "society"—i.e., the federal judiciary *speaking* for society—considered unacceptable under the "evolving standards of decency" which underlie the constitutional test.

Until the mid-1960s, the courts declined to exercise jurisdiction over claims concerning conditions within state prisons. The cruel and unusual punishment clause was deemed applicable only to penalties as they were inflicted by the *courts*; for the most part, the courts deferred to the authority of state and prison administrators in the sphere of prison conditions.[10] Given that the Thirteenth Amendment explicitly exempted the condition of incarcerated convicts from the constitutional ban on involuntary servitude or slavery, the courts accepted the view that duly convicted prisoners did not generally possess the legal right to attack the conditions of their incarceration.

The elevation of the rights of the accused by the Warren Court inevitably led to similar expansion in the actionable legal rights of prisoners. Initially, the courts confined their intervention to specific instances of cruel treatment applied to a specific prisoner—e.g., use of the whipping strap; confinement without food for extended periods of time; or confining a prisoner in conditions where he was deprived of light, ventilation, or sanitary facilities for maintaining personal cleanliness. This limited judicial role allowed the courts to redress the kind of malicious and extraordinary punishments which the Eighth Amendment *was* intended to prohibit, but without undermining the ability of the states and their prison administrators to maintain control over fundamental state corrections policy.

However, the runaway judicial activism of the 1970s did not spare the prisons from intrusions into spheres of activity which historically and constitutionally had been left to legislative and state regulation. The federal courts quickly leapfrogged from redressing specific instances of cruel and unusual *punishment* to roam at will in the broad field of *general prison conditions*. The question was no longer whether the guards or the warden had inflicted cruel and unusual punishment on a prisoner, but whether the general living conditions of entire prisons measured up to some vague and elusive standard of "evolving human decency" and "civilized norms." Within a decade, prisons in the vast majority of the 50 states were either decreed unconstitutional, bludgeoned into "consent decrees" which effectively conceded unconstitutionality, or submitted to interminable litigation which offered little or no promise of ultimate vindication. Almost overnight, the legal norms and presumptions governing prison conditions had been turned on their heads.

To a large extent, this judicial revolution amounted to the *retroactive* imposition of standards upon state prison authorities. Prisons designed and built 10 or 20 years ago could hardly have reflected standards which had not even been thought of, much less promulgated as law, at the time of construction. But many federal judges archly dismiss such practical exigencies as irrelevant and unpersuasive. The moment a prison is subjected to judicial review under the pretext of the Eighth Amendment, rational considerations of cost and feasibility are the first casualties.

The key element in the expansion of federal judicial power in this area has been the judge-made standard of judicial review known as the "totality of circumstances" test.[11] The "totality" test is a marvel of judicial invention, in that it enables a federal court to declare that the conditions prevailing within an entire prison are unconstitutional despite the absence of a single act or practice which is unconstitutional in itself.[12] Under this approach, the whole is greater than the sum of its parts. It is remarkably similar to other broad standards of legality concocted by the federal judiciary—such as the "effects" test in voting rights cases or the "disparate impact" test in employment discrimination cases—in that a variety of perfectly lawful defects in prison conditions can create a "penumbra" of unconstitutionality which somehow permeates the whole prison. It does not take a skeptic to perceive that the "totality of circumstances" test is not a *standard* at all, but rather a convenient device for *avoiding* the constraints of rigorous, objective standards.

The "totality" test becomes especially significant at the remedy stage of prison conditions litigation. If the courts confined their jurisdiction to specific, identifiable acts or instances of malicious punishment, they would be confined by the specific nature of the violation in fashioning a remedy. But by its very nature the "totality of circumstances" test circumvents such constraints and amounts to a license for the courts to impose their ideological preferences on entire state prison systems. They then decree broad and costly reforms which *must* be achieved within specified time limits, and appoint a "Special Master" to ride herd over state prison officials as they struggle to effectuate the Utopian visions of the courts. When embattled prison administrators plead financial impossibility, courts mechanically invoke the simplistic maxim that cost considerations simply cannot be taken into account when there are constitutional violations to be remedied. Again, judicial isolation from the harsh fiscal realities of state government allows the courts to assume a lofty, moral posture which bears no relation to the urgent practical problems which must be sensibly resolved in the grimy trenches of prison administration.

A CASE IN POINT: THE RHODES DECISION AS AN EXERCISE IN FUTILITY

In June of 1981, the Supreme Court handed down a decision which should have trimmed the sails of the lower federal courts in their expansionist interpretation of the Eighth Amendment.[13] Instead, many lower courts either openly scorned the Supreme Court's restrictive admonitions[14] or casually distinguished away the actual holding to proceed apace with their arrogation of prison supervisory powers.

In *Rhodes v. Chapman*, an all but unanimous Supreme Court (Justice Thurgood Marshall alone dissenting) reversed a Sixth Circuit ruling that "double-celling" practices—housing two prisoners in a cell originally designed for one—in an Ohio state prison constituted cruel and unusual punishment. The decision should have been highly significant in its impact because it was the High Court's first occasion to assess claims that *overall* conditions of confinement at a particular prison violated the Eighth Amendment.

The Court reiterated the general standards governing cruel and unusual punishment claims, which focus on three particular factors:

- unnecessary and wanton infliction of pain;
- punishment grossly disproportionate to the severity of the offense; and
- punishments which are totally lacking in any penological justification.

The decision also reaffirmed the principle that application of the Eighth Amendment must reflect "the evolving standards of decency that mark the progress of a maturing society."

Significantly, though, the opinion stressed that such judgments "should neither be nor appear to be merely the subjective views of judges".[15] As in the capital punishment cases, the courts must look to history, the action of state legislatures, and other indicia of prevalent *popular* norms (as opposed to the norms of "experts" or those of the "progressive" bar) for objective criteria truly reflecting the standards of society. Justice Lewis Powell's opinion emphasized that:

> [C]onditions that cannot be said to be cruel and unusual under contemporary standards are not unconstitutional. To the extent that such conditions are restrictive and even harsh, they are part of the penalty that criminal offenders pay for their offense against society.[16]

The Supreme Court flatly rejected the various factors cited by the district court as evidence that double-celling gave rise to cruel and unusual punishment: that the prison population was 38 percent over design capacity; that "several studies" recommended that each inmate have at least 50–55 square feet of living quarters; and that the double-celling in the Ohio prison had evolved from a temporary expediency into an established practice. Justice Powell's opinion then went directly to the basic flaw in the prevalent approach used by the lower courts to reach their decisions on prison overcrowding:

Perhaps they reflect an aspiration toward an ideal environment for long-term confinement. But the Constitution does not mandate comfortable prisons, and prisons...which house persons convicted of serious crimes cannot be free of discomfort. Thus, *these considerations properly are weighed by the legislature and prison administration rather than a court.* There being no constitutional violation, the District Court had no authority to consider whether double-celling...was the best response to the increase in Ohio's statewide prison population.[17]

Finally, after acknowledging that the courts cannot shirk their constitutional authority to remedy specific instances of cruel and unusual punishment, Justice Powell's opinion went out of its way to admonish the lower courts as follows:

[C]ourts cannot assume that state legislatures and prison officials are insensitive to the requirements of the Constitution or to the perplexing sociological problems of how best to achieve the goals of the penal function in the criminal justice system: to punish justly, to deter future crime, and to return imprisoned persons to society with an improved chance of being useful, law-abiding citizens.[18]

Although the *Rhodes* decision did not *explicitly* foreclose resort to the "totality of circumstances" test, its reasoning and result strongly pointed in that direction. The decision rejected the district court's "totality" analysis and pointedly stated (in language that subsequent lower court decisions predictably characterized as mere *dicta*) that such considerations were properly reserved for the legislatures and prison authorities. The Court's failure to condemn explicitly the "totality" test was probably the price exacted for negotiating the strong 8 to 1 majority vote. If so, the price was too high. Many lower courts proceeded to seize upon those parts of the decision which recognized a judicial duty to rectify genuinely cruel and unusual conditions of confinement while all but ignoring the admonition that the complex questions of how best to accommodate and maintain discipline over increasing prison populations are for the state legislatures and prison authorities to decide.

Thus, in *Walker v. Johnson*,[19] Judge Stewart Newblatt of the Eastern District of Michigan (a 1979 Carter appointee) felt compelled to state that "This Court disagrees with much of the *Rhodes* statement [concerning the constitutionality of double-celling]." The judge then proceeded to mandate "constitutionally acceptable" levels of yard time and law library access for inmates at a Michigan prison—the very kinds of prison management detail which the Supreme

Court had admonished the courts to refrain from tampering with.

Similarly, in *Smith v. Fairman*,[20] Judge Harold Baker on the U.S. District Court for the Central District of Illinois (another Carter appointee) held that double-celling at an Illinois State Prison *was* unconstitutional, the *Rhodes* opinion notwithstanding. While Judge Baker's decision was later reversed by the Seventh Circuit, other district court decisions rejecting *Rhodes* have been approved by the U.S. Court of Appeals. In *Toussaint v. Rushen*,[21] for example, the U.S. District Court for Northern California dismissed the impact of the *Rhodes* opinion by citing a subsequent *district court* opinion which said that double-celling *was* unconstitutional after all, and the Ninth Circuit affirmed.

The blatant resistance to the Supreme Court's modest attempt at restraint in the *Rhodes* decision aptly demonstrates the extraordinary hubris of many lower federal courts. Not content with encroaching on the authority of the executive and legislative branches, they do not even flinch at challenging the authority of the highest tribunal within their own branch when it interferes with liberal orthodoxy. It thus appears that *no* governmental institution within our "constitutional" system is presently equal to the task of curtailing the runaway prerogatives of the lower federal courts.

Perhaps the ultimate in judicial arrogance can be seen in the remarkable position taken by the Tenth Circuit in *Battle v. Anderson*.[22] There, after concluding that there were no remaining constitutional deficiencies within an Oklahoma State Prison—indeed, the dissent stressed that its facilities were "not only fit but most comfortable for prisoners"—the Court of Appeals nonetheless held that the District Court should maintain continuing jurisdiction over the prison "until it can say with assurance. . .that there is no reasonable expectation that unconstitutional conditions will recur."[23]

In short, the federal judiciary now is exercising jurisdiction for the openly stated purpose of supervising and monitoring the administration of a prison that passes muster even under the amorphous "totality of circumstances" test. The institutionalized and pervasive nature of this judicial supervision was openly proclaimed by the district court and approved by the Court of Appeals as follows:

> [T]he determination of constitutional conditions must inherently involve a continuing review of population figures, as one of the multiple relevant factors. The court must stand ready to act should *any* factor casually swing the balance separating constitutional from unconstitutional conditions.[24]

The Court openly characterized its remedy as *"indefinite relief,"* and just as openly flouted the *Rhodes* decision's admonition to defer to the good faith and competence of state prison administrators.

Cases like *Battle, Walker,* and *Smith v. Fairman* confirm that even the feeble gesture at judicial restraint reflected in the *Rhodes* decision is doomed to failure. A federal judiciary swollen with liberal Carter appointees[25] has found every imaginable device to avoid compliance with anything less than a definitive Supreme Court ruling that judicial intervention in general questions of prison supervision policy is unconstitutional.

PRIORITIES AND CONSTITUTIONAL PERSPECTIVE

Judicial usurpation of the power to control and supervise state prison policies reflects a distortion of at least two basic constitutional principles. It disregards the Tenth Amendment's requirement that powers not expressly granted to the federal government are reserved to the states. It also undermines the constitutionally mandated separation of powers, in that the court's broad, ongoing supervision of prisons has extended far beyond the Article III limits which restrict the courts to deciding only litigable cases or controversies. Such judicial intervention amounts to *de facto* judicial legislation.

The federal courts have achieved their dominance in the field of prison reform by transforming the cruel and unusual punishment clause from a shield against acts of malicious and barbarous punishment into a sword wielded against state legislatures and prison administrators in the name of "across-the-board" penal reform. Judicial activism under the banner of the Eighth Amendment is an especially inappropriate response to the pervasive problem of overcrowded prisons, because those conditions are neither the result of "cruelty" on the part of states, nor are they "unusual." Overpopulated prisons are caused by the tragic confluence of an unacceptably high rate of serious crime and limited state financial resources—resources which must meet the demands of countless critical governmental services in addition to funding adequate prison facilities. When prisons in nearly every state in the Union are populated beyond their design capacities as a direct result of these conflicting societal pressures, to hold that such conditions constitute "cruel and unusual" punishment emasculates the very specific and discrete objective of the Eighth Amendment.

At least some recent federal decisions have recalled the critical point: For overcrowded prison conditions to rise to the level of cruel and unusual punishment there must first be a causal relationship between those conditions and some serious *culpability* on the part of the state.[26] It follows that where crowded conditions reflect nothing more than the influx of too many convicted criminals into prison facilities which are necessarily limited by available financial resources, then the issue is not properly one of cruel and unusual punishment. Instead, it is a complex *policy* issue of resource allocation, which the unelected and inexpert judiciary has neither the proper authority nor the competence to decide. The courts should limit their role to rectifying specific instances where prisoners are deprived of the minimum necessities for civilized incarceration—food, medicine, clothing, sanitation, shelter, and personal safety—while refraining from second-guessing state officials on such nice questions as the ideal minimum for living space or desirable levels of "yard time" or work opportunity.

To the extent that overcrowded conditions may sometimes give rise to incidents violating the minimum necessities requirement, the courts should not view such incidents as giving them license to fashion across-the-board prison reform orders. The occurrence of one constitutional violation does not invest a court with authority to preempt state power to deal with the multi-faceted societal problem of overcrowded prisons. This point is especially critical because there is much more at stake in prison conditions litigation than the well-being and comfort of the plaintiff convicts. The judicial perspective has focused obsessively on the rights of prisoners, to the exclusion of the countervailing considerations of law enforcement, deterrence, prison discipline, and state fiscal imperatives.

To contend that the federal courts have dangerously exceeded their jurisdiction in dealing with overcrowded prisons is not to minimize the serious nature of that problem. An immediate commitment to relieving overpopulated prisons is demanded not only by basic humanitarian concerns but, more importantly, by considerations of effective law enforcement and corrections policy. When prisons become so crowded that prisoner safety and prison discipline are genuinely threatened, society itself is threatened. Such conditions chip away at the foundations of prison security, predispose some judges against prison sentencing, and breed a class of hardened recidivists who are virtually beyond rehabilitation.

But the undisputed severity of the problem hardly justifies the unchecked judicial activism which has dominated the field—without achieving significant success—for the past decade. Aside from the basic fact that the Eighth Amendment does not empower the courts to impose their ideals of penal reform upon the states, the courts lack both the competence and the representative character which are needed to formulate a balanced solution to this complex problem. Judicial insensitivity to state revenue and budgeting constraints is an especially compelling reason why the problem of crowded prisons cannot be resolved by the courts. Any court-ordered prison reform which fails to take into account the state's budgetary constraints is ultimately doomed to failure.

The remedy for overcrowded prisons must also be carefully fashioned to avoid any consequences which undermine the ultimate state responsibility of preserving the safety and security of the citizenry. Interim remedies such as alternative sentencing for nonviolent offenders, "intensely supervised" probation programs, and early release measures triggered by "emergency" levels of overcrowding must be subjected to stringent safeguards which will prevent the release of dangerous criminals who belong behind bars for the full period allowed by law. Preemptory court orders which impose inflexible and unrealistic constraints on prison administrators too often disregard this critical consideration, often with tragic results.

Ultimately, prison overcrowding is but one manifestation of the broader problem of excessive crime. Only by achieving substantial progress in the drive to reduce serious crime can society reduce the task of our correctional institutions to sane and manageable proportions. The fact that the incidence of serious crimes dropped by 7 percent and 2 percent in 1983 and 1982 respectively suggests that genuine progress may already be underway.[27] It is no coincidence that this progress has occurred during a period when stricter law enforcement and sentencing policies have been visibly on the rise. These circumstances should remind everyone concerned that the ultimate priority of deterring and reducing violent crime must not be thoughtlessly compromised in society's efforts to cope with the problem of crowded prisons.

REFORM PROPOSALS

Under the current Eighth Amendment theories of the federal judiciary, a sudden increase in the rate of violent crime can have the grimly ironic effect of liberating hordes of convicted felons from prison to prey on society. The influx of prisoners created by the new crime wave would create "constitutionally intolerable" conditions in our prisons, and the federal courts would feel "compelled" to order accelerated release of other violent felons to relieve the overcrowded conditions.

This is the point where excessive judicial activism undermines the most basic function of government—the preservation of law and order. Our Constitution provides the legislature with the power to halt this dangerous drift toward government by judicial fiat, and it is time for Congress to reassert its democratic prerogatives.

The most controversial (but also the most direct) means to halt judicial excess in prison conditions litigation would be for Congress to limit federal court jurisdiction in that area. While those who have a vested interest in perpetuating federal judicial control over the critical decisions in our society would attack such legislation as unconstitutional, we believe that the Constitution clearly vests such authority in Congress. The Congress which has the power to constitute (or abolish) lower federal courts surely has the power to limit and regulate their jurisdiction, and the decisions of the Supreme Court indicate as much.[28]

Such legislation could be modeled on the Norris-LaGuardia Act,[29] which restricts the power of federal courts to issue injunctions in cases growing out of labor disputes. The statute could provide that, in cases challenging prison conditions under the Eighth Amendment or derivative statutes, no federal court shall have jurisdiction to issue injunctive relief or other mandatory orders which would, directly or indirectly:

- compel prison authorities to release any prisoners who would not otherwise be released;
- set numerical limitations on the number of prisoners who may be confined in any prison or system of prisons; or
- compel prison authorities to provide any amenities, benefits, privileges, or facilities the deprivation of which does not in and of itself constitute cruel and unusual punishment.

The foregoing, of course, are merely suggestive of the type of jurisdictional restrictions which ought to be considered. The statute should also expressly prohibit the kind of indefinite, continuing jurisdiction asserted by federal courts in cases such as *Battle v. Anderson*. Jurisdiction would terminate upon a showing that the particular constitutional violation in issue had been corrected.

Another approach would be for Congress and the state legislatures to establish legislative standards for minimally acceptable conditions in the prisons. Such standards could be modeled on the "minimum necessities" test adopted by some courts, and would be flexible enough to accommodate the practical demands of housing growing prison populations caused by increased crime. Because such standards would presumptively reflect the *representative* judgment of the legislatures as to prevailing popular norms, the courts would be hard-pressed to second-guess them. The Supreme Court has repeatedly indicated that legislative standards are persuasive indicators of what is permissible under the cruel and unusual punishment clause.[30]

The legislative standards approach has its risks, however. Pro-prisoner lobbies such as the ACLU would expend every effort to shape the standards to maximize the "rights" and amenities of prisoners. Unless law enforcement advocates are prepared to mobilize the mass support of large pro-law enforcement constituencies, legislative standards could conceivably produce a cure worse than the disease.

A final possibility for curbing judicial excess in prison supervision would be to "defund" the entrenched civil rights lawyers who have turned the field into a virtual cottage industry. As noted above,[31] groups such as the ACLU are collecting literally millions of dollars in statutory attorney fees from the states as a reward for their assaults on the efforts of embattled but conscientious prison administrators. These fees are authorized by the Civil Rights Attorney's Fees Award Act,[32] which provides for attorney's fees as part of the prevailing party's costs in cases brought under the various civil rights acts. The funding of radical advocacy through statutory attorney's fees goes hand-in-glove with excessive judicial activism in prison reform. Judges who support the ACLU's agenda are in a unique position to sustain it with their power to award shocking attorney's fees.

It is time for Congress to relieve the taxpayer of the burden of indirectly funding the ACLU's radical prison reform agenda through statutory attorney's fees for their interminable lawsuits and "monitoring" activities. This could be done by repealing the Civil Rights Attorney's Fees Act or by restricting the amounts or types of fees which could be awarded. Groups such as the ACLU are apt to be more selective in bringing their suits, and less vexatious in their extreme, across-the-board approach to prison litigation, if they can no longer assume that the courts will order the states to foot their massive legal fees. The truly legitimate suits will continue, but the ACLU and similar groups will no longer have a blank check to pursue their dangerous assault on the very legitimacy of incarceration for convicted felons.

REFERENCES

Prisons, Priorities, and Judicial Fiat: The Need for Constitutional Perspective by Daniel J. Popeo and George C. Smith

1. New York *Times*, April 23, 1984, p. 1.
2. New York *Daily News*, April 23, 1984.
3. *Ibid.*
4. 15 *Criminal Justice Newsletter*, No. 9, p. 2 (May 1, 1984).
5. Although FBI statistics report a 7% decrease in serious crime for 1983. 15 Criminal Justice Newsletter, *supra*, p. 7. As Attorney General Smith stated, "It is no coincidence that the decrease in our crime rate came at a time when more criminals are behind bars than ever before." *Ibid.*
6. The ACLU's National Prison Project's Report of Activities for the Quarter ending December 31, 1983, proudly proclaimed that the ACLU received the following legal fees and costs from state government defendants for attacks against state prison systems on behalf of criminals: Over $100,000 in Rhode Island; $110,00 in Maine; over $90,000 in Florida; $124,000 in New Mexico; $250,000 in Virginia; over $700,000 in Colorado (legislative approval was pending); and $15,000 in the District of Columbia.
7. For instance, it has been held that "double-celling" conditions which may in themselves be constitutional can become unconstitutional if they are associated with riots, violence, or psychological disturbances. *Toussaint v. Yockey*, 722 F.2d 1492 (9th Cir. 1984). Under this approach, the existence of cruel and unusual punishment turns not on what the state did but on how the prisoners' *respond*. It takes little imagination to appreciate how this approach serves to undermine prison authority.
8. U.S. Dept. of Justice (Bureau of Justice Statistics), *Report to the Nation on Crime and Justice*, p. 80 (Oct. 1983).
9. *Rhodes v. Chapman*, 452 U.S. 337, 101 S. Ct. 2392 (1981).
10. *Banning v. Looney*, 213 F.2d 771 (10th Cir.), *cert. denied*, 348 U.S. 859 (1954); *United States ex rel. Lawrence v. Rogen*, 323 F.2d 410, 412 (7th Cir. 1963).
11. *Pugh v. Locke*, 406 F. Supp. 318, 329 (M.D. Ala. 1976), *aff'd in part, remanded in part sub nom Newman v. Alabama*, 559 F.2d 283 (5th Cir. 1977).
12. *Laaman v. Helgenoe*, 437 F. Supp. 269, 322–23 (D.N.H. 1977).
13. *Rhodes v. Chapman, supra* n. 9.
14. *E.g., Walker v. Johnson*, 544 F. Supp. 345 (E.D. Mich. 1982).
15. *Rhodes, supra* n. 9, 452 U.S. at 346, 101 S. Ct. at 2399.
16. *Ibid.* at 347, 101 S. Ct. at 2399.
17. *Ibid.* at 349, 101 S. Ct. at 2400 (Emphasis added).
18. *Ibid.* at 352, 101 S. Ct. at 2402.
19. *Supra*, 544 F. Supp at 361.
20. 528 F. Supp. 186, 201 (C.D. Ill. 1981), *rev'd*, 690 F.2d 122 (7th Cir. 1982), *cert denied*, 103 S. Ct. 2125 (1983).
21. 553 F. Supp. 1365, 1379 (N.D. Cal. 1983), *aff'd sub nom Toussaint v. Yockey*, 772 F.2d 1492 (9th Cir. 1984).
22. 708 F.2d 1523 (10th Cir. 1983).
23. *Ibid.* at 1537.
24. *Ibid* at 1540 (Emphasis added).

363

25. An August 1983 "Guide to Federal District Judges" published by *The American Lawyer* revealed that 35 percent of all federal district judges sitting at that time were Carter appointees. Over 56 percent of the federal district judges were appointed by Democratic presidents, even though as of 1983 the presidency had been occupied by Republican presidents for 11 out of 15 years since 1968. As of 1983, only 12 percent of the district judges were Reagan appointees. [Editor's note: Assuming President Reagan secures confirmation of his nominees, a prospect which seemed clouded in early 1986, it was expected to be well into 1986 before President Reagan—after nearly six years in office—matched Jimmy Carter's appointments in just four years. Even once Reagan judges match their predecessors in numbers, they will face the daunting prospect of correcting hundreds of dubious precedents. *See* articles on the "judges war" throughout 1986 in *Judicial Notice*, a publication of the Free Congress Foundation's Institute for Government and Politics.]

26. *Haywood v. Younger* 718 F.2d 1472 (9th Cir. 1983).

27. 15 *Criminal Justice Newsletter, supra* n. 4, p. 7. However, the preliminary date for the FBI's *Uniform Crime Reprots* (1985) showed a 1985 *increase* of 4 percent. *See, Judicial Notice*, May 1986. The 1984 decrease was only 1.9 percent (2.8 percent per 100,000 population). [Editor's note: Counting crime can get confusing. *See* "Households Touched by Crime, 1985," *BJS Bulletin*, June 1986. This intriguing study found that the percentage of U.S. households touched by crime fell to the lowest level in a decade in 1985, partially offsetting the FBI's bad news about the increase in the crime rate.]

28. U.S. Constitution, Article I, Section 8, clause 9; and Article III clauses 1 and 2. *Ex Parte McCardle*, Wallace 506 (1869) *Lockerty v. Phillips*, 319 U.S. 82 (1943); *Levering & Garrigues Co. v. Morrin*, 71 F.2d 284 (2nd Cir. 1934), *cert. denied*, 293 U.S. 595.

29. 29 U.S.C. Sec. 101.

30. *Gregg v. Georgia*, 428 U.S. 153, 176-87 (1976); *Rhodes v. Chapman, supra*, 452 U.S. at 347-48.

31. *Supra* n. 6.

32. 42 U.S.C. Sec. 1988.

22

COSTLY PRISONS: Should the Public Monopoly be Ended?

by James K. Stewart

The national elections of 1978 and 1980 and the changes in public attitudes they revealed hold a clear message for the future: the pendulum is swinging toward a greater role for the private sector in American life. The American people have raised fundamental questions about the relations between the public and private sectors, and their changing views will inevitably be reflected in public policy.

—William Baroody, Jr.[1]

If the sixties and seventies were the era of transforming social problems into government programs, then the eighties will be seen as the time when the government's role in many areas of our national life was reassessed and redefined. More and more Americans realize that government alone cannot—and was never intended to—completely meet the needs of society.

As governments at all levels have attempted to contain costs and maintain essential services, public administrators have turned increasingly to the private sector to obtain expertise in dealing with specific problems or to deliver a variety of services. Evidence of the trend can be seen in the movement of private enterprise into what has traditionally been the public arena—dealing with "public" problems such as health care, housing, and environmental control.

Now privatization is being considered seriously in providing one of the oldest and most traditional functions of government—our jails and prisons. Public agencies have had a virtual monopoly in the corrections field. As with most monopolies, there has been little incentive to strive for greater effectiveness and efficiency. Greater private sector involvement in corrections holds the potential for introducing more sophisticated management techniques and expertise, with the promise of greater economy and flexibility in response to changing correctional needs.

The benefits of bringing the discipline of competition and market choices to what has been public sector monopolies is becoming evident, for example, in the public health care field. County hospitals have a reputation in many locales for poor care, low skills and costly administration. Skyrocketing medical costs and dissatisfaction with the quality of care has stimulated an accelerating trend from county administered and staffed toward private health care programs and facilities. The availability of such options is helping to meet the need for lower-cost, more efficient medical care.[2]

Concern over costs and performance also plague corrections. As policymakers look to the private sector for improving corrections management, a number of issues require serious consideration. Certainly the most basic is the question of the role of government. In a free country, the right to impose punitive sanctions—forcibly to deprive individuals of their liberty—is an awesome responsibility. That responsibility may be delegated—but not relinquished—to others. The collective government, with its checks and balances, remains accountable for setting policy and assuring that policy is followed.

THE CRISIS IN CORRECTIONS

Today, our corrections system is in crisis. Most of our prisons and jails are overcrowded and outdated. Many are more than 100 years old. Such facilities are more costly to maintain, requiring extra personnel and thus increasing the burden on taxpayers. Court orders mandating improvements in antiquated conditions have become commonplace. As a result the federal government, the states and local governments are faced with either releasing prisoners or providing adequate facilities for them using public funds.

How did we arrive at this point in corrections? It is important to understand the genesis of the problem.

In 1980, crime rates in this country reached an all time high, after climbing virtually steadily throughout the sixties and seventies. *Yet while crime soared, risk of imprisonment dropped to half what it had been in 1960.*

In the past several years, there has been a dramatic turnabout in our government's attitude toward crime and criminals. Citizen pressure for longer sentences and stricter penalties by judges have changed the risk of going to prison for the violent predator. We have seen a welcome downturn in the crime rate. At the same time, there are today almost half a million serious felons in our prisons, up nearly 40 percent in the past five years.[3]

Because a significantly larger number of convicted predators are now actually in prison, it is reasonable to conclude that we now have a sufficiently large proportion of serious criminals in prison to make some impact on the crime rate. In short, incarceration works as a crime prevention strategy. We know that, while in prison, a criminal cannot commit additional crimes.

Unfortunately, however, we are still reaping the consequences of policies of the sixties, when imprisonment as a crime control strategy was dismissed. During those years, many states imposed a building moratorium on new prison construction on the premise that prisons were so-called "schools for crime."

The spurious argument posited that most criminals released from prison are rearrested frequently for serious crimes (sometimes more grievous than the original one). Accordingly, the argument went, the stay in prison had a negative effect on the predators' behavior. But proponents of this notion never considered the victims saved from criminal attack as a benefit of imprisonment. As a result, a moratorium on new prison construction gained considerable acceptance and prison capacity remained static over virtually two decades. In recent years, states and localities have found themselves in a desparate predicament of too many victims and too many serious criminals—and not enough prisons to house them.

Over the next 10 years, new prison construction will gobble up an estimated $5 billion at the state level alone. Given the enormity of these public expenditures in today's fiscal climate, it is more crucial than ever that the investment in prison construction achieve the greatest return in terms of increased public safety.[4]

PRIVATIZATION AS A POLICY OPTION

Elected officials, policymakers and corrections administrators throughout the country are searching for ways to ensure the wisest investment of limited public resources in meeting corrections needs. For many, the search has led them to private enterprise.

The private sector is no stranger to the corrections field. Historically, the shire-reeve, or sheriff, of the Middle Ages contracted with unsalaried jailkeepers who, in turn, charged the prisoners for their confinement. In the modern era, when confinement replaced corporal punishment in the Nineteenth Century, private companies were the most frequent employer of convict labor.

More recently, private organizations have for some time furnished specific institutional services, such as health or food service, and have operated facilities and programs for those just released from prison, e.g. halfway houses, work release and drug rehabilitation programs. What is new about today's growing interest is the possibility of a greatly expanded role for the private sector—in prison industries, in financing for new construction, and even in the operation and management of minimum to medium-security institutions.

These new avenues for privatization—from financing to operation and management—are still largely in the embryonic stages. There is increasingly wide interest in the overall concepts and substantial media attention to the idea of "prisons for profit." Both government and private firms, however, are moving cautiously to explore whether privatization is mutually advantageous. For government, the crucial policy consideration is: Can public benefit be derived by contracting with the private sector to support corrections? Proponents believe that privatization offers flexibility, efficiency and the discipline of the free market. Others voice concern about the propriety of delegating social control powers that have traditionally resided with government.

To examine the issues and give policymakers and corporations credible data on quality of service, costs and effectiveness of private sector involvement in corrections, the National Institute of Justice in 1984 began to investigate the potential of private sector resources to meet the increasing demand for correctional facilities and services. The Institute published a report, *The Privatization of Corrections*, to analyze the major issues in the privatization movement and report on the practical experience to date. Our researchers contacted corrections departments in all 50 states, as well as many private firms involved in correctional operations and construction financing.[5]

The report was released to the public at a National Forum on Corrections and the Private Sector, held in Washington, D.C. in early 1985. The National Institute of Justice convened the Forum to allow state, local and Federal government agencies and officials and the private sector to join together in a common debate and search for solutions to the nationwide problem of prison and jail crowding.

This chapter draws upon these sources of information, as well as other research sponsored by the National Institute of Justice, in summarizing some of the major considerations that should be weighed in thinking about new roles for the private sector in our corrections systems.

The chapter focuses on the four major ways the private sector has or might increasingly become involved in corrections:

- Participation in prison work programs;
- Providing specific services or dealing with specific types of offenders;
- Financing new construction or rehabilitation of outmoded facilities; and
- Managing jail or prison facilities.

PRIVATE SECTOR PARTICIPATION IN
PRISON INDUSTRIES[6]

Prison costs have escalated four-fold during the past 15 years. It now costs some $20,000 to house an inmate for a year. This is an unbelievable expenditure of public funds. Is this 400 percent increase in costs of prisoner services necessary or is it an artifact of the system? For slightly less money—$18,500 to be exact—we could send the inmate around the world on the *Queen Elizabeth II* luxury liner! Instead of paying their "debt" to society, prisoners are adding to the debt of each and every one of us by sitting idly in prison consuming our tax dollars.

How can we reduce some of this burden? Prison industries managed or operated by the private sector hold promise of providing productive work for prisoners, enabling them to pay some of the cost of their imprisonment, to make restitution to the victims of their crime and to provide some support to their families on the outside, thus reducing the cost of public assistance to these dependents.

The ideal of the prison as a workplace operating at a profit, defraying the costs of the institution and providing work experiences resembling those on the outside has been eloquently championed by the Chief Justice of the United States, Warren E. Burger. Never before has a Chief Justice taken so strong and active a role in trying to remedy deficiencies in our nations's correctional system.

We still have a long way to go to realize Chief Justice Burger's concept of "factories with fences" rather than "warehouses with walls." Since 1980, however, private sector involvement in prison industries has been gaining. Over the past 10 years, almost half the states have adopted legislation calling for some form of private sector involvement in their prison work programs. The Crime Control Act of 1984, strongly supported by the President and the Attorney General and passed by Congress, authorizes up to 20 projects to sell goods in interstate commerce, a crucial requirement for most businesses.[7]

Despite this progress, however, the anticipated benefits of private sector involvement are not yet being realized to a significant degree. Institute research identified private sector work initiatives in only nine states, although momentum is gaining. At least seven additional states are exploring private sector projects; at least 19 businesses serve as the owner-operator, key investor or central purchaser for one or more prison-based industry. And yet the number of inmates involved in prison work programs of any kind remains small—about 34,000 state prison inmates. Only about 1,400 were participating in private sector programs as of early 1984.

Although neither corrections nor the private sector are moving vigorously toward a cooperative and mutually beneficial relationship, there are some encouraging examples.

Inmates at the state prison in Stillwater, Minnesota, manufacture disk drives and wire harnesses for a subsidiary of Control Data Corporation. This Corporation has computer assembly plants located in South Korea, Taiwan, and Hong Kong, where they have a reputation for high quality control and inexpensive labor. Surprisingly, however, Control Data found the performance of motivated prisoners to exceed that of foreign labor.[8]

In Florida, a single non-profit corporation, PRIDE, now operates all 43 prison industries' programs in 17 institutions within the state. The legislature had watched inefficiencies mount as costs escalated in the prison industry program. Under the discipline of a fixed investment and using a large idle labor pool, the private non-profit corporation has completely overhauled the products and programs, turning a resource-depleting operation into a program that now generates some revenues. It has the potential for becoming significantly self-funding, which would relieve the state of Florida from paying out millions.

The issue of competition with "free workers" remains a concern. By paying prisoners a competitive wage and taking advantage of the diversity of markets offered by private sector involvement, the possibility of unfair competition in one area is eliminated. Even the most optimistic projections for prison industries envision employment for approximately 100,000 out of the 450,000 inmates now in prison—an imperceptible percentage of the labor market. Moreover, it's important to remember that inmate earnings go to defray the costs of incarceration, repay victims, and help support the prisoner's families—all of which help to lower the tax burdens on working men and women.

There are burdens to doing business within the prison environment. These include the training and scheduling problems inherent in dealing with a workforce whose daily routine involves frequent interruption for such activities as inmate counts or treatment programs. While these circumstances appear to have been successfully accommodated in places like Arizona, Minnesota and Florida, the question remains whether many private sector firms can recoup costs and make a profit at less than current costs without some incentives by states, ranging from absorbing administration and transportation costs to tax and capitalization incentives.

Neither corrections nor private enterprise are clamoring for the market opportunities in prisons. However, reduced regulation may change the equation for the benefit of all.

CONTRACTING FOR SERVICES

The most thoroughly tested kind of private sector involvement in corrections—and the least controversial—is contracting for the purchase of specialized services such as medical treatment, food preparation, or special treatment programs for drug or alcohol abuse.

The responsibility for care and security remains with the state. However, contracting permits competition, delegation, and flexibility in service not possible in a government monopoly. As clients, states specify the service performance level and the compensation the contractor receives. The contractor then must perform within agreed-upon costs. Through careful management and cost control, the contractor is able in many cases to make a profit. Most make enough money to sustain their continued participation within corrections.

Contracting also permits periodic review and development of new services—a flexibility that is virtually impossible with government institutions whose established workforce tends to hold past practices as binding and accordingly are subject to very little change.

The decision to contract with private industry can be stimulated by a number of factors. Corrections administrators may decide that turnover or lack of skills among the inmate labor pool make it impossible to assure acceptable levels of quality in food service, for example, or maintenance. Or a prison may be under a consent decree to improve medical services. Or the labor costs and administration of a program may be too expensive or cumbersome. Or the service personnel may be of poor quality and the prison has been unable to attract competent, skilled personnel, such as doctors.

371

Research by the National Institute of Corrections reports that the most frequent specialized services provided by private firms are health services, education/vocational training, and staff training.

Private contracting generally has improved efficiency and services and reduced costs where real competition exists. In general, corrections agencies are satisfied with the services they contract for. Some report that they would not return to direct service provision in these areas themselves. Greater cost effectiveness in the privately-purchased services is the reason given for their satisfaction. Seventy-four percent of the agencies surveyed in the study said they had realized staff savings through contracting, while 54 percent reported saving money.

It is important to note, however, that not all agencies realized savings. Of those responding to the survey, 17 percent said contracting had exceeded normal agency costs. However, typically the increased costs were agreed to and realized improvements that were satisfactory to agency managers and in some cases were mandated by the courts.

Costs are not the only criterion, of course. More than 60 percent of the agencies said they received a better quality of service from the private sector, and 32 percent reported a decrease in liability because of improved conditions.[10]

The decision to contract out is one that each jurisdiction must make based on its own particular needs and considerations. If the decision is affirmative, then researchers and experienced corrections administrators all agree that the most essential consideration is monitoring the contractor to ensure effective performance. This includes both assessing compliance with service objectives as well as monitoring and review of fiscal management and accountability.

But monitoring and accountability do not begin with the award of the contract. At the very outset of the decision to contract, there should be careful planning and setting of specified objectives. Unless government knows what it wants, it cannot expect the private sector to fulfill expectations. Background checks on a private vendor's competence also should be done, just as any prudent buyer of a product or service would do. And the issue of liability of the public agency for the private firm's performance—including insurance and bonding requirements—should be rigorously analyzed.

From the private sector's perspective, corrections services are seen as a market they have just begun to tap and an opportunity to provide some services more cost-effectively. As one executive of a Fortune 500 company noted, prison managers have had neither the opportunity nor the necessity to acquire the business skills necessary to run work and training programs. Competition and the requirement to be effective or face extinction has not been part of the tradition of corrections.

PRIVATE FINANACING OF CORRECTIONAL CONSTRUCTION

Faced with the prospect of a $5 to 10 billion investment of public funds for adequate space to meet public safety demands, local and state government officials are looking for new options to speed financing and provide flexibility that can accommodate fluctuating demands for prison space. Creative financing techniques for construction represent another example of potential private sector assistance to state and local governments in desperate need of prison and jail space. With corrections systems both overpopulated and underfunded, officials are searching for solutions. The financial community has developed a variety of lease financing alternatives to the conventional general obligation bonds.

Traditionally, state and local governments have financed correctional construction through available cash reserves (current or accumulated revenues) and/or through general obligation bonds. Cash—or the "pay-as-you-go" approach—eliminates the need to borrow and thus avoids interest charges and long term liabilities. General obligation bonds are generally acknowledged to be the least expensive and most secure type of borrowing for state and local governments. They are, however, subject to debt limitations and voter approval.

Over the past several years, the combination of rising construction costs, insufficient cash reserves, constitutional and statutory debt limitations, and the "taxpayer's revolt" have combined to limit the ability of states and localities to finance construction through conventional methods. And even if voter approval of construction bond referenda seems likely—not always the case with corrections facilities—referenda requirements mean substantial delays. And delay translates into increased construction costs. California, for example, reported needing about $1.3 billion for new prison construction. Assuming a 5 percent inflation rate, the 8- to 10-month delays typically associated with general obligation bonds would increase total construction costs in the range of $43 to $54 million.

Thus, it is not surprising that governments are turning to the private sector for access to financing alternatives not subject to debt ceilings or referendum requirements. National Institute of Justice research has found the most widely discussed arrangements to be lease contracts. These most often take the form of lease/purchase agreements, in which the government purchases the facility from the "lessor" over time, much like an installment sale.

While comparatively new in corrections, the lease/purchase technique is not a dramatic new departure in government financing. It has been used successfully to finance new office buildings in California, port construction in Oregon, schools in Colorado, and telecommunications systems in Montana and Ohio. Most frequently, the "lessor" is a legal entity (public works board, facilities authority, or non-profit corporation) established specifically to issue revenue bonds or certificates of participation to support the desired construction. The role of financial investment houses in marketing the new issue is not unlike their role in marketing general obligation bonds.

The unit of government, as "lessee," operates the facility and annually appropriates funds for the lease payments. When the revenue bonds or certificates are fully paid, the government obtains title to the facility. However, because this approach does not rely on new taxes, the government must use other funds for the lease payments. This, in turn, may require cuts in the jurisdiction's annual operating budget.

In many states, use of lease/purchase arrangements for prison and jail construction must be legislatively authorized. According to the National Institute research, enabling legislation has been passed in California, Illinois and Ohio, and introduced in Arizona and Missouri. California, Kentucky, and Minnesota were evaluating proposals for lease/purchase, but Ohio was the only state that had acquired beds through lease/purchase financing.

Some of the major sponsors of lease/purchase agreements were Merrill Lynch Capital-Markets, E. F. Hutton, and Shearson Lehman American Express. They reported significant activity at the local level: a $30.2 million jail and sheriff's facility in Colorado, a $50 million jail project in Philadelphia, a $5 million jail project in Tennessee, and a large project in Los Angeles County for a jail and criminal justice training center.

Lease financing offers a number of advantages. Such arrangements *avoid debt limits* because, as leases, they contain non-appropriation clauses giving the government the right to terminate the lease at the end of any year. They *do not require voter approval* because they do not pledge new taxes to support the lease/interest payments. They offer the government *flexibility to negotiate the terms* of the lease and also *savings in both* set-up-time and costs. Some variable or *floating rate* packages currently offer attractively low interest rates. In some cases, the funds raised by issuing such bonds or certificates may be invested at a higher rate of interest, so that the issuer can earn a profit while the facility is being built.

Both philosophical and financial questions have been raised about private financing alternatives. Because lease/purchase contracts do not have to meet debt ceilings and referenda requirements, some contend that the government is limiting citizen participation in corrections policy and assuming long-term obligations without voter approval. However, it is important to remember that the officials involved are elected representatives of the people. If they set policies or enter agreements contrary to the will of the people, they can be "unelected"; thus the voters still have ultimate approval of decisions made. In fact, most policy making occurs by our representatives rather than through referendum to the people.

Some accounting authorities also voice concern about the "off balance sheet technique." They say that lease/purchase should be considered an installment sale and reflected on the government balance sheet, thus affecting debt capacity.

At the same time it must be recognized that often the public simultaneously demands stronger penalties for offenders while refusing to authorize additional funds for inmate housing in secure facilities. Clearly the voters must understand the link between mandatory sentencing, longer prison terms, and increased space requirements—in short, the additional revenues to pay for prisons. So too must administrators understand that the voting public feels that better management of current resources and reordering of priorities can accommodate new demands on prisons, and help to keep taxes down.

Lease/purchase is not the solution to this policy dilemma. Rather it is another option that government can consider, particularly in local jurisdictions, where taxing authority is increasingly restricted.

Obviously, there are financial tradeoffs that must be carefully weighed by government entities considering lease/purchase. The primary financial concern centers on interest rates. Fixed rate lease issues require a higher interest rate than general obligation bonds because they are not backed by the "full faith and credit" of the state or county and are therefore viewed by the financial community as a less secure investment. While a one percent difference in interest rates may seem small, the high costs of large correctional facilities means that a jurisdiction can pay $1 million or more extra each year over the life of the lease.

On the other hand, variable or floating rate issues, while currently much less expensive, have the inherent risk of sharp increases in the interest rates should there be an upturn in inflation. For states or counties willing to take the risk, the cost—at today's rates—can be significantly lower than general obligation bonds. At the National Institute of Justice conference on corrections and the private sector, finance industry representatives suggested that where general obligation bonds were feasible, they were preferred—as a more secure long-term commitment for construction financing.

Two particular types of lease arrangements have stimulated considerable interest and discussion in the corrections field. The first focuses on eliminating all obstacles to swift completion of a new facility. The government entity executes a single lease agreement with a private firm which then handles design of the facility, financing arrangements, and construction. Upon completion, the private firm leases the prison or jail back to the governmental unit. The method eliminates the time normally required for competitive selection of an architect, procurement of an underwriter, and public bidding for construction of the facility.

While being actively marketed, the technique has not yet been tested for correctional construction. Some legal counsel to private firms believe it will face serious court challenges over compliance with public bidding laws and with the intent of public works legislation. Equally important, while the single package avoids the string of seemingly unending re-hearings, the system may work to cut out smaller firms and actually limit competition. One alternative might be to create project teams—constellations of firms that together can handle the entire task.

The second leasing alternative initially prompted great interest among investors. Under this option, the private sector would finance construction of a correctional facility. Unlike the lease/purchase arrangements described earlier, the private firm or group of investors would retain an equity interest in the facility—i.e. hold a majority interest in ownership of the prison or jail, which they then lease to the government.

The approach offered dual tax advantages. Investors in government buildings were able both to earn tax-exempt interest income, and as equity investors, to realize the tax benefits of accelerated depreciation. Recent tax reforms, however, have eliminated the accelerated depreciation write-off, thus reducing the attractiveness of the investment. As a result, market participation has declined rapidly. Proponents of the changes in the tax laws viewed the dual investment benefits as "double dipping." The new legislation permits such investors to receive the depreciation benefits only if they earn taxable income *operating* the facility. While elimination of the tax benefits for private ownership of correctional facilities has curtailed interest in such financing opportunities, it may stimulate interest in *ownership and operation* of facilities where tax benefits are still available.

PRIVATE OPERATION OF CORRECTIONAL FACILITIES

Contracting with a private vendor both to provide and to operate a correctional facility may be one way to expand corrections capacity without imposing any burden for facility construction on the government. However, the proposition that private contractors should manage prisons and jails for mainstream adult offenders—whether in privately-owned facilities or in existing public institutions—has stimulated intense debate and sharply divided opinion. The National Sheriff's Association, whose members are primarily responsible for county jails, has expressed opposition. Sheriffs, of course, are elected to be responsible for jails. If the private sector circumvents that responsibility, then it violates the peoples' will. However, sheriffs also could make the decision to delegate management and operations because they have the legal responsibility. In these situations, the sheriff is still responsible and oversees the contract performance.

Many in the corrections field, however, are willing to explore the concept. The executive director of the American Correctional Association has stated, "We ought to give business a try."

That view appears to be echoed by the public. At the National Institute's conference, a report on emerging public opinion on the issue of privatization suggested a generally favorable trend. This conclusion is based on analysis of media coverage of privatization by a consulting group that monitors public trends.[11]

Despite the media bombardment and the intensity of the debate in correctional circles, "prisons for profit" is, as yet, a catchy headline—not an objective asessment of the reality.

However, there are some projects underway that give an indication of the acceptability of private management of facilities. The following table summarizes major developments in contracting for facility management during 1984 at the federal, state, and local level.

At the federal level, the Immigration and Naturalization Service is an active customer for contract confinement services, primarily for short-term detention of illegal aliens prior to hearing and deportation. The numbers of persons deported can vary dramatically. Thus the flexibility of private management, and a daily per person occupancy rate, may achieve better service at lower cost than the flat rate charged by government facilities. According to INS, they are achieving good results, due in large part to a carefully-crafted statement of work and monitoring of the contractor's adherence to uniform standards.

Two other federal agencies have responsibility for the growing problem of illegal aliens, and have turned to private sector contract facilities for housing these populations. The U.S. Marshal's Service, responsible for the custody of aliens who are material witnesses, has plans to add 100 to 150 beds through contracting with the private sector. In 1984, the Bureau of Prisons, which has jurisdiction over sentenced aliens, issued a solicitation for a 400–600 bed facility.[12]

At the local level, where the fiscal crunch is really felt, there is both developing interest and controversy over the prospect of private jail facilities. Despite opposition from sheriffs, hard-pressed local jurisdictions may provide fertile ground for entry of the private sector into facility management and operation. Corporate providers reported that a number of proposals were under consideration in the southern and western regions.

In late 1984, Hamilton County, Tennessee, became the first county in the nation to contract with a private company for the operation of a primary adult facility. Corrections Corporation of America, which has been one of the most active firms in this emerging market, took over operation of the County's penal farm. The Silverdale Facility houses more than 300 male and female offenders. While the majority of persons there are sentenced males serving a year or less, Silverdale also includes local, state and federal prisoners, with some current inmates serving sentences of up to six years in length.

Only a few months of operation were available for assessment of

Facility Management Contracting Ability in Early 1984[a]

Federal Contracts	State Corrections Contracts	Local Jail Contracts
Immigration & Naturalization Service	**Secondary Adult Facilities**	Legislation enabling private jail operations was pending in Colorado and had passed in New Mexico and Texas.
4 facility contracts for aliens awaiting deportation were operating (in San Diego, Los Angeles, Houston, Denver), providing a total capacity of 625 beds.	28 states reported the use of privately operated pre-release, work-release, or halfway house facilities. Largest private facility networks found in California, Massachusetts, Michigan, New York, Ohio, Texas, and Washington.	While the National Sheriff's Association registered formal opposition to privately operated jail facilities, corporate providers reported significant interest and a number of pending proposals for jail operations in the Southern and Western regions.
3 facility contracts were nearing award (in Las Vegas, Phoenix, San Francisco), providing another 225 beds.	**Primary Adult Facilities**	
2 additional facility contracts offering a total of 270 beds were planned in the near term (Laredo and El Paso, Texas).	No contracts reported for the confinement of mainstream adult populations; however, the Kentucky Corrections Cabinet issued an RFP in late 1984 to contract for minimum security housing for 200 sentenced felons.	In Hamilton County, Tennessee a private contractor took over the operations of a local work house holding 300 males and females awaiting trial or serving sentences up to 6 years in length.
U.S. Marshals Service		
2 small (30-bed) facilities operated uner contract in California.	Two interstate facilities for protective custody prisoners planned by private contractor.	
Plans to open a larger (100- to 150-bed) contracted facility in Los Angeles for alien material witnesses.		**Shared Facilities**
Federal Bureau of Prisons	**Juvenile Facilities**	One private organization in Texas planning to construct and operate a facility that would serve local detention needs as well as the needs of federal agencies responsible for confining illegal aliens.
Plans to operate a 400- to 600-bed contracted facility for sentenced aliens in the Southwest region. (Project delayed due to siting difficulties.)	A 1979 survey of private juvenile facilities found 1,558 privately operated residential programs holding a total of 28,678 juveniles, 9,603 of whom were adjudicated delinquents.[b] Only 42 institutions were classified as strict security and 333 as medium security.	
A 60-bed facility in La Honda, California operated under contract for offenders under the federal Youth Corrections Act.	Departing from the small, less secure settings characteristic of contracted juvenile facilities, a private contractor operates the Okeechobee (FL) Training School for 400 to 500 serious juvenile offenders.	Other proposals have called for the development of regional jail facilities that would serve multi-county detention needs.

[a] Reported in phone contacts made in January/February 1984 with additional follow-up at later points in 1984.

[b] *Children in Custody: Advanced Report on the 1979 Census of Private Facilities*, U.S. Department of Justice, Office of Juvenile Justice and Delinquency Prevention, Washington, D.C., 1980.

Source: *The Privatization of Corrections*, National Institute of Justice, February 1985.

the Silverdale experience. However, the contract cost per inmate is 10 percent less than the county cost,[13] yet, as part of the contract, the corporation made a $1 million capital investment to renovate parts of the facility.[14]

At the level of state adult corrections with its longer terms, higher security requirements and more complex service needs, the concept of contracting for prison operation has met with a cautious reception. In early 1984, the NIJ survey found 28 states using privately operated facilities for secondary housing, such as half-way houses. No state Department of Corrections reported contracts for prison operation in use or actively being planned. In late 1984, however, the Kentucky Corrections Cabinet issued a Request for Proposals for minimum security housing for 200 sentenced felons, the first such venture to involve the private sector in housing a mainstream population of state adult offenders.

There was considerable interest on the part of state officials learning about the pros and cons of facility management, and to draw upon the experience with private contracting in other areas of public administration, such as health care and environmental protection. At the NIJ conference in 1985, a number of participants expressed interest in facility management contracts, particularly for offenders with special needs. One private security firm has announced plans for two such facilities—maximum security prisons in Pennsylvania and Idaho, which would accept protective custody inmates from any state.

Whether these developments will lead to wider use of management contracts for secure adult facilities is not yet clear. In Kentucky, no proposal was selected for funding, and the Corrections Cabinet has issued a revised RFP. In Pennsylvania, construction of the proposed protective custody prisons has been delayed by legislators' concerns about the state's liability for a privately owned and operated facility of this nature.

KEY ISSUES IN PRIVATIZING CORRECTIONS

The experience in these two states suggests the careful analysis and assessment of the issues that should be part of decisions about the appropriate role of the private sector in corrections management. According to the National Institute of Justice research, the issues can be framed as political, administrative, legal and financial.

Political issues include debate about whether such functions as the

380

classification, discipline, and control of inmates (including the potential use of deadly force) can appropriately be delegated to a private contractor. Many believe that only government (or employees acting under policy direction) can use force against another and accordingly it cannot be delegated. The use of force is a profound responsibility, one that both police and the courts have grappled with in defining appropriate limits.

Is force exclusively a government employee function subject to government review? In fact, our society has already delegated the use of force to nongovernmental entities—private security personnel, and staff in secure psychiatric wards of hospitals. However, this delegation is subject to the same review processes and judicial evaluation as government officials are. Concerns over the delegation of social control can, in the final analysis, be resolved only by carefully defining the limits to be placed on contracted functions and the policies and procedures to be followed. Protection of personnel, public and inmates themselves is the priority governing the use of force.

Some voice concern that the "bottom line" perspective of business may conflict with the public interest. Will the profit motive fuel a drive to keep corrections populations at the maximum level? There is also the potential for graft and corruption if private firms attempt to use their influence to secure contracts.

A potentially volatile issue is the reaction of public employees and corrections managers when corrections jobs are "privatized." Opposition from unions and staff can be minimized if the government agency establishes formal programs to assist displaced workers. Los Angeles County, for example, has combined early planning, retraining (for which 5 percent of all cost savings through contracting are set aside), aggressive job referral, contracts which give public employees the right of first refusal to the "privatized" job, and negotiation with the union to ease the impact on employees.[15]

There are also concerns that traditional public reluctance to have a correctional facility in their community may be intensified if that facility is privately operated. On the other hand, corporate providers often have more experience in dealing with the public on such matters as zoning issues and may prove more adept at responding to community questions and concerns than government agencies.

Administrative issues center on quality, accountability, flexibility, and costs. Because private providers are under competitive pressure to perform and free of civil service restrictions, many believe that the quality of privately provided services is likely to be superior. Others question whether there will be sufficient market pressure to sustain improvements over the long term.

Strong monitoring, on-site inspection, and careful rebidding procedures are the key to ensuring effective performance—and should be carefully designed at the outset of a contract. Accountability also requires a clear definition of roles and responsibilities in the contract document and continuing efforts to monitor contract performance. Corrections departments will remain accountable for contracted services and need to adapt supervisory practices to create an effective public-private alliance.

Most observers agree that contracting offers public agencies the ability to respond to immediate needs with greater flexibility and speed than is typically possible under government operation. The experience of the Immigration and Naturalization Service (INS) in contracting for private construction and operation of detention facilities for illegal aliens has demonstrated substantial time savings over standard agency procedures in bringing new facilities on-line. The INS facility in Houston, operated by a private contractor, was built in six months at a cost of $4 million. Immigration officials say the federal government would have needed up to 5 years to do the job because of competitive bidding and other regulations.[16]

Will contracting for facility management limit the government's ability to change course in corrections management and policy-making over the long term? The answer is uncertain, but clearly the issue needs to be considered in planning the types of facilities and contract arrangements best suited to a given jurisdiction.

Legal issues include authority, liability, security and contract specificity. Even where states and counties have statutory authority for service contracting, legislative amendments may be required to permit contracts for primary facility operations, or specific language may be needed to open contracting to profit making organizations.

Liability also is a critical concern. There is no legal principle to support the premise that public agencies and officials will be able to avoid or diminish their liability merely because services have been delegated to a private vendor. It is imperative to ensure that contractors observe appropriate staff selection and training standards.

Actions taken by the private sector can place a government at financial risk if harm results. Consequently, government administrators must maintain careful supervision and policy approval. The delegation of security functions, for example, is of crucial concern in the debate on the appropriate roles and liabilities of the government and its private providers. One approach might be to have positions that may call for the use of restraining or deadly force (e.g., perimeter security) retained by the government although the policy may increase the operating costs.

The role of the public agency in internal disciplinary procedures also needs to be considered and specified in both the contract and operating regulations. Adequate staff training and supervision, frequent review and inspection, written client complaint procedures, and periodic inmate surveys are useful techniques to ensure the accountability of providers.

Another legal issue involves the private holding of prisoners from other states transported to serve time in another state. What is the government's liability and control over this kind of operation?

Perhaps the most important legal issue is one raised earlier in this chapter: the development of explicit contractual standards of performance. Both research and experience underscore the crucial role of highly specific and detailed contractual standards in ensuring safe, secure, and humane facilities.

Financial issues also loom large in the privatization debate. Proponents say that private vendors can operate equivalent facilities at lower cost, due largely to staffing efficiencies possible in the absence of civil service regulations, lower private-sector pension and benefits costs, and market incentives to increase productivity. Critics fear that the costs of private management will escalate once vendors become established, and point to the burden of monitoring private providers as a hidden but potentially large cost of management contracting.

As yet, there is only very preliminary data to inform the debate. The privately operated facilities utilized by INS appear to represent a modest cost savings over those operated by the agency. Conversely, when the National Institute of Corrections sponsored an evaluation of the first large juvenile facility to be privately operated (a training school for 400–500 serious juvenile offenders), the evaluator reported that private operation did not result in significant cost savings.[17]

Cost issues are likely to remain a murky subject in the short term. Much more comprehensive methods of analyzing cost data, especially the full costs of government operations, are needed before accurate comparisons of public and private sector corrections operations can be made. Isolating the true costs of publicly operated

383

facilities is difficult. Government budgets typically do not include the costs of capital investment, debt maintenance, and other elements of facility costs. Thus, the per diem cost per inmate in public facilities may be artificially low, and actual savings in privately constructed and operated facilities may be greater than they initially appear.

Cost comparisons also are difficult because public and private facilities may serve different populations with different security requirements and service needs (particularly if private facilities deal only with lower risk offenders).

Costs will differ if private vendors are to be held accountable for running institutions that meet professional standards. At the NIJ conference, for example, private contractors stated that their institutions would adhere to the American Corrections Association Commission on Accreditation standards, including standards on space and crowding. Public institutions may not be able to adhere to similar standards since they cannot refuse to accept prisoners. Precisely because of their crowding, however, the costs per inmate in public facilities may be artificially lower.

POLICY RECOMMENDATIONS

While definitive answers about many aspects of privatization are not yet available, research suggests that further experimentation with privately managed facilities may be warranted to achieve several goals:

• To avoid permanent facility expansion but still accommodate near-term population shifts.

• To test new practices without making permanent commitments or laboring under bureaucratic constraints.

• To acquire greater geographic and programmatic diversity than is typically possible under a centralized agency.

• To satisfy unique or highly specialized treatment needs that cannot be efficiently handled in a general purpose institution (e.g. AIDS patients, mentally ill, etc.).

• To develop interjurisdictional facilities unencumbered by the politics of geography.

The National Institute of Justice report, *The Privatization of Corrections*, which this chapter has drawn upon, has been widely distributed to give both public and private sector decision-makers the best available information on the privatization movement in corrections. In addition, the Institute is making available materials from the 1985 recent National Forum on Corrections and the Private Sector so officials can examine the relevant issues in the context of their own jurisdictional needs and problems.

Soon to be published is a detailed analysis of both the impediments and the incentives to increased private sector participation in prison industries. Because prison industries is a critical and potentially promising arena for private sector involvement, NIJ research funds are supporting preliminary work at the National Center for Innovation in Corrections. The Center was recently established at George Washington University with the mission of increasing prison industry and educational programming—creating the "factories with fences" envisioned by Chief Justice Burger.

Our research to date has highlighted a number of questions which jurisdictions considering alternative financing techniques for prison or jail construction need to address. The Institute has funded a feasibility study to determine whether the type of financial programs utilized by investment firms to develop and market alternative financing packages can be usefully adapted to help jurisdictions determine when such financing would be beneficial and/or select among options offered.

The National Institute of Justice also is considering working with one or more states planning facility management contracts for mainline adult populations, so that their experience can be documented and shared with other jurisdictions throughout the country.

Research is also being conducted by a NIJ Visiting Fellow on detailed local experience with both innovative financing techniques and new building technologies which might be applied for both time and cost savings in prison and jail construction.

In fact, the NIJ Forum was the first public opportunity for leaders to share lessons learned about building techniques. Some prison officials have recently utilized construction methods known heretofore only in private industry. Prefabricated concrete panels were brought to a prison site in California and erected into a new prison in 17 months for $50,000 per bed. A comparable but traditionally constructed California facility cost $90,000 per bed and required 38 months for completion. Both are typical of what is required by contemporary standards for maximum security, single cell facilities. An even more striking example came from the less costly market area of

Florida, where a 336-bed prison was constructed with new methods in just 10 months at a cost of only $16,000 per cell.[18]

As this chapter suggests, the private sector has much to offer corrections. New ideas, new products, new techniques—in short the vitality and flexibility of successful business practice—can be brought to bear on corrections. Public officials can learn from their private sector counterparts effective techniques for mobilizing resources to meet immediate needs, to adapt services rapidly to meet changing circumstances, to experiment with new practices, and to meet specialized needs with an economy of scale. In our efforts to realize these benefits, we should keep in mind that the challenge is not to replace public corrections with the private sector, but to develop a corrections system that uses both public and private strengths to their best advantage.

It seems that more information is needed to increase our confidence in the performance of the private sector in corrections. The only way to get that information is through careful evaluation in the natural market place of many states. The results can inform and then guide public and private sector collaboration in moving forward to the benefit of all.

REFERENCES

Costly Prisons: Should the Public Monopoly Be Ended? by James K. Stewart

1. William Baroody, Jr., preface to Jack A. Meyer, *Meeting Human Needs: Toward a New Public Philosophy* (Washington, D.C.: American Enterprise Institute for Public Policy Research, 1982).
2. Senator Mitch McConnell (R-KY), remarks at "National Forum on Corrections and the Private Sector," National Institute of Justice, February 20-22, 1982, Arlington, Virginia.
3. *Prisoners in 1984*, Bureau of Justice Statistics, April 1985 (Washington, D.C.: U.S. Department of Justice).
4. Joan Mullen, Kent Chabotar, Deborah M. Carrow et al., *The Privatization of Corrections*, February 1985, Abt Associates for the National Institute of Justice, Washington, D.C.
5. *Ibid.*
6. This section is not an exhaustive review of the issues involved in prison industries, because the topic is treated more fully in Richard Abell's chapter in this book.
7. George E. Sexton, Franklin C. Farrow and Barbara J. Auerbach, *The Private Sector and Prison Industries*, National Institute of Justice, Research in Brief (Washington, D.C: U.S. Department of Justice, 1985).
8. Private communication with Richard Mulcrone, General Manager/Operations, Correction Systems Division, Control Data Corporation, at "National Forum on Corrections and the Private Sector," *supra* n. 2.
9. J. Floyd Glisson, President, PRIDE, Remarks at panel discussion during "National Forum on Corrections and the Private Sector," *supra* n. 2.
10. Camille G. Camp and George M. Camp, *Private Sector Involvement in Prison Services and*

Operations, Criminal Justice Institute for the National Institute of Corrections, February 1984 (Washington, D.C., U.S. Department of Justice).

11. Dr. Judith Schloegal, staff director, National Center for Innovation in Corrections, remarks at panel discussion, *supra* n. 2.

12. Joan Mullen, *et al.*, *supra* n. 4.

13. "Jails Run by Private Company Force it to Face Question of Accountability," New York *Times*, February 19, 1985.

14. *Supra* n. 4.

15. Lynn W. Bayer, Office of Chief Administrator, Los Angeles, California, remarks during panel discussion, *supra* n.2.

16. *Supra* n. 4.

17. Robert Levinson, American Correctional Association, remarks during panel discussion, *supra* n. 2.

18. Charles de Witt, Research Project, Visiting Fellowship Program, National Institute of Justice (Washington, D.C., U.S. Department of Justice, 1985).

23

PRISON LABOR:
A Neglected Resource
by Richard B. Abell

Private sector involvement in prison industry work programs is a concept which is good currency. But, what is it? What is meant by this term which gives it such wide acceptance?

To many, it refers to the application of private industry expertise and skill, through advice and consultation, in the problem-solving, decision-making functions of prison industry such as can be seen in the Federal Prison Industry Program. To others it means the authority to sell, and the sale of prisoner-made goods in interstate or intrastate commerce, whether by public or private corporations. The term has been used to denote the acquisition of private sector capital to purchase facilities, equipment, and other needed production resources. For some, private sector involvement is the paid management of prison industry factories by private sector professionals. And, for others, the term means the displacement of public ownership and public management in favor of the private sector which employs prison labor, or some form of mixed public/private venture.

This chapter deals principally with the introduction of private enterprise in its many forms into the prison sector for the purpose of interstate commerce. We will review the history, current activity, specific operational projects, and possible future directions of the range of private sector involvement in prison industries.

However, before exploring the status of the new models, both the Federal Prison Industries system and the current status of state prison industry operations warrant brief discussion.

THE FEDERAL PRISON INDUSTRIES SYSTEM

The Federal Bureau of Prisons was established by Act of Congress on May 14, 1930 and directed to develop an integrated system of institutions to provide custody and treatment of sentenced offenders based upon their individual needs.

The Federal Prison Industries, Inc., (FPI) was established in 1934 by Act of Congress, as a self-sustaining corporation keeping prisoners constructively employed and providing job training.

Between the end of FY 1982 and May 10, 1985, the FPI (also known as UNICOR) has achieved a 6.6 percent increase in the percentage of federal prisoners employed in its industries' factories. Of the 34,170 incarcerated prisoners, 39.4 percent (13,412) were employed within the 70 factories operating in 41 of the 46 Bureau of Prisons' institutions. The five largest industry operations within the UNICOR system are textiles, wood/metal office furniture, electronics, printing and sign making. Inmates are employed in the fabrication of canvas mailbags, parachutes and clothing. Office furniture is manufactured and rehabilitated and electronic cable harnesses are assembled by employed prisoners.

FPI operates basically as a traditional state-use industry employing prisoners in government-owned and operated factories in which inmate workers are paid token wages (which range from $.44/hour to $1.10/hour) and sales are limited to federal government agencies. Production is diversified to minimize competition with private industry. Unlike traditional state-use industries, UNICOR has developed and operates within a set of sustained goals and objectives designed to help accomplish the mission of the Bureau of Prisons. The goals include: maintenance of facilities and inmates, protection of the community, assisting inmates in preparing for release, achieving productive and profitable prison industries and achievement of economic benefits which reduce or offset government expenditure.

Within this framework UNICOR has been able to establish long and short-range planning objectives to meaningfully involve the skill and expertise of the private sector; and to utilize, to the maximum extent possible, the prisoner workforce to accomplish industries' goals. For example, five years ago, the Bureau of Prisons targetted the employment of 40 percent of its prisoners in UNICOR operations. As we have noted above, that goal is within .6 percent of being achieved.

The growth of UNICOR relates to its role in furthering the mission of the Bureau of Prisons. Past experience indicates that change will occur in a planned, orderly and well-managed fashion. It is unlikely, however, that these changes will include privatization of UNICOR. In a recent report to the Congress, the Department of Justice's Justice Management Division Evaluation Staff recommended UNICOR not pursue direct participation in a private prison industry program.[1] UNICOR is essentially a self-sustaining quasi-federal government corporation. Tax dollars are not used to support the corporation; the corporation supports itself through its profits or it goes under.

STATUS OF THE STATES

All 50 states have prison industry programs in one or more prisons. About 9 percent of all state inmates are employed in prison industries. Prison industry activities are a combination of product production/repair and services. The most common activities involve license plate manufacture, printing, data processing, furniture and upholstery production/repair, metal fabrication and agriculture. These products and services are generally sold to state agencies and local governments (often the first priority being the state Department of Corrections) and non-profit organizations.

Pay schedules within traditional state prison operations range from $0–$1.00 per hour. The most common form of compensation is the "payment" of time reducing the prisoner's length of incarceration.

Few states have developed long-range strategic plans guiding their administration of prison industry work programs. Long-term employment objectives are seldom established. Long-range market and product development plans are an exception rather than a rule. Development of planned institutional prison industry work programs as a means for achieving correctional goals or program strategies is infrequent. As reported in a recent Department of Justice study, ". . . in most cases these 'correctional industries' were neither correctional [sic] nor industries in the private sector sense of the term."[2]

The literature describing the history, growth, and condition of prison industry work programs suggests a plethora of reasons for their status. Those explanations include repressive federal and state legislation, absence of managerial and worker expertise, absence of markets, poor equipment, insufficient capitalization, featherbedding and inadequate facilities.

There is an element of truth associated with each explanation, yet there is no agreement among policymakers, administrators or managers as to whether these reasons are causal or symptomatic. Efforts to resolve these debates and firmly establish a set of causal factors which would form the basis for planned change remain stymied by the absence of wide agreement defining the purposes of state corrections in America.

391

THE RESOURCE

At the end of 1984 there were 463,866 people incarcerated in state and federal prisons in this country. This marked the tenth straight year that the prison population increased over the previous year according to the Bureau of Justice Statistics in their Bulletin, "Prisoners in 1984." In each of these 10 years the size of this group reached an all-time high.[3]

Using a minimum figure of $10,000 per year to maintain each of these prisoners, the annual cost to this country's taxpayers of supporting this population exceeds $4.5 billion. Yet often overlooked is the benefit which taxpayers receive in terms of reduced crime by ever-larger numbers of the predator/criminal class being locked away from potential victims. Some analysts believe that recently declining crime rates may be partly explained by an increasing prison population.

Inmates sentenced to prison enter a completely controlled environment. The opportunity to earn money legitimately is limited both by the scarcity of paying jobs and by the level of wages which is paid for those which do exist. Fewer than 10 percent of the prisoner population are employed in state operated prison industries which pay from $.00 to $1.00 per hour depending upon the prison system. While a larger proportion is employed in institutional support activities such as food service, laundry and maintenance, the wage levels are generally lower than in prison industries.

The low levels of wages are generally justified by the rationale that all of the inmate's basic needs are provided by the state without charge. In fact, it can be argued that the level of disposal income available to wage-earning prisoners, even at these wage levels, is probably as high or higher than that available to a significant portion of the law-abiding and employed citizenry.

However, the real losses engendered by this state of affairs are not incurred by the inmates but by others, primarily taxpayers and victims. For example, not only are taxpayers saddled with the cost of the prison system , but the inmate's families may also become welfare recipients. Victims rarely receive financial reparations or meaningful assistance because there are inadequate funds available to pay victim compensation, restitution or to support victims services.

Work has played a significant, albeit ambivalent, role in American corrections. Political debate has seldom focused exclusively on inmate workers or on the work of inmates as ends in themselves. Rather, the role of work in American corrections has been defined by the results of debate defining the purpose of corrections.

There has recently been created the opportunity to change this situation and to provide inmates with employment at pay levels which necessitate the payment of state and Federal taxes and which also permit contributions to family support, partial reimbursement for room and board and payment of restitution to victims.

Before examining this opportunity in detail it is appropriate to review briefly the history of prison industry to determine not only how it reached its current state but also to understand some of the forces that shaped its development.

HISTORY

Work has played a significant, although controversial, role in this country's prisons since their inception. In the first prisons, work was viewed as a fundamental aspect of prison life but treated in a markedly different fashion. In the early Nineteeth Century in the Pennsylvania system founded by the Quakers, work was performed in solitude and in silence to maintain an atmosphere conducive to penance. On the other hand, work in the Auburn system in New York was a congregate activity resulting in the development of the prison factory with the objective being a self-supporting institution.

The rationale of the Auburn system struck a responsive note in the other states and it soon became the model which others strived to emulate. "The original aim of prison industries, which for many years overshadowed every other prison policy, was to make prisons self-supporting. In former times, the success or failure of many wardens depended on their ability to meet this test and many of them met it successfully even though they may have failed in all else."[4]

There developed four different methods for employing prisoners:
• The lease system in which inmates were released to private contractors who provided food, clothing, shelter and security for the inmates and in return paid the state a specified amount for their services;
• The contract system in which private industries contracted with institutions for inmates to work in shops which they operated and paid a per capita fee to the state;
• The Peace-Price system which was a variant of the contract sys-

tem but with reimbursement to the state dependent on the quality and amount of shop output; and

• The state-account system in which the state operated the shop itself and employed the inmates directly, a forerunner of today's prison industries.[5]

The lease system gradually fell into disfavor because of the excesses of certain of the contractors in the management of the inmates and the abysmal working and living conditions provided which caused public outrage when publicized.

As the other systems flourished, there was opposition from segments of private industry and labor who were threatened by what they perceived as unfair competition using low-paid inmate workers. Restrictive state legislation was enacted to protect various industries from the incursion of prison-made products into their markets.

Ultimately, this opposition reached the national level led by the garment and cordage industries. In 1925 a national study was commissioned to examine the problems "...in the hope of proposing Federal restrictive legislation."[6]

Although the opponents of prison industries were unsuccessful in that effort, in 1929 they did cause Congress to pass the Hawes-Cooper Act[7] which allowed the states to regulate the entry of prison-made goods by removing the protection of the interstate commerce power of the federal government. "By making this law effective in 1934 Congress gave to prisons a 5-year period in which to adjust themselves to these new conditions."[8]

However, during this time a new effort was mounted by the Roosevelt Administration against prison industries through the National Reconstruction Administration code provisions which prohibited distribution of their products. Prison administrators thereupon retaliated by creating their own Prison Labor Compact. "This Compact, administered by a committee having the functions of a code authority was a voluntary agreement of some 32 states, including substantially all of the prisons selling their products to the public, to observe code hours of work in the respective industries and to sell at fair market prices."[9]

Despite this effort the opposition continued, and in 1935 Congress passed the Ashurst-Sumners Act[10] which barred the transportation of prison-made goods into states whose laws prohibited their entry and also required the labelling of prison-made goods as such. Then in 1940 the Sumners-Ashurst Act[11] was enacted to make it a federal crime to introduce prison-made goods into interstate commerce except for agricultural products and goods for state use.

In addition to barring the private sector market to prison industries, Congress also severely restricted access to the federal government market through the Walsh-Healy Act of 1936[12] which barred the use of prison labor on all government contracts exceeding $10,000.

As all of these pressures took effect the impact on prisons was to increase idleness and relegate the industry's program to the status of a make-work operation. There was a brief respite during World War II when prison labor became a significant contributor to war production even though the size of the prison population dropped markedly as military service became an accepted alternative to incarceration as well as the basis for early release.

After the war, however, conditions reverted to their pre-war status, including a return of the prison population to its pre-war size. Idleness again became the hallmark of the country's prisons.

Another post-war development affected the role of work in prisons as well. The notion that rehabilitation was the proper objective of prisons became popular, accompanied by a variety of programs called "treatment." These were designed to deal with whatever aspect of inmate character or behavior that was most suspect at the time. Work then became valuable only as a means to an end and was regarded as a "program" by clinicians who had little sympathy with or understanding of the work ethic. With the removal of economic self-support as an accepted corrections purpose, the methods for achieving both rehabilitation and reintegration were freed from economic reality. Advocates against constructive, productive, profit-oriented work in correctional facilities were successful almost without fail in abolishing meaningful prison industries.

So industrial programs limped along as prison administrators viewed them as baby-sitting operations to which as many inmates as possible were assigned with little concern about efficiency, cost-effectiveness or productivity.

By the mid-Twentieth Century, rehabilitation of offenders within institutions totally supported by taxes allocated from state and local government had become the accepted purpose of corrections. Rehabilitation remained in good currency until the late 1960s, when reintegration emerged as a somewhat subtle, yet significant, change in the purpose of corrections. While strategies of rehabilitation sought to emulate the treatment models of medicine and social work, reintegration strategies sought to design free world social, economic and psychological skill development opportunities. The concept of reintegration is currently a hotly debated topic.

Then in the mid-1970s several apparently unrelated developments coincided to produce a renewed public interest in the purpose of corrections:

- The rapid expansion of the prison populations;
- A general loss of confidence in most of what had been labelled "treatment," "rehabilitation," "reintegration"; and
- A rethinking of generalized priorities to more specific ones regarding corrections by state governments as a result of shrinking tax revenues.

It was into this environment that the Law Enforcement Assistance Administration (LEAA) established its interest to work within state prison industries. It funded a major study of state prison industries to identify the causes of its many problems and to develop a work strategy which would be successful in the prison environment. The study created a model which was referred to as the "Free Venture" prison industry. Essentially, it was based on the adaptation of several precepts of successful private sector business practices to prison industries.

LEAA then provided funds to six states to develop Free Venture Industries which they did with varying degrees of success. According to the LEAA contractors responsible for program management there were three primary purposes of this effort:

> ...First, to transform traditional prison industries from instructional workshops to more realistic business environments housed within correctional facilities; second, to test the feasibility of various short-term strategies for changing prison industries; and third, to pave the way for a more fundamental change, both in prison industries and ultimately in the operation of the prison itself.[13]

An independent evaluation also funded by LEAA concluded:

> "...the impact of Free Venture programs upon host institutions has been positive. Industries which differ from traditional prison industry programs along the dimensions of the Free Venture model (e.g., higher wages related to productivity, longer work days, etc.) have been well received by inmates and contributed to institutional tranquility and stability without adversely effecting (sic) other programs.[14]

In 1979, Senator Charles Percy (R-IL) was instrumental in providing for legislative authority to exempt up to seven non-federal prison projects from provisions of the Walsh-Healy Act and the Sumners-Ashurst Act. This authority permitted an expansion of the market for non-federal prisoner made goods by the removal of constraints against the purchase of goods by the federal government and against the Interstate commerce of prison-made goods.[15]

This section, called the Prison Industries Enhancement (PIE) Program authorized LEAA to certify up to seven demonstration projects which met several conditions:

- Inmate employment was voluntary;
- Inmates were paid wages not less than those which were paid for comparable work in the locality where the work was performed;
- Organized labor was consulted;
- An assurance that free labor within the community would not be subject to displacement nor would any existing contracts be impaired;
- There did not exist a surplus of labor within the community in the occupational areas which were to be included in the project; and
- Inmate workers had "...not solely by their status as offenders, been deprived of the right to participate in benefits made available by the Federal or state government to other individuals on the basis of their employment, such as workmen's compensation."[16]

States participating were authorized but not mandated to make deductions from inmate wages not to exceed 80 percent in the aggregate for any of the following purposes:

- Federal, state and local taxes;
- Room and board;
- Family support; and
- Contributions to crime victim support.

Once certified, the projects were exempted from the restrictions which prohibited the movement of prison-made products in interstate commerce and those which prohibited federal agencies from purchasing products made by inmates in prisons other than those operated by the federal government itself. Unlike Free Venture, there were no funds provided in connection with this program. In essence, this measure was simply an expression of endorsement for an orderly and controlled demonstration of the impact upon private industry, upon working Americans, organized labor and upon correctional practices from limited deregulation of federal restrictions on the marketability of non-federal prisoner made goods.

CURRENT PIE PROJECTS

There are currently four PIE projects operating: two in Minnesota, one in Kansas and one in Utah. There were several projects which were subsequently decertified for inability to continue in compliance with the requirements. There are also a number of projects which are now awaiting certification under the new 1985 guideline.

The Kansas Operation is a wholly owned and operated private sector sheet metal fabrication shop located in Lansing, Kansas serving male and female inmates confined in the Kansas Correctional Institution, a co-correctional facility. Zephyr Industries has managed to survive in an area with a generally depressed market for metal products. The Utah graphics center, operated by Utah Correctional Industries in the State Prison in Draper, Utah, produces reflecting signs. The Minnesota State Prison at Stillwater has an assembly of computer periphals operated by Minnesota Correctional Industries on contract with Control Data Corporation. This project has continually produced a profit since its inception. The other Minnesota project, at the same facility, manufactures farm implements such as manure spreaders and other light metal fabricated farm products.

As of March 31, 1985, participating states reported that inmates employed in the various projects had earned $2,975,167, paid $240,615 in Federal taxes, and $54,504 in state taxes. In Kansas and Utah, $302, 621 had been contributed to room and board (Minnesota does not have this deduction). Authorities in Minnesota and Utah report inmates have authorized approximately $900,135 be sent for family support.

There has been virtually nothing collected for victim compensation. Until recently deductions for this purpose were limited to court-ordered restitution and judges rarely impose restitution on offenders sentenced to prison. In Minnesota legislation is currently being considered which will authorize the Commissioner of Corrections to deduct money from inmate earnings for the purpose of supporting victims assistance programs administered by the Department of Corrections.

The Reagan Administration proposed, and Congress authorized, an expansion of the program from the original seven demonstration projects to 20 as part of the Comprehensive Crime Control Act of 1984.[17] There has been a great deal of recent interest in this concept sparked in part by the strong support given it by Chief Justice Warren Burger who has spoken frequently in favor of the prisons of the future as "factories with fences" to provide employment opportunity to the inmates in contrast to the idleness and make-work programs too common today.

In 1984, Reagan Administration appointees in the Office of Justice Assistance, Research and Statistics (OJARS) within the Department of Justice, now the Office of Justice Programs (OJP), conducted an assessment of the impact achieved by the Prison Industry Enhancement Program. This assessment concluded both positive and negative results. On the positive side it was determined that:

• Exemption of the federal restrictions which prohibited the interstate commerce of prison-made goods and would prohibit federal agencies from purchasing non-federal prison-made goods did provide a meaningful incentive for participation by the states;

• Adequate protection of the interests of free workers and organized labor representatives was provided by the authorizing legislation and administrative procedures;

• Adequate protection of the interests of inmate workers against "mismanagement" was provided by the authorizing legislation and administrative procedures; and

• The introduction of constructive, productive, profit-oriented work in contemporary correctional facilities did not cause problems for the participating prison administrators beyond their willingness or ability to resolve.

On the negative side it was determined that:

• No financial support for either victim compensation or victim services was being collected or transferred to state victim program agencies;

• Interests of private businesses and representative trade associations were not being adequately protected;

• The operational activities of designated projects were not being reported in an organized, disciplined, and predictable manner; and

• The role of the federal government in prescribing how projects must be administered and managed was overly intrusive into the affairs of the state governments.

The consequence of this assessment was a total redesign of the program guideline. Reagan Administration appointees directed that designated projects provide financial support to either state victim compensation or state victim assistance agencies. The revised guideline also requires that businesses potentially affected by the activities of designated projects be consulted. Most importantly, it was required that the program leave to maximum state discretion the development and use of procedures and methods to meet guideline requirements and achieve revitalization of their prison industry operation.

DISCUSSION ON THE FUTURE

Before speculating on the future, it would be helpful to examine some of the implications and dynamics of the private sector in creating work programs for inmates.

Although rarely articulated, there are several important assumptions underlying support for private sector joint ventures with prisons:

- Constructive work is increasingly seen as a means for achieving a reintegrative mission of prisons, e.g., the development of good work habits;
- Providing constructive work for which a fair wage is paid to prisoners is valuable to inmates' families, victims of crime, and to the inmate workers; and
- Private enterprise is better able to provide efficient productive work programs for prisoners than is the public sector.

There is a growing general awareness of the importance of the work ethic in our society today despite some of the doubts that may have been cast upon it in the past. Psychologists, sociologists, and economists agree that work is important, not only for the material benefits it provides, but also for the psycho-social benefits as well. It provides a focus for life; enables people to better relate to others; it supports reality in determining one's expectations and roles, and offers opportunities for self-actualization and a sense of positive accomplishment in accordance with the generally accepted Judeo-Christian values of our Western Civilization.

The role of constructive work in prison has only recently emerged; it has not run long enough to have any results available in terms of follow-up of participants after release. Any such studies (*e.g.*, recidivism) are difficult to carry out because of the problems of tracking people who have been discharged from prison as well as the methodological difficulties for study design. This challenge has not yet been taken up, however, it must be.

The opportunity to work in a setting which is based on real life measures of performance, such as profit and loss, dollars and cents, quality of work, and deadlines provide many inmates an introduction to the world of work. It offers not only the chance to earn money, but also to test themselves against the same forces which test the rest of us daily.

There is obviously much more to functioning effectively in a free society as a law-abiding citizen than simply holding a job. There is a limit to what fundamental changes can be made during incarceration in a person's outlook on life and his ability to cope with all the challenges which life holds. However, there is a potential benefit to society in the expectation that inmates who have had an opportunity to develop work skills, work habits and an understanding of what it takes to obtain and keep a job, will be able to be productively employed after release. It must be remembered that great numbers of inmates (and perhaps a majority) have never developed proper work habits. Considering the low probability of a criminal serving his full sentence, we must realize that as a group we are talking about those actually serving time for their transgressions against society.

The prison industry concept, as discussed here, will hopefully facilitate the development of the beginning of a free enterprise ethic among inmates. By earning money, inmates with families can contribute to their support and maintain meaningful family relationships. They can begin to accumulate funds to use when they are released. In short they can begin to learn their community responsibilities within our family value system.

Employment in Prison Industry Enhancement projects at the minimum wage level or above will provide financial support to state victim compensation or victim assistance programs. Inmates whose earning capacity during incarceration is enhanced by action of the state should share a portion of these earnings with those who suffered from their criminal behavior. The paucity of resources available to victims to help cope with the aftermath of their experiences underscores the need for inmates contributions. In addition, the payment by an inmate to victims of crime reinforces the criminal lesson of restitution and accountability for one's actions.

Economically motivated work may provide for the movement of at least some of the inmate population from the welfare society of the prisons to partial self-support.

We also work upon the assumption that the private sector can provide more efficient and productive work programs than the public sector. This does not suggest necessarily that those in the private sector are more able managers, but rather that there are structural aspects of the private sector which enable it to create and maintain more efficient industrial activity than the public sector.

One particular advantage of the private sector is the size of the market available. Three of the existing PIE projects are in fact managed by public sector employees but through certification use the broader base of the private sector market to achieve financial viability. At the same time the private sector market enforces a discipline in terms of quality and delivery requirements which results in prison shops operating in the same manner as would their counterparts in private enterprise.

Where the private sector actually serves as the employer, there are the advantages in terms of managerial flexibility (lack of restrictive public agency laws and practices as is the case with personnel, procurement, for example) and the entrepreneurial spirit.

But just as the private sector has no monopoly on talent and dedication, neither does its presence guarantee success. There are inherent difficulties in operating a production enterprise in a prison with an inmate workforce. There can be mandatory cell confinement which disrupts production schedules. There is turnover as inmates are paroled, transferred to other institutions, or subject to disciplinary action for activities not related to the job. There are security restrictions which can affect incoming or outgoing shipments, operating procedures, and hours of work. The concerns for security can never be underestimated. Prisons are usually not located in or near metropolitan areas. Lack of work skills pose continuing training problems and may require redesign of operations. Supervisors are continually subjected to inmate testing and manipulation. After all, the prime issue in prison is security and the associated issue of managing idleness.

It should also be noted that for all of the benefits such work programs may bring to a prison, prison administrators must cope with the problems of adapting traditional prison practices and procedures to the demands of shop managers intent on making a profit. In short, it is a difficult and demanding environment in which to operate a business. Notwithstanding the above, there is a dollar to be made by private enterprise in prison industries.

If the underlying assumptions of what we have been discussing are reasonable, then the future of the concept deserves careful consideration.

In December 1984 there were 26 prison-based businesses with significant private sector involvement inside 17 prisons in 10 states and operated in connection with 19 private firms. These businesses, located in prisons ranging from small community-based facilities to large, rural maximum-security institutions, employ almost 1,000 prisoners or 0.2 percent of the total prison population of the United States.[18]

In a sense, we have not yet determined if we are within the Indian summer of the past or the cutting edge of the future. In fairness, until realizing the economic recovery during the first term of the Reagan Administration, our national economic situation was not conducive to starting new industrial operations. With less than 100 percent of factory capacity in the country being used it was difficult to approach companies to suggest expansion into prisons. With the unemployment rate over 10 percent in the late 1970s, jobs for prisoners was not a politically attractive objective. As the economy has picked up during the ongoing recovery, so has the interest of the business community picked up in prison industries.

Several states have expressed intent to the Department of Justice to submit applications for certification under the new private sector-prison industry enhancement certification program guidelines. Each of these states have reported active interest on the part of one or more companies in some type of working arrangement. Local units of government are now eligible to participate and there are several which may become involved as well. The new guidelines expanded the definition of "project", so that state prison industries' systems can now apply for a single department certification. This not only encourages the states to develop more prison industry plants, but also significantly cuts down on federal red tape. With increased national visibility arising out of more public discussion of the concept of utilizing prison labor as a resource, and at least two recent national conferences devoted to the privatization of corrections, more and more private enterprise companies are becoming aware of the opportunities.

It is likely then that there will be an expansion both in the production projects certified under the PIE program and those service operations not needing such exemption. However, this growth is likely to be gradual and centered in a relatively few states. "Twenty-one states have statutes specifically authorizing the private sector employment of prisoners or the contracting of prisoner labor by the private sector, or both."[19]

There needs to be a blend of circumstances to bring the industries concept into fruition in a particular place. There must be available space in or adjacent to a prison; there must be legislative authorization and departmental management must actively support the concept. An appropriate business partner must be available, interested, aware of the opportunity and willing to make the necessary commitment. It is not easy to bring all of these factors together in the right place at the right time.

To date there has been little thought given to the policy implications of the prison industry system except as it relates to the field of corrections. For example, there has not been serious consideration of this concept being used as an economic development program or as a potential factor in reversing the flight of American industry to Third World supply sources. Relatedly, there has not been sufficient thought given to this idea as a companion to the enterprise zone proposals of Congressman Jack Kemp (R-NY). The PIE requirements require the payment of wages comparable to those paid for similar work in the locality as do most of the state laws which authorize private sector business joint ventures with prisons. This is a *sine qua non* in order to prevent unfair competition and the protection of non-criminal working men and women.

A tantalizing question which may be ripe for discussion: What about the plant which has decided to move all or part of its operations to a Third World nation to take advantage of cheap labor? Would it be appropriate to consider the payment of wages comparable to those paid for similar work in the locality in which it would otherwise be performed (The Third World)? Could it be a legitimate objective of this program to use inmate labor as a means of keeping some industry here which might otherwise leave the country? If so, what protection could be provided to avoid employers using this threat as a ploy to use cheap labor in unfair competition against American labor?

There may be some advantages to manufacturers to consider this alternative. They would not incur the shipping costs involved in overseas supply sources. There are currency control and exchange problems in some case which could be avoided. Tariffs, or the threat of them, can affect costs. There are cultural differences to consider in doing business in foreign countries. There is also our mutual interest in keeping work in this country even if it is in prisons. There would certainly be a national interest in offsetting even a small portion of the trade deficit.

A well designed economic analysis, reviewing the feasibility of using inmate labor in this manner as well as discussion of various alternative ways of dealing with the complex issues involved, could contribute significantly to the growth of prison-based businesses in the future. This warrants further study and evaluation.

CONCLUSION

History records that the achievement of correctional purposes has been the driving force defining the role of work within the correctional environment. Though work can serve other prison purposes, an emerging implication to states participating in the Prison Industry Enhancement Program seems increasingly to define the role of constructive work as necessary and sufficient in its own right—not subordinate to nor dependent upon any particular correctional purpose or philosophy. The validity and correctness of work as a social value is no more or no less than the validity and correctness of imprisonment as the accepted value for enforcing sanctions against criminal behavior in our society. Penal policies have historically attempted to deny work as a social value within the prison environment for many reasons. The Prison Industry Enhancement Program and the utilization of private enterprise is challenging these antiquated policies. Likewise, there is a growing body of thought that the incarcerated criminal should pay as high an economic portion as possible for his incarceration and for the social damages ancillary to that incarceration. There is an affirmative duty on the part of the criminal to those, both individually and collectively, whose rights and properties he has violated. There is also a growing recognition that private enterprise can assist in prison management through pursuing its own natural profit-making goals.

Experience from the certified projects is validating the observation made by Gordon Hawkins that "the failure to develop efficient systems for the utilization of prison industries is not due to the inherent intractability of the problem, indeed, when the difficulties which are commonly said to stand in the way of its solution are analyzed, it is clear that taken singularly, not one of them represent an insuperable impediment."[20]

As these projects continue and expand, we may soon find ourselves closer to achieving self-supporting correctional institutions, inducing work habits upon inmates, providing reparations to victims, introducing the genius of private enterprise into the public prison system, enhancing our historical work ethic, enhancing accomplishment of prison management objectives and, paradoxically, completing the full circle of a journey of correctional philosophy which began in colonial times.

REFERENCES

Prison Labor: A Neglected Resource by Richard B. Abell

1. *Feasibility of Implementing a Private Prison Industry Program in the Federal Prison System*, Report to Congress, Office of Controller's Evaluation Staff, Justice Management Divison, May 1985 (Washington, D.C.: U.S. Department of Justice).

2. *Impact of Free Venture Prison Industries Upon Correctional Institutions*, University City Science Center, Law Enforcement Assistance Administration (Washington, D.C.: U.S. Department of Justice, 1981), p. 82.

3. *Prisoners in 1984*, Bureau of Justice Statistics, April 1985 (Washington, D.C.: U.S. Department of Justice). The increase continued into 1985. Preliminary data found 505,037 people incarcerated in 1985. *Prisoners in 1985*, BJS, June 1986. [Editor's note: The surge in prison population shows no signs of abatement. A record 528,945 inmates were in state and federal prisons at the end of June 1986. BJS press release, September 14, 1986.]

4. Jack Schaller and George Sexton, "From Plates for Profit to Tags for Treatment," unpublished paper, April 19, 1976, American Institute of Criminal Justice, p. 2. *See* U.S. Department of Justice, the Attorney General's Survey of Release Procedures, Volume V, *Prisons* (Leavenworth: Federal Prison Industries, Inc. Press, 1940), p. 210.

5. *Ibid.*, pp. 2–3.

6. Howard B. Gill, "Technical Proposal for a Study of the Economic and Rehabilitative Aspects of Prison Industries," unpublished paper (Entropy Limited, 1974), p. 5.

7. 49 U.S. 11507

8. Prison Industries Reorganization Administration, *Progress Report*, May 15, 1937, p. 1.

9. *Ibid.*, pp. 1–2.

10. 40 Stat. 494.

11. 18 U.S.C. 1761.

12. 49 State. 2036, 41 U.S.C. 35 (d).

13. American Institute of Criminal Justice, *The Prison Industries Enhancement Program*, final report for Office of Justice Assistance, Research and Statistics (Washington, D.C.: U.S. Department of Justice), p. 2.

14. *Supra* n. 2.

15. Justice System Improvement Act, 18 U.S.C. 1761, § 827, P.L. 96-157.

16. *Ibid.*

17. P.L. 98-473, Title II.

18. Criminal Justice Associates, *Private Sector Involvement in Prison-Based Businesses: A National Assessment*, National Institute for Justice, April 1985 (Washington, D.C., U.S. Department of Justice), p. 35.

19. *Ibid.*, p. 73.

20. Gordon Hawkins, "Prison Labor and Industries," in Michael Tonry and Norval Morris, editors, *Crime and Justice: An Annual Review of Research*, Volume V (1983), p. 123.

24

CRIME AND PUNISHMENT IN MODERN AMERICA:
Some Concluding Thoughts
by Jack Kemp

It was on rotting prison straw that I felt the first stirrings of good in myself. Gradually, it became clear to me that the line separating good from evil runs not between state, not between classes, and not between parties—it runs through the heart of each and every one of us and through all human hearts. This line is not stationary. It shifts and moves with the passing of the years. Even in hearts enveloped in evil it maintains a small bridehead of good. And even the most virtuous heart harbors an un-uprooted corner of evil.

—Aleksandr Solzhenitsyn[1]

Evil exists. No law can change human nature. The Soviets have tried for almost 70 years to produce their "New Soviet Man," and the Russian people are still pretty much like the rest of us would be under such an unnatural system. Our Judeo-Christian heritage teaches us that we cannot eliminate crime altogether because some hearts will always turn to evil. But it is the first responsibility of government to protect citizens, families and children from these predators. They can and must be prevented from harming others.

Our judicial system must be designed to protect the law-abiding citizen. Part of this protection is the protection of the accused from violation of their rights. But we can never allow our concern for criminals as individuals, our hope that they can be rehabilitated, to violate the right of all Americans to live and work in safety.

As painfully detailed in the essays of this book, there are flaws in our present criminal justice system. Two-thirds of the crimes committed are not reported to the authorities. Barely one-fifth of all crimes result in arrest. And of those arrested, some cases are not prosecuted. Other defendants jump bail. And when a case ends in a guilty plea or conviction, still more criminals are placed on probation. Sentencing varies by state, by judge, and over time. Equally devastating to the task of deterrence is the time lag between the crime, trial, conviction and sentencing which can make the final punishment appear to the criminal to be more the result of bad luck than the direct result of his criminal behavior.

It is time to raise the costs of crime and reduce its rewards. The essays in this book demonstrate that this is not accomplished by increasing the length of sentences. The certainty of arrest, conviction and punishment are just as important. The financial rewards of criminal activity must be reduced. Judicial and congressional restrictions on some of the most egregious interpretations of the *Miranda* decision[2] have increased the people's power to introduce non-coerced confessions, leading to the imprisonment of dangerous felons and reducing the costs of criminal trials. Allowances for good-faith exceptions to our nation's strict rules on search warrants help ensure that it need not be the case that "because the constable blundered, the criminal goes free." Limits on the use and abuse of the insanity defense have begun to close that loophole through which dangerous and vicious individuals have been loosed on new victims. And the appointment of new judges who take the law and the rights of victims seriously has begun to turn the tide against crime. President Reagan and Attorney General Meese are dedicated to appointing highly qualified judges who take the "letter of the law" seriously and believe in the perpetual relevance of our constitution.

The Comprehensive Crime Control Act of 1984,[3] the anti-racketeering laws and the strengthening of criminal forfeiture have all reduced the rewards of criminal behavior, particularly for members of organized crime networks and drug traffickers. The increasing application of the principle of restitution at the state level and the imposition of financial penalties for crime against property is an encouraging development. The Sentencing Improvement Act (S. 1644) has been introduced by Senators Bill Armstrong (R-CO) and Sam Nunn (D-GA) to bring this principle to federal law.[4]

The death penalty serves as punishment, deterrent and prevention of future crimes. There are some crimes for which the severest of penalties is appropriate. Justice demands the death penalty for those who have willfully and wrongly taken a life and for those who endanger the lives of millions through treason or espionage. As for those who argue that the death penalty does not deter future murders the proper answer is simply: nonsense. Too many murderers have been released to kill again for us to allow that argument to be taken seriously.[5]

There is a growing body of law that empowers crime victims to sue parole boards and others who knowingly free murderers, even those who admit that they will kill again. A company that released a product they knew would kill would find no sympathy from a jury. Those who exhibit a similarly cavalier attitude towards releasing vicious killers should be held accountable.

There has been progress in our war against crime. Crime, and particularly violent crime, has decreased since 1980. Yet it remains at an unacceptably high level—almost double that of crime in the 1960s. This epidemic remains a barrier to an American renaissance, the realization of the American dream of opportunity, prosperity and safety for oneself and one's family. Crime and the fear of crime remain a heavy tax on those whose neighborhoods are unsafe. I am a firm believer in initiatives that would improve the economic base of our neighborhoods, especially in areas where poverty and crime go hand in hand. I believe that the Enterprise Zone Act[6] that I have introduced along with Robert Garcia of New York will reduce the tax and regulatory burdens that now inhibit job creation in our cities and rural areas. But besides the paycheck that such opportunity would bring to our neediest citizens must go the security of knowing that a worker can safely get that paycheck home and that his or her family will be safe at home and in the streets. We can only guess at how many breadwinners have been frustrated from reaching their dreams, providing for their families and helping their neighbors by the present high rate of crime.

How then are we to build on the accomplishments of the past few years? What are our goals and purposes? How should we judge whether past and future reforms are truly bringing us a safer and more just society? I have often observed that the measure of the compassion of America should not be judged by how many American families are on welfare, but by how many families do not need welfare. I suggest that we ought to judge the success of new laws, new court guidelines, and sentencing provisions not by how many individuals we have in our nation's prisons, but by how few Americans must be imprisoned.

In addition to the common-sense realization that the degree and certainty of punishment make a difference in the decision making process of criminals, as well as other Americans, I believe that two trends bode well for future serious reforms. The first is the belated recognition that the victim is the first and foremost casualty of crime. Yes, society as a whole has an interest in "maintaining the King's peace," but a woman who is robbed of her social security check in Buffalo is right in perceiving herself, not the state of New York, as the victim of crime.

409

Thus restitution for crime victims has rightly gained public support.[7] The idea that a burglar should return stolen goods, pay for damage to the house he broke into and pay his victims for the time lost from work to appear at a trial meets with universal support from the American people. Many are surprised to learn that this is not already the case in all property crimes. There is, of course, a reason that the concept of restitution appeals to America's sense of justice. It is based on our Judeo-Christian heritage, as well as the rule of reason. In both the New and Old Testaments those who have stolen from their neighbors are required to restore the stolen property and repay them twice or four times over to compensate for the loss. Restitution also provides an alternative to imprisonment for nonviolent criminals, reducing the need for taxpayers to continue building prisons (at the cost of $70,000 for a new jail cell) and paying $16,000 to keep *one* prisoner incarcerated for a year.[8]

The need to focus more on victims' rights can also be seen in the sad fact that, as recently as 1979, no state allowed victims to testify at the sentencing of criminals. Today, 32 states make provision for the victims of crime to be heard prior to sentencing, and some states have taken the further step of *requiring* victims to be heard when a criminal is up for parole.[9]

The American people have always rooted for the perceived underdog. Throughout the 1960s and 1970s the criminal justice system worked as if the criminal was the underdog, facing the awesome might of the state. The victim of the crime, however, found that he or she had fewer rights than the accused. Moving to the point where the rights of crime victims are equal to or greater than those of the accused is a positive development.

We must also make the prevention of crime a higher priority. Recent studies have shown that a very small number of criminals are responsible for the bulk of violent and property crime. Professor Marvin Wolfgang of the University of Pennsylvania found in 1978 that of 9,945 males studied, 627 of these young men, or just over six percent, had been arrested for five crimes each and accounted for almost-two thirds of all crime committed by this group.[10] The identification and incarceration of career criminals, and the targeting of police and court resources on putting those individuals behind bars, reduce the number of criminals our criminal justice system must handle. States are beginning to rethink the policy of ignoring juvenile crime records in the sentencing of adults. I would suggest that such records be kept for five years after a teenager reaches the state's age of maturity and not be sealed permanently unless he has remained "clean" during that period.

The second heartening trend is the greater public interest in the criminal justice system. Mothers Against Drunk Driving have demanded and received reform in how our judges treat this dangerous crime. Dan Popeo's national court watch program has put judges on the alert that their actions and decisions are not immune from public scrutiny. Too many of our judges at all levels have drifted away from their simple yet profound mandate to dispense justice for the benefit of all. Rather, some have focused their efforts on more esoteric—and less important—pursuits.

The hard work of judicial reformers such as Pat McGuigan, the editor of this book and the director of the Judicial Reform Project, and Mrs. Roberta Roper, the guiding force behind the Stephanie Roper committee, have helped bring American people back into the decision making process they should never have been excluded from in the first place.

The strong popular response to the drift of our courts can also be seen in the proliferation of "Neighborhood Watch" organizations that now band citizens together in 2,500 neighborhoods nationwide. Citizen concern about the high level of crime has changed the view of the American people towards their law enforcement officers. In the 1960s, many seemed to have lost faith in America and the ideals of her people. Those who defended our freedoms and our unique role in the world were often the objects of hostility. But today we have renewed our commitment to the principles America stands for, including a strong sense of respect for those who protect our freedom. Citizens are increasingly willing, indeed eager, to work with their local law enforcement officers in protecting themselves, their homes and their families.

Just as war is too important to be left to the generals, criminal justice is too important to leave to law school professors and tenured judges.

It is not from the experts and practitioners in our courts that we will see the demand for positive change and reform. The citizens of California, using their right of initiative, overwhelmingly passed the Victims Bill of Rights Initiative of June 1982 over the objections of the legal establishment.[11] The Comprehensive Crime Control Act of 1984 and other anti-crime legislation considered by Congress were strengthened by the contributions of many of the scholars represented in this book and by the hard work of thousands of police officers, prosecutors and victims' rights organizations who have taken to heart the common law tradition that the law must serve the cause of justice and the people.[12]

Reforming our judicial process—the sentencing of criminals and the treatment of victims and witnesses—raise issues of basic fairness. We cannot maintain respect for the law when citizens hear and read about those who "beat the system" by exploiting a technicality. The momentum behind President Reagan's tax reform initiative stems from the belief of many honest taxpayers that others are not paying their fair share by taking advantages of loopholes and tricky investment schemes. So, too, do many citizens perceive that the law is unfairly and unevenly applied—that victims are ignored and witnesses are neglected. The support necessary to encourage citizens to join forces with the police in combatting crime is often lacking. This is not only unfair to citizens who are dissuaded from reporting crimes to the police and testifying in court, but also to those young Americans who all too often see criminals evade the costs of punishment, only to continue terrorizing their neighbors.

As we move forward in enacting the Reagan Revolution, the creation of a true American Opportunity Society where families are free to pursue their highest aspirations, to provide their children with education, values and principles, to prosper economically and spiritually, we must defend their freedom and security against those criminals here at home and those foreign enemies who would rob them of their liberty. The price of liberty, as Jefferson warned, is indeed eternal vigilance. And the popular demand for reforming our criminal justice system, the growth in size and strength of victims' rights groups, the increased intellectual power brought to bear on this question as witnessed by the sound thinking of the contributors to this book—all bear witness to the fact that we Americans are still willing to pay the price to remain a free and strong people.

REFERENCES

Crime and Punishment in Modern America: Some Concluding Thoughts by Jack Kemp

1. Aleksandr Solzhenitsyn, *The Gulag Archipelago.* Quoted in *Religion and Society Report* (March 1985).
2. *Miranda v. Arizona*, 384 U.S. 436 (1966).
3. P.L. 98-473.
4. *See* the excellent Armstrong-Nunn essay, Chapter 20 in this book.
5. *See* Senator Strom Thurmond's essay, Chapter 13 in this book.

6. The Enterprise Zone Jobs Creation Act, H.R. 1955, was introduced before the 99th Congress in March 1983. It has the support of President Reagan and secured 261 co-sponsors.

7. Although restitution is addressed in many of the essays in this book, in particular *see* Armstrong/Nunn, *supra* n. 4, and the analyses of Dr. Herb Titus (Chapter 16) and Daniel Van Ness of Prison Fellowship (Chapter 15).

8. In many instances the annual cost of keeping a prisoner is even higher. However, there is some evidence that privatization in some jail and prison systems is having an impact in reducing the costs of incarceration. *See* both Richard Abell's essay, Chapter 23 in this book, and James K. Stewart's analysis (Chapter 22).

9. Maryland is the most recent state to take this step, thanks to the work of Roberta Roper and members of the Stephanie Roper Committee. For background, *see, Judicial Notice* May 1986 and September–October 1984.

10. *See* Eugene H. Methvin, "The Proven Key to Crime Control," *Reader's Digest*, May 1986, p. 7.

11. For the fascinating background on passage of this citizen initiative, *see* issues of the *Initiative and Referendum Report* through early 1982.

12. And, the substantive reforms of drug statutes nearing congressional passage in the fall of 1986 flowed from this same sense of popular intensity and leadership from law enforcement.

CONTRIBUTORS

Richard B. Abell is Deputy Assistant Attorney General, Office of Justice Programs, U.S. Department of Justice. Abell has served on the faculties of West Chester State College and the Delaware Law School, and was an Assistant District Attorney in Chester County, Pennsylvania. Abell holds a B.A. in International Affairs from the George Washington University, and earned his J.D. from GWU Law School. He is the Attorney General's representative on the Federal Prison Industries Board of Directors.

William L. Armstrong is the Republican Senator from Colorado. He serves on the Banking and Housing and Urban Affairs Committees in addition to his work on both the Budget and Finance Committees. Before coming to the Senate, Armstrong served for two terms in the U.S. House of Representatives, and for seven years in the Colorado state legislature. Armstrong came to public service from the broadcast media, and served as director and vice president of the Associated Press Broadcasters Association.

Frank G. Carrington is an attorney, consultant on the rights of crime victims, and one of the founders of the victims rights movement in America. Executive Director of the Victims/Assistance Legal Organization (VALOR), Carrington formerly served as President of Americans for Effective Law Enforcement, and was a member of both the Attorney General's Task Force on Violent Crime (1981) and the President's Task Force on Victims of Crime (1982).

Pete du Pont completed his second term as Governor of Delaware in 1985. Du Pont began his political career in 1969 in the Delaware General Assembly. After serving for six years as Delaware's Congressman in the U.S. House of Representatives, he was elected Governor in 1976. He is the founder and former Chairman of GOPAC and the National Leadership Council, national party organizations involved in state legislative and party building effects. Pete du Pont is also Chairman of the Hudson Institute, the public policy research organization founded by the late Herman Kahn, and is a partner in the Wilmington firm of Richards, Layton & Finger.

Du Pont holds a B.S. degree from Princeton University, and earned his J.D. at Harvard.

Bruce E. Fein is President of Bruce Fein and Associates, and a Visiting Fellow in Constitutional Studies at the Heritage Foundation. He was a Senior Vice President (Telecommunications and Information Group) at Gray and Company in the nation's capital. He was General Counsel at the Federal Communications Commission and, for two years, Associate Deputy Attorney General at the U.S. Department of Justice. Before that, he served for many years as an attorney in various units of the Department of Justice. The author of many articles in both scholarly and general interest publications, Fein is Supreme Court Editor for *Benchmark*, a publication of the Center for Judicial Studies.

Charles E. Grassley is the senior Senator from Iowa, and is a member of the Senate Judiciary Committee. He is Chairman of the Committee's Subcommittee on Administrative Practice and Procedure. Grassley received his M.A. from the University of Northern Iowa in 1956. He previously served as a member of the Iowa state legislature, and as a member of the U.S. House of Representatives. Grassley contributed to both *Criminal Justice Reform: A Blueprint* (1983) and *A Blueprint for Judicial Reform* (1981).

Abraham L. Halpern is Director of Psychiatry at United Hospital in Port Chester, New York. He is also Clinical Professor of Psychiatry at the New York Medical College. The author of many scholarly articles on the insanity defense, Halpern is a member of the New York state Commission of Corrections Medical Review Board. He is President of the International Academy of Law and Mental Health, and Past President of both the American Academy of Psychiatry and the Law and the American Board of Forensic Psychiatry.

Paula Hawkins is a Republican Senator from Florida, the first woman ever elected to that position. Hawkins is Chairman of the Senate Drug Enforcement Caucus and is a member of the Committees on Labor and Human Resources; Agriculture, Nutrition and Forestry; and Aging. Hawkins was a leading sponsor of the historic Missing Children Act, which led to establishment of the National Center for Missing and Exploited Children.

416

Lois H. Herrington is Assistant Attorney General in the Office of Justice Programs at the Department of Justice. Among her many duties, she chaired the President's Task Force on Victims of Crime, and supervised the work of the Attorney General's Task Force on Family Violence. For many years, Herrington was a prosecutor in Alameda County, California, with substantial background in sexual assault investigations and juvenile justice issues. Herrington earned LL.B. and J.D. degrees from Hastings College of Law in San Francisco.

L. Stephen Jennings received his B.A. degree in political science from Hiram Scott College, Scottbluff, Nebraska, and is a candidate for a M.S. degree in administration of justice at the University of Pittsburgh. He is contributing editor of *CRIME* Magazine. He is completing work on a book, with David Jones, on conservative approaches to crime control.

David Jones is a professor of interdisciplinary studies in law and justice at the University of Pittsburgh. He holds an A.B. degree in United States history; a J.D. from Albany Law School of Union University; and a Ph.D. from the School of Criminal Justice, Nelson A. Rockefeller College of Public Affairs and Policy, State University of New York at Albany. The author of six books and numerous articles, Jones is editor in chief of *CRIME* Magazine.

Jack Kemp has served as a Republican congressman from Buffalo, New York since his election in 1970. Kemp was a quarterback in professional football for thirteen years. He holds a B.A. from Occidental College and has pursued graduate studies at Long Beach State University and California Western University. He is Chairman of the House Republican Conference and is a member of the House Appropriations Committee. The author of *An American Renaissance*, Kemp is the Founder of both the Campaign for Prosperity, a political action committee, and the Fund for an American Renaissance, a public policy research organization.

Benedict J. Koller is currently Director for the American Legislative Exchange Council's Juvenile Justice Reform Project. He received his B.A. from Thomas Aquinas College in Santa Paula, California and his J.D. from Santa Clara University School of Law. He is a member of the California Bar.

Patrick B. McGuigan is Director of the Judicial Reform Project at the Institute for Government and Politics in Washington, D.C. He is the co-editor of five books on legal policy issues, and is the author of *The Politics of Direct Democracy in the 1980s*.

Edwin Meese III is Attorney General of the United States. Previously, he served at the White House as Counsellor to President Ronald Reagan. Meese is a graduate of Yale University and holds a law degree from the University of California at Berkeley. He served as a lawyer, educator and public official, and as a business executive in the aerospace and transportation industries. Meese also served as Deputy District Attorney of Alameda County, California. A frequent lecturer on legal policy issues, Meese was a contributor to *Criminal Justice Reform: A Blueprint* (1983).

Gerald P. Monks is presently the Executive Director of the Professional Bail Agents of the United States (PBUS). He received a B.A. in Math from Texas A&M University, M.B.A. from Columbia Pacific University and Ph.D. from Columbia Pacific University. Past President of PBUS, Monks serves on the Pre-trial Advisory Committee of the Bureau of Justice Statistics, the Houston Chamber of Commerce Criminal Justice Research Committee, and as a Consultant for the American Criminal Justice Research Institute.

Sam Nunn, a Democrat, is the senior Senator from Georgia. First elected in 1972, Nunn is the ranking minority member of the Armed Services Committee. He also serves on the Governmental Affairs, Intelligence and Small Business Committees. An attorney and farmer, Nunn served four years in the Georgia state legislature. He holds A.B. and LL.B. degrees from Emory University in Atlanta.

Jon S. Pascale is an Attorney/Advisor at the U.S. Civil Rights Commission. He formerly served as Assistant Director of the Judicial Reform Project at the Institute for Government and Politics. Pascale holds a Bachelor's degree from Fairfield University in Connecticut, a law degree from Syracuse University, and served as an appellate lawyer in the U.S. Army's Judge Advocate General Corps.

Daniel J. Popeo is founder and general counsel of the Washington Legal Foundation, America's largest public interest law and policy center. Popeo received his B.A. from Georgetown University and his law degree from Georgetown Law Center in 1975. Before founding the Washington Legal Foundation, Popeo worked at the White House, Department of Justice and the Department of the Interior. The author of several monographs and many articles, Popeo was a contributor to *Criminal Justice Reform: A Blueprint* (1983).

Alfred S. Regnery is Vice President and Publisher for Regnery Books, as well as an attorney with the Washington, D.C. firm of Leighton & Regnery. Regnery served as Administrator of the Office of Juvenile Justice and Delinquency Prevention (U.S. Department of Justice) for three years. A graduate of Beloit College in Wisconsin, Regnery earned his J.D. from the University of Wisconsin Law School. After serving as counsel to Senator Paul Laxalt (R-NV), Regnery was Deputy Assistant Attorney General for Land and Natural Resources at the Department of Justice. Regnery was a participant in the 1983 Conference on Criminal Justice Reform.

George C. Smith is Director of Litigation at the Washington Legal Foundation. He is author of a major monograph on the death penalty, *Capital Punishment 1986: Last Lines of Defense* (1986). Smith received his B.A. (*magna cum laude*) from Penn State University and his J.D. from Duke University School of Law.

William E. Spaulding is a lieutenant in the Lousiville, Kentucky Police Division. Presently he is commander of the criminal intelligence unit. A member of the board of several organizations and a frequent instructor on criminal justice issues, Spaulding holds a Bachelor of Science degree in Police Administration from the University of Louisville, and a Master of Science in the Administration of Justice from the same institution.

Kenneth W. Starr is a judge on the U.S. Court of Appeals for the District of Columbia Circuit. He is a graduate of George Washington University and earned an M.A. in political science from Brown University. Starr holds a law degree from Duke University, and was a partner in the firm of Gibson, Dunn & Crutcher. From January 1981 until October 1983, Starr was Counsellor to Attorney General William French Smith. Starr is a member of the Judicial Fellows Commission, the Chief Justice's Task Force on Prison Industries and the Judicial Conference Committee on the Bicentennial of the Constitution.

James K. Stewart has served as Director of the National Institute for Justice (NIJ) since 1982. At NIJ, Stewart's activity is directed toward narrowing the gap between research and practice in the criminal justice system. A frequent instructor and guest lecturer at colleges and universities before joining the Department of Justice, Stewart is a veteran of 15 years with the Oakland, California police department, including service as Commander of the Criminal Investigations Division. Stewart holds a Master's degree in Public Administration and a Bachelor's degree from the University of Oregon. A graduate of the FBI's National Academy, Stewart is a member of the Advisory Board of the National Center for Innovations and Corrections.

Strom Thurmond is the President *pro tempore* of the United States Senate and Chairman of the Senate Judiciary Committee. A Republican from South Carolina, Thurmond's career has included service as a teacher, athletic coach, education superintendent, city and county attorney, state senator, circuit judge and Governor of South Carolina. Senator Thurmond holds 17 honorary degrees and is a decorated veteran of World War II.

Herbert W. Titus is Vice President of Academic Affairs and Dean of the School of Public Policy at CBN University in Virginia Beach, Virginia. Founding Editor of the *Journal of Christian Jurisprudence*, Titus is the author of *God, Man and Law: The Biblical Principles* and was a participant in the Conference on Criminal Justice Reform in 1983. Titus holds a Bachelor's degree in Political Science from the University of Oregon, and a J.D. from Harvard. He has taught at Oklahoma University, the University of Oregon and Oral Roberts University.

Daniel W. Van Ness is President of Justice Fellowship, a Washington D.C. organization formed by Charles W. Colson and Prison Fellowship to promote criminal justice reform. The author of *Crime and Its Victims: What We Can Do* (Intervarsity Press, 1986), Van Ness has conducted extensive state and federal lobbying on this issue, as well as public education campaigns. Prior to working with Justice Fellowship he practiced law in Chicago for six years.

J. Clifford Wallace is a judge on the Ninth U.S. Circuit Court of Appeals, where he has served since 1972. Prior to joining the circuit court, Wallace served as a federal district court judge. After receiving his LL.B. from the University of California at Berkeley—Boalt Hall, Wallace practiced law in San Diego, California for fifteen years. Judge Wallace holds a bachelor's degree (with honors) from San Diego State University.

Kurt W. Wolfgang is the Director of Intergovernmental Affairs for the National District Attorneys Association. Formerly a prosecutor in Prince Georges County, he earned his J.D. from the University of Baltimore, and his B.A. from the University of Maryland Institute of Criminal Justice and Criminology. Wolfgang is also a member of the board of directors of the Stephanie Roper Committee, a Maryland-based grass roots organization lobbying to improve the rights of victims of crime.